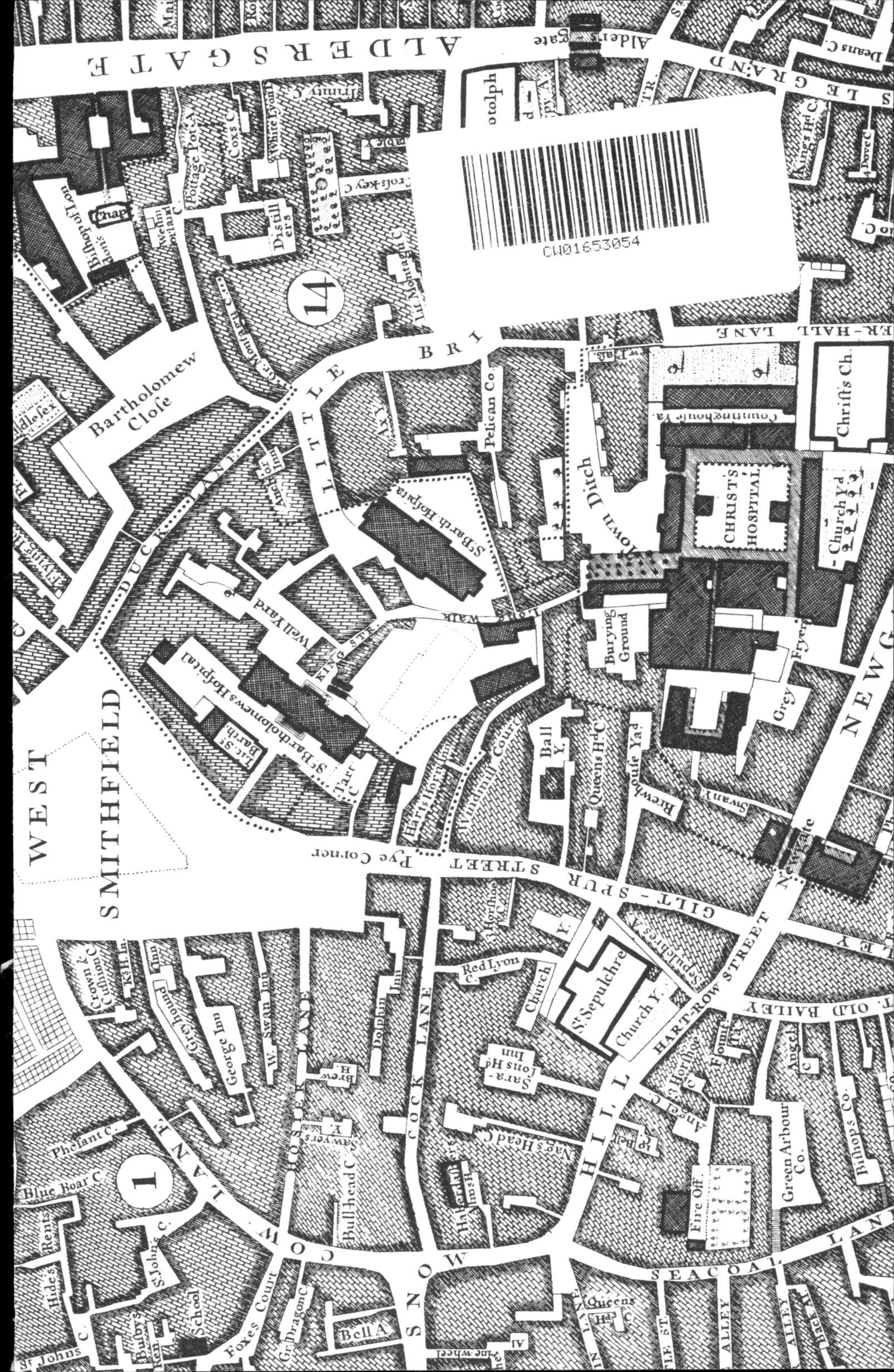
ALDERSGATE
Aldersgate
S. LE GRAND
Deans C.
Kings Hd. C.
Bishop of Lon.
Chap.
Distillers
Cross-key C.
14
Gt. Montague C.
Lit. Montagu C.
Bartholomew Close
LITTLE BRITAIN
DUCK LANE
LANE
Christ's Ch.
CHRIST'S HOSPITAL
Church Yd.
Counting house Ya.
Town Ditch
Pelican Co.
St. Barth. Hospital
Well Yard
KING ST.
Cloyster Walk
St. Bartholomew's Hospital
Lit. St. Barth.
Burying Ground
Grey Fryers
Ball Y.
Queens Hd. C.
Brewhouse Yd.
Swan Y.
Windmill Court
Hartshorn Inn
Tart C.
WEST SMITHFIELD
Pye Corner
GILT-SPUR STREET
Newgate
NEWG
Red Lyon C.
Church
St. Sepulchre
Church Y.
Sepulchres A.
HART-ROW STREET
OLD BAILEY
COCK LANE
HOSIER LANE
Dolphin Inn
George Inn
Greyhound Inn
W. Swan Inn
Crown & Cushion C.
Brew H.
Sawyers Y.
Sara-cens Hd. Inn
Nag's Head C.
SNOW HILL
Angel C.
Green Arbour Co.
Bishops Co.
Fire Off.
Phesant C.
1
Blue Boar C.
COW LANE
Bull head C.
Haberdashers Almsh.
SEACOAL LANE
School
St. Johns C.
Foxes Court
Gr. Dragon C.
Bell A.
Queens Hd. C.
ALLEY
St. Johns

# THE STORY OF FITCH LOVELL

SIR AMBROSE KEEVIL, K.B.E., M.C., D.L.
Chairman and Managing Director 1959-63;
President 1963-69; Hon. President from 1969

SIR GRAHAM ROWLANDSON
M.B.E., J.P., F.C.A.
Chairman 1958-59

HUGH BERNARD FITCH, C.C.
Chairman 1921-53; President 1953-58

SIR ROLANDE WALL, M.C.
Chairman and Managing
Director 1963-66

R.E. BLANNING
Chairman and Managing
Director 1967-69

SIR CHARLES HARDIE
C.B.E., F.C.A.
Chairman from 1970

# THE STORY OF FITCH LOVELL

## 1784 - 1970

*by*

AMBROSE KEEVIL

PHILLIMORE
London & Chichester

1972

Published by

PHILLIMORE & CO. LTD.,
Shopwyke Hall, Chichester, Sussex.



ISBN 0 85033 074 2

*Text set by Phillimore in 11 pt. Press Roman*
*Printed in Great Britain by*
*Fletcher & Son Ltd, Norwich*

## CONTENTS

## Appendices

## ILLUSTRATIONS

# FOREWORD

IT MAY BE difficult for those now employed in the food industry to realise how, even 30 years ago, the trade was divided into strict compartments. It was rare for an importer to engage in wholesaling, still more rare for a wholesaler to have retail shops. These rigid trade customs made it difficult for a firm like Fitch Lovell to be created until recent years.

Fitch Lovell Ltd. was formed from a merger of Fitch & Son Ltd. and Lovell & Christmas Ltd. It is not, to use a modern, ugly word, a conglomerate, but rather a gathering under one umbrella of over 50 allied firms in the food industry. It has grown as a result of the natural development of that industry, a development governed by the increasing standardisation of products, the invention of new methods of preserving food, the acceleration of communications, and from a need for more capital, due to the falling value of currency. The large groups which have been formed as a result of these factors have enabled some firms to survive when they otherwise could not have. They have enabled others to expand. They have also made it possible for the companies' staff to be better cared for, their customers to be better served and their investors to be adequately rewarded for their faith.

Although, in its present form, Fitch Lovell is a comparatively new firm, its history goes back nearly 200 years, and I have often been asked, both by members of our company and its business associates, why there is no published record of this old-established firm. When I retired from active participation in the company's daily business and had more time available, I agreed, as a result of continual pressure from my various colleagues, to write, not a history, but the story of Fitch Lovell, provided that I could interpose odd memories of individuals and some reflections on my 60 years' association with the firm.

Many of the younger generation reading this story will consider the sums of money invested in, or loaned to, different ventures also the turnover and profits of old times to be very small compared to the figures of today. They should remember the effect of inflation in recent years which has distorted money values. They will be able to make a comparison if they compare today's prices and wages with those of the times mentioned in the story.

House rents 3s. to 5s. a week, butter 8d. a lb., meat 4d. a lb., cigarettes 6d. for 20, beer 1d. a glass, whisky 3s. 6d. a bottle, with wages for male manual workers 30s. a week and senior partners or directors about £1,000 a year.

I remember when at a Military Staff College, during the First World War, that an Australian Colonel, who was also a leading industrialist, saying to me 'There is a dividing line in material success. Anyone earning over £5 a week can be considered to have arrived'. My experience is that it was far more difficult to earn £1,000 in the '20s and the '30s than seven times that amount in the '60s and '70s.

We have inflation because most people like it but those who suffer are the old people – both the so-called 'working class' and those who by thrift saved something each year to provide for their retirement and have found their savings disappear with the depreciation of the currency.

Today there is much glib talk of capital gains but during 100 years of deflation they were practically non-existent, if we wish to have a balanced judgment we must not be deceived by the evil effects of inflation which tend to breed a generation of shallow people with paper profits and few values other than sharpness, and extroversion.

One of the most difficult tasks has been to find early records as, during Hitler's war, Smithfield, in London, was more or less devastated, and the heavy raids in the region of the docks in Liverpool, Southampton, Bristol, Manchester and Glasgow – where the wholesale food trade is naturally situated – destroyed many priceless records.

I doubt if the story gives sufficient credit to those, who during the war, carried on their somewhat unglamorous, but nevertheless vital work, often in conditions of great danger. Fire-watchers' devotion to duty saved many of our buildings and some watchers gave their lives in the service of their company. The overcoming of the problems of food distribution, often, during the height of the Blitz, from burning or badly-damaged buildings, is an epic which will probably never be told.

Although early records are scarce, plenty are available from later periods but I must admit that I under-estimated the amount of research needed. Some 2,000 sets of minutes, apart from piles of documents, letters and other material, were made available to me. I doubt if this story would have been finished without the help and encouragement of numerous people.

This simple tale tries to show the changing background of an industry which is the biggest in the country, (over 20% of the money spent in the United Kingdom is spent on food), to trace its gradual development from the filthy Shambles and Stinken Lane of London to the hygenic and almost palatial factories and supermarkets of today, and to show how forward-looking men, always striving, sometimes stumbling by the way, created one of the big companies of our time.

Many of the founders of our firm had similar beginnings. But a moment's reflection will show how natural it was that this should be so. The growth – the vast growth – of London and the big cities outside the Metropolis following the Industrial Revolution, was bound to attract young men from the impoverished countryside, and what more natural than that many should be attracted to the food trade, for 'the farm was the basic factor in providing food'.

Often of a merchant one has heard the remark, 'All he has to show for his life is a Sales Turnover ledger'. There is some truth in that. Certainly this story could have been twice as long had it included a mass of figures relating to sales, profits and percentages. I have relegated such details to the Appendices preferring to illustrate the body of the text with photographs showing the differences between olden days and today and with maps clarifying the numerous references to Smithfield and the streets of the City of London, the areas where Fitch Lovell began and upon which its growth has centred.

I wish it had been possible to mention hundreds of individuals instead of a few score by name, because businesses, like nations, are dependant on individuals, particularly on those who lead. However, there is nothing to prevent other members of our group from writing their own stories and going into greater detail than I have done.

So many have helped with information, documents and in other ways, it is not feasible to mention them all and therefore I have decided to mention none, but I ask them to accept my sincerest thanks for all they have done, especially the ladies who, often in their spare time, have cheerfully typed out the text and mastered the difficult task of understanding my handwriting.

AMBROSE KEEVIL

---

I would like gratefully to acknowledge the assistance I have had from the principals of the various companies, and to thank Michael Morris for his help with the preparation of the text.

1

## THE BACKGROUND

FITCH LOVELL LTD. is a large tree with many branches. To tell its story takes us back in time through nearly 200 years and, in space, across the five continents. It also takes us into the hearts of men, for behind each of the enterprises, some modern, some old, which have come to make up Fitch Lovell, stand men of vision and courage who saw the opportunities and went forward to seize them, and by their hard work and good judgment translated those opportunities into achievements. Such men were John Cary Lovell and Edwin Fitch, George Wall and Hervy Stanley Rowlandson, Clement Keevil and George Beale, Auguste Noël and Ernest Beer, Bob Gunner and many others.

Although a firm believer in the importance of the individual in business, I realise there are external factors which create the opportunities for such men to take. These factors range from political and social developments to technical innovations, and their importance is obvious. No men, however able, could have developed a dairy industry in New Zealand before enough settlers had arrived there to man the farms and dairies, or before the techniques of refrigeration had advanced sufficiently to enable dairy products to be shipped half way round the world.

Of all these 'external factors' none has been more important than the growth in population of the United Kingdom. When the story opens in the late 18th century, this country had only seven million people. Today there are 54 million. Such a rapid population growth has made inevitable the importing, production and distribution of food on industrial lines. The development of Fitch Lovell and similar great concerns to organise the food industry also became inevitable.

Not only did the population grow, it became increasingly concentrated in vast cities remote from the countryside, and this urban concentration of the population, the result of the Industrial Revolution, has left its mark on the food industry.

The countryside too has changed. During the 18th century agriculture emerged from the primitive state in which it had lain for many hundreds of years. The work of men like Viscount Townshend and Robert Brightwell made possible the production of cheaper food on a larger scale. Even so, Britain had already become a net importer of food by the end of the 18th century. Increased home production coupled with unrestricted imports, although essential for the feeding of the growing population, led to severe agricultural depression. This spelt disaster for the yeomen of England, and many of them sent their sons to the cities, where they were ideally qualified to organise the new food trade. Much of this happened within the memory of my own father. My grandfather, Peter Keevil, was one of the yeomen of England, springing from a family with occupation of land going back for 700 years. I remember my father telling me how, in his early days, his father said to his family, 'Children we may not have enough to eat this winter'. No fewer than six of Peter Keevil's sons came to London from their native Wiltshire to found businesses, most of them in the food trade. Many of the firms from which Fitch Lovell has grown started in the same way. The Fitches came from Essex, the Lovells and the Gilhams from Somerset, the Beales from Warwickshire and the Walls from Derbyshire.

Then, as now, London was the greatest city in the kingdom, and it was to London that most of the hopeful young countrymen came. The rural exodus to our company was led by young James Fitch, who said goodbye to Great Dunmow, Essex, in 1777. He found that the food trade in London had hardly changed since medieval times. The only retailers allowed to trade were those who had been apprenticed to a freeman of the City, and who, on completion of their apprenticeship, had themselves taken up the freedom of a City Company or Guild. The Lord Mayor and his Court were still virtual dictators of trade within the City walls and for up to seven miles outside. Price control was exercised from the Guildhall, and it was an offence to offer goods for sale other than in the markets. No one was allowed to own more than one shop selling poultry, butter or eggs. As always when control is too rigid,

black marketeers had appeared. These traders went outside the limits of London to buy from the farmers before they could reach the markets.

Beneath the Lord Mayor were the great City Companies, whose powers over their members make modern Trade Unions look like boys' clubs. Freemen engaged in selling food had to belong to the appropriate Livery Company, Butchers', Poulters', Grocers', Bakers' or Fruiterers'. Curiously enough the cheesemongers of the City never had their own Company. They seem to have been taken under the wing of the Clothworkers. Edward Whinnell, to whom James Fitch was apprenticed, was a Freeman of that Company. Of all the Companies, the Grocers' was the foremost in the 18th century, controlling not only grocers but also druggists, confectioners and tobacconists. The Grocers' Company, like the others, had wide powers. Its officials could enter warehouses and shops to inspect merchandise and test for purity and they controlled the weights and measures that were used. They could throw into prison any merchant found guilty of selling damaged or adulterated goods.

One of the prime concerns of these City authorities was the maintenance of open markets. The principal and probably the most ancient of the flesh markets was the Shambles on the north side of Newgate Street. Another, called the Stocks Market, stood on the present site of the Mansion House. From earliest times a market for the sale of live horses and cattle was held on certain days of the week at Smithfield, or Smoothfield. After the Great Fire, in 1666, meat was sold wholesale in Eastcheap, the butchers living in the adjoining houses, but such was the congestion there that the City Corporation rebuilt the Leaden Hall for the sale of meat and other victuals.

The Fleete Market near the Fleet River (which was an open sewer and one in which a Bromley barber 'was found one morning stuck with feet in air and frozen to death'), was opened just before James Fitch came to London and functioned until 1829. Built to replace the Stocks Market it was mainly for the sale of vegetables, corn and fruit. The Fleet River was covered over to provide for a meat and vegetable market and occupied the centre of the whole length of Farringdon Street. It consisted of two lines of shops, covered over and provided with skylights. Other markets included Covent Garden Market and Newgate Market, which in the 17th century had developed from the New Gate Shambles, adjacent to the site of the present Old Bailey. It was here that my family firm had its origin and even today Keevil and Keevil head their notepaper, 'Established in Old Newgate Market 1797'. It was through the sale of corn and meal in this market and the surrounding tenements, where the market salesmen lived, that the Newgate-Smithfield area gradually developed into the centre for the general provision trade, while Eastcheap and Mincing Lane remained the centre for groceries.

It is important to remember that these markets were not confined to the wholesale trade, which was a 19th-century development. Covent Garden Market, for example, started in an informal way with the villagers of Kensington, Hampstead, Chelsea and other London suburbs, bringing their fruit and vegetables for sale in Inigo Jones's piazza. This market did not need to be as strictly controlled as the others, because the sale of fruit and vegetables did not create the mess found in the meat and poultry markets.

There, the disposal of entrails and putrid meat was a source of continual trouble. The extent of the problem is well conveyed by the names of streets adjoining the New Gate Market, more eloquent than any description: Butchers' Hall Lane, Chicken Lane and Stinken Lane.

The archaic, tightly controlled trading system of markets and City Companies was about adequate for James Fitch's London, with its population of 800,000, but the centuries-old pattern of trade, in which the country people brought their surplus produce on pack horses or in waggons for sale in London, was soon overwhelmed by the sudden growth in population. The Freemen were constantly appointing buyers outside the seven mile limit. Imports were arriving uncontrolled from abroad and as the 19th century progressed the Lord Mayor and the City Companies were forced to abandon their attempts to control the capital's trade. The way was open for outsiders, like John Cary Lovell, to enter the City and revolutionise the food industry.

Despite the decline in its authority the Corporation continued to supervise the markets, which grew in importance during the 19th century and became exclusively wholesale. They handled large quantities of produce, much of it imported, and dictated the price of commodities throughout the country, and beyond. A big international trade grew up, and without refrigeration or reliable fast transport, the commerce was ruled by the London wholesalers who built up large business-houses by their ability to recognise fine produce and to judge the state of the market. Many of them were the same young men who had come to London earlier in the century and taken to the provisions trade because of their knowledge of farming and familiarity with horses, which they used to pull their delivery vans. Some of these men eventually found themselves, half a century later, at the head of important joint stock companies, providing finance for producers all over the world.

It was far from certain that Smithfield would become the centre for all this activity, although there was a cattle market there. New Gate Market was the main meat market of the capital in the first half of the century and in 1836 the City Corporation and the House of Commons decided that Smithfield was too near the centre of London and proposed that a new cattle market should be built in Islington. The move was strenuously resisted by the market traders. The authorities were adamant however, and a new market was built on 15 acres of land at Islington. The project failed, despite the fact that the traders reluctantly agreed to support it. On an average market day soon after the new market opened, 20,000 beasts were sold at Smithfield and only 3,000 at Islington. In defiance of both Corporation and Parliament the traders continued to use Smithfield and in 1841 the area available there for the live market was enlarged. However, as the volume of business continued to grow, congestion grew too and the Corporation became determined to move the cattle traders out of Smithfield. In 1855 the government gave the Lord Mayor permission to open the Caledonian Market, north of King's Cross. This time the authorities won. Smithfield, vacated, remained an open site. Shutters went up on the surrounding warehouses and the public houses became empty.

The unnatural quiet at Smithfield lasted for 13 years. By 1868 New Gate Market had become hopelessly congested. It was impossible for this market to expand on its confined site, so the Corporation decided to erect a large dead meat and poultry market at Smithfield, and made another approach to Westminster. Opened in 1869 the new market established the New Gate-Smithfield area as the food distribution centre for the whole of southern England. It remained so right up to the Second World War. Between 1870 and 1889 other provision markets were also opened. Round the markets the salesmen established their offices and, side by side with them, the general provision wholesalers became established in warehouses which were on the sites of those coffee-houses and inns where, in former times, countrymen used to sell their produce.

The growth of London inevitably drew food from a wider and wider area, and by the mid-19th century imported food was beginning to become important as basic commodities could no longer be produced in sufficiently large quantities on English farms. Dairy produce was imported from Holland and Belgium; then, in 1842, when the ban on imported livestock was lifted, live cattle flooded in from the Continent and Ireland and, increasingly, from America, both North and South.

It was the perishability of meat and dairy produce which held up the development of this importing business, and a vital factor in Fitch Lovell's story is the development of the two main techniques for preserving food – canning and freezing. For centuries the only methods of preserving perishable foods were brining, dry salting, the addition of spices and herbs, partial cooking, storing in caves and drying in the sun. For one reason or another, all these methods were unsuitable for use in large volume trade. The first steps into canning and freezing were made by Frenchmen; the first viable canning process being evolved in 1810 by one Appert, while Charles Tellier invented the first successful ice-making machine.

During the Napoleonic Wars when France was cut off from colonial supplies of the cane sugar used for preserving fruits, Appert, a skilled chef who ran a food preserving business near Paris submitted to his government a prize-winning account of a process he had invented. A copy of this account found its way to London, where one Peter Durand immediately took out a patent for, 'an invention communicated to me by a certain foreigner residing abroad'. He sold it for £1,000 to the firm of Donkin & Hall, which began using soldered tinplate containers, instead of the glass jars suggested by Appert. The new process was so successful that when in 1815 Sir Edward Parry set out to explore the Arctic, Donkin & Hall did much of the provisioning of his ships. One of these, *The Fury*, was caught in the ice and put part of its canned stores on shore. One of the tins was picked up by Captain Ross's later expedition and kept by his descendants, who did not open it until 1938, when the contents were found still to be well-preserved.

Canned foods did not begin to reach the shops until 1830. They were slow in selling because of their price. Corned beef cost 1s. 8d. per lb. and salmon 2s. 3d. (the rent of a whole house at that time might be only 2s. 6d. a week). Prices were so high because even a skilled man could only fill 100 cans a day. Moreover, the cans were made from rolled sheets of wrought iron, using at least five times the amount of metal used nowadays. Their lids were fitted by placing a sheet of metal across the top of a can and hammering it down over the side. The lid was then soldered on. These early cans were so heavy that a lifting ring was sometimes fitted to make their handling easier and they could only be opened with a hammer and chisel. It is hardly surprising that they did not appeal very much to the housewife!

Alternative methods of canning began to be used in America about 1860 after Pasteur discovered that bacteria, not air, caused food to decay. The practice of leaving vent holes in the can was then discontinued. The real breakthrough, which established the tin can as one of the symbols of our modern way of life, was made in America when a German immigrant called Max Ames invented the method of canning which used double seams made airtight by a sealing gasket of rubber solution applied to the ends. The first British Ames factory was not set up until 1927 and only after the Second World War did canned goods become an established part of our everyday diet.

Refrigeration was however slow to develop from Tellier's original ideas and the first commercial freezing works was not established until 1861, and only in 1879 did the development of refrigerated ships enable meat to be shipped from Melbourne to London. The first consignment, which weighed 40 tons, was actually frozen on board the ship. The voyage took 96 days and when the meat arrived at Smithfield it was found to be in excellent condition. The beef sold for 4d. a lb.

The success of this experiment opened the way for the shipment of vast quantities of meat, not only from Australia but also from New Zealand, the United States, and, above all, from the Argentine.

Butter too could now be imported from any distance, and by 1918 the largest single source of Britain's butter was half way round the world in New Zealand. Refrigerated railway wagons began to come into use and imposing cold stores sprang up around Smithfield and in the vicinity of the major ports.

The advances in techniques of food preservation combined with the rapid development of steamships and a home government devoted to a cheap food policy brought imports to Britain from every corner of the globe, and the importance of this new trade was recognised in 1887 by the foundation of the Home and Foreign Produce Exchange near London Bridge. (The Exchange still survives as the London Provision Exchange.)

By the late 1880s butter was being imported in large quantities from Normandy and Brittany, a trade which had begun during the seige of Paris in 1870. In the north of England people acquired a taste for Kiel Butter, so called because it arrived in northern ports in wooden casks stamped *Kiel*, the name of the port of shipment, (in fact most of this butter was Danish). By the turn of the century butter was also being imported from Australia, New Zealand, the Argentine and Russia, and by the early years of this century large amounts of cheese were also imported from Australia, New Zealand, the Argentine and Canada, as well as from Europe, and right up to 1939 there was a big international trade in eggs, which came to Britain from Russia, the Baltic, China, Egypt, Argentina, North Africa, France, Italy and Denmark. The traffic in poultry, although smaller was almost as wide.

By 1900 a fairly stable pattern of trade had emerged, with the importers and wholesalers established in the great London and provincial markets drawing supplies from all over the world. Competition was fierce and profits were low, the wholesalers' prosperity being founded on the volume of the business they were able to handle.

Further changes were to come. The very advances in food preservation, transport, finance and organisation, which made possible the complicated trade patterns of the turn of the century, also made possible the gradual standardisation of products and prices and the stabilisation of markets. These changes were to make the highly specialised skills of the wholesaler less and less important. Already, by 1900, the growth of multiple shops was well under way and in the 1930s great integrated companies like Allied Suppliers, and Unigate began to appear. These companies expanded rapidly, as did multiple shops in every field, helped by the low value of property and low rents. The standardisation of packaging made possible mass advertising of branded food, selling it long before it reached the shop. Traditional wholesaling was becoming an expensive luxury and far-sighted firms like Fitch Lovell diversified out of it as quickly as possible.

Two world wars have had a profound effect on the food industry, forcing successive governments to abandon the policy of cheap food and under the system of farm subsidies British agriculture has revived to an extent unknown since the Napoleonic Wars. Devastated by bombing, Smithfield has never recovered its position as the centre for the provisions trade. Most of the important firms have moved their warehouses and depots out of Town; (traffic congestion has also played a part in this move, which has been mirrored in other great centres like Liverpool and Glasgow); although Smithfield Market and the other markets continue, they have lost their supreme importance as ever larger quantities of food move direct from importer, manufacturer and producer to retailer.

Prosperity, high wages and inflation have also had their effect on the food trade. The well-off can no longer obtain domestic servants to cook for them. Attracted by high wages more and more women take jobs outside their homes, so a demand has been created for convenience foods and labour-saving gadgets. Nowadays the typical domestic servant is in a factory making washing machines, the typical shop assistant working in a cannery. A whole new food manufacturing industry has sprung up.

The demand for convenience foods has been further stimulated in recent years by the introduction of quick frozen foods. This preservation technique was introduced to Western civilisation by Col. Clarence Birds Eye, an Arctic explorer who learned about quick freezing food from the Eskimos who dropped their food in the ice. By means of quick freezing a wider range of food can be preserved for longer periods than it could by means of old-fashioned refrigeration. With the spread of the home deep-freeze the consumption of frozen food is likely to grow even faster in the future.

One must accept the changed conditions, which have affected Fitch Lovell as they have every firm in the industry. At the same time I feel that we are the poorer for the loss of the enterprising owner-proprietor. Inevitably relations between staff and employer have changed. The family atmosphere of the old private firms, where the senior partner or chairman considered himself responsible for the welfare of his staff and their families, has largely disappeared. The men who built up those firms have all passed and with them many others who managed and developed their concerns and still found time, as was considered right and proper in those days, to take a leading part in local affairs and in the work of churches, charities and hospitals.

These leaders, and others 'which have no memorial' laid the foundations which the present generation has had the good fortune to inherit.

# 2

## JAMES FITCH TO FITCH & SON LTD.

BEHIND YOUNG JAMES Fitch when, for the first time one midsummer morning in 1784, he took down the shutters of what was now his own shop in Leadenhall Street, stretched many generations of masters and apprentices. His mind was doubtless little bothered by any considerations of the kind; he knew that he was but recently out of his own apprenticeship, was his own master and aspired to greater things than his predecessors had achieved. Those predecessors had lived and conducted their cheesemongery either in the same building where James now stood, (and where 34 years later his great nephew would recall, as an early childhood recollection, the sight of James's coffin draped with a Union Jack standing in the shop), or in a building two doors further east. The choice of shop and dwelling on the north side of Leadenhall Street, adjacent to St. Katherine Cree, must surely have been dictated by the survival of the district from the Great Fire of London

Prior to 1666 earlier generations had been cheesemongers in the parish of St. Mary at Hill to the south, a district completely gutted by the Fire. Tiring perhaps of delays in rebuilding and being doubtless anxious to start trading on his own, since he had only been made free in 1664, the master of the firm then existing seized the opportunity offered by the premises in Leadenhall Street. Here, and in the other building mentioned, business was uninterruptedly carried on for some 160 years until, on recovery from the disastrous slump following the Napoleonic Wars, a larger shop and warehouse with dwelling above was bought in 1828 by James's nephew and sometime apprentice, George Fitch, at what was then 66 Bishopsgate Within.

The memory of the Gate persisted for many years after its demolition and those 'Within' the City walls considered their address superior to those 'Without'. 66 became in course of time 99 Bishopsgate and here during 101 years of occupation members of two generations of the family were born, the last, in 1873, being Hugh Bernard Fitch, later to be first Chairman of the public company formed in 1920 and afterwards first President of Fitch Lovell Ltd.

During the first 50 years' trading under the name of Fitch various members of the family came and went as partners; James had very soon taken his brother William into partnership but the latter died in 1801; the articles of partnership of his nephew George are dated 1812. In 1818, at the date of his uncle's death, George was 38 and his eldest son Frederick, then aged four, was the diarist who later recorded the impressive sight of his great-uncle's coffin. For a few years George's younger brother Thomas was a partner and it was the two brothers who negotiated the purchase of the larger Bishopsgate premises. In 1836 Thomas withdrew and Frederick at the age of 22 took his place. Thereafter the style of the firm became George Fitch and Son and later just Fitch and Son, the name which survives to the present day.

The partnership of father and son was not destined to last long since George, through ill-health, retired in 1841 and died the following year. Frederick's diary, as might be expected of an ambitious young man with an ailing father, reveals them at cross purposes in the few years they worked together, the father much too conservative in the son's opinion and doubtless George thought his son far too incautious.

Once on his own, Frederick put out a very carefully worded circular over the name of 'G. Fitch and Son', enumerating the goods he sold and the deliveries made and in what districts. As this appears to be the earliest surviving list of his provisions it is worth quoting in full.

> The finest Fresh Butter from the Vale of Aylesbury – a locality unequalled in this or any other country for dairy produce – Dorset Butter, Parmesan, Stilton, and Cheshire Cheese, Bath Breakfast Bacon as agreeable for its delicious relish as it is for its wholesome properties – Bath Chaps, Berkshire Collared Heads – a novelty – German Sausages, York Hams and Ox Tongues are among the articles we have the honour to offer to Public Notice.

To Families residing in the neighbourhood we beg to intimate that we have three simultaneous deliveries of Butter and Eggs at 8 o'clock in the morning.

One down Bishopsgate Without and the Streets and Squares adjacent as far as Shoreditch.

Another to the North West through Broad Street, Finsbury Circus and Square, etc. to Artillery Place.

And the third up Bishopsgate Within, Leadenhall and King William Streets, and Cheapside with the Places and Squares adjacent.

We have also regular deliveries by our own Cart in and about the following places: Hackney, Clapton, Stoke Newington, etc. on Tuesdays and Saturdays.

Islington, Regent's Park, and the West End on Fridays.

Stepney, Limehouse, Bow, etc. on Mondays and throughout London daily.

It is interesting to note that, though relegated to a *post scriptum* 'Shipping Orders' were 'executed to any extent'. It was through this activity and also because Frederick was of the same religious persuasion as Dr. David Livingstone, the explorer, that the two men met and struck up friendship; The degree of special pleading to which this relationship gave rise appears in extracts from Livingstone's letters from Africa which were used as advertisements; writing from the Zambesi in 1859 he says 'The hams you sent kept admirably; the bacon too was in good condition. Hams supplied by other houses to the Expedition were not good' (!) The following year he wrote; 'Two of them [hams] were saved for the long journey into the Makololo Country; and were still as good as when they came out two years before'.

In such papers and advertisements as have survived no mention is made of any date of establishment of the business until the mid-1850s. It may be that about this date it became fashionable to specify the number of years a firm had been trading – if such was ascertainable. James can certainly never have thought of himself as 'establishing' a business and even though his nephew George lived to see more than 50 years' trading under the name of Fitch he apparently made no public claim to whatever merit long establishment is thought to confer.

Frederick, too young to have heard from James personally about his start in trade, whatever he may have heard from his own father George, waited until he could claim 70 years' continuous trading before making a point of it in his advertising. In an advertisement marked in Frederick's hand 'Mar 26/55' the wording 'Established 1784' is used for the first time. Thereafter it came to be accepted as in fact the date of commencement of trading.

Frederick's eldest son, Edwin Frederick, who had been born in 1839, joined his father in the firm at the age of 22. Just before this event Frederick, in conformity with the Early Closing Movement, put out a notice dated 21 September 1860 in which he 'respectfully announced that on and after Monday October 15th the Establishment will be closed at 8 o'clock every evening excepting Saturdays; and then at 10 o'clock'. He further hoped that 'this boon to the Assistants will occasion no inconvenience to customers'.

The year 1863 was noteworthy in as much as Frederick received his first Royal Warrant as Purveyor of Bacon to His Royal Highness the Prince of Wales, dated 2 March; and, as is the habit of new brooms, Edwin lost no time in putting his ideas into practice. On 15 June a notice was published – the Prince of Wales's feathers and appropriate wording filling all the left margin – stating that

> Messrs. Fitch and Son beg to inform their friends that their premises, 66 Bishopsgate Within, are about to be rebuilt. They leave them on July 1st, and take possession of them again October 15th following. In the interval their business will be carried on at No. 63, at the corner of Camomile Street, and immediately opposite their present premises. They deem themselves particularly fortunate in having secured so eligible a situation, involving so little or no inconvenience to their customers.

Incredible though it may seem, in these days of mechanisation, computers, productivity talk and the rest, 105 days sufficed for the demolition of the old building and the erection of a new one comprising ground floor and four floors above.

Frederick now lived at Highbury New Park but Edwin and his wife moved into the upper floors of the new building and continued to reside there until after the birth of their fourth child 10 years later.

Unfortunately the rebuilding, an occasion that must have been the cause of much rejoicing at the time, was almost certainly also the reason for the destruction of all the early Company Account Books. Only a Journal of 1818 has survived – perhaps because it was some way connected with the year of James's death. The new broom in some respects only too well did his imagined duty.

As a result nothing is known with certainty of the goods sold in very early years, but it may be presumed that they resembled those quoted in the list above, with, in addition, very probably the great cartwheels of Essex cheese. As an article of trade these disappeared in the early years of the 19th century but since James's father was an Essex farmer, the supposition does not seem unlikely. A son with an outlet in London for farm produce would clearly be an asset.

With the removal of Edwin and his family to a house on Stamford Hill in about 1875, much more space became available for office staff. The Bishopsgate premises extended back to Helmet Court, which itself gives on to Wormwood Street. This rear portion was allotted to the developing Export and Shipping Department; from here and from the warehouse in what was then Bridge Road, Limehouse, now West Ferry Road, customers all over the world, as well as shipping companies, were supplied. The growing trade of Southampton and Liverpool occasioned the opening of export warehouses in both those ports.

Under Edwin a number of branch shops were also established in outer London, but bad choice of managers and general lack of supervision made this early experiment in 'multiples' a failure.

In 1880, Frederick, who had been trading for 44 years, retired, leaving Edwin sole partner for the next 10. Frederick lived on until 1909, dying in his 96th year. Having been born before the Battle of Waterloo, when a galloping horse was the fastest means of transport, he lived to see the inauguration of railways, the birth of the internal combustion engine, and the early essays in flight. His diary never makes mention of any static quality in 19th-century life. For him, now that the Industrial Revolution was well under way, orderly progress seemed inevitable and would eventually bring about a Utopia, where Victorian virtues would have their reward. (Frederick's grandchildren saw the last years of the century in quite another light; for them, as year succeeded year, nothing ever seemed to change and impatience seethed.)

Stanley Fox Fitch, Edwin's eldest son, joined his father as partner in 1890 at the approved age of 23, as previous generations had done. (As a bachelor he resided in rooms over the premises at Bishopsgate and indeed continued to occupy them after his own retirement and until several years after the Kaiser's War. The crusty temperament for which he was reputed was never apparent to the numerous nephews and nieces who made their way to the City during school holidays to lunch with him and be generously tipped.)

Edwin's wife died in 1891, an event which changed his whole manner of life, although he did not retire from the firm until 1907, when its Home Department became a Private Limited Company – Fitch & Son Ltd. – of which his sons Stanley and Hugh were the principals.

A year earlier, in 1906, the Export Department had also become a Private Limited Company, under the title Fitch & Son (Export) Ltd., energetically guided by Charles and John Baker. As a young man John Baker had sailed before the mast and he brought an unwonted and refreshing outlook to the Department's affairs. He joined Fitch to look after the delivery vans and horses. He had been doing this job, and driving a horse van, for Hudson Bros. of Southsea, and when he was offered the job at Fitch he wrote on 20 September 1895 accepting, but regretting that he was unable to come for a fortnight because Hudsons' 'have no one else to see to the horse carts'. 20 years later when Fitch became a public company his name appeared on the prospectus as Vice-Chairman. Hugh Fitch often said he considered John Baker to be one of the most remarkable men he had known.

The formation of the two companies was accompanied by a complete reorganisation of the firm. H.S. Rowlandson, the son of a representative who had been with the partnership since 1869, became Secretary. A newcomer to the Home Department was E.F. Ashelford, who greatly developed the hotel and restaurant supply trade, and thus, while retail business was still being done at Bishopsgate a footing was gained in the West End by the acquisition of Bellamy Bros.' shops, three of which stood between St. James's Street and Charing Cross.

Fitch became a public company in July 1920. The prospectus was advertised in *The Daily Telegraph* and *The Evening Standard*. The first directors were: H.B. Fitch, Chairman; E.F. Ashelford, Managing Director; H.S. Rowlandson, Director and Secretary; E.C. Beale, John Baker, Charles Baker, E.A. Crawford and J.T. Muncaster. The original share issue was 80,000 8% £1 preference and 80,000 £1 ordinary shares. The number applied for was 67,251 preference and 64,980 ordinary. Assets in 1920 were put at £226,000, the profits for the preceding eight years having varied between £15,800 and £42,800.

1. Smithfield – London's famous cattle market in the 'good old days'

2. Newgate Market, 1856. From a drawing by T. Hosmer Shepherd

The [illegible]

James Fitch Cheesemonger

1784 To Cheesemongery Goods as per Bill from 29 September 1784 to the 23d December following both inclusive — 17 8 9

1785 To Cheesemongery Goods delivered at the Workhouse as per Bill from the 7 January 1785 to the 24th March following both inclusive — 19 1 10

1786 To Cheesemongery Goods deliverd at the Workhouse as per Bill from the 26 March to the 23 June following both inclusive — [illegible]

To Cheesemongery Goods deliverd at the Workhouse from the 4th day of July 1786 to 25th day of September 1786 both days inclusive — [illegible]

1787 To Cheesemongery Goods deliverd at the Workhouse from the 1st day of January 1787 to the 24 Day of March 1787 both days inclusive — 19 6 1

To Cheesemongery Goods delivered at the Workhouse from the 27th June 1787 to 26th September following both Days inclusive — 18 17 8¼

1788 To Cheesemongery Goods delivered at the Workhouse from 29th March to 21st June 1788 both Days inclusive — 16 14 7

3. James Fitch: Account, 1784-1788

4. A selection of trade cards from Fitch & Son

5. The Home & Foreign Produce Exchange, London, 1891

A COPY of this PROSPECTUS HAS BEEN FILED with the REGISTRAR OF JOINT STOCK COMPANIES.

NO PART OF THIS ISSUE HAS BEEN OR WILL BE UNDERWRITTEN.

*Application will be made to the Committee of the Stock Exchange for permission to deal, after allotment, in the Shares offered herein.*

The Subscription List will close on or before Saturday, the 10th day of July, 1920.

# FITCH & SON, LIMITED

**(Amalgamating Fitch & Son, Ltd., Fitch & Son Export Ltd., George Partridge & Co., Bellamy Brothers, and the Fairoak Dairy Produce Co.)**

(*Incorporated under the Companies Acts,* 1908 *to* 1917.)

## SHARE CAPITAL:

| AUTHORISED: | | ISSUED: (including shares to be allotted in part payment of Purchase Price). |
|---|---|---|
| £150,000 | in 150,000 8 per cent. Cumulative Preference Shares of £1 each | £150,000 |
| £150,000 | in 150,000 Ordinary Shares of £1 each - - - - - | £150,000 |
| £300,000 | | £300,000 |

## ISSUE OF

## 80,000 8 per cent. Cumulative Participating Preference Shares and 80,000 Ordinary Shares.

| PAYABLE | FOR THE PREFERENCE AND ORDINARY SHARES: |
|---|---|
| 2s. 6d. | per Share on Application, |
| 7s. 6d. | per Share on Allotment, |
| 10s. 0d. | per Share within two months after Allotment. |
| £1 0s. 0d. | |

6. Part of the Prospectus of Fitch & Son Ltd., 1920

Of the directors, E.C. Beale had been many years with the Home Department and was almost of retiring age. He was given a directorship to complete his career. The Baker brothers have already been mentioned; Charles soon retired owing to ill health, but John remained as a sort of elder statesman for another ten years. Crawford and Muncaster represented the active Export and Shipping Department.

Even after the formation of the public company the essentially family nature of the business persisted. The shareholders were almost all employed by the company and, as in previous generations the principals had been known to all as 'Mr. Frederick', 'Mr. Edwin', or 'Mr. Stanley', so 'Mr. Hugh' when he became the first Chairman retained the familiar epithet, by which he was always addressed.

Such was the situation as the company entered the rapidly changing world of the 1920s. The days when everyone knew everyone, together with their family history, and which had made firms like Fitch's family ones in the widest sense, were rapidly vanishing. Growth and the rush and pressure of new American methods eliminated the easier-going ways that had existed before 1914.

## 3

# FITCH TO FITCH LOVELL (1920-1958)

THE PRIME MOVER in the transformation of Fitch & Son Ltd. from a private to a public company and of its activities afterwards was Hervy Stanley Rowlandson, although he was only the Secretary and a very junior director of the firm.

H.S.R., as he was known, was an extremely able man with a first-class brain. He joined the firm in 1893 and advanced from Office Boy to Clerk, thence to Office Manager and in the end to the Principal Director. He was the most influential figure in Fitch's until his death in 1956, for he combined to an unusual extent the expertise of an accountant with the instincts of an alert trader.

His main contribution to Fitch & Son was to forsee in the '20s that, if the company was to continue viable, it would have to diversify out of its staple business of retail and secondary wholesale provisions. (Foresight was something for which H.S.R. will always be remembered. 20 years before his death he wrote in detail how his funeral service was to be conducted and included a summary of his faith and philosophy to be read at it.) The two main areas into which he led the company were the growing factory-made cakes industry and the manufacture of the new product, plywood. Although these activities did little to improve Fitch's profitability at first, they were to contribute much in later years, particularly during the war.

H.S. Rowlandson and his family held a large personal interest in both the bakery and the timber companies. Indeed Fitch was content to leave minority interests, which were sometimes substantial, in many of the ventures in which it became involved. The policy reflected H.S.R.'s own belief that directors and employees ought to have a personal interest in the profitability of the venture in which they worked. As far as companies bought by Fitch were concerned, H.S.R. regarded a continuing financial interest on the part of the vendor as a form of insurance if the vendor was staying on as manager. Without this continuing shareholding he might be tempted to take his cash and leave, and the future of the concern be jeopardised.

Fitch kept its policy of permitting and even encouraging these minority interests for more than 40 years, and the system seems to have worked well. The policy was regularised at the Annual General Meeting of 27 May 1942, when the following motion was passed unanimously:

> That this meeting of the Company do hereby approve and endorse the action of the directors in acquiring in the past or in the future any personal interest in any business or businesses acquired by the Company and no director being so interested shall be liable to account to the Company for any profit or other benefits so acquired.

Nearly all these holdings have now been sold, because of a desire by the holders to capitalise on their position, or to retire, or perhaps through their lack of confidence in the business in question. Modern professional thought is not in favour of minority shareholdings even by executives, but the fact remains, however, that without these holdings Fitch Lovell would not have been able to grow into the important company it is today.

To return to the early days of the new company – in the 1920s, before the flotation of Fitch, H.S.R., who always had an eye for a bargain, had managed to acquire Bellamy of Jermyn Street, George Partridge – bakers' sundriesmen – and Fairoak and Foxhole Farm – farmers and butter-blenders. It was decided to sell the Fairoak premises in August 1920, the asking price being £35,000. (They are still unsold and their valuation in 1965 was £30,000, which shows that values of properties do not always rise.) As soon as the public issue was made H.S.R. continued his search. In 1922 Fitch & Son acquired the wholesale grocers Gold Bros. & Nash for £4,500 and John Radmalls, bacon distributors, for rather less than asset value. In 1926 it bought a minority interest in the Southwark Bacon Drying Co. and purchased the goodwill of Webb Sons & Clarke, wholesale provisions, for £1,000; it took over the Norfolk Poultry Packing Company and also bought an interest in the Scottish textile firm of Wilson & Glenny with which M.F.B. Fitch was connected by marriage. Another company taken over by Fitch was H.J. Webb & Co. of Smithfield, importers of rabbits and salesmen of provisions. (This firm still exists as Webb & Fowler Ltd., but has sold its market tenancies.) The Managing Director of Webb Sons & Clarke, A.H. Jones, joined the Fitch board, which later was further strengthened by the election of J.H.T. Clayton, who had been with the firm's Home Department for many years. It was through my association with Clayton that Keevils' merged with Fitch some 10 years later.

Despite this expansion, 1931 was a poor year for Fitch & Son and it was decided that 'in view of the bad times through which the company is passing that directors' salaries should be reduced and that Christmas boxes to directors be discontinued'.

Among all the little businesses with which Fitch became associated in these years, the name of Stephen Siratsky stands out, not so much because of his contribution to Fitch's profits, but through the scale and style of his activities. Siratsky shot across these rather gloomy years like a comet. Before the war he had been a partner in Brill, Siratsky & Co., the Russian poultry importers and he was to become the outstanding man in the European poultry world. He was a tall, elegant man speaking several languages and had an intimate knowledge of Eastern Europe and America.

Strangely enough, he was a close friend of my brother, C. Percy Keevil. They were exact opposites in many ways, but between them in the late '20s and the '30s, they more or less dominated the European poultry trade, Stephen with his ability to obtain and maintain supplies, and Percy with his uncanny judgment of markets.

Siratsky decided in 1921 to work through Drabble Baranoff & Sieffert of Tooley Street, importers of Russian and European poultry and eggs, whom Fitch & Son had purchased earlier that year. Fitch agreed to back his operations. On the whole it was a most fortunate association for Fitch. Siratsky's activities contributed substantially to their ailing profits. In 1925, both Siratsky and Maynard his co-manager at Drabble, were invited to become directors of Fitch.

Fitch early in 1923 had no less than nine different small companies or branches, but the results were meagre. With the value of hindsight it is not difficult to understand why. 'The original business was not kept up to date, the newer businesses were too small and changes of management were frequent. Head Office appears to have interfered too much with the trading managers. Administration was efficient, but the ability to make worth while profits was lacking.

Although none of the companies seem to have contributed much to the Group profits it was mainly because of wise property operations, not unconnected with the companies, that Fitch's financial position in 1939 was, in spite of everything, somewhat better than it had been in 1920.

Another generation of the Fitch family was on the way and Hugh's only son Marc, representative of the sixth generation, entered the firm in 1927, becoming a director in 1930 at the age of 23, the age at which it was customary in the Fitch family for a member to become a Partner. He began work with the subsidiary, Drabble Baranoff Sieffert & Co. Ltd. Drabble's was obtaining large supplies of poultry from Eastern Europe, particularly Hungary, and in 1925 it had reached an agreement with a Soviet agency, Solosoyus Ltd., for the sale of 50 trucks of poultry. This importing business, although profitable, needed large sums to finance it, and was straining Fitch's resources. The overdraft rose to £100,000, and when the Russians offered to increase their supplies in return for a loan of £60,000, Fitch's directors had to say 'no'.

Thanks to Siratsky, however, Drabble's continued to give Fitch good profits until 1934. In that year, when the parent firm's timber and bakery sections were both doing badly, Siratsky failed it, and although the poultry business did better in 1936, relations between Siratsky, suavely criss-crossing Europe buying and selling huge quantities of poultry, and the Board of Fitch & Son, nervously watching him from London, began to deteriorate. Finally he decided to sever his connection with the firm and begin trading on his own account.

Meanwhile, the Bishopsgate shop, which, in earlier days, City merchants had been in the habit of visiting themselves, buying provisions to be carried out to their waiting carriages, found its retail trade gradually dwindling as the carriage gave way to the motor car and outer London acquired its own retail shops.

Gone were the days when, in frock coat and four-in-hand, Edwin had received his distinguished customers, proferring to each, for instance, a cheese-iron which it was intended they should plunge into the Stilton he had himself selected, having a lifetime's knowledge of the idiosyncrasies of every aristocratic palate. To buy less than a whole Stilton for households of those days was scarcely to be considered.

Thus, through the change and movement of trade it came about that, in September 1929, Fitch's business moved to '80/81 St. Martin's Lane, in the West End. The Bishopsgate building was sold to J. Lyons & Co. Ltd. for £50,000; a last bottle of champagne was drunk in the room in which Hugh had been born, the glass was broken in the old grate, and 101 years' occupation came to an end.

Much of the optimism felt as Fitch moved into St. Martin's Lane was soon dispelled. Far from improving, the trading climate grew steadily worse. In 1933 the directors were unable to recommend a final dividend on the ordinary shares, and in the following year an Extraordinary General Meeting was summoned to reorganise the company's capital. The 8% preference shares were reduced to 6% and the right of preference shareholders to participate in the surplus profits of the company was annulled. In return, they were given one ordinary share for every 10 preference shares held. At the same time the ordinary shares were written down from £1 to 10s., £50,000 was written off goodwill and £30,000 off investments.

In 1935, profits before tax were only £12,500. Even so, the company managed to pay 3% on the new 10s. ordinary shares and thereafter things began to pick up a bit and the dividend was raised to 5% in the following year. In 1937 and 1938 profits approached £15,000 but fell sharply to £7,500 in 1939 when there was again no dividend. E.F. Ashelford, the Managing Director resigned.

He had held this position since the launching of the company in 1920. Like John Baker, the Vice-Chairman, he had come from Hudson Bros. A first-class salesman, which was most important in those days of fierce competition, he had been introduced to Fitch by my father, Clement Keevil. H.S. Rowlandson had already resigned as Secretary in 1938 and been succeeded by G.S. McDonald, who had done so much to make the bakery section profitable.

It is easy to criticise and anyone whose business experience falls only within the inflationary period since Hitler's War may find the failure of pre-war companies to earn profits hard to understand. but they should realise that the commodity price index has risen from 225 to 539 over the last 20 years, whereas between 1920 and 1938 the same index fell from 336 to 125, while London Bank Clearings per head are today 37 times greater than in 1900.

It is now a matter of history that the war, though vastly destructive of both life and property, brought the long depression of the inter-war years to an end. Although Fitch's hotel-supplying business was badly hit, and the ship supply and export trade virtually ceased, the bakery and timber interests suddenly picked up.

K. Norman, Fitch's main timber firm, was appointed an importing agent for the government and, as might be expected in time of war, sales of cakes rapidly improved. The bakery division was helped further by arrangement to supply N.A.A.F.I. and the loss to the provisions section of the export trade was partly made up by Fitch's being a member of the Ministry of Food's distributing organisation for poultry and rabbits, which assured it a profit in those trades.

The company's liquid position changed dramatically. The pre-war overdraft disappeared and before long Fitch was able to make an interest-free loan of £15,000 to the government. By the end of the war, government loans and tax certificates amounted to £360,000. In addition, the company had more than £50,000 in the bank.

In 1941, Fitch had used some of its new wealth to buy a majority holding in the West Country firm of Hales Home Bakeries and, as the war ended, it was in a position to acquire some really substantial businesses. It is at this point that I enter the story, for Fitch & Son decided to obtain a majority interest in Keevil & Keevil. (The full story of this merger is told in a later chapter.) My brother Percy stayed on as Chairman of Keevils' and I joined the Fitch Board and formed the Fitch Provisions Co-ordinating Board. The company was reorganised into divisions: bakery, provisions and timber. This was the first attempt to organise according to their functions the various companies under the Fitch umbrella.

Fitch followed the purchase of Keevils with another good investment when it bought the Far Famed Cake Co. These two investments further strengthened its good financial position. Fitch was now poised to begin its dramatic climb from being a comparatively small, director-controlled firm, to becoming one of the principal companies in the food trade and one of the major companies in the country. *The Times 1000 List 1971/1972* cites it as being the 82nd largest U.K. industrial company.

At the end of the war, although the shares were publicly quoted, none were sold on the Stock Exchange in 1945. It was therefore decided to activate a market in the shares, and with this end in view the directors made a pool of shares available to the public through the firm of Chapman & Rowe, to which the company was introduced by Hugh B. Robinson, who had recently returned from a prisoner-of-war camp in Germany. (As a senior partner in the old-established firm of Fenn & Crosthwaite, he is still the company's stock-broker and has rendered many valuable services over the years.)

At the same time it was also decided to make a rights' issue to provide more shares for the market and to give a good bonus to existing shareholders. This was done in June 1946, when a rights' issue of 1 in 3 shares at 20s. was made, in view of the fact that the dividend had been raised to 17½%. The success of the issue was assured as the directors held the controlling interest. In fact it was over-subscribed. The shares opened at 30s. and rose to 65s. within a year, while ordinary dividends mounted to 25% plus a 2½% capital bonus. As the shares had risen so much it was then decided to split the 10s. shares into 2s. 6ds. units, in order to make them more marketable. Each shareholder was given a 3 to 1 bonus.

While new life was thus being injected into the company's finances its management was strengthened by an influx of young men demobilised from the Forces. Many of them proved to be of marked ability. Three, Norman Lambourne, Clement Keevil and John Gilpin, were to become directors of Fitch Lovell. The excellent performance of the shares spread a keen and exciting atmosphere throughout the company. Even those sections which were not benefiting from the continuing controls and licences managed to increase their business and their profits, but after the initial spurt, marked by the buying of Keevils' and Far Famed, it proved difficult to make any immediate headway with the firm's expansion plan. Since Fitch was already established in importing and wholesaling it was chiefly looking for good buys in manufacturing and retailing. While controls continued and profits were not hard to come by, established companies were most reluctant to sell. Moreover, proprietors who were willing to sell invariably wanted to retire themselves, because they were fearful of what would happen when the fat years of control come to an end. Naturally Fitch did not want to buy a company in a field in which it possessed no expertise itself only to find the management skills which it had purchased slipping through its fingers.

Fitch was particularly drawn to the idea of bacon curing and began negotiations with Collins of Evesham, but these came to nothing. Fitch did manage to acquire the old-established bacon wholesaling firm of Impey & Dyke. (The full story of the bacon-curing division is told later.) On the retail side things moved slightly faster, and in October 1947 a group of 15 retail grocers' shops called Partners Stores Ltd. was bought and two years later the foundations were laid of the company's large retail meat chains. (Details of both these developments are contained in later chapters.) We also had a look at a large grocery chain about this time, but the price being asked for it was too high.

Meanwhile Fitch & Son was rapidly reorganising to cope with the big increase in the company's business since pre-war days. In July 1946 monthly turnover figures for the provision section were presented to the Board for the first time, a practice which was soon followed by the bakery and timber sections. These simple figures were the beginning of the detailed analyses with which the Board are now presented. Then in 1947 the Board decided to publish consolidated profit accounts although these were not yet required legally. Profits for the year ending March 1947 were £218,000, rising to £294,000 in 1948 and an upsurge to £424,000 in 1949. The largest contributor was the bakery section. These figures are astonishing compared with the £7,500 profit returned in 1939, less than a decade before.

In 1948 Norman Lambourne whose drive and initiative had been of great benefit to the bakery interest, was appointed a director and John Gilpin became Company Secretary.

In September 1949, the first attempt was made to start a group insurance department, although this did not really materialise until Fitch Lovell Insurances Ltd. was formed 18 years later. That such ideas were being considered in 1949 is evidence of the alertness and virility of the company at that time. In the same year a Group Pensions Scheme was inaugurated. Although commonplace today, such schemes were unusual 25 years ago.

The continued buoyancy of the company opened possibilities to raise its authorised capital. In June 1949, when current assets showed a surplus of more than £600,000, three-quarters of which was in cash and other liquid forms, it was decided to make a script bonus of 2 in 5 to ordinary stockholders bringing the number of ordinary shares in issue to over one million. In January 1950, the authorised capital was increased to £500,000, and a £50,000 bonus issue was made to ordinary shareholders in 5% £1 preference shares on the basis of 1 to 22.5 shares held. £50,000 was the limit a company was allowed to issue at the time without government permission. A further £50,000 was issued in the same way the following year.

Efforts were continually being made to organise the buying and trading in provisions on a group basis, but this never proved satisfactory, and the different companies in the provisions section still tended to go their own way. This was partly because some of the provision companies, particularly Fitch Home, remained the responsibility of directors who were not in the provision section. Fitch Home was run from St. Martin's Lane which was also the Head Office, and naturally those residing there who had supervised Fitch Home for a generation did not want to relinquish control.

Such difficulties are quite common during the initial growth of an old-established company. In fact this problem was not too severe at Fitch because of the friendly personal relations which existed at Board level, so progress was only hindered for a year or two at the most.

While these internal problems were being overcome, decontrol was creeping up on the company. By 1950 canned goods under the Ministry of Food's unit voucher scheme were not all taken up and the supply of rationed bacon began to exceed demand. Stocks of free canned goods began to accumulate. Points rationing was ended in July 1950 and poultry was decontrolled in July. From then on free markets were established rapidly in almost every commodity. Inevitably, decontrol led to a set back for the company. Profits dipped slightly in the next three years, but fell steeply in 1954 to £210,000, less than half the peak figure in the years of control. The effect of falling prices and increased competition was felt in every sector, with the bakery interest particularly hard hit. However, the difficulties were surmounted and, since 1954 the group has not looked back.

Before the decrease in profits had really begun, the Annual Report for 1951 was still able to say '. . . our policy of decentralised interests and participation in the trade at all levels has amply justified itself'.

Rising overhead costs at this period caused a report to be circulated to the directors pointing to the necessity of limiting the expenses of sales, warehousing and transport on the wholesale side to 2½% to 2¾%. (This reads like a fantasy in 1972.)

That summer the company considered the increase in trade was justifiable to apply to the Capital Issues Committee for an issue of rights shares. In due course consent was obtained and 2 shares in every 5 were issued as rights to the ordinary shareholders at 10s., although the market price was approximately 14s. The 2s. 6d. shares which had been split from the original 10s. shares gave the right to 1 vote for every 4. (While on the subject of shares, it is interesting to note that the price of Fitch 6% preference shares reached 30s. about this time and the 5% preference exceeded 20s. Those prices are about 40% higher than the level at which similar shares stand today. It shows the deterioration in the demand for fixed-interest stocks in an inflationary age.)

As well as issuing new shares, the directors showed their conviction that the profits' setback would prove to be only temporary by pressing on with their plans for expansion. A site near London was bought on which they decided to build a bread-baking plant, and in order to help the bakery business out of its difficulties a group of retail cake shops called Crisps Bakeries was purchased. In 1953, the retail meat chain was enlarged and T.M. Cox invited to manage it. In the early days of 1954, our long expressed wish to enter the bacon manufacturing field was finally realised through Bywaters of Birmingham.

The health of H.S. Rowlandson gave some cause for anxiety in 1952, and the Chairman, Hugh Fitch, suggested a remodelling of the Board. He proposed he should retire as Chairman and become President, that S. Graham Rowlandson, the son of H.S.R. who had been the auditor and financial advisor for some years should become Chairman, and that Norman Lambourne and I should become Managing Directors. The proposals were accepted unanimously and as S. Graham Rowlandson could not continue as auditor in view of his appointment, it was agreed that his Junior partner H.D.B. Laughlin should form his own firm and take over this work.

With this reorganisation accomplished, we continued to modernise the company's administration. It was decided that in future a report on the progress of each division should be given at every Board meeting. In January 1953, we set up a small committee of three senior directors to be known as the Group Salaries Committee which would decide on the salaries and commissions payable to senior executives and directors. Over the years numerous alterations had been made to the Articles of Association and it was agreed that a completely revised set of Articles under the Companies Act should be prepared, and also that the capital of the company should be raised to £750,000.

The provisions trade in the United Kingdom proved to be particularly slow at recovering from the setback of decontrol. Results of Fitch Home in particular were unsatisfactory and a committee was set up to investigate. In the year ending March 1953, Fitch Home lost £12,000 and it was decided to search for a new manager. Numerous efforts were made to find firms which might strengthen the provisions section but without success. Many good pre-war firms had not adapted themselves to post-war conditions and in others there was a lack of management continuity. The problems of the wholesale food trade were shown about this time by a report based on returns from 121 wholesale provision and grocery firms in the United Kingdom which showed that the net average profit on sales turnover of the trade in 1952 was 1.21% and 0.93% in 1953. The figures are not much better today.

In the light of those figures, Fitch's desire to diversify is not surprising. In the other fields, things began to improve. The bread bakery was built and reached its production target very quickly, and by March 1955, the bakery group was producing good profits again. The retail side did well and the first self-service store was opened in Drury Lane in the spring of 1954, 'as a basis for experiment in this rapidly increasing type of business'. Although the Company was in the forefront of the supermarket revolution with the Drury Lane shop, it was not until 1961, seven years later, that a concerted thrust was made in this direction. The fact is that the company was too busy digesting the businesses it had acquired and moving them into offices, factories and warehouses, at last being rebuilt after the war, to have the energy for a move into supermarkets at this time. It was an arduous and exacting time and on the whole the company did far better than the average in surmounting its difficulties. Yet it still did not have a sufficiently broad basis to make really spectacular advances.

Meanwhile, a new manager had been found for Fitch Home, and R.G.J. Evans joined the company through the introduction of T.M. Cox. He had not previously been engaged actively in secondary wholesaling and was a little nervous as to how he would achieve sales as his experience had been mainly in buying in the wine trade. He proved to be an apt learner and it was not long before he became master of his job. He turned the loss at Fitch Home into a profit, improving the results steadily, month by month until today, Fitch Home, together with Wholesale Catering Services for which he is also responsible, is one of the most successful organisations in the group. He has proved that it is not difficult for a man of real ability to succeed in an industry with which he is unfamiliar.

In January 1955, the new Chairman began asking for monthly profit figures. Up to this time six-monthly figures were all that had been provided, and there were difficulties at first. These were soon overcome, and it has proved most beneficial to know the position of each company month by month.

S. Graham Rowlandson was a non-executive Chairman, and he made it clear that he had accepted the Chairmanship on the condition that his other business interests would not be affected. He promised that he would not knowingly do anything detrimental to Fitch in the event of a conflict of interests. Two long-serving directors retired during 1954, E.A. Crawford resigned after nearly 60 years with the company, and J.T.H. Clayton also gave up his seat.

The profits showed a substantial improvement in March 1955. They climbed to £364,000, compared with £210,000 the year before. It is noteworthy that sales turnover for the last two weeks of 1954 exceeded the turnover for the whole 12 months ending March 1945.

In 1955, I thought the time had come for the Board to develop its policy of expansion in greater detail. Accordingly a memorandum based on my ideas was drawn up. This was presented to the Board on 15 June 1955, and approved in principle:

1. Manufacture. Extension of existing premises, acquisition of an Egg Station, and as general trade develops possible acquisition of other factories or prepackaging plants.

2. Importing and Agency. Acquisition of an Agency business when a suitable opportunity occurs, being careful that this is not a personal business, as are so many importing businesses.
3. Wholesale. Maintenance and if possible gradual improvement without extension unless something extraordinary is offered.
4. Retail Sales.
   (a) Extension of Groceries and Provisions in London area and to the South and South-West.
   (b) Acquisition, if possible, of retail branches based on Fairoak linking up with the London Southern extension.
   (c) Gradual extension of the meat branches from London to the North West.
   (d) Extension of Bywaters in the Midlands and towards the branches of extending from London.
5. Liaison. Liaison if necessary along the lines adopted with Lovell & Christmas, Elkes and R.W. Smith.

It has been suggested that our expansion was delayed because we were sticking to a preconceived plan. This one had been in my mind since 1936.

It is certainly true that our growth was not as rapid as it might have been, although well above average for the industry. On the other hand, by growing at a slightly slower rate we have been able to ensure that the structure of the company is soundly based with new interests properly consolidated and management control streamlined. In this way we have avoided turning the group into a mere holding company. Obviously there are different opinions on this point. However, the memorandum of 1955 enables us to compare the group's intentions 15 years ago with what has been achieved. It is clear that many of the objectives set out in 1955 were realised three years later when Fitch merged with Lovell & Christmas, particularly in the manufacturing, importing and retail fields. As far as retailing is concerned, the memorandum is notable for failing to mention supermarkets, which are now an important group activity. In general retailing interests have developed quite differently to the way envisaged at that time.

On the manufacturing side, prepacked poultry has become much more important than was foreseen in 1955, although Percy Keevil had forseen it in 1938 and then was making some tentative experiments.

One way of preventing Fitch from turning into a holding company was to make sure that outstanding executives in the subsidiary companies were promoted to the main Board, thus ensuring the

Board possessed trading ability in all the activities in which the group was engaged. Accordingly R.E. Blanning was invited in July 1955 to explain the plans for the development consequent on Bywaters' new factory. The directors were greatly impressed with the lucidity of his statement at a Board Meeting concerning the extension of Bywaters' factory and he was elected to the Board in January 1956. About this time G.S. MacDonald who had done so much before the war to place the bakery companies on a profitable basis retired. H.S. Rowlandson's health was slowly deteriorating and he died in March 1956. The President, Hugh Fitch, said it was 'the end of an era'. H.S.R. had given devoted service to the company for 63 years.

Profits continued to pick up. They rose to £481,000 in 1956 and £510,000 in 1957, the first time they had topped the half a million mark. During the year the Queen conferred a Knighthood on the Chairman, S. Graham Rowlandson, in consideration of his political and public services. The return to better profits encouraged the Board to increase the capital of the company again. A successful application was made to the Capital Issues Committee in November 1955 to issue 400,000 ordinary shares at 10s. on a basis of 1 in 4 rights. In November 1957 a scrip bonus of 1 for 1 ordinary shares (two million shares) was made from the share premium account. At the time the Board still held control. Although this had obvious advantages, it did not aid expansion, and consideration was continually given to the creation of 'A' non-voting ordinary shares, but it was not until 1960 that the company issued partial voting 'B' shares.

During these last few years of the existence of Fitch & Son as an entity there were few outstanding events. Our energy was devoted to putting the company in the best possible shape internally. It was as though we were clearing the decks for the large merger which was just around the corner. We acquired a provisions firm, Robsons of Bournemouth, and went into a poultry packing scheme with Allied Suppliers in Northern Ireland. We opened a similar poultry packing plant of our own at Abbotshay in Hertfordshire. Internally, Fitch Home began producing better figures than it had done for 20 years, and the new bread plant showed a good profit. In fact it did so well that we could not refuse a large offer for it from Ranks in 1958. Heavy capital commitments were entered into at Hales Home Bakeries for factory extensions and new machinery, the conversion of the shops of Hale & Partners, formerly Partners Stores Ltd., into self-service continued, although the group still had nothing which could be called a supermarket.

A factory extension at Bywaters' of Birmingham was opened. In fact with the single exception of the timber interests, Fitch in 1958 presented a picture of soundness and strength which was reflected in the record £629,000 before tax profits for the year ending in March.

The Fitch dividends were covered no less than four times, which looks strange compared with the average of 1.5 times in 1970, so it was from a comparative position of strength and liquidity that it was learned in the summer of 1958 of the sudden activity in the shares of the well-known provisions and manufacturing company of Lovell & Christmas.

7. James Fitch: Founder of Fitch & Son

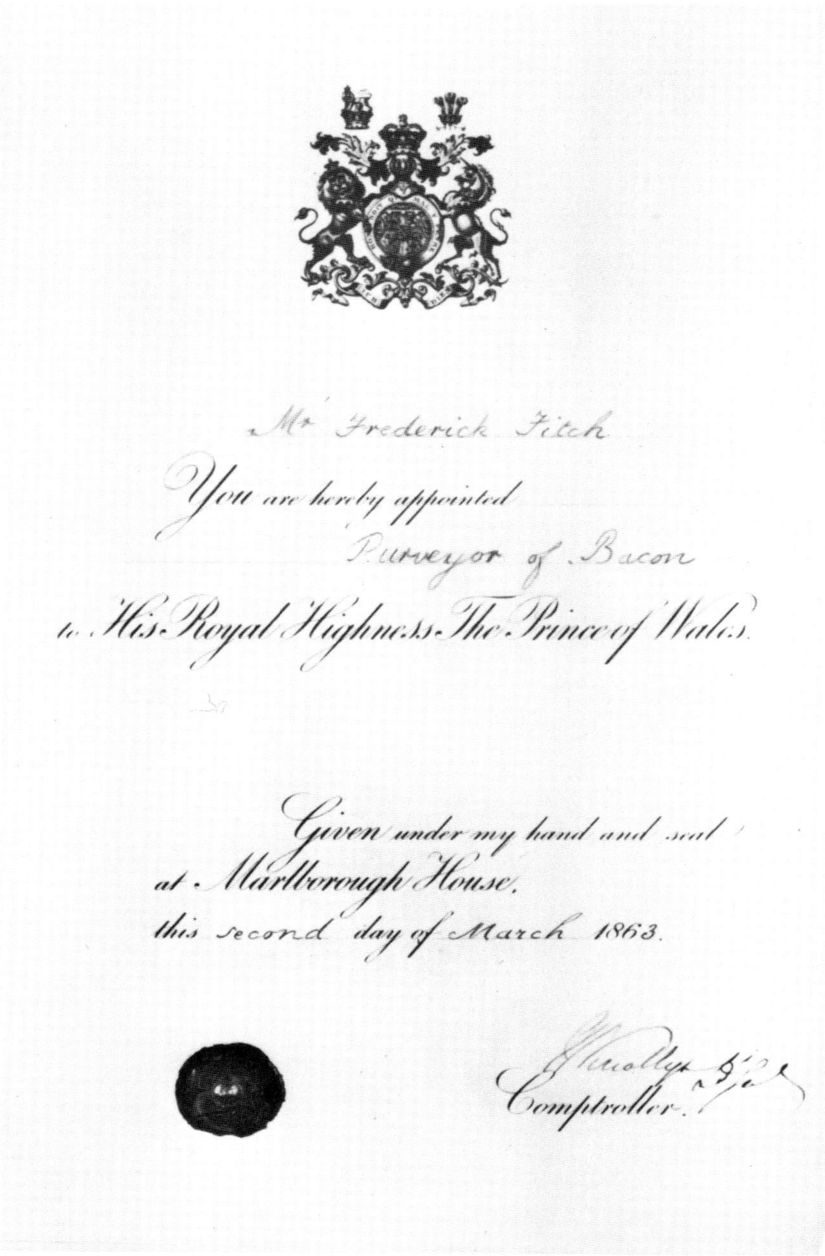

Mr Frederick Fitch

You are hereby appointed

Purveyor of Bacon

to His Royal Highness The Prince of Wales

Given under my hand and seal

at Marlborough House,

this second day of March 1863.

Comptroller.

8. Royal Warrant, 1863, to Frederick Fitch

9. Fitch and Son, 1890:
Premises at
Bishopsgate Within, London, E.C.

10. Fitch and Son Ltd., 1930: Premises at
St. Martin's Lane, London, W.C.2

11. H.S. Rowlandson
Director, Fitch & Son Ltd.,
1921-1956

12. G.S. MacDonald,
Director, Fitch & Son Ltd.,
1939-56

13. N.F. Lambourne
Director, Fitch & Son Ltd., 1949-58
Vice-Chairman and Managing Director,
Fitch Lovell Ltd., 1958-62

4

## JOHN CARY LOVELL – SKETCH OF A GREAT VICTORIAN

BEFORE WE CONSIDER the merger which was to bring the modern company of Fitch Lovell into being, we journey back to mid-19th-century Somerset in search of the Lovells. When Spencer Lovell set out on a similar quest in 1900 he found a family remarkable for their energy and drive going back to the 15th century. This energy was not always well applied. It drove Viscount Lovell to hire 2,000 German mercenaries in the 16th century to support the Pretender Lambert Simnel in his abortive attempt to wrest the crown from Henry VII. Spencer Lovell heard of Sir Thomas Lovell, who became a trusted henchman of Henry VIII. He was told of a Captain Richard Lovell, who became a fugitive during the Wars of the Roses. (His skeleton was found in a bricked-up chamber at Minster Lovell.) Another Lovell, John, was said to be the coxswain of the pinnace which rowed Nelson out to the *Victory* at the start of his last voyage. Within the memory of one elderly informant of Spencer Lovell, was Captain John Lovell, known as the 'Devil of Walton', whose two hobbies were drinking and running after his wife through the streets with a knife.

Tablets to the memory of less colourful, but more pious, Lovells can be seen to this day on the walls of the cloisters of Wells Cathedral. Not all these people were necessarily the direct forebears of the founders of Lovell & Christmas. However, bearing in mind that for centuries families moved only short distances from their place of birth, it is quite reasonable to assume they are all connected in some way with William Lovell who lived at Wick Farm, Glastonbury from 1790 to 1850, the true ancestor of the firm of Lovell & Christmas.

He was only a small farmer, and like all his neighbours suffered from the severe agricultural depression of the early and mid-19th century. How he – and they – fought their way out of their troubles can only be described as a classic tale of human enterprise. One Saturday evening in 1844 William Lovell and a number of other farmers met in the bar parlour of the market inn at Shepton Mallet to discuss and complain of the prices they were receiving from the London dealers in Newgate market and Smithfield. The farmers were sure they were not getting a fair deal. Helped no doubt by the refreshment they consumed, they continued talking into the early hours of Sunday morning. The only thing to be done, they decided, was to send someone to London on their behalf to see if they could do better by dealing directly with the market buyers. But it would have to be someone they could trust, preferably a farmer, one of themselves in fact. Above all, he would have to be a man of energy to carry through such a difficult enterprise.

The man the Somerset farmers chose to entrust with their produce was William Lovell. A few Sundays later he climbed on board the mail coach armed with a list of the produce being offered by the farmers who supported the plan. That night he arrived at *The Cross Keys Inn,* St. John Street, Smithfield. The next morning he rose early despite his fatiguing journey and proceeded on foot to call on various retailers in and about the City. William Lovell soon proved that his friends had been wise to choose him to represent them. By the end of the week he had sold all the goods on his list. On Saturday he paid his bill at *The Cross Keys* and took the coach back to Shepton Mallet.

There were more than a few jugs of ale and cider consumed in the bar parlour of the market inn that night. So pleased were the farmers with the prices which William Lovell had obtained for them that they decided there and then that he could continue selling for them. What was more they undertook to help Mrs. Lovell look after the farm during William's absences in London.

The arrangement worked well for four years. Then in 1848 William decided to devote his whole time to the business in London. He gave up his farm and took rooms over a tobacconist's in Farringdon Street and then moved to 66 Snow Hill where he remained until his death in 1864. Soon after his arrival in London he was joined by his wife, his daughters Mary Cary, Ann and Phyllis Cary, and his three sons, William, Samuel and John Cary. There have been four William Lovells in the firm of Lovell & Christmas. William Lovell of Wick Farm will be referred to as William (I), his eldest son as William (II), and the William Lovell who became Chairman of Lovell & Christmas Ltd. between the wars as William (III).

The day the brothers left the farm for the last time was vividly remembered by the youngest, John Cary, not because it was a momentous step in the history of the family, but because of the rain. It was the sort of day we tend to forget about in our romantic notions about travel before the coming of the railways and the motor car. The three boys, travelling outside the coach, became so wet that they were actually sitting in pools of water. When the coach made one of its stops, one of the brothers jumped down and bought a grid-iron to sit on.

We do not know how the Lovell family took to the City after the broad acres of Somerset. London was more accessible to the countryside in the 1840s than it is today and there was not a better place for a country family to settle than Smithfield. There was no need at that time for anyone near the market to feel homesick for the sounds and smells of the farmyard. Nor would there be any shortage of country folk in the ale houses and inns around the market to tell them how things were down on the farm. Incidentally, both Farringdon Road where William Lovell first stayed, and Snow Hill where he settled are within a few hundred yards of West Smithfield where Lovell & Christmas and the Fitch Lovell group have their modern headquarters. These streets and the others in the area, King Street, St. John Street, Charterhouse Street, Hosier Lane and Cock Lane are rich in Fitch Lovell associations, and to help the reader follow the story I have included a simple map of the area as it was 200 years ago. I have also included a family tree of the Lovells involved in Lovell & Christmas as Appendix VIII.

William Lovell (I) was now approaching 60. He does not seem to have considered that the business which he began would survive his approaching retirement, for he apprenticed his eldest son, William (II) to a linen draper by the name of Bridges in Tottenham Court Road. Meanwhile the Lovells became friendly with another Smithfield family, by the name of Christmas, and one of the Lovell girls, Mary Cary, married a Christmas boy, Josiah. Young William did not take to the drapery business and before long he decided to enter his father's trade and joined him. In 1851 he went into partnership with Josiah Christmas's brother, Charles. Together they opened a warehouse at 44 Snow Hill, down the road from William's home. Charles Christmas was a retail cheesemonger with a shop in Hampstead Road. They began trading as Christmas and Lovell, and a balance sheet dated November 1852 shows the capital of the firm at £200 equally provided by the two partners. No mention is made of William (I) and we must assume that, at the age of 61, he had retired.

The partnership of Christmas and Lovell proved to be a false dawn. In 1857 it was dissolved. Apart from other difficulties a clerk they employed had embezzled £250, a considerable sum of money in those days, more in fact than the capital which the two men had put into the business six years before. A letter survives which Charles wrote to William in 1857 about the missing money (see Appendix XI).

It was by no means the end of William (II)'s career in the wholesale provision trade. Nor, surprisingly, was it the end of his association with the Christmas family. In 1856 no sooner had he broken with Charles – who went back to his shop – than he went into partnership with his brother-in-law Josiah. They marked the change in brothers by changing the name to Lovell & Christmas, but otherwise, things went on much as before. The firm still traded from 40 Snow Hill, and the business continued to consist of the sale of West Country produce, mainly cheese. The West Country connection was made still stronger by the injection of fresh capital during these years from relatives in Somerset. The new partnership proved to be founded on rock. Josiah stayed with William until his death in 1884.

As the 1850s drew to a close the firm of Lovell & Christmas began to prosper – William was able to afford to hunt. Edward Lovell, in his booklet *Lovell* describes him as a fine sporting type, a typical John Bull, always happy on or near a horse. The rapid increase in the firm's business caused considerably jealousy in the trade and some competitors took to calling the partners unpleasant names. William (II), quick of temper, expressed his disapproval so forcibly that he was summoned for assault. The magistrate passing sentence regretted that he was obliged to inflict a fine of 20s. and costs. He said that in the circumstances he would have done the same as William!

Increasingly however, it was not the name of William Lovell that was on the lips of their anxious competitors, but that of John Cary Lovell. He was only 12 or 13 when he joined the business, but such was his drive and ability that he began to dominate the firm before he was out of his teens. His partners recognised his worth, and more and more, they left decisions to him. John Cary Lovell was so important, not only to Lovell & Christmas but to the provisions industry on a global scale, that we must pause in our story of Lovell & Christmas to take a closer look at him. There is no understanding the course which the firm took without first understanding the extraordinary man who steered it for so many years.

At the beginning of this chapter I wrote that energy seemed to me to be the most characteristic Lovell quality. John Cary had it to a limitless degree. He stands out in an energetic age as a man to whom nothing seemed impossible. As I have written, he began his working life while scarcely in his teens after a formal education remarkable only for its brevity. Without any hesitation he proceeded to educate himself. He had an insatiable appetite for reading. All the spare time he had from the business at Snow Hill – which was little enough – he spent on his books.

He was a strong sturdy boy and later in life, one of his sons wrote that he could take a 56 lb. weight by the ring in his hand and write his name on the wall with a piece of chalk. He was fond of wrestling and boxing – useful arts in the early days of the Ostend rabbit trade when sometimes the only way of defending a good place for the Lovell & Christmas van on the wharf, when the rabbit boats came in, was by making use of a good pair of fists. Once at Epsom races he thought a bookmaker had done him out of 10s. He promptly seized the unfortunate man and forced him to make good – no doubt to the delight of the onlookers. However the story illustrates more of John Cary Lovell's character than his sheer strength of body and of purpose, because when he got home he found the missing half sovereign in the turn-up of his trouser. He at once went back to Epsom to find the bookmaker but without success. He worried constantly about the small sum of money that he had wrongly obtained and continued to make efforts to find the bookmaker. Another story told about John Cary Lovell's physical strength concerns the night his house was burgled. He heard noises and came down to see what was happening only to find himself seized in a powerful grip. After a long struggle he overcame his opponent who turned out to be not the burglar but a policeman, the burglar having made his escape while the owner of the property and the arm of the law were locked in combat.

John Lovell married at the age of 24 and his wife bore 12 children in 18 years. Not content with this family, large as it was even by Victorian standards, he made himself responsible for the support of 14 more children, the orphans of two of his sisters who died without means. By the time of his marriage he was assuming the leadership of the firm, although he was the youngest of the partners. He was a born leader, although, like many such men he was not always easy to work with. Edward Lovell writes: 'there was nothing saint-like or heroic about John Lovell, he was very human and had his faults'. Undoubtedly he liked his own way, had a quick temper and, in the words of Edward Lovell 'collaboration was not congenial to him'. Nevertheless he was a kind man, strictly just and considerate especially to the young, as I have good reason to remember from the dealings which I had with him when I was only 18.

He was a great sportsman, keen on cricket from his earliest days. He used to play on Kennington Green and became a member of the Old Surrey Club and Ground. All his children had to be able to swim and ride horses almost before they could walk. He was fond of whist and bridge and played a good game of chess. In his constant search for education he went to hear Charles Dickens reading his novels and subsequently read every word of the author's published works. He used to read extracts aloud to his children. Spencer Lovell wrote – 'What a treat it was'. He had no taste for music, but bought a box at the Albert Hall and took his children in turn to the concerts. At one time he took a great interest in Sunday School work and built a large institute for working men where they could read and play games as a counter-attraction to the public houses. He provided the Tulse Hill Hockey Club with a ground and supported them right through until they became one of the largest and strongest clubs around London.

It is hard to believe how he found time for all these activities. He used to rise between four and five o'clock each morning, drive to the office with a fast trotting horse, and very often not return home until nine or ten o'clock in the evening. He was a man who never wasted a minute. He could make up his mind very quickly, and he had the ability to carry figures in his head and do rapid calculations without the need to write them down.

In spite of his many outside interests, his business was at all times his prime consideration. He had no use for people who came to chatter to him during business hours. He only occupied himself with his hobbies when he was away from the City. Nor were his business interests confined to Lovell & Christmas, which he made into the leading firm in the trade. He also inspired and improved the great drapery firm of Thomas Wallis and Hodgson's Brewery Company at Kingston. Somehow he also found time to administer the finances of St. Bartholomew's Hospital. All this was done without modern means of communication.

Indeed the achievements of John Cary Lovell and the other great Victorians now seem scarcely possible. They were a tough race, but there is no reason why young people today endowed with brains good health and the will should not emulate them.

By the time he was 35 years old, he was well and truly established. Following the fashion of the successful merchants of those days, he decided to move out of the City. He built a house, St. Ronan's, at Tulse Hill, near Streatham and brought his family there. It was his family who paid the price for his incessant activity. His sons wrote in admiration of him, but they said they saw little of him when they were young. Edward wrote that he was really 'only the man who carved the joint on Sundays'. He says that the Sunday dinners were not too happy as there was too much education and particularly mental arithmetic about them. As they grew older John found more time for his sons. He began to take great pains with their cricket, running and swimming. Edward recalls that he would take them to a bar after a visit to the baths, and give them sponge cakes and port wine. He says that it was not until they grew up that they appreciated their father's qualities, his character and his generosity.

His wife, who had been in poor health for a long time, died in 1884. He had to relinquish sport for a time. But even bereavement could not make him stay still. On a Sunday afternoon, in the months after her death, he would say to his children 'get your hat', and set out for a walk – nearly always to some distressed person. It was a prime duty for him to look after those who, through no fault of their own, had fallen on evil times.

It was after his wife's death that he founded his cricket club, with a team mainly composed of members of his family. The standard of play was reported to be well above average. He himself was a useful underarm bowler. Even at the age of 60 he was able to take wickets in good club cricket. He became interested in horse racing and often on Derby Day he would hire a four-in-hand coach and take all his family to the races.

In business he was strict and hard to please, but his justness, underlying generosity and complete fairness made him a much loved leader. He was ruthless even to old servants for slackness and carelessness but would quickly forgive a serious blunder if it was made through over-zeal. He could never overlook acting or posing or hypocrisy of any kind. He had no use for social climbers. His business judgment was first class, and his instinct for an opportunity unfailing. He foresaw that the growth in the population would require food to be imported and he steered Lovell & Christmas from being small agents for West Country produce, to being food importers on a massive international scale. He was always thinking of the future. He had an instinct for seeing the heart of a problem and he always refused to be swathed in a mass of figures. Looking back one can see that he was perhaps impetuous. No sooner had he an idea but it must be put into action, often without heeding the advice of more cautious people. He seems to have been unduly generous in the advances he made to shippers in all the exporting countries. But these advances played a key role in securing the supplies which were the life-blood of the firm. The fact remains that in their own sphere, the dairy produce business, Lovell & Christmas became in 30 years the leader in the world for the distribution of these products.

New Zealand, the Argentine and Denmark would probably have become in the course of time, great exporters of butter and cheese. The historical fact remains that it was John Cary Lovell who provided the initial encouragement which enabled their export industries to be founded.

He realised early the potentials of property and obtained a remarkable knowledge of values in the City of London. As Almoner of St. Bartholomew's, he was able to put this knowledge to the service of the community. John Lovell became known to an ever widening circle, and was asked to stand for Parliament on several occasions. He always refused, saying that he did not have the right temperament. He would say that he was not suited to listening to long arguments. His method was to think quickly and act at once.

He was a Liberal for many years but ultimately turned from Gladstone in disgust. Lord Salisbury and Joe Chamberlain were more to his liking.

With the growth of the firm. John Cary Lovell became more prosperous. In the year he formed Lovell & Christmas into a public company, 1896, he bought a place at Eddington in Kent. He made a cricket ground there and started a second team which often played against his original Lovell team.

Lovells was one of the first companies to install telephones. It had a direct line from Smithfield to the docks. This telephone line provides an amusing anecdote of the days when the Chairman knew everyone of the company's hundreds of employees. John Cary knew that the man in charge of the dock work was fond of slipping out for a drink, so one day he rang up and asked to speak with Bill.

'Bill', he said, 'you've been drinking'.

'Oh no Sir'.

'Bill, I can smell your breath.'

'Well, I've only had one glass, Sir.'

He realised early the tremendous potential of refrigeration and wherever possible constructed cold stores on the firm's premises and continually enlarged them. He loved horses, but he foresaw that the internal combustion engine would supplant them and he began experimenting with motor vehicles for delivery work long before other firms had begun to appreciate the revolution in transport which lay just over the horizon.

He was not fond of public speaking, but he became an admirable, if somewhat autocratic, chairman. He was particularly good at a difficult meeting when there were objectors to be dealt with. He possessed – or acquired – the gift of a really good chairman: people went away from his meetings happy and satisfied.

He was a very generous man, surprisingly so in one so determined and relentless. When he died his executors found many I.O.U.s signed by his friends for considerable sums. On most of them he had written 'not to be pressed'. He was particularly generous to rivals in business and the records show that several important wholesale provision firms were assisted and even kept in business through him. He took one of his competitors who had failed, set him up in business again and cancelled the debt which the man owed to him. Spencer Lovell heard this rival say of him, 'what a marvellous man'. Equally remarkable was John Lovell's treatment of the firm of Isaac Beer & Sons.

Ernest Beer, in his history of the firm entitled *Isaac Beer and his Sons* wrote about the sad state of the business about 80 years ago.

> . . . Isaac Beer had now reached the age of seventy six and was failing in health; his position was questioned by certain creditors and matters became steadily worse. At this juncture an amazing thing happened; the man who had been his sternest opponent in the Ostend Trade – John C. Lovell – hearing of his misfortunes came to his help. I well remember when, late one evening, I was in the outer office finishing off the day's work, and my father, as was his wont, sat poring over his accounts in the inner room, that I was astonished to see this great gentleman enter and ask to see him. He had come to offer £2,000 without guarantee or security.

It is difficult in these days of giant companies and a welfare state to imagine the prevailing tone of those Victorian days. Life was harsher, competition infinitely more severe, finance always difficult for the family firm, and little sympathy available for the man or firm which failed. The cynic may say that John Cary Lovell's assistance to his fellow wholesalers was not entirely without self interest. By keeping them in business he helped to ensure outlets for the goods which were arriving in ever larger quantities. But I think that would be an unfair interpretation of his motives. I am sure he acted through pure humanity. Certainly the trade thought so, for he kept its regard and even its affection throughout two generations.

All through business life, John Cary kept a firm hand on expenditure and stocks. Almost at every board meeting he stressed the need for liquid cash and low stocks. In 1898 he said '. . . if there is one thing more favourable than another it is a small stock'. Like many of his time he was fond of slogans. His favourite is reputed to have been 'cut your losses and keep in the market'. We, who are traders, know that this is easier said than done, but he believed in doing what he said. He was never a desk-bound leader. He travelled widely overseas to visit the firms and shippers and encourage them.

The last years of his life were unhappy in many respects. He had an accident one night when visiting a sick friend. He fell and dislocated his thigh. The injury was never quite put right, and for years he was always in some sort of pain. However it did not prevent him from applying himself vigorously to all his interests.

He was greatly saddened by the loss of two sons early in the First World War. He was burdened with anxiety at the knowledge of three other sons, six grandsons and 10 nephews in the services. For the first time in his life he was inclined to be pessimistic. He was rather bitter in his criticisms of the way the politicians were conducting the war.

He was appalled by government control of the food trade. He considered it interference in his business. His son Edward wrote: 'I shall never forget the look on his face when he first realised that he had to take orders instead of giving them'. Although he was depressed, he soldiered on until his death in 1919 at the age of 79.

He remained very much in charge right up until the end. He took the chair on the 30 September, a fortnight before his death, when he approved the formation of Lovell & Christmas (Canada) as a limited company.

His passing was greeted with numerous tributes from all over the world. Perhaps it is most fitting to quote what was said of him at the company's annual general meeting the following year.

> . . . during the 24 years he acted as our chairman, his strenuous work, clear-sighted judgment and splendid organising ability were largely responsible for bringing Lovell and Christmas to its present state of efficiency. It is no exaggeration to say that, by all who came into contact with him, including in a way competitors, he was looked upon as one of the most straightforward and honourable merchants in the City of London. We who were more intimately acquainted with him knew him also as a fine sportsman, a true friend and comrade and essentially an English gentleman in the best sense of the word.

I conclude this brief outline of the life of a distinguished entrepreneur in a past and different age with words written by his son:

> The fact that there were more than 200 motor cars at his funeral did not impress me, but the sight there of many women, and even men, with tears on their cheeks, told me that his loss was genuinely mourned.

## 5

## LOVELL AND CHRISTMAS AS PARTNERS

THE FIRM of Lovell & Christmas was still operating in the mid-19th century from Snow Hill, dealing in West Country produce and young John Cary Lovell was beginning to make his mark. In 1862 they moved from Snow Hill to 35/36 King Street, nearly opposite the entrance to Hosier Lane. In those days King Street (now Smithfield Street) had buildings on both sides. The north side was demolished when the site of the present Central Poultry Market was needed for the building of the original Poultry Market. The Corporation of London offered compensation to the residents and businesses in the street. The amount of compensation was the subject of litigation between Lovell & Christmas and the Corporation. The firm won. However it still had to move. It purchased *The King's Head* public house at 12 West Smithfield, and the business moved there in 1872. Lovell & Christmas is still there, and passers-by can see the reliefs of *The King's Head* which adorn the pillars on the frontage.

As I have written, John Cary Lovell at an early age foresaw the importance of imported food and he directed the firm into the Ostend trade. The Ostend boats used to arrive at Brewers' Quay in the Pool of London laden with produce from Holland and Belgium. Ostend butter and Ostend rabbits became important commodities, and Lovell & Christmas quickly became principal agents.

Having begun as commission salesmen for West Country produce, it was natural for them to become agents rather than trading importers, who were rare in those days. Lovell's and a firm called Devine became the leaders in the Ostend trade, followed by Isaac Beer. The butter would arrive in long coffin-like cases, made up into 2 lb. rolls. But it was the rabbits which formed the bulk of the business. At one time Lovell's was handling 250 cases, each weighing 2½ cwt., in every week.

The work at the wharf was strenuous. The traders would gather there with their vans as the bleak dawn was breaking over the river. There would be jostling and pushing for position. Tempers were often short at that hour in the morning. The one thing they all dreaded was fog, which meant the boats would be delayed. There was no refrigeration then, and the highly perishable rabbits would have to be quickly sold off to costermongers either on the spot or back at Smithfield. At the best of times the vans would be loaded as fast as possible and the teams of horses would gallop away at full speed to try and get to the shops first. It was a race which Lovell's was good at winning, and sheer physical toughness played a part. I have already said that John Cary was proficient with his fists, but his eldest brother, William (II) was apparently more renowned for his strength. Those were rough days, 100 years ago in Smithfield and on the wharves. They make the present times seem rather tame. Harry Lovell, who will appear frequently later in the story, evidently inherited these attributes for he boxed for the Army in India.

It was the custom in the trade in those days for the principal in a firm and the other partners to travel round the shops in broughams and call for orders which were executed later by carrier. Lovell & Christmas realised that it could provide a much quicker service if the partners actually took the goods round themselves. So they began to use stout two-wheeled vans instead of the broughams. As business grew, larger single horse vans were introduced and then pair horse vans. The partners usually drove their own teams and naturally became expert horsemen. Years later at a four-in-hand meeting J.W. Christmas was greeted with the words, 'Here comes the cove what drives the rabbit van'.

My father, Clement Keevil, who owned a store in South London from about 1871 to 1874, told me many times how John Cary Lovell would come running into the shop, holding a testing iron, followed by a man with a cask of butter. He would dig the iron into the butter saying, 'Try this, it is good'. Then he would arrange a price, leave the cask, run out again to the van, take the reins and drive away. The whole incident would last about a minute, while others might take half an hour to make a sale.

Lovell & Christmas stopped importing rabbits at the time of the First World War. For more than 50 years, they had received supplies from Paul Carbon of Ostend. Years later he remained a friend of

Lovell's. On 21 February 1936, Paul Carbon wrote to William (III) to offer sympathy on the death of George V. In the letter he recalls a visit paid by William (III) and John Cary to Ostend before the 1914 War and regrets that, should they come again, he would be unable to offer the same hospitality because 'les allemands ont pris et but toute ma cave'.

Although the Ostend trade was important, it was relatively small. The real breakthrough for Lovell & Christmas came in 1870. It was caused by events, not in the Low Counties, but in France as the result of the Franco-Prussian War of 1870 and the siege of Paris. The siege, which meant starvation for the citizens of the capital also meant distress for the farmers and traders who marketed their produce there. The leading people in the important French butter trade at this time were a firm called Bretel Frères of Valognes in Normandy. If their business was not to collapse, an alternative market had to be found quickly. There was no refrigeration in those days, and no way of storing large quantities of butter. Bretels approached Mahier of Cherbourg, probably shipping agents, who in turn contacted Lovell's. Quick to spot an opportunity the London firm agreed to handle Bretels' butter, and so began an amazing business, which, at its height, involved the chartering of special ships from France to Southampton nearly every day of the week, with special trains to meet them and rush the butter to London. Turnover rose to £30,000 a week, which would have meant sales of about 250 tons of butter a week.

The organisation needed in the 1870s and 1880s to sell and distribute a highly perishable product shows how far Lovell's had advanced. People often say how trade is changing in the mid-20th century, and how important it is to keep up to date. I sometimes think we hardly know the meaning of the word change when I reflect upon the speed at which John Cary and his colleagues worked. Of course, although they had to make up their minds quickly, they were not bedevilled with the modern practice of referring matters to committees which often cause delay and lead to compromise.

These years, the '80s in particular, saw the rise of Lovell's to a dominating position in the trade. John Cary never seemed to put a foot wrong. As supplies from the West Country, Jersey and Belgium became inadequate, other sources were quickly tapped. As well as from France, Lovell's imported from Ireland, Denmark, Sweden and other European countries.

In Denmark and Sweden Lovell's dealt with the firm of Edward Walther. In 1898 he presented the firm with the certificate reproduced as Plate 16. It is beautifully contrived in gilt and colours and it commemorates the 'one thousandth consecutive weekly consignment of Swedish or Danish Pure Butter'. It goes on to say 'no contract, agency or subsidy whatever having at any time existed; the sole motive which has actuated the continuance of relations having been a mutal good understanding'.

The very high reputation which Lovell's enjoyed for fair dealing was undoubtedly the reason for its leading position as agent for overseas suppliers. Even now, some 70 years later the weekly dairy reports prepared by Peter Gomersall are models of fairness, and give to buyers and sellers all over the world a true perspective and unbiased view of the market. They deservedly enjoy a very high reputation through the world.

The Normandy butter trade, like the Ostend rabbit trade, was more or less killed by the First World War. It was fitting, perhaps, that German guns which had signalled the start of this commerce should sound to end it. The flavour of French butter was much appreciated in southern England. Many of us remember well the Bretel Blues and Bretel Reds with their 2 lb. rolls packed in 24 lb. boxes, and feel something is missing in the hygenic blended butters of today, which we found, or so our memories tell us, in the natural flavours of Bretel from the pastures of Normandy.

French butter was undercut by butter, not from English farms or those of other neighbouring European countries, but from a little country on the other side of the earth. How the farmers of New Zealand managed to produce butter and ship it half way round the globe and still sell cheaper than local produce is one of the great stories of modern commerce. It is a story closely woven with the history of Lovell & Christmas.

Lovell's claim, that it was the first firm to import butter from New Zealand, is supported by P.J. Peterson in his history *Pioneering 100 years under the Southern Cross.* A forbear of his became Lovell's first agent in New Zealand. He says a young Englishman by the name of Victor Chapman was the first to think of sending butter to England. He wrote back to the Old Country and asked who were the best firm of importers to deal with. He was given the name of Lovell & Christmas. The date was around 1880.

A consignment was dispatched in 40 lb. tins with the tops soldered on. Lovell's reported that it arrived in fair condition but it had melted crossing the equator and then firmed again as it neared England. But they said it had undoubtedly been good butter when packed.

Lovell's asked for further shipments to be sent, suggesting that this time the butter should be packed in 60 lb. firkins of wood with one inch of salt at the top and bottom. This was done and a good report was received. However it was a risky and expensive method of shipment and only suitable for small quantities. At the beginning of the 1880s, refrigerated transport was just beginning to be a practical proposition.

The New Zealand Government realised that refrigerated exports of farm produce to England could lead to a new era of prosperity and development for their struggling settlers, and in 1881 they offered a bonus of £500 for the first 25 tons of butter and 50 tons of cheese exported and sold in a foreign market at such prices as should show that the articles were of fair quality. In 1882 the sailing ship *Dunedin* left Port Chalmers for England with a shipment of frozen meat and a small quantity of butter. She reached the London docks with her cargo of 700 tons in 98 days. *The Times* described the achievement as 'prodigious'. The butter was sold at 11½d. a lb.

John Cary Lovell at once realised that an important new source of supply had emerged. He quickly sent a letter to Peterson, who was based at Springhill, New Zealand asking him to act for Lovell's. He sent a draft for £3,000 to start with and £1,500 four weeks later. Peterson sent several consignments but he was afraid of the risks and he asked Lovell's to send its own man out to handle the trade on the spot. J. Kowin was dispatched on the next boat – the SS *Coptic*. He reported that he had arrived in a wonderful country and he was sure everything grown there could be sold in London. Getting it there fresh was the problem. Peterson wrote that Kowin eagerly sought after 'butter, cheese, mutton and fowl'. After a quick inspection he went back to London on the *Coptic* and returned to New Zealand on her next voyage armed with ample funds to advance to suppliers.

By this time a number of co-operatives were starting and Kowin went round and obtained consignments of their whole season's output. He was a popular man, described as Peterson as 'a typical

14. John Cary Lovell,
1840-1919

15. Henry Reynolds, Founder of
New Zealand Co-operative Dairy Co. Ltd.
in 1886. Client of Lovell & Christmas Ltd. in
the Argentine, 1900

1879 Certificate. 1898

I, Edward Walther; hereby certify that on this the 27th day of November, 1898, I have despatched from the Sound The One Thousandth consecutive weekly consignment of Swedish or Danish PURE BUTTERS

To LOVELL & CHRISTMAS, LIMITED, WEST SMITHFIELD, LONDON. Formerly the Firm of Lovell & Christmas

This regular business has always been done voluntarily by me, no contract, agency or subsidy whatever having at any time existed, the sole motive which has actuated the continuance of relations having been

A Mutual Good Understanding

As I consider the occasion one remarkable enough for record, I now avail myself thereof to pledge my good wishes and best thanks to the above mentioned House, whose reputation and well-known success I believe to be mainly attributable to the fair principles exercised by them in the conduct of their business.

Copenhagen, Denmark.
Helsingborg, Sweden.

24th November 1898.

Edward Walther

16. The Certificate from Denmark, to mark the 1000th weekly consignment of Swedish or Danish butters

FOUNDERS OF LOVELL & CHRISTMAS, 1851

17. William Lovell

18. Josiah Christmas

19. W.G. Lovell, C.B.E.
Chairman, Lovell & Christmas Ltd.,
1919-43

The Subscription List will Open on Monday, the 27th inst., at 9 a.m., and will close on or before Tuesday, the 28th inst., at 4 p.m.

# LOVELL & CHRISTMAS,

**LIMITED.**

*Incorporated under the Companies' Acts* 1862 *to* 1890.

## SHARE CAPITAL - £350,000,

TO BE ISSUED AS FOLLOWS:

| | |
|---|---|
| **40,000 Ordinary Shares of £5 each at par** ... ... ... ... ... ... | **£200,000** |
| **30,000 Preference 6 per cent. Shares of £5 each at 10s. premium** ... ... ... | **150,000** |
| | **£350,000** |

**Four per cent. Mortgage Debenture Stock, £200,000.**

Of this Stock only £150,000 will now be issued, leaving £50,000 to be issued should further increase and development of the business require it.

Power is reserved to the Directors, at their option, to redeem the Debenture Stock by annual drawings of not more than £10,000 in each year at the price of £110.

Interest on the Debenture Stock will be payable on the 14th January and the 14th July in each year.

The Company will receive the profits of the business from the 1st July, 1896, and the Vendors will be entitled to interest at the rate of £4 per cent. per annum from such date until payment of the balance for the time being due in respect of the purchase money payable to them in cash.

**Messrs. ROBARTS, LUBBOCK & Co., 15, Lombard Street, London, E.C., as Bankers to the Company, will receive Applications for 26,660 of the above-mentioned Ordinary Shares, 20,000 of the above-mentioned Preference Shares, and £100,000 of the above-mentioned Debenture Stock on the enclosed Forms.**

The Vendors will in consideration of the purchase take 13,333 Ordinary Shares, 10,000 Preference Shares, and £50,000 Debenture Stock (being the largest amount allowed by the rules of the Stock Exchange consistently with obtaining a quotation), and the balance of £343,335 in cash.

THE PAYMENTS FOR EACH OF THE ISSUES WILL BE AS FOLLOWS:—

***Ordinary and Preference Shares:***

| | ORDINARY. | PREFERENCE. | |
|---|---|---|---|
| **On Application (per Share)** ... | **10s.** | **10s.** | |
| **On Allotment „** ... | **£1 10s.** | **£2** | *(Including 10s. premium)* |
| **On the 31st August next** ... | **£3** | **£3** | |
| | **£5** | **£5 10s.** | |

***Debenture Stock:***

| | |
|---|---|
| **On Application** ... ... ... | **10 per cent.** |
| **On Allotment** ... ... ... | **30 „** |
| **On the 31st August next** ... | **60 „** |

The Preference Shares will be entitled out of the profits of the Company to a Cumulative Preference Dividend of six per cent. per annum, and will also be entitled to rank in respect of Capital in priority to the Ordinary Shares.

THE TRUSTEES FOR THE HOLDERS OF THE DEBENTURE STOCK WILL BE:

JAMES HUDSON, Nutfield, Surrey, Esquire.
JAMES ADAMS HEWITT, 12, Palace Gardens Mansions, Kensington, W., Esquire.

20. Part of a Prospectus for Lovell & Christmas Ltd.,
1896

John Bull'. He was famous for his rendering of *The Village Blacksmith.* Kowin successfully represented Lovell & Christmas for 11 years. His practice was to return to England every year and see the consignments sold. He always left for New Zealand in the autumn, thus successfully avoiding the winters of both hemispheres.

The story goes that other firms in London were puzzled as to where Lovell's was obtaining this new influx of produce, and one year they sent a man to follow Kowin on his annual migration. When he returned the spy told them of the co-operatives in New Zealand. The following year a contingent of travellers went out and called at the various dairies and co-ops all round the country. However, they did not have much success. Lovell's had been first on the scene, and had made sure of the suppliers' loyalty with liberal advances, and a proven record in the London market.

Meanwhile the injection of capital by Lovell's and, in the end, by its competitors brought prosperity to rural New Zealand, just as the New Zealand Government had hoped. But the butter was still being made more or less as it always had been. For the New Zealand dairy industry to take real advantage of the country's climate and the productive capacity of the land, some way of producing butter more quickly, and above all, more cheaply, was needed if New Zealand was to compete effectively in the British market.

The man who pioneered the making of butter by factory methods was Henry Reynolds, always known as Harry. He was a Cornishman who emigrated to New Zealand and met an American who showed him how butter was being made at that time in California. He at once realised that the Californian system could be adapted to give New Zealand the really low-cost mass-produced butter needed to compete in England. With the help of the American, Mr. Gemmell, he set up a small factory at Pukekura and on 3 November 1886 the first 100 lbs. of factory made New Zealand butter was churned.

He chose an anchor as the symbol of his product. It is still the symbol used by the New Zealand Co-operative Dairy Company Ltd. He succeeded in raising further capital, some of it almost certainly from Lovell's, and in spite of the difficult economic conditions of the time, opened another factory, and by the early '90s his organisation had grown to two factories and eight creameries.

While Harry Reynolds was slowly developing the dairy industry in the Upper Waikato region, another pioneer, Wesley Spragg had been organising farmers in the Lower Waikato. After early conflicts and then understandings with Reynolds, Spragg's New Zealand Dairy Association bought out the Reynolds interests, thus laying the foundations for the modern New Zealand Co-operative Dairy Company.

Undoubtedly Lovell & Christmas were involved in this operation, for their minutes for the year of the merger, 1896, show large loans to both parties. At the time of writing, New Zealand *Anchor* butter is still the largest selling brand of butter on the British market. But there remains the possibility that we may yet rediscover the taste of Normandy butter with the advent of Britain as a member of the Common Market.

The winding up of his affairs in New Zealand was by no means the end of Harry Reynolds. On the advice of Lovell & Christmas he moved to the Argentine. (The story of his role in starting yet another dairy industry in partnership with Lovell's is told in a later chapter.) In 1936 the New Zealand Co-operative Dairy Company celebrated the golden jubilee of *Anchor* butter by publishing a commemorative brochure. The editor writes: 'Let 11,000 suppliers and over 1,100 employers be upstanding to toast the memory of Henry Reynolds, Cornishman, farmer, visionary and English gentleman'.

Meanwhile back in London the growth of the business through the firm's interests in Europe and New Zealand led to a need for bigger premises. In 1877 they purchased *The Cross Keys* public house in St. John Street, together with the stabling. It must have been a proud day for the Lovell brothers, for it was at *The Cross Keys* that their father had stayed on his first night in London when he came up from Somerset to try and sell his neighbours' produce 33 years before. The stabling was on two floors, and there was room to park the vans under cover in the spacious yard. Unlike *The King's Head,* the public house itself continued to be licensed. Someone once mistook the entrance to the yard for the way into the bar. He was bitten by one of the guard dogs and sued Lovell & Christmas. He was given short shrift by the Magistrate in court. 'Don't you know', he was told, 'by the law of England a dog is entitled to his first bite gratis? The case is dismissed'. *The Cross Keys* was eventually let to Watneys, and the stabling was sold in 1922 to the Union Cold Storage Company.

The main business continued to be conducted from 12 West Smithfield, and it was the custom of the partners and staff to take their meals on the premises. 1889 was a milestone in the history of the firm. In that year a branch was established in Manchester and Lovell & Christmas made their first acquisition. They bought the firm of Vanderhaege & Co. of Charterhouse Street and carried it on as a subsidiary. This business was originally founded by the Devines, who were the big people in the Ostend trade when Lovell & Christmas started. There was no doubt who were the big people in 1880. Vanderhaege's amalgamated with S. Phillips many years later and continued to trade as Phillips & Vanderhaege.

In 1889 a new partnership deed was drawn up. It was to be the last, for within a few years Lovell & Christmas was to become a limited liability company with shares quoted on the London Stock Exchange. Before describing that turning point in the company's history, it is worth pausing a moment to look at the system which it used in 1889 to distribute the profits.

According to a letter from John Cary Lovell to William Lovell (II) dated 30 July 1889, and headed St. Ronan's, Tulse Hill, the profits were to be divided into eights. So many would go to William Lovell (II) and his sons, so many to John Cary Lovell and his sons, and so many to J.W. Christmas. The idea was that William and John Cary would divide their shares with their sons as they thought fit, and that J.W. Christmas would do the same with his brother Alfred. The partners had the right to transfer part of their shares of the partnership to the members of their family when they considered the right time had arrived. Today, in an era of limited liability companies, this may seem a strange arrangement. However, it was not unusual in the days of family partnerships. In those times, everyone worked for the benefit of the firm and therefore of the family. The father or eldest member had practically autocratic power over the family. It worked well with Lovell & Christmas and with many other firms in the energetic and disciplined times of England's commercial supremacy during Victoria's long reign.

However, the system had one big drawback. When a partner died it was necessary for the remaining partners to find large sums in cash for the beneficiaries of the deceased partner. Two of the three partners in Lovell & Christmas died within a few years of each other, Josiah, as I have written, in 1884, and William (II), the senior partner, in 1894. So it was decided to make the partnership of Lovell & Christmas into the company of Lovell & Christmas Ltd.

The flotation took place in 1896. The company was capitalised at £350,000, made up of 40,000 ordinary shares of £5 each and 30,000 6% preference shares of £5 each at a premium of 10s. Also £200,000 4% mortgage debenture stock was authorised but only £150,000 was issued leaving £50,000 in reserve against future requirements. The directors had power to redeem up to £10,000 per annum at £110 by drawings. The vendors, the partners, took in part payment for their interest the largest amounts allowed by the Stock Exchange rules.

Several interesting names are connected with the flotation. The brokers were Sidney J. Lovell & Co., now the firm of Popham, Lyon & Smith who still, after 70 years, act as one of the brokers for the company, Sidney Lovell was a cousin of William G. Lovell (William III). The solicitors were Pontifex Pitt & Hewitt. James Hewitt was one of the trustees for the debenture holders. Spencer Lovell was employed at Pontifex's. He was a son of John Cary. Later he left Pontifex, and with two others of the firm, established Lovell, White & King, now of Serjeants Inn, E.C.4, today the solicitors of Fitch Lovell and many of their associated companies. They have developed into one of the leading firms of solicitors in the United Kingdom. At the time of the flotation, Pontifex Pitt seem to have been solicitors and advisors to most of the firms in the Smithfield area and various partners have acted as trustees for the estates of many directors. They still carry out work for certain of the Fitch Lovell companies.

Edgar Lovell, although not mentioned in the prospectus could well have been consulted. He was a member of the Corporation of Lloyds and a well known insurance expert. His firm is still in existence and today is known as Adams, Golding & Co. It is noteworthy that one Lovell was in Law, another on the Stock Exchange, and another in Lloyds. One can detect the influence of John Cary Lovell behind this judicious spread of family expertise.

The bankers were Roberts, Lubbock & Co. and the London and Midland Bank, Manchester. The original directors were: John Cary Lovell (Chairman), Josiah Christmas, Lionel Lovell, Alfred Christmas, Ernest Lovell, William G. Lovell (William III) and Edward Driver Lovell. The Secretary was H. Soden. The head office was registered at 12 West Smithfield and it is still there today.

The properties listed in the prospectus in addition to the registered office, were *The Horns* Public House and *The Cross Keys* Hotel, both in St. John Street, with stables for 82 horses and standings for 47 vans. There were also two leaseholds in the Smithfield area and the Manchester headquarters in Fennel Street. The average net profit for the previous ten years was £38,000.

The arrangement for the payment of directors was unusual. They would take no fees until after the ordinary shareholders had received a dividend of 8%. Then they would be entitled to one third of the surplus profits, the balance being available for dividend, reduction of debenture debt, extension of business connections and otherwise at the discretion of the directors.

The prospectus states:

> It has been found that where large trading concerns have been formed into companies and the customers have been allowed to participate as shareholders, extension of business has followed. This has been notably so in the case of Thomas Wallis & Co. Ltd. and Hodgsons Kingston Brewery Co. Ltd. of which Mr. J.C. Lovell has for some years acted as Chairman and it is anticipated that similar results will follow in the present case.

It was an obvious appeal to customers to become shareholders which was in fact most successful. The prospectus continues:

> The concern ... holds direct Agencies for the sale of butter, cheese, eggs, rabbits and other provisions from nearly every country where these articles are produced, including Normandy, Brittany, Ireland, Denmark, Sweden, Finland, Holland, Belgium, Italy, Australia and New Zealand, and arrangements have been concluded by which consignments will soon be received from the Argentine.

It was a far cry from the bar parlour of the Somerset market town 52 years before.

There the story of William Lovell coming to town in 1844, the rise of John Cary Lovell, the partnership of Christmas & Lovell and the partnership of Lovell & Christmas comes to an end and we go forward to study the progress of Lovell & Christmas Ltd., the leading distributors and merchants of dairy produce in the United Kingdom. This study will not be difficult as all the Minute Books since 1896 are in existence as well as a scrap-book of all public records published of the company's activities.

# 6

## LOVELL & CHRISTMAS LTD.

1896, THE YEAR of the birth of the limited liability company was also the year in which the firm began the enterprises in Canada and the Argentine which were to absorb much of its energies in the decades ahead. The year 1896 is a turning point in the telling of our story too. Up to now it has been possible to gather the activities of Lovell & Christmas within the compass of one narrative. From now on this will no longer be feasible. I will here, therefore, continue the broad history of the London company, with only passing references to its growth in the provincial areas of Britain, to the firm of Rutzou, which Lovell & Christmas took over in 1925, to Canada and the Argentine. All these activities are dealt with later.

How calm Lovell & Christmas Ltd. appears at the turn of the century, a great Edwardian merchant house in its heyday, with the rough and tumble of Brewers' Quay left far behind and the uncertainties of the 20th century waiting in the wings for the coming of the Great War. The stability and prosperity of the firm were personified by the figure of the Chairman, John Cary Lovell.

He was growing, it is true, a little more stately, a little older every year, but with his seemingly indestructible presence at the Annual General Meeting each July there was no reason to believe that change was on the way. It was his custom to remind the shareholders how well off they were, and as they listened to him reporting the profits year after year, they agreed with acclamation.

Yet changes were underway. Indeed commerce was undergoing what was little short of a technological revolution. As far as the business of Lovell's was concerned, the most important development was the growth of refrigeration, which not only made possible the import of perishable food from distant countries, but also completely changed traders' approach to the market. No longer was it necessary to take any offer at the end of a day to sell perishable goods before they became valueless.

Lovell's wasted no time in adopting the new technology. Cold storage space for 300 tons of produce is mentioned in the firm's 1896 prospectus. In 1898 extra space was provided in West Smithfield and Greyhound Yard and in 1900 the West Smithfield premises were rebuilt and cold storage space there extended to 400 tons. Meanwhile, by 1899 the firm was exploring the possibility of using insulated trucks to carry Bretel Butter on the Southampton to London railway.

In March 1900 the company signed a contract for the installation of electric light, and at about the same time arranged for a telephone line to be fixed between 12 West Smithfield and the London Docks. This alone began a revolution in communications every bit as profound as the modern preoccupation with computers.

It was not only on the technological side that Lovell's was abreast, even ahead, of the times. From 1889 directors were allowed two weeks' holiday in the summer and another week as and when convenient. (The usual holiday allocation at this time was one week.)

John Cary Lovell made it quite clear that the directors had not forgotten how to do a day's work. 'There are no ornamental directors among us', he told one meeting. 'There are always two or three directors on the premises to do business', he declared on another occasion. Indeed at the time of the flotation, two Lovells, William Lovell (II) and Edward Driver Lovell actually gave their addresses as '12 West Smithfield' for the prospectus. The holiday concession to directors was followed in 1904 by the even more unusual decision to give old servants of the company a half day's holiday a week.

Meanwhile the company was forging ahead overseas, and not only in Canada and the Argentine. This was an era of generous financial aid to suppliers. The spirit in which Lovell's handed out money is epitomised in one agreement made in which it was stated, 'the Company are pleased to let them keep the money as long as they want it'. These advances, which played so large a part in giving Lovell's its competitive edge, were financed entirely out of its profits. In 1895, the year before flotation, the firm made £40,000 net. Year after year John Cary was able to report better and better results. In the five years to 1902 loans and investments almost tripled their value. In that year agents were appointed in South Africa, New Zealand and Siberia and a contract, later guaranteed by £10,000, was signed with the Danish Produce Export Co. Despite all this varied activity, the Chairman was able to tell shareholders, '. . . we know from one week to another what we are doing and at the end of every month, our exact position'.

Although no agent was appointed in Australia until 1912, for some years before that Lovell's had been doing a substantial trade in the import of Australian butter, under the brand name of *Golden Churn,* and by 1905 was exporting this butter to South Africa, a business which was almost certainly the beginning of Lovell's entrepôt trade.

Most of the firm's Siberian trade was also in butter. In 1905 the war between Russia and Japan caused a setback to this trade, but in the following year Lovell's was back in business in Russia and making loans to suppliers there, although it turned down one request for 6,000 roubles from a firm called Ptcheliakoff because its shipments were not sufficiently large. Lovell & Christmas's big contact in this part of the world was a man named Otto Hansen, who first appears in the records in 1909 and seems to have been Lovell's agent throughout Russia and in the Baltic states. It was to him that Lovell's turned when the firm of Ptcheliakoff justified the Lovell directors' caution in refusing it a loan in 1906 by later getting into difficulties and owing the company £2,500. Hansen was given a power of attorney and despatched to Rybensk, the town where Ptcheliakoff operated, to sort out the muddle. The scale of the firm's trade with Russia may be gauged from the fact that although the major commodity imported was butter, Lovell's also at one time took out an insurance policy for £10,000 in respect of eggs cold stored in Russia. The firm also helped Hansen to set up an experimental plant for making 'English' Cheddar cheese in Siberia. Russian bacon is also mentioned often in the company's records, but without any indication of the quantities received.

The story of growth abroad was matched by that of growth at home. In 1904, Lovell's took an interest in George Bowles Nicholls, important Smithfield wholesalers, and its near neighbour. (Many years later this firm became part of Peter Keevil & Sons Ltd. It is now owned by Associated British Foods.) In 1906 the informal loans which John Cary had made to Isaac Beer & Sons (see page 170) were regularised under an agreement by which Lovell & Christmas was to receive one fifth of Beer's profits for a period of seven years. The most important development at home during this time was, however, the merger in 1906 between Lovell & Christmas and the Liverpool firm of George Wall & Co. This crucial event, which is fully dealt with in a later chapter, transformed Lovell's from a firm of London importers into a national concern, but at first, although there were suddenly a lot of unfamiliar Wall faces on the Board, the merger had surprisingly little effect on the activities of either company.

After agreeing to the merger and increasing the capital to one million shares at an Extraordinary General Meeting, Lovell's settled back to trade much as before. The Chairman kept calling for reductions in stocks, the profits kept going up. All the offices of the company closed on the day of Edward VII's funeral. £100 was donated to victims of *The Titanic* disaster, and although bad debts continued to be such a feature of the period that the directors decided to set up a permanent reserve fund of 10% of all monies owing, they still found themselves able to make substantial donations to charities. There arose a small difficulty over the question of directors' remuneration. As I have said, they had decided in 1896 not to take any payment unless the dividend exceeded 8%. Unfortunately it was often below this. The shareholders pressed the directors to amend the Articles to allow fees to be taken and when the directors refused, the shareholders at one meeting voted them £3,000 to be divided between them. Incidentally, it is interesting to note that at this time the trading year ended on 30 June, a notice of the accounts was sent to shareholders a week later and the Annual General Meeting held in the middle of July. The Chairman clearly meant what he said when he told shareholders that the directors knew the exact position of the firm at the end of every month. (I wonder how many companies today are ready to hold their A.G.M.s less than three weeks after the end of their trading year.)

In 1914 the Lovell & Christmas A.G.M. was held as usual in July. The Chairman reported the usual increase in profits. Business was growing in Siberia. An extra £10,000 had been put into reserve against investments. Trade in London was moving further and further into the suburbs and the Chairman said the firm was making more and more use of motors.

Historians of this period are fond of taking August 1914 as a watershed between two epochs. On the level of international politics this it was, but in the rather less exalted field of everyday commerce with which we are concerned life went on, for a time at least, much as before. It took the business community, and for that matter, all ordinary citizens, some time to realize the awful extent of what was happening. (One must remember that Great Britain had not been to war on this scale since Napoleonic times. What everyone remembered was the Boer War 15 years before.)

As far as Lovell's was concerned, all that happened immediately was an increase in shipping charges and an irritating delay in passages to the Argentine; (ships bound for Buenos Aires developed a habit of sailing via the Cape in order to land horses and mules for the army); so when the directors met to consider what they should do about the war they never considered the possibility of shortages, rationing, or government controls. Their main concern seems to have been about a possible collapse in demand, and their rather surprising decision was to clear stock, and work from hand to hand, not buying except when absolutely necessary and keeping cash in hand. They considered the question of employees who might be killed and decided to pay their widows up to, but not exceeding, half their husbands' wages for the duration of hostilities.

During the first year of the war the company's business was still mainly unaffected. 63 of the London staff volunteered. The company made payments to them and to all other volunteers from the staff. It donated £1,000 to charity and the Chairman reported record profits of £91,000. These proved an embarrassment at this time, when there was much talk about people's doing well out of the war. 'We are not profiteers', the Chairman declared. The truth of his assertion was more than borne out by the Board's decision of the previous year to run down stocks rather than increase them, but as further proof of its patriotism the company proceeded to buy large amounts of War Loan 5%.

The first signs of trouble did not come until 1916, when the price of fodder for horses began to cause great anxiety. So did the large number of staff volunteering for the forces. The company was increasingly staffed by old men and retired directors. Old George Wall, the founder of the Liverpool company returned to take a more active part in affairs, although he had never really retired, and monthly board meetings were suspended for the duration of the war.

For the first time there began to be concern for the health of John Cary, the Chairman. He was now 76 and was much burdened by the death of two of his sons in action and the danger facing the other members of his family who were at the Front. The unfamiliar problems facing the firm were beginning to wear him out. He was finding great difficulty in taking the amount of leisure his health required. Accusations of war profiteering depressed him still further. Government control of food was growing all the time. It was beginning to commandeer supplies and place restrictions on freight. John Cary's son, William G. Lovell was loaned to the Ministry of Food as Director of Butter and Cheese.

John Cary began to be absent, almost for the first time, from Board meetings, and in July 1918, he was not well enough to take the chair at the A.G.M. In spite of his poor health he immersed himself in plans to form a trust for the relatives of employees killed or incapacitated during the war. William (III) took the chair in his absence. There were anxious inquiries from shareholders who were disturbed at the absence of John Cary Lovell for the first time since the formation of the company. One shareholder called him a commercial genius and said, 'he must spare himself and regain his health and so be with us for many years'.

Within a month he was indeed back at work. The Armistice four months later lessened the burden of his worries, but the wish of the shareholder for many more years of life for John Cary Lovell was not to be fulfilled, and he died the following October at the age of 79 after a business career lasting more than 60 years, during which he had built a small partnership dealing in West Country cheese into the foremost company in the United Kingdom in their particular business. He was active right to the end. He chaired the A.G.M. in July and a meeting of the Board on 30 September. Those few of us still living who knew him remember John Lovell even now with great admiration and much affection.

He was succeeded by his son William (III), newly released from the Ministry of Food with a C.B.E. to his credit. William Lovell was a very different type of man, particularly called to memory for his courtesy and integrity. He was devoted to the business and gave limitless time to it, but perhaps he did not possess the steel beneath the charm of his father. Perhaps also he did not have John Cary's trading ability and intuition.

Certainly he relied on others who were themselves possibly not too astute as traders. They tended to be accountants somewhat removed from the sphere of marketing. He remained as Chairman right through the years between the wars until his death in 1944, in fact his chairmanship covered the most difficult years the company has passed through. He was thoroughly conversant with the provision trade. After leaving school he spent 18 months with Bretel Frères in Normandy. He went right through the offices from the bottom and later became a first class salesman. Selling came naturally to him. He visited regularly the far distant countries from which the company drew its supplies. He continued the important work of his father at St. Bartholomew's Hospital and at Hodgson's Brewery. In the City of London Police Reserve, in which he served for a number of years, he rose to the rank of Commandant and retired with the unusual rank of Honorary Commandant. He was a good and respected Chairman of the company for more than 20 years.

Despite the difficulties of the latter years of the war, the company was in excellent shape when he took office. Its balance sheet was strong and its world wide business almost intact. The main casualty was the young but growing business with Russia and Siberia killed by the Bolshevik Revolution. Otto Hansen, at a loose end, and still bursting with energy was appointed agent for Norway, Sweden, Denmark and Finland. Elsewhere, in spite of wars and revolutions, normal commercial transactions continued. Offices on the second floor at West Smithfield, which are now the offices of Fitch Lovell Ltd., were let at £100 per annum in 1916 to James Preston, who later became West Butchers and is now known as West Layton Ltd., part of the Fitch Lovell group. In January 1919 Lovell & Christmas made a big loan to World's Stores to enable them to purchase another chain of provisions shops called Walkers Stores. It was the beginning of Lovell's interest in the retail trade. (World's Stores is one of the components of the modern Fitch Lovell interest known as Key Markets, and the whole story of World's Stores and the Group's retail development is told in another chapter.) In the same year, £90,000 was paid for a factory for the English Margarine Co., a subsidiary of George Wall & Co. Additional agencies for bacon and butter from Denmark were negotiated.

The main problem facing William (III) in 1920, his first full year in office was decontrol. As the various commodities were freed by the post-war government, every effort was made to ensure that the company's position was as strong as it had been before the war. This entailed visits by the Chairman to many of the supplying countries, and his efforts were successful.

The capital structure of the company was altered during this year. The orginal £5 preference and £5 ordinary stock were converted into £1 stock, and stockholders received an extra four stock units for every one they held. At the same time, a direct financial interest was taken in Isaac Beer to replace the guarantees formerly given. 20,000 £1 ordinary shares were acquired by the issue of £20,000 of the new Lovell & Christmas £1 stock units and an extra 5,000 shares were purchased at 21s. This investment still remains on the books of the company but it has been increased by the issue of scrip bonus shares.

J.G. Elliott – later to become the first Chairman who was not a member of the Lovell family – had by now become the company's accountant. He had been closely associated with William (III) at the Ministry of Food. He held an Australian accountancy qualification and was a forthright man of definite views and considerable energy. There is little doubt that the new Chairman relied on him to a considerable extent. He was elected a director some three of four years later.

It is noticeable that after the death of John Cary, the minutes, which had been terse and to the point, became diffuse and more like management memoranda. They continued to be written in a neat copperplate hand. H. Soden, who was named as the company's secretary in the 1896 prospectus, died in 1917 after writing the minutes for 21 years. He was succeeded by Mr. Young.

If I were to pick a year which marked the end of Lovell & Christmas's Edwardian prosperity, I would not choose 1914, nor 1918, nor even 1919, the year of the first Chairman's death. It was in 1921 that the company first experienced the adverse trading conditions which were to be the main feature of the inter-war period. For the first time a drop in profits was reported. They fell in this year to £107,000. The reason for the reversal was a sudden drop in the price of butter and cheese. The two commodities fell about 30% because of the big increase in world production, since the end of the war, which was now beginning to make itself felt in the markets. Butter fell from 3s. to 2s. a lb. Cheese dropped from 1s. 8d. to 1s. 2d. Naturally the directors began to take a hard look at costs. They found that overheads in London were as high as 2% of the sales' turnover!

With prices so low it was essential to obtain the cheapest supplies possible. As far as butter was concerned, Russia still seemed a promising source, but no business had been done there since the Revolution. Lovell & Christmas bided its time and its patience was rewarded with an agreement with Centrosojus (England) Ltd., the Russian Government Agents. Lovell's loaned them £20,000 and deducted £1 on every cask of butter received until the loan was paid off. These supplies began to be received in 1924.

It is an amusing sidelight on Lovell's flexibility that, while perfectly at home negotiating with this Communist agency, it was at the same time still dealing with that splendid pre-revolutionary entrepreneur Otto Hansen. He was now in Latvia, and the company advanced him £10,000 for Latvian dairies. (He was getting a commission of 1d. a bale on bacon received from his contacts.) The following year another Soviet concern, Selosojus, was loaned £50,000 to develop butter-making capacity in Russia and with even handed impartiality Lovell's accepted a proposal from Hansen to loan £15,000 to Central Savebena for a bacon factory in Riga. Further money was later loaned to this company and a form of mortgage obtained, but there was difficulty in getting fire insurance from an English company and Lovell's support of the Capitalist system in Riga was not entirely successful in other ways, for, a few years later, the bacon factory had to call a meeting of creditors. However, consignments to Lovell's continued and nine years later the mortgage deeds arrived in London. Things at the bacon factory went from bad to worse nonetheless. The local manager was found to be misappropriating funds, although the fidelity guarantee was invoked it was not paid in full.

Dealings with the Communists were not easy either, although there was certainly no suggestion of default on their part. Just before the General Election of 1931 International Communism was alleged to be poised to take over the country. Spurred on by a virulent press campaign this rumour caused intense anti-Soviet feeling, which affected the demand for Siberian butter. This was a serious matter for Lovell's, who had 100,000 casks to sell. Once again however, it took the long view in its relations with Russia. It granted a loan of £60,000 and shipments were resumed in 1932.

I mentioned in the last chapter that France was no longer a material source of supply for butter after the First World War. The end of the Cherbourg-Southampton trade was not however the end of Lovell's activities in France, and in partnership with Bretels it switched to selling butter in France itself. The original principal of the firm, Adolph Bretel had died in 1913, but relations with his successors continued to be good, and Lovell's bought a 40% interest in a firm of Parisian provision merchants in equal shares with Bretel. The Paris house was Mionnet et Cie. The joint control with the Mionnet family was not entirely successful, and so in October 1922 the entire firm was bought, including fixtures and machinery for 540,000 francs. It is not known if Bretel Frères retained their 20% interest. Monsieur Mionnet was given a contract as manager or *directeur* for 10 years, and the firm became known as the Paris branch. Elsewhere agents were appointed in Hamburg and Berlin. 'Our San Francisco office' is mentioned in correspondence of the same period but no further reference to it can be found in the records.

Back in London, the company was slowly developing the familiar office structure of modern business. A committee of the Board was formed to prepare a plan for staff life insurance and pensions. Approval in principle was given in June 1923. Employees who reached the age of 65 and who had served continuously for at least 20 years were to be paid a retiring allowance of half the previous 20 years' remuneration with a limit of £200 per annum.

A costing department was inaugurated in October of that year under J.G. Elliott. One of their first projects was to cost horse drawn vehicles against motors. It was discovered that the cost on turnover of horses was 3.84% and motors 3.38%. In the light of this information the directors did not in fact turn all their horses out to grass and go knocking on the door of Morris Motors. Instead motor transport continued to supersede horses in the gradual way it had done ever since the first lorries were purchased in 1909. Horse drawn vans were still being used for in-town deliveries in 1938.

During the early '20s, Lovell's became involved in the condensed milk business in Ireland, first of all through a firm called Cleeve Bros., and then through the Condensed Milk Company of Ireland. In 1924, J.G. Elliott and another director, Robert Graham, visited Ireland and as a result it was decided to buy £50,000 7% preference participating ordinary shares at £1 and make a loan of £30,000 to the Condensed Milk Co. which was associated with Cleeves. It held some 13,000 shares in Cleeves, and Lovell's decided to buy 12,700 of them for £15,000 so as to obtain majority control – the price also included an interest in a toffee factory at Battersea in London.

In the next stage of this complicated transaction, the Condensed Milk Co. of Ireland proceeded to buy the Newmarket Dairy Co. In order to enable it to do this, its nominal capital had to be increased to £250,000. Lovell's then owned, after extra payment, 133,000 out of the 189,000 shares issued. Two years later, in 1926 a further £200,000 was guaranteed for the Condensed Milk Company of Ireland. It was proving a trying and not too profitable business, and fortunately a couple of years later it was sold for a satisfactory price to the Eire Government.

Ventures like the purchase of the Irish business were having an adverse effect upon the company's financial position in the mid-'20s. By June 1925 Lovell & Christmas was running an overdraft of £810,000. It also had a loan of £200,000 to be repaid. There had been a considerable deterioration since the death of John Lovell.

At the suggestion of its bankers the company raised fresh capital by issuing £250,000 £1 preference shares at £1, and 250,000 £1 ordinary shares at 30s. Lovell & Christmas was now capitalised at £2 million. Looking back it seems strange that the company was able to continue the indulgent policy of giving such generous advances to suppliers. It was a policy which was dangerous enough in the pre-war days, and was inappropriate to the changed conditions of the late '20s. Even the General Strike of 1926 and the first signs of approaching depression did not deter the firm. Apart from other difficulties, there were serious losses in ventures in Europe at this time. I have already mentioned the bacon factory in Riga. There was also trouble about a loan to a Polish bacon factory and an attempt to set up an egg packing business in Roumania ended in disaster. (That story is told in Chapter 8). Lovell & Christmas must have done extremely well with its established trade in this period to absorb these various losses. The Chairman revealed about this time that the net profit on agencies, the staple business of the company was about one third of one per cent. He added, 'but enormous turnover in butter and cheese imported from every producing country in the world enables us to exist'. In 1928 alone Lovell's received consignments of 17,000 tons of butter and cheese

21. G.P. Gomersall,
Director, Lovell & Christmas Ltd.
from 1952

22. Arthur G. Locke,
Vice-Chairman and
Managing Director,
Lovell & Christmas (Northern) Ltd.

23. Lovell & Christmas Ltd.: Motor Delivery Service and Horse and Van Delivery Service at Smithfield

24. Lovell & Christmas Ltd.: Modern Butter Packing Factory

25 and 26. Lovell & Christmas (Northern) Ltd.: Blue Cap Foods Division modern factory

from New Zealand. The dairy factories there and in Australia were becoming more and more interested in selling their produce rather than consigning it, and Lovell's had to follow the trend of the day, although traditionally preferring to act as agents. Despite the changes and difficulties in marketing it has remained in the lead for distribution and packaging of butter and cheese from those two countries.

In 1928 Lovell's was approached by Lunham Bros. Ltd., bacon curers in Eire. They offered to guarantee supplies to Lovell's in return for an injection of capital. Lovell's agreed and took up debentures, preference shares and some ordinary shares. The association continues today. At this time the Hamburg Office, opened only six years before, was closed and the Paris Branch was sold to Barthelmy et Cie., although Lovell's retained a small interest in it.

Perhaps the happiest feature of these difficult years was the success of experiments which had been going on for some time in the production of pre-packed processed cheese. Marketing of the product began in 1925. The brand name, *Blue Cap* was chosen and each packet carried the picture of a smiling dairymaid wearing a blue bonnet. Backed by newspaper advertising, coupon schemes and even door-to-door canvassing to push up sales, the venture was a real success.

With the fall in prices on the London butter and cheese markets, overseas suppliers became more and more interested in opening their own selling floors in the United Kingdom. Lovell & Christmas's agency business, which was its mainstay, began to look vulnerable. The Chairman, rightly, saw the increase in the manufacture and sale of *Blue Cap* products as a form of insurance. By the early '30s the firm was selling *Blue Cap* butter as well as cheese, and the products, said the Chairman, helped materially in the achievement of better results in these difficult years.

The company demonstrated its confidence in the future by building, in 1928, a new freehold building in Hosier Lane, Smithfield. Lovell House, with its extensive warehousing and cold storage accommodation still stands (although it is now occupied by the Union International Ltd.). The building, faced in white, is an uncompromising example of the style of its period. To celebrate its opening the company published its first publicity brochure, lavishly illustrated with pictures of the company at work. The text is clear and concise, its message summed up in the opening paragraph:

> You have goods to sell, and we have the organisation for selling them quickly and at the best price.

The brochure is clearly aimed at overseas suppliers, there are pictures of Australian eggs in storage, of cheeses being checked for quality in a Lovell & Christmas warehouse, and of boxes of Dominion butter being sampled on the Butter Floor at Smithfield.

Lovell & Christmas's delivery service is a big feature of the brochure, which points out that motor deliveries are made daily to customers.

> An expert salesman accompanies the lorry and delivers the goods as he sells. This is a very great convenience to the smaller shops in the suburbs; they are enabled to receive their butter and other produce fresh from our cold store. They get just what they want, when they want it, at the price that is ruling upon that day. On the other hand, our large buyers are able to draw direct from our cold stores, so that we have equally quick facilities for supplying one box of butter or one crate of cheese to a suburban grocer, or 5,000 to some great chain store buyer.

The point is driven home by a series of pictures. Butter and cheese is shown being loaded on to lorries in the early morning at Smithfield under the watchful eye of a bowler-hatted overseer. They were beautiful vehicles with fixed starter-handles, headlamps mounted on a bar in front of the radiator, and solid tyres. A lorry is shown driving along a country road. The next picture shows the lorry outside a small grocer's shop. Three men, all wearing bowler hats, are standing at the tail of the lorry discussing the wares, while a fourth wearing a flat cap, waits inside for the sale to be completed in order to deliver the goods into the shop. The caption reads 'Selecting Empire Butter. Getting to business at a typical country shop'. In the centre of the brochure are two truly magnificent pictures. Across the top of the double page, an entire fleet of old lorries is drawn up in front of the Lovell & Christmas premises in West Smithfield. The caption is 'Our Motor Delivery Service at Smithfield'. Below is an endearing picture entitled 'Our Horse and Van Delivery Service at Smithfield'. It is interesting to note that the lorry men all appear to be young and clean shaven. The van men are older, moustachioed and clad in aprons.

The brochure goes on to extol the efficiency of the office, saying that a telephone call is enough to bring a shopkeeper fresh supplies 'in an hour or two'. There are two pictures of the clerks at work. In the Stock Book Department they are shown seated at long desks on high stools. In the Day Book and Ledger Posting Department they are busy at their typewriters. There is not a single woman in sight.

The brochure ends with a final appeal for 'continuous and regular consignments'. It offers advances on the shortest notice and upon the most liberal basis possible. 'Consign your produce to us', the brochure adds, 'and judge us upon the results we obtain'. On the very last page Branch Houses and Agents are listed: Liverpool, Manchester, Bristol, Cardiff, Birmingham, Newcastle, Glasgow, Aberdeen, Leith, Dundee, Belfast, Dublin, Cork, Montreal, New York, Paris, Rotterdam, Brussels, Copenhagen, Riga, Auckland, Hawera, Palmerston North, Invercargill (New Zealand), Melbourne, Sydney, Brisbane, Cape Town, Buenos Aires.

We must after this story of progress and success, return to the appalling trading conditions of the late '20s and '30s as the great Depression settled over Europe. One reaction to the difficulties was a scheme engendered by a well known finance house to form a joint trading company with other leading dairy produce importers. Although the idea had not originated with Lovell's the firm was not averse to it, provided its interest was safeguarded. Discussions took place, dragged on into the summer of 1931 and then, as so often happens, enthusiasm wained and the scheme was abandoned.

The firm's brochure was scarcely in the hands of suppliers before the blizzards of the Depression began to blow in earnest. Prices were lower than they had been in 1914. Best New Zealand butter went down to 7d. a lb. and cheese to 4½d. at first-hand value. Apart from the strain of collapsing prices the company was subjected to a double squeeze on its business as overseas suppliers tried to sell direct in the United Kingdom and tariff barriers excluded the company from selling abroad. The closure of the Paris Branch (already mentioned) and of the New York office (closed as a result of the high tariffs imposed by the United States' government) were described by Lovell's Chairman as, 'a bitter pill'. He also had to report stock losses due to falling markets. There were changes on the Board. Lionel Lovell had retired in 1927, after 55 years in the firm. Now P.T. and G.V. Wall also retired. Old George Wall, the last of the founding fathers of the company, died in 1929, at the age of 85. At this difficult time however, the Board also gained a new and valuable recruit in Rolande Wall, one of George's grandchildren. He had already distinguished himself in Liverpool and was to prove one of the company's ablest leaders.

Meanwhile Lovell's despite the Depression, still somehow managed to find cash for advances and investment, although on a reduced scale. Early in 1933 credits of £80,000 were opened for the Soviet agency Selosojus against a promise of consignments of 150,000 casks of butter. Two months later, however, an embargo was placed on the import of Russian butter so the credits were withdrawn. The Board of Trade eventually granted the firm licences for advances but it is uncertain if they were sufficient to cover the advances Lovell's wanted to make. However, the company was able to finance an extension to a small bacon factory in the Isle of Wight and to buy a small meat factory in Yeovil. Prices were low at this time and Lovell's would probably have been better advised to buy something really good, but its real interests remained in obtaining overseas suppliers. In this it excelled.

To facilitate its development plans for Hosier Lane, the company bought *The Wheatsheaf Inn* and other properties towards the end of 1934. Meanwhile the Board was having to give a lot of attention to the affairs of Cleeves Ltd., the condensed milk and confectionery business in which Lovell's had become involved in 1924. It was not a trade in which it felt at home and eventually in 1939 the confectionery part of Cleeve's was sold to Mace's Confectionery Co. Ltd. while the condensed milk section was formed into a new company, Charles Cleeve & Co. Ltd., in which Lovell's retained an interest.

Before it had had time to solve the problems associated with Cleeve's Lovell's found itself involved in the internal difficulties of Isaac Beer's, with which it had been associated for more than a generation and of which it now owned a good portion. The Chairman, William Lovell (III) was also a Beer's shareholder. Both he and Lovell's therefore were worried to learn of a lack of harmony on Beer's Board. Mr. Ernest Beer, the Chairman, approached William (III), as an act of courtesy, to ask for his blessing on a merger between Beer's and a neighbouring company, George Bowles Nicholls. Other members of Beer's did not support the idea of this merger. In the end Ernest decided to sell his 90,000 shares to Lovell's for 6s. 6d. each and retire. Edward Shephard took the chair of Beer's in his place.

As the shadow of Hitler's War began to loom over England in 1938, Lovell's directors decided to prepare duplicate share registers. These and other vital papers and records were deposited with the National Provincial Bank in East Grinstead, Sussex. Architects were engaged to prepare places for the protection of staff and the business generally in the event of War, and later, with hostilities imminent, the firm's accountants said they were worried about the extent of its overseas advances and recommended that Lovell's prepare for the worst by forming a special, extra reserve fund of £80,000. The company's directors evidently had a much more realistic idea of what war was going to mean than had their predecessors in 1914.

Immediately war was declared, Rolande Wall was seconded to the Ministry of Food, where he had a distinguished career, (of which more later). I became Chairman of the Ministry of Food's London Area for Provisions and Groceries and Lovell's made available to me office space at 12 West Smithfield, which I used throughout the worst of the bombing. It is now the office of E.M. Canevali, the Chairman of Lovell's.

As war broke out, Lovell's decided to separate its importing and manufacturing business from its wholesaling activities, and formed a new private company, Lovell & Christmas (Wholesale) Ltd., to which the trade and goodwill of the wholesale section was transferred. Together with Isaac Beer, Lovell's also formed a special company, with a nominal capital of £100, called Emergency Food Supplies Ltd., 'to provide for the distribution of foodstuffs from depots in outlying districts in consequence of the disorganisation which might result from the war'.

Lovell's board was right to suppose that this war was going to affect its business even more radically than had the previous one. The company suffered heavily from the bombing, as in addition to the devastation of the Smithfield area, its main premises in both Bristol and Liverpool were severely damaged. Trade was resumed with surprising speed amidst the rubble. Nevertheless, the bombing, the general dislocation of trade and the rapid call-up of staff placed heavy burdens on the firm. One idea to ease the situation was a proposal that Lovell's merge with Beer's, George Bowles Nicholls, Trengrovic & Nathan and their subsidiary companies. The various boards seemed willing, but the project came to nothing.

The difficulties of wartime trade were appalling. How John Cary Lovell would have managed I cannot imagine. From almost the first day of the war, the Ministry of Food exercised stringent controls, of quite a different order from those operating during the First

World War. They changed the whole nature of Lovell's business and the firm became simply a first-hand distributor for the Ministry and registered wholesalers to its retail customers.

More than 1,000 employees were in the Forces and, as in the previous war, the company drew up a scheme for their remuneration. Married men with more than 12 months' service were to have the difference between their service pay and the company's made up.

Like his father a generation before, the Chairman was soon feeling the strain of guiding the firm under the appalling wartime conditions. J.G. Elliott was elected as Vice-Chairman to ease his burden. Still feeling that the Board was too weak to cope with the tremendous problems, William (III) asked the Minister of Food if he would release Rolande Wall, as his services were urgently needed by the company. The Permanent Secretary of the Ministry, Sir Henry French, replied that the work Wall was doing was of national importance and his loss would seriously affect the Ministry, so he hoped the company would not press for Wall's return. Under the circumstances, the Chairman acceeded to Sir Henry's request.

On 28 December 1943, William (III) for the last time took the chair at a meeting of directors. A charming and conscientious gentleman, untiring in his efforts, he died a month later, almost exactly 100 years after his grandfather had begun trading in London. He was succeeded by a man who had no connection at all with the families of Wall, Lovell or Christmas.

J.G. Elliott, who had joined the firm after the First World War as an accountant, was elected Chairman in February 1944, and Rolande Wall, although still serving at the Ministry, became the firm's Vice-Chairman.

When in 1945, the War ended, government controls continued and the company became fearful about what would happen to its huge agency business when freedom of trading was restored, so it decided to develop the manufacturing side. During the war it had become associated through its Liverpool subsidiary with a canning business in Northern Ireland. This association was now developed.

A new subsidiary, Lovell Wall & Co. Ltd. was formed to exploit the new technology of quick frozen foods. The company began to deal in citrus products, and in 1948 Lovell's became agents for large quantities of canned goods from Australia. In spite of this diversification, the firm decided, in 1945, to expand its property holding in the Smithfield Market area and bought the freehold of 4/5 West Smithfield.

In 1946 Rolande Wall was welcomed back, at last, from the Ministry of Food, although in fact he continued to act for the Ministry in an advisory capacity and undertook journeys for it to the United States and South America in the following year.

He returned to the company just in time, for in 1947 the health of the Chairman, J.G. Elliott, broke down and Sir Rolande took the chair at the Annual General Meeting in 1947. Although Elliott returned to his desk in due course, he retired in 1951 when Sir Rolande was elected in his place.

In 1947 Lovell's published its second publicity brochure. It provides an interesting contrast with the first. It is written in English and French and well illustrated with aerial photographs of the cities in which the main offices are situated, and on the cover is a splendid picture of a Lovell & Christmas lorry going down Ludgate Hill, with St. Paul's behind it and bomb damage to one side. Indeed, history and the Blitz are two of the brochure's main themes.

Instead of the simple sales message of the 1929 publication, the 1947 brochure contains notes on the history of the company, together with some delightful old drawings and prints of Smithfield in days gone by. There is much about the bomb damage and difficulties of the war and about the service provided by the company to the nation in two world wars, but there is no appeal for business, and no mention of 'advances on liberal terms'. The truth is that in 1947, with decontrol not even in sight, there was little point in a direct sales message, and the purpose of the brochure was simply to keep the Lovell & Christmas name alive among the suppliers. Nevertheless, the text reveals some interesting statistics. At that time, the company employed 117 travelling salesmen and depot salesmen. 'In normal times, when unhampered by restrictions on the use of petrol, customers are visited at least once a week'. There were over 180 vans and heavy lorries as well as 64 cars for the use of sales representatives. Main centres were linked by teleprinter. Cold storage capacity in London is given as 203,000 c.ft. The Liverpool cold store had a capacity of 43,000 c.ft. and cold store facilities existed both at Bristol and Birmingham.

One new development mentioned was the St. John's Laboratory 'where we can test the various goods that are offered to us and in addition offer a technical service to shippers and customers who may require chemical or bacteriological examinations. This department is supervised by a Scientific Adviser of long and wide experience'. He was Osman Jones, F.R.I.C. His name appears at the beginning of the publication under those of the previous chairmen.

Further down the same page it is announced that the paid up share capital was at this time £1,500,000. Reserves were £700,000 and the total capital employed was £54 million. Elsewhere the brochure gives an interesting list of the products handled by the firm. They were 38 and ranged from the familiar butter, bacon and cheese, to more exotic commodities like dried nuts, honey, olive oil and game. Even the editor, A. Gordon Lovell did not think the list fully comprehensive, for he ends it, 'rice, pulses, etc. etc.'.

Under the conditions of the time it is not surprising that the latter years of J.G. Elliott's chairmanship were unspectacular. Although much was done towards reshaping the company and its various activities, in many ways the business needed to be re-built almost from scratch, and on his assumption of the chair Sir Rolande immediately set about this work. D.W. Elliott, J.G.'s son, resigned from the Board, to facilitate the reorganisation and in February 1952 A.J. Beney, F. Bernau and G.P. Gomersall were appointed as directors.

In the 18 years that have passed since then, A.J. Beney has retired, F. Bernau has died, and G.P. Gomersall has become Vice-Chairman of the firm. Gomersall, known everywhere as Peter, has been a tower of strength, particularly to the dairy produce side of the business. His pre-war experience was with the New Zealand Dairy Board and with Amalgamated Dairies. During the War he served for five years as Assistant Director of Imports at the Ministry of Food and joined Lovell's in 1949. Since then he has not only become Vice-Chairman of the firm, but also been for some years Chairman of the Butter Packers' Association and, in 1965, an outstanding Chairman of the London Provision Exchange.

In 1952, Lovell's adopted new Articles of Association and its pension scheme for employees of all grades was changed and brought up to date. At about this time also the practice of writing the Board's minutes in longhand was discontinued and thereafter they became much more concise and dealt mainly with policy. Mr. Young, who had been the firm's Secretary since 1917, when its first Secretary Mr. Soden died, retired in 1947 and was replaced by two men; one was A.H. Williams, the other A.J. Beney.

As everyone waited for the long-expected final decontrol of food, modest expansion continued. Philips & Co. the Smithfield market company acquired two new stalls. Later they were sold to Keevil & Keevil and in 1957 a new company was formed on a 50-50 basis with Keevils', which is still in existence. Agents were posted overseas to various countries and visits paid to Australia and New Zealand. Sir Rolande Wall was distinctly impatient to get back into the real business for which Lovell's was so well placed, and in September 1953 urged the government to proceed with decontrol of all foods as quickly as possible. He pointed out that the government were still the sole importers of the staple foods. Then, as decontrol got underway at last, he forecast lower prices, but said he was slightly nervous of the administrative difficulties, stating, 'After fourteen years of dealing with permits and ration documents, it is not an easy task to adjust the administration of a large organisation such as ours to the methods of freedom'.

One of the problems was finance for the larger volume of business which began to flood in, but Lovell's floated a debenture issue which met with a good reception.

Meanwhile, Lovell's was pressing on with its plans to increase its output of frozen and canned food, and began its financial involvement with Frozen Foods (Ditton Court) Ltd. which was to end in purchase of the company and its establishment under a new name as an important manufacturing unit. 1954 was a busy year with negotiations for new premises in Liverpool, Glasgow and Southampton, and a reorganisation at Bristol. K.O.G. Huntley was appointed a director and began his distinguished career with the company which only terminated with his death 16 years later.

A few years afterwards in 1958 E.M. Canevali, who had directed with such success the Liverpool company, of which he had been a director for eight years, was appointed to the parent board. His career is worth studying, he joined the Liverpool company in 1927 as a boy of 14 at 7s. 6d. a week. After war service in the Royal Navy, he was elected a director of Liverpool in 1950. Then, as mentioned, to the parent board in 1958, he became the Vice-Chairman in 1962, and succeeded Sir Rolande Wall as Chairman on 25 May 1963, and was appointed a director of Fitch Lovell in 1964.

Apart from his outstanding business career he has achieved the happy distinction of playing both tennis and golf for his native county of Cheshire.

S.E. Sharpe, who was responsible for the dried fruits division of L. & C. and who had worked and schemed so hard to make it a success, was also appointed a director.

Dried fruits were one of the earliest diversifications from dairy produce and Lovell's received its first consignment of Australian raisins in 1929. The involvement in this trade demands the same skills which enabled Lovell's to become supreme in butter and cheese, an ability to judge the quality of the product and get it to the market at the right price and above all to attract and maintain the confidence of the suppliers.

Steadily and surely over the years Lovell's improved its position, receiving each year a bigger quantity, and early in 1968 approximately, 6,000 tons of fruit a year were being handled. S.E. Sharpe had visited with success both Australia and Persia.

As the 1950s advanced the company was becoming more successful and more profitable. This was evidently noticed in financial circles because early in 1958 unusual activity began in Lovell & Christmas shares on the London Stock Exchange. It became obvious in the spring and early summer that someone was acquiring large numbers of the company's shares, and it began to be feared a 'take over' was being planned.

However, as told later in this story, Lovell's came to an agreement with its friends Fitch & Son and a merger of the two firms resulted.

An extract from Sir Rolande's review of 1958/9 is worth noting '. . . there has been complete harmony in our relations, economic and trading advantages have already resulted. There is no doubt they will continue to accrue'.

Prior to this, in August 1957, the Good Housekeeping Institute granted the Institute's Certificate for Canned Meats to *Spam*. This is the first mention of *Spam* in the official records and in September of that year negotiations were concluded with Hormel's for a licence to manufacture and sell *Spam* in the U.K. and other European countries for a number of years, this in addition to the agreement whereby Lunham's in Eire produced *Spam*.

The Bank of England approved the payment of a royalty to Hormel's which over the years has amounted to over one million dollars. The excellent understanding and goodwill existing between Hormel and L. & C. has been generated by E.M. Canevali on his various visits to the senior officers of the American company, and on their visits to England. This is truly business in the old Lovell tradition of mutual respect and understanding based on a letter of agreement.

The profits of L. & C. exceeded £400,000 for the first time in 1960, and the King George V Cup which had been presented for competition among Factory Managers in New Zealand was won outright and the Board decided to give a replacement trophy at a cost of £150.

During this period a 50% interest was taken in Gevato at Driebergen, Holland. This was a most successful connection, but in 1969/70 the shareholding was sold whilst maintaining the full selling agency for their products and De Haan (Foods) Ltd. Abram, near Wigan, was taken in part settlement.

Record profits were again attained in 1961/2. The major undertaking of moving to Erith from Smithfield occupied much time. E.M. Canevali became Vice-Chairman, it was a pleasure for me to vacate this position to make way for his promotion. At the same time S.F. Collins was appointed to the Board. The following year Sir Rolande Wall, on his assumption of the Chairmanship of Fitch Lovell relinquished that of Lovell's in favour of Canevali, and Peter Gomersall became Vice-Chairman. He is referred to in the Annual Report as 'one of the leading personalities in the Dairy Produce Trade'.

When E.M. Canevali was appointed Chairman on 25 May 1963, he issued a challenge to all companies in the L. & C. Group to increase their future profits by 10% each year (known as Mr. Ten Percenter) so that in the next decade they would exceed one million pounds. I am told they hope to achieve this within the 10 year period.

Fitch Lovell early in 1966 had acquired McElderry & Moffett Ltd., the well established bacon curers in Northern Ireland, through the good offices of Rothchilds and decided that the company should operate under the aegis of Lovell & Christmas, who had already interests in that country. This has proved a happy and rewarding association with Mr. Tom McElderry a first class and most capable colleague.

The new Chairman, besides inspiring the companies, began several tidying operations and among other things the interest in Barthelmy of Paris was sold and the balance of shares in Phillips & Co. (Smithfield) was purchased from Keevils'; at the same time he was achieving his 10% overall profit increase.

He decided to reorganise the Board in 1967 and I made way again, as was only right, to allow the younger generation to assume responsibility. Fred Lovell was elected (he is a great grandson of John Lovell and a member of the fourth generation to sit on the board) and also G.A. Dickman, the Manager of the bacon division. H.E. Williams who had been 47 years with the company retired and J.H. Connolly succeeded him as Secretary. A.J. Beney also retired as a director to help with the reorganisation.

It is interesting to note that one other Lovell of the fourth generation holds an important position in the company, namely, Kingsley Lovell the son of Gordon, of whom so many hold affectionate memories.

Each year the company has continued to hold its Spring Luncheon at the Savoy. This has become, perhaps, the most important social function in the Provision Trade, and to which practically every leading personality and firm is honoured to be invited, and those who are in London from distant countries and able to come, are wholly delighted at the hospitality and impressed with the extent of L. & C. connections and their happy relations with suppliers and customers.

Arthur Locke, of whom mention is made elsewhere, became a member of the parent board in 1965.

1966 saw a record profit of £660,000, and up to the time of these records in 1970, there has been sustained activity in a period of inflation, rationalism and swiftly changing trade conditions. It is greatly to the credit of the Chairman, the Vice-Chairman, the Board and the Staff that the company has emerged stronger than ever and still holds a dominant position in the trade in England, Europe and beyond.

Several important changes since 1969 have taken place which I hope will be recorded by some future historian, but it is well to note a continuing number of further visits to Canada, the U.S.A., Africa and Asia by the Chairman and his principal colleagues.

If the spirit of the great and restless John Cary Lovell is able to perceive his company today, those who lead it, its wide ramifications and the great esteem in which it is held throughout the world for its integrity and efficiency, he could justly say, 'You have been given a charge to keep – well have you kept the same'.

But this could not have been achieved without the wonderful team spirit, fostered particularly by Sir Rolande and carried on splendidly by the present Chairman, Vice-Chairman and their associates.

# 7

## I

## LOVELL & CHRISTMAS OUTSIDE THE METROPOLIS

LOVELL & CHRISTMAS was rather slow to establish itself in the growing provincial cities of Britain. Almost certainly, it held back because of the personal preference of the first Chairman, John Cary Lovell. He was tireless in his search for new sources of supply in distant parts of the world, but he was a London merchant, and as far as he was concerned, the supplies, from New Zealand, the Argentine, Russia or France were destined for the great markets of the City and nowhere else. So it was that by 1906, 10 years after the flotation of the public company, Lovell & Christmas had only a single branch in Manchester and a sales office in Liverpool.

The Manchester branch had been established in 1880 at 5 Fennel Street, with Samual Broadbent as Manager. Stephen Head was sent from London to organise the office and assist with sales. Each Tuesday, one of the younger Lovells, either L.B. or Albert went from London to cope with the rush of business on market day. In 1882 E.J. Lovell, having spent 12 months behind a counter in the shops of Hudson Bros. in the Strand and Ludgate Hill, went to Manchester and there remained for 20 years. The business at 5 Fennel Street was done in a cellar and as it progressed it was transferred to 4 Fennel Street on the opposite side of the road where there was a fine selling floor, with a cellar below and a cheese floor above.

In the 1900s the need to expand the company's interests at home became more and more important. In 1906 the younger members of the Board proposed that Lovell & Christmas should amalgamate with a well-established northern firm based in Liverpool. At first, John Cary Lovell was opposed to the merger. He went to Liverpool and inspected the business and the books himself, and realising that the younger men who favoured the move were the ones who would have to conduct the business in the future, he agreed to support it. On 21 May 1906 a meeting was called of all shareholders owning 100 or more shares. The Chairman did not think there was any need to worry the shareholders, but he considered it would be a courteous gesture to call a meeting. He outlined the benefits he thought the merger would bring. Finally he said to the assembled shareholders, 'I shall not tell you the name of the firm until you approve'. They did. Then John Cary Lovell announced that Lovell & Christmas proposed to amalgamate with George Wall & Company Limited, wholesale grocers and manufacturers of margarine. A report of this meeting was then sent out to all shareholders and the consent of the preference shareholders, who then held votes, was obtained by referendum. A full report of the merger was given in the May 1906 edition of *The Grocer.*

George Wall, the chairman and founder of the firm was a man of some standing in the City of Liverpool. As well as being an Alderman of the City he was a Justice of the Peace, and President of the Liverpool Provision Exchange, which at that time was the hub of the provision trade in the North of England. His election to that position is a measure of the esteem in which he was held by his fellow traders. Yet like so many of the founders of Fitch Lovell, he had started from scratch.

He was born about 1845, the son of a Derbyshire farmer. Apprenticed to R. Orme & Co., a firm of grocers in Bakerwell, he was only 18 years old when he decided to begin on his own. He opened a shop at 9 Great Homer Street near to one of Liverpool's markets and worked day and night. It soon became clear that he was a most intelligent trader and his business prospered. He launched out into the wholesale trade and within nine years opened premises in Williamson Street in the centre of the city. 12 years later they had become too small for the growing business and had to be extended. His two sons, Percy T. Wall, and Charles G. Wall came into the business which spread into Wales and large areas of the North of England. George Wall had two nephews, Charles T. Wall, and G.V. Wall. The latter joined his uncle, but Charles T. was interested in the margarine trade and owned the Cheshire Creamery in Birkenhead. Later he secured a large factory outside Liverpool at Broadgreen to increase his production. Thus, towards the end of the century, there were two family firms, George Wall, and C.T. Wall's margarine company. It was decided to amalgamate the two, and C.T. became a director of his uncle's company.

George Wall retired officially in 1913, but continued to come to the business and help in many ways for another 16 years. When he died at the age of 85 he had completed a business career lasting no fewer than 70 years.

When George Wall's amalgamated with Lovell's it ceased to trade as a company but 34 years later the name still appeared on the stationary below Lovell & Christmas. Even in 1969 some of the old customers insist on making their cheques payable to Geo. Wall & Co. One casualty of the amalgamation with Lovell's was George Wall's original shop in Great Homer Street. One of the terms of the agreement was that there should be no retail businesses, and so the shop was sold. The Liverpool firm was certainly not swallowed up in the merger, however. In 1911 five out of the ten directors of Lovell & Christmas were members of the Wall family. The other five were Lovells. In the next generation, the Wall family were to produce one of the distinguished men in the story of Fitch Lovell.

Among the young men to return from the First World War, in which some of the staff lost their lives, was G.R.P. (Rolande) Wall a grandson of the founder. He had distinguished himself with the Royal Field Artillery and was awarded the Military Cross 'for gallantry and devotion to duty in action'. Rolande Wall was appointed a director of Lovell & Christmas in 1930, became Vice-Chairman in 1946 and Chairman in 1952. He became Vice-Chairman of the newly formed Fitch Lovell group in 1958 and Chairman in 1962. He still remains on the board of Lovell & Christmas and has been elected a Life President as a tribute to the great services he has rendered for nearly 50 years. His name has appeared continuously since 1919 in the history of Lovell & Christmas. He served it well not only in this country, but also in Canada, the Argentine, Australia and on the Continent.

On the outbreak of the Second World War he was seconded to the Ministry of Food as Assistant Director of Butter and Cheese. His personal qualities were well suited to the work of the Ministry and he advanced steadily and surely until he became the Commercial Secretary, responsible for the purchases of all food. In the end he was made a Deputy Secretary. It is understood that he was the only trade member to reach this high and important position. He received the honour of knighthood in 1946 for his services to the nation.

27. Gordon W. McLean,
President and Managing Director,
Lovell & Christmas (Canada) Ltd.
from 1961

28. Montreal staff of Lovell & Christmas (Canada) Ltd.,
with the Chairman of Lovell & Christmas Ltd., E.M. Canevali

29 and 30. Lovell & Christmas (Scotland) Ltd.:
Warehouse, old and new

31. Part of the Glasgow cheese store, accommodating 2000 tons

32. J.D. Holgate,
Chairman of Rutzou Limited
from 1937-71

33. Presentation of the Fitch Lovell Golf Challenge Cup 1971:
E.M. Canevali, Chairman of Lovell & Christmas Ltd.,
receives the Cup from Fitch Lovell Chairman, Sir Charles Hardie

Rolande Wall is a diplomat by nature and was able to accomplish much which more forthright men could never have done. He was indefatigable in visiting the various depots and factories and he was held in affection to an unusual degree by the staff. A modest man who shirked the limelight, he was shrewd and possessed good judgment. It was rare that he did not achieve a goal when he was sure it was in the best interests of the firm. He is a great gentleman, whom to know is to admire.

Relations with another member of the Wall family were not so happy. Serious differences arose between the London Board and C.T. Wall, the one who had started the margarine business. He was not satisfied with the terms of the merger. He was also being reprimanded for not attending Board meetings. The differences were taken right up to the House of Lords, when the action was withdrawn after a period of disagreement lasting nearly six years. The litigation cost Lovell & Christmas more than £4,000.

C.T. Wall's margarine business was in fact sold soon after the First World War to Jurgens. By this time it was known as the English Margarine Company Ltd. It won a place in the history of the margarine industry by the way it successfully competed against the giants of the trade. By 1917 it was producing 1,000 tons of margarine a week, approximately one eighth of British production. The works were sold for cash and shares in Jurgens, who were anxious that Lovell's should not sell them and depress the Bear Markets of those days.

The manager of English Margarine was V.D. Graae, a Dane noted for his genial temperament. It has been maintained that he was appointed a director of Lovell & Christmas as a nominee of Jurgens. He certainly did become a director of Lovell's for five years after the sale, and before assuming the chairmanship of the Maypole Dairy Company in which Jurgens were interested. He did much to improve Maypole, as he had already improved Lovell & Christmas.

Because of its independent roots, the Liverpool Branch of Lovell & Christmas, as Geo. Wall & Co. was now known, tended to pursue an independent and aggressive trading policy. In May 1913 it negotiated a 10-year agreement for the supply of skimmed condensed milk with a consortium consisting of Cleeves Bros., R. Lehmann, Van den Bergh Van Heels Condensed Milk Co., and Lovell's itself. It was active in the sugar market, and early in 1914 12,000 tons were sold short. In 1924 the Board was disturbed by a loss approaching £10,000 on sugar deals in the course of the year. Liverpool is not mentioned by name, but almost certainly its activities were the cause. Instructions were issued that the buying of any article in excess of normal requirements must be referred to the Board for approval. In fact Liverpool had made good profits out of this type of trading – matters only tend to come to the notice of the Board when they go wrong. In 1939, for instance, Rolande Wall made heavy forward sales of canned hams to Canada which made what he describes as 'embarrassingly high profits' because of the war. The hams came from a ham canning plant started by the branch in Williamson Street, Liverpool. The branch also began the packing of butter into a consumer pack. The office in Glasgow was expanded, a branch was opened in Cardiff, and offices were established in Belfast, Hanley and Grantham.

The significance of the merger with Geo. Wall & Co. Ltd. is now clear. It was the beginning of the transformation of Lovell & Christmas from an importing and wholesaling business receiving supplies mainly from overseas, into a much more complex trading organisation with important interests in domestic food manufacture and distribution.

While the Liverpool business thrived, the Manchester Branch languished. Just as the secret of Liverpool's success lay in its independence, so the cause of Manchester's failure may have been its dependence on London. Remember that it was the custom for members of the Lovell family to travel to Manchester each week on market day in the early years of the branch's history. From those days onward, the minutes of the Board record little about Manchester except trouble. In 1898, all the Branch's travellers resigned after a dispute. In 1905 the directors recorded their opinion of Manchester with a refreshing frankness. 'Expenses are out of all proportion to the business done, and gross profits absurdly small.'

Things improved when Robert Graham became manager of the branch. In 1920 he was in Canada and America looking for business, and on his return it was decided to improve the status of Manchester by forming the branch into a limited company and making it the headquarters for the Danish bacon agency. Graham was also invited to accept a directorship on the London Board. Despite these measures, apprehension over the running expenses and low profits continued. In later years, Liverpool and Manchester found themselves frequently in danger of competing in sales and distribution. Eventually an arrangement was made whereby the two organisations split the North of England between them, Liverpool, for example, taking the Nottingham area, and Manchester taking Yorkshire.

In 1929, Rolande Wall joined the London Board, but his first interest lay with Liverpool, and it was mainly due to him that Liverpool was able to record very good results. By this time Liverpool had been streamlined under the name of Lovell & Christmas (Liverpool) Ltd. (It became the policy in the '30s to form branches into limited companies.) The goodwill of the grocery side of the business had been sold to Morris & Jones Ltd.

As I have said, Rolande Wall left for the Ministry of Food on the outbreak of war, leaving W.J. Studholme as the Senior Director in Liverpool. He, and the Liverpool staff soon found themselves in the front line, for, on 20 December 1940, the Williamson Street premises were hit by incendiary bombs and completely gutted. Everything was destroyed: goods, butter-making machinery, ham canning machinery, office furniture and most of the records. Fortunately, the customers' records and the main ledgers, although charred, were still legible. The safes containing them had fallen through the burning floor and crashed to the basement, intact.

Studholme, his regular male staff almost all gone to war, was faced with the task of keeping the business going after this devastating blow. He rented offices from Lloyds' Bank, and the ledger staff began sorting out their charred documents in a private house in the suburbs. For the moment, nothing much could be done about the ham canning, but the butter-packing plant was transferred to the warehouse in Peter's Lane.

Incredibly, under these conditions the Liverpool branch continued to expand: before the war an interest had been taken in an egg packing station at Preston and now another egg packer, who operated in Lancaster, was taken over, while in 1940, the branch made its first contacts with New Forge Ltd., of Northern Ireland. Today, *Newforge* is the brand name of a wide range of Lovell & Christmas's canned goods

In 1929 R. Clement Wilson bought a factory in the Newforge area of Belfast. At first it processed bacon by-products into sausages and pies, but in 1936, when Wilson built a new factory for this business near Lisburn, the Newforge factory was renovated and converted for the processing of various foods, which were sold under the brand name *Newforge*. One of the principal lines was Ulster Fry, a German type of sausage sold to the trade for slicing as a bacon substitute, bacon then being in short supply. The visking cases for these sausages came from America and supplies were interrupted on the outbreak of war and so it was that the factory was able to obtain an allocation of cans. The Newforge company, now canning not only meat but soup and vegetables realised it needed more sophisticated distribution arrangements and at this point called in Lovell & Christmas (Liverpool) as its sole distributors. Lovell's put £20,000 into the business, W.J. Studholme paid frequent visits to Belfast and very friendly relations were built up between the two firms. In these Rolande Wall played an important part.

Wilson's found its finances were stretched by the big contracts it received to supply the forces and Lovell's prompt payment for the goods it sold was a great help. Wilson's also foresaw a lean time ahead when its military contracts would come to an end and these fears for its future led the firm to rely still more upon Lovell & Christmas.

Wilson's fears were well founded. The Northern Ireland government stopped passing orders to the firm and without the official contracts, supplies of raw materials became difficult to obtain. The company therefore turned to the production of quick frozen foods.

Lovell's was also interested in extending its production of canned and frozen foods and was experiencing difficulty in finding the extra capacity it needed, but in May 1954, Lovell's was offered 85% of the output of Frozen Foods (Ditton Court) Ltd., a Kent firm to which it had lent £18,000 on mortgage. Having secured these Kentish supplies, Lovell's turned its attention again to Belfast and entered into negotiations for the purchase of the brand name *Newforge.* An agreement was reached under which the name became Lovell's property, while Wilson's continued to manufacture for Lovell's under the *Newforge* brand name. Of course Wilson's could no longer call itself Newforge Ltd., and so changed its name to Robert Wilson & Sons (Food Industries) Ltd. At the same time, in order to protect the name on the Register of Companies, a small, nominal company was formed by Lovell & Christmas under the name of Newforge Ltd.

This arrangement, reached in 1955, continued for about three years and when it ended the production of *Newforge* canned fruit and vegetables was transferred to Ditton Court, which had become a subsidiary of Lovell's in September 1958. In March 1960 this firm became fully integrated into the group and its name was changed to Blue Cap Foods (Kent) Ltd. Since then, under the leadership of S.E. Sharpe, the Lovell director responsible for its canned and dried fruit division, Blue Cap has prospered and *Newforge* became one of the leading brand names in the country. Robert Wilson went into voluntary liquidation in 1965.

When this Irish digression began, Lovell & Christmas (Liverpool) was expanding its business, against all odds, during the war. It later continued its diversification into food manufacture. The two egg packing businesses were amalgamated in new premises especially built at Garstang, halfway between Preston and Lancaster, and another packing station bought at Hoole, near Preston. At this plant the firm later branched out into poultry farming with a view to making the packing station self-supporting. In 1952 it started a plant for freezing liquid egg in a factory at Bootle and in the next year restarted ham canning, which it decided to move out to the Bootle factory.

By 1957 the ham business had outgrown these premises, so a large depot and factory at Gateacre was bought from John Irwin Ltd. (Strangely enough both this plant and the Bootle factory had originally been built for making jam.)

The seal was finally set on the establishment of Lovell & Christmas (Liverpool) as major food manufacturers when an agreement was reached with the American firm Hormel's to start canning *Spam* at Gateacre. This plant has been continually enlarged and improved and today, under the name of Blue Cap (Foods) Ltd. and the enthusiastic direction of George Newell, it is the meat canning factory for the entire Fitch Lovell group and up-to-date in every respect. More than 200 million tins of *Spam* have been made.

Meanwhile, in 1964, a new main distributing depot was built for the group, next door to the Blue Cap (Foods) Ltd. Gateacre factory and replaced the old premises in Peter's Lane Manchester. Now only a cheese factory remained in the city.

The next logical step was to create one company to cope with the ever increasing business, so in 1967 Lovell & Christmas (Northern) Ltd. was formed incorporating the Liverpool and Manchester businesses, with group responsibility for meat processing, canning, cheese packaging and for the offices and warehouses in Nottingham, Stoke-on-Trent, Cardiff, Belfast, Newcastle-on-Tyne and Leeds.

As will be realised this new company was the basis for servicing about half of the United Kingdom. Two years later the cheese factory was moved to Gateacre – this is now a large and impressive centre where in addition to the foregoing, Blue Cap Foods manufactures *Spam* and other products.

The main obligation for this major reorganisation rested on Arthur Locke, the managing director, who had dealt admirably with a difficult and complex operation which happily has proved most successful.

The merger with George Wall's which had had such important consequences in England, had also given Lovell & Christmas a foothold in Scotland. In 1903, George Wall had appointed William Semple as his agent in Glasgow. He was very successful in selling dairy produce to the wholesale and multiple trade and was rewarded by being appointed manager of the Stoke-on-Trent branch. Wall then engaged A.A. Jackson as Scottish representative and took a small office at 9 Wilson Street, Glasgow. Jackson was energetic and soon had to engage staff. He opened a store and office at Leith and appointed agents in Dundee and Aberdeen. Supplies bound for Scotland from abroad were all arranged by Liverpool, although most shipments were sent direct to the Clyde or to Leith.

It was this embryo organisation, only three years old, which came with the Liverpool business into the newly-merged firm in 1906. From the day of the merger the organisation based in Glasgow became more and more independent of Liverpool until finally it was reconstituted as a separate company.

It was through Liverpool, however, that Glasgow became a centre for home-produced cheese. Arrangements were made in 1921 with Andrew Letters of Stranraer, a noted expert and cheese buyer to consign Scottish Cheddar cheese. By the end of 1922 some 600 tons had been handled. Percy Wall of Liverpool was so pleased with the quality and the quantity that Andrew Letters was engaged as manager for Scotland of a home cheese department. The trade increased and a large store was acquired in College Street, Glasgow. At this time, the name of Walter Thornley is mentioned as one who was very active in sales, and the Scottish office continually pressed London and Liverpool for bigger allocations of butter and cheese.

It was particularly anxious to obtain Siberian butter, which was much in demand by the biscuit manufacturers. Walter Thornley was appointed assistant manager to Jackson in 1925, and Andrew Letters concentrated on procuring supplies.

Permission was given for Glasgow to sell direct to London and they had great success in supplying Peter Keevil, Nurdin and Peacock, Harrods, Selfridges and other leading firms. The London demand was mainly for White Cheddars, and it became necessary to take a new house in Bell Street, Glasgow with 100,000 square feet of storage space in which 60,000 cheeses were stacked two deep on the floor. It is believed to have been the largest store used by the Ministry of Food in Scotland during Hitler's War.

In May 1931, Lovell & Christmas took over the Scottish firm of National Milk Products Ltd., which was a maker of processed cheese. The manufacturing side of the business was discontinued and the sales staff were used to sell Blue Cap products. 19 years later, Lovell & Christmas (Scotland) Ltd. was formed by changing the name of National Milk Products Ltd.

The Scottish Milk Marketing Board was formed in 1933, but ran into difficulties straight away because hundreds of cheese-making farmers ceased making cheese themselves and sent their milk to the Board. It only had a few creameries and was forced to make cheese twice and even three times a day to save the milk. It lacked adequate storage facilities and had no staff for turning and caring for the newly-made product. Meanwhile supplies accumulated fast.

Hearing about the Board's troubles, Andrew Letters paid a visit to its marketing officer and offered to care for and clear the whole accumulation on a consignment basis. The Board was delighted to have these responsibilities taken off its hands, and Rolande Wall came up to Glasgow and completed the arrangements.

In 1934 Jackson retired and Andrew Letters became manager for Scotland. George Thomas was seconded from Liverpool to help with the growing business. His exceptional ability to select cheese was of particular value to Glasgow.

At about the same time, the Scottish Milk Marketing Board began to make its own butter. It found marketing difficult and in a year or two sold the selling rights to Lovell & Christmas for £700. This arrangement continued until the outbreak of war.

During the war, activities in Scotland were confined mainly to dealing in rationed goods and such unrationed commodities as were obtainable, and storing goods for the Ministry of Food. On the conclusion of hostilities, the Scottish Milk Marketing Board decided to develop its butter making and chose the name of *Scottish Pride,* suggested by Lovell & Christmas. Once again, the marketing was given exclusively to Glasgow.

In 1947 Glasgow began prepacking butter in conjunction with Cow & Gate and Aplin & Barrett at a factory in Hillington. This joint service company operated under the name of Rockville Ltd. In the same year, Liverpool invited Andrew Letters to become a director of the Board of Lovell & Christmas (Liverpool) as the Scottish and Liverpool trade was so interwoven.

Glasgow had a long association with the firm of Rogerson and Black of Kirkcudbright, cheese factors and bacon curers, and in 1950 it bought a controlling interest. It was in this same year that the Scottish business was formed into a company as Lovell & Christmas (Scotland) Ltd., Sir Rolande Wall became Chairman, Andrew Letters became Managing Director, and Walter Thornley a director.

The expansion of the business continued under its new structure. In 1954 a firm of bacon curers, John McCaskill Ltd., was acquired and it was decided to consolidate all the Glasgow activities, including John McCaskill, in one place, and so new premises were bought at Soho Street, Glasgow. In the same year, George Thomas was appointed an executive director. The company moved into its new premises in 1957. The following year Andrew Letters retired, and Walter Thornley was appointed Managing Director.

In 1960, Unigate, the successors to Cow & Gate, decided to pull out of the joint butter packing company set up in 1947, and so Lovell & Christmas (Scotland) Ltd. decided to begin packing butter itself at Soho Street.

The Scottish company needed to vacate Soho Street by 1974 because of redevelopment, and so the search began for a new and permanent home. At last a suitable place was found in the new town of East Kilbride, and so Scotland followed the example of both London and Liverpool and left its congested metropolitan birthplace. The move to East Kilbride was completed in November 1969. The turnover figures show the achievements of Lovell & Christmas (Scotland) since its formation in 1950. In that year turnover was £1,020,000. In 1969 it was £5,860,000. The achievements of the Bacon Division are even more remarkable. Its turnover was only a few thousand pounds in 1950, by 1970 it was running at £2,500,000 a year.

There is one area of Lovell & Christmas's business in the United Kingdom over which the ghost of George Wall does not preside, and that is the small but profitable branch at Bristol. It was formed in 1928 and from the beginning it had no connection with the Liverpool company. The most that can be said is that the success of the merger in the North encouraged the directors in London to consider branching out in the West of England too. Very little is known about the early years of the branch or the manner of its establishment, because all the pre-war records were destroyed by enemy action in 1940.

We do know the beginnings were small. The manager lived in a flat over the office and the orders were delivered by one hired horse and cart. The bacon foreman, who joined the branch later, was one of the pioneers of the Labour movement. He attended meetings with Ernest Bevin and other trade union visionaries in the *Old Star Coffee House.*

The first Manager was S.L. Ostler, and under him the business expanded steadily, especially in Devon. On his retirement H.W. Hydge became responsible. It was while he was Manager that the offices and warehouses were completely destroyed during the first heavy air attack on Bristol in 1940. The two firewatchers, Otridge and Cook, escaped with injuries and are still on the staff 30 years later. The office black cat, a great favourite, was rescued from the smouldering ruins three days later in a pitiable state, but to everyone's delight was nursed back to health and established himself with dignity at the temporary premises to which the company migrated.

Gerald Chilvers was appointed Manager shortly after the destruction of the premises and continued as such for 25 years. In the early days of his business career, around 1920, he was a personal assistant to me at Keevils' and our friendship has lasted for 50 years. He was the son of the well known Rev. H. Tydeman Chilvers, the subject of a biography entitled *The Last of the Puritans*, and Baptist minister at Spurgeon's Tabernacle in London. Gerald had high standards, both in business and in private life. He was a good leader with the rare quality of delegation. By the time he retired he had built up the smallish Bristol business to a point where a fleet of 19 lorries was needed to distribute the produce sold.

He was succeeded by L.L. Bull, under whose enthusiastic guidance Lovell & Christmas (Bristol) Ltd., continues to expand.

## *II*

## *THE ARGENTINE*

LOVELL & CHRISTMAS opened in the Argentine in the same year that it began in Canada, 1896, the year of its formation as a public company. The prospectus issued for the flotation includes the brief statement '. . . arrangements have been concluded by which consignments will soon be received from the Argentine'. Now, three-quarters of a century later, the Canadian venture is flourishing, while the Argentine business is no longer in the group.

The two countries were curiously similar 75 years ago. Both were large, primary-producing areas, with European populations and a potential for future development. Canada has realised this potential differently from the Argentine. One reason for this difference has been the Latin American country's political instability and the chronic inflation from which its currency has suffered. It was this inflation that drove Lovell & Christmas to cease its Argentine operations. Not that its business there was ever easy. The operations between 1896 and 1962 were the subject of more entries in the Lovell & Christmas minute books than any other activity of the company.

In the first 25 years or so of its business with the Argentine Lovell's followed its usual practice. It sold produce, in this case butter, in London on commission basis and made liberal advances to the foreign producers, in some cases taking debentures as safeguards. The first of these advances was given to a Mr. Schoek. Its size is not recorded, but in November 1896 a 'further sum of £700' was sent to him. Van den Berg's also advanced him £300.

Lovell & Christmas cannot however have been happy about its first Argentine protegé because it asked the Sansinena Company and also the Anglo-Argentine Bank to ascertain 'what Schoek had been erecting in Buenos Aires'. The result of these enquiries is unknown, but fears must have been allayed because in the following September Schoek was advanced a further £2,250 against a mortgage on a butter factory. The mortgage was for £7,000. A quarter of this was in trust for Van den Berg. Within six weeks however, the Argentine Bank was instructed to stop all credit and do everything in its power to protect the mortgage. The following month a power of attorney was executed in favour of the bank's manager and Lovell & Christmas's secretary was told to 'send it by the mail leaving today'. As in Canada, the company had not, initially, put its faith in the right man.

The new agent was none other than Henry Reynolds, the pioneer of the New Zealand dairy industry. Right up to 1924 he was to be known as 'our man in the Argentine' by everyone who worked in the Lovell & Christmas head office. When Henry Reynolds arrived in South America the dairy industry there was in its infancy, hence the importance of capital from England. There was clearly plenty of scope for an expert like Reynolds, in the organisation of butter factories. According to Harry Lovell, Reynolds came to the Argentine on the advice of his father William (III) after Lovell & Christmas had purchased his interests in Auckland.

The following year, 1900, Reynolds was negotiating with another local firm, the Union Argentina. As with Schoek, the aim was to obtain secure supplies in return for an advance. Reynolds was told to write to Union Argentina and tell it the terms on which Lovell & Christmas might advance money. The Union Company seemed agreeable, but this time London was determined not to take a chance. In June 1900 Lionel B. Lovell set sail for Buenos Aires armed with full powers to make a deal with the Union Argentina.

Finally, Lovell & Christmas loaned it £7,000, which was approximately two thirds of the cost of setting up a butter factory, which Henry Reynolds was to manage. Three years later, A.G. Christmas went out to the Argentine with instructions from the Chairman, John Cary Lovell, to expand the Company's interests in the country. The result was an agreement with Dr. Faina Santamarina of Santamarina & Co.

According to Harry Lovell, the Santamarina family owned very large tracts of land in the best part of the Province of Buenos Aires. Lovell & Christmas agreed to lend Dr. Santamarina £25,000 to expand the butter industry in his part of the country. The loan was to be repaid in three years, and during that time Lovell &

Christmas would have the sole agency for the butter in the United Kingdom or elsewhere. Once again, Henry Reynolds the butter expert would be involved in seeing that the investment in butter manufacture was correctly organised. In February 1904 Reynolds was consigning butter at the rate of 80s. per cwt. f.o.b. In June 1905 the agreement with Santamarina was extended for another year, to expire in 1907 instead of 1906. It seems that Santamarina was finding the repayment of the loan difficult. Things can hardly have been going well, because as soon as the extension to the agreement expired, the butter factory was sold. Since the London head office had to agree to the sale, Lovell & Christmas presumably still had an interest in the firm. The factory fetched £10,000.

By this time, Lovell & Christmas had been involved in the Argentine for more than a decade. Some of its investments had been successful, others less so. In July 1908 it decided to participate in the formation of a company which was to shape Lovell & Christmas's interest in the Argentine for more than 50 years. The name of the company was the River Plate Dairy Company. It was a partnership between local capital and Lovell & Christmas, with Henry Reynolds taking a big executive part. There was one significant departure from the terms under which Lovell & Christmas had become associated with the original Mr. Schoek, the Union Argentina and Dr. Santamarina. This time Lovell & Christmas bought share capital in the new company, as an entry in its minute book makes clear.

> That Lovell and Christmas Ltd. subscribe for £10,000 obligations of the new company to be redeemed at the rate of £1,000 per annum, the new company having the option to pay off the balance at the end of six years. Lovell and Christmas Ltd. further to buy £5,000 at par. The new company to undertake to consign to Lovell and Christmas Ltd. all butter exported to Great Britain until all obligations are paid off.

That investment of £5,000 was a most significant factor. It was a sign that the directors of Lovell & Christmas had at last found a company through which they were prepared to work on a long term basis. It was a commitment which was to lead in time to the River Plate Dairy Co. being a wholly-owned subsidiary.

The company was promoted in the Argentine by Runciman & Co. an English merchant banking firm in Buenos Aires who floated government loans and limited companies and administered estates.

According to Harry Lovell they, 'enjoyed a very high prestigate among the Argentinians in the old days when England meant something'. Runciman's retained a substantial interest in the R.P.D.C. themselves.

The new company quickly established itself as an important part of the growing dairy industry in the Argentine. Four butter factories and a large number of creameries were established in the provinces of Buenos Aires, Santa Fe and Entre Rios. Eventually a local distribution network was also set up.

(It is worth pausing here to explain briefly how the dairy industry in the Argentine was organised. It all began with the farms which produced the milk. Many dairy firms owned their own land and cattle. The R.P.D.C. had a fine herd which was sold during Hitler's War, and the company never became deeply involved in the farming stage of production. This proved a weakness during the years of inflation. Creameries were established in the milk producing areas.

A creamery consisted of a separator, a casein manufacturing plant and a piggery. The cream was sent to the butter factory, the skim made into casein and the whey fed to the pigs, who are often referred to as the 'creamery drainage system'. By the '30s the R.P.D.C. had breeding establishments in each area to keep the creameries supplied with young pigs. It was found that Berkshires did best, and pedigree stock were brought out from England from time to time to improve the breed. Except when there were epidemics of Hog Cholera and Foot and Mouth disease, the pig account always showed a good profit.

A good economical creamery needed 7,000-10,000 litres of milk a day on average, but many were run on less than half that amount. The butter factories received the cream from the creameries, and made it into butter which was then either exported or sold locally. Some of the cream had to travel long distances in hot weather and often arrived in bad condition, hence the rather poor quality of some Argentine butter.)

During the 1914-1918 War, Runciman's were appointed agents for the Ministry of Food, and it was arranged that R.P.D.C. should supply the Ministry with butter. The shipments were organised by Rivero Haedo of Runciman's who later played an important part in the R.P.D.C. story.

After the war, in 1919, the R.P.D.C. paid a dividend of 8% to Lovell & Christmas. It is the first dividend recorded, and probably the first that the company paid. Two years later, however, the Board in London received a less agreeable communication from the Argentine. Reynolds wrote to them that the River Plate Dairy Co. was in a serious financial condition. It was in debt to the tune of £250,000. He suggested that a way out of the trouble might be to sell a factory in Santa Fe which would raise £150,000, but he pointed out the commercial danger of allowing it to fall into other hands. A much better solution, Reynolds suggested, would be for Lovell & Christmas to come to the rescue.

A considerable sum of money was involved and the Board hesitated. Cables went back and forth and Reynolds was called to London. Eventually London agreed to a loan of £150,000, the exact sum that Reynolds hoped to raise by the sale of the Santa Fe factory. Reynolds returned to Buenos Aires with a power of attorney containing the terms on which the loan would be made. The R.P.D.C. was asked to sell some land, the Estancia El Carmen, and repay £50,000 out of the proceeds. The loan was to be secured by 15 6% debentures of £10,000 each on all the remaining properties. Repayment was to begin five years after the loan in instalments of not less than £20,000. Reynolds was given the power to arrange other terms which he might think desirable in the interests of Lovell & Christmas. One of these was a guarantee that a certain percentage of R.P.D.C.'s produce should be offered to Lovell & Christmas. The loan was duly paid in February 1923 and the documents lodged with the bankers.

This was the last major business transacted by the redoubtable Henry Reynolds for Lovell & Christmas. In 1924 he retired, and his position was taken by Rivero Haedo. His appointment had been made by the new Chairman of Lovell & Christmas, William Lovell (III) who visited the Argentine in July 1923. Reynolds was succeeded as trustee for the £150,000 worth of debentures by Robert and Malcolm Begg, who also took over the power of attorney which Reynolds had been given at the time the debentures were arranged.

Robert Begg was a director of R.P.D.C., he was also what the Argentinians call a *sindico,* more or less equivalent to a trustee for the shareholders. He was a good friend of Lovell & Christmas. Robert Begg was also a director of another dairy firm, Magnasco.

It is worth mentioning that Lovell & Christmas continued to receive supplies from other companies in spite of its involvement in R.P.D.C. This occasionally led to difficulties. During his 1923 visit, William (III) agreed that Lovell & Christmas would in fact limit itself to three correspondents in the Argentine, R.P.D.C., Magnasco, and a third firm called Wesley.

This arrangement was not enough to keep Lovell & Christmas clear of the rivalries between the Argentine dairy firms. Trouble began the following year when Henry Reynolds' son Harry tried to start a butter factory in the Tandil district in partnership with Wesley. Harry Reynolds (II) was a director of the R.P.D.C. and wanted Lovell & Christmas to finance the factory. In the matter of founding new butter factories, he saw himself as the natural successor to his father, he was a charming man, liked by everyone, but not of the same calibre as his father. Cables passed between William (III) and Rivero Haedo about the scheme. It became apparent that Magnasco had a strong interest in the Tandil district. If Lovell & Christmas financed Reynolds (II) they were in danger of losing all Magnasco's consignments, and the newly-established factory would have to face strong local competition.

The problem was only resolved by another visit to the Argentine by William (III). He agreed that Lovell & Christmas would finance Harry Reynolds (II) in a factory situated where it would not compete with existing interests. It would be placed under the supervision of Rivero Haedo and Robert Begg who would report progress to London.

Comfortable local arrangements like this one were rudely shattered in the late 1920s by the appearance of the Vestey Group. They were intent on obtaining refrigerated butter freight for their *Blue Star Line*. Up to then it had been carried by the Royal Mail and Holder Brothers. Vestey bought a dairy company, Elowson and Wester and entered active competition for milk and cream.

Returning from the Argentine in 1929, the Chairman of Lovell & Christmas, William (III) said that the position had become precarious. Although the R.P.D.C. were still doing well in their retail trade, their export sales were resulting in heavy losses. Other companies were in the same position and many of them were thinking of closing down. He considered that they would have to come to some arrangement with Vestey's or leave the Argentine altogether. He advocated an approach to Vestey's. Before that, he thought Lovell & Christmas should place itself in a stronger position by buying sufficient shares in R.P.D.C. to give it 51% interest. This would cost £175,000.

William (III) then approached Vestey's and asked if they would be interested in an amalgamation of interests if Lovell & Christmas became the majority shareholder of R.P.D.C. The interview was friendly, and Vestey's cabled its manager in the Argentine to see Rivero Haedo and investigate methods of working closely together.

Meanwhile Lovell & Christmas set about buying the R.P.D.C. shares. With the help of the Bank of London and South America it acquired practically the whole of the company's share capital by September 1929, although the price was higher than it had intended to pay. From its bankers Lovell & Christmas obtained the £350,000 necessary for the purchase. Later Haedo was instructed to dispose of excess shares, leaving Lovell & Christmas with approximately 60% of the share capital, but this was never done.

The way was now clear for an agreement with Vestey's. What it came down to was an arrangement whereby Lovell & Christmas agreed to ship butter on the *Blue Star Line*, and Vestey's promised not to compete for milk in the areas where the R.P.D.C. was operating. The two groups were further bound together by the joint purchase of La Euskara, a small butter factory in Buenos Aires. Its produce was to be shipped to Britain by Blue Star on consignment to Lovell & Christmas. Although in itself too small to be a financial success, it was the shape of things to come. It was impossible to give Blue Star the total consignment of R.P.D.C. as well because their ships were not always available at the right time, but it was agreed that they would be given the bulk of the shipments. This arrangement worked smoothly for most of the '30s.

Now that Lovell & Christmas owned R.P.D.C., it naturally wanted a more direct hand in the company's affairs, and it was decided to send out a member of the Lovell family as President. The job was first offered to Gordon Lovell, but he turned it down because his wife objected to leaving England.

So it was that the job went to Harry Lovell. Appropriately enough, there was a revolution in progress in the Argentine as he sailed into Buenos Aires. It was a difficult assignment. He was being put into a company in a distant land whose language he did not speak. All he knew about butter was how to pack and sell it. Perhaps he was fortified by the memory of his father's early exploits in the Argentine. (When attached to Bretel Frères in France as a learner William Lovell (III) had been sent to Buenos Aires and Rio to sell tinned French butter as at that time there was practically no butter made locally. Not only did he sell the butter, he also found time to join a British expedition up the Amazon and became a fellow of the Royal Geographical Society.)

Harry Lovell found the R.P.D.C. in pretty good shape, with Rivero Haedo in complete command. It took Harry Lovell about six months to acquire a knowledge of Spanish and some idea of what was going on. It became clear that provided all went well there was no reason why the R.P.D.C. should not make reasonable profits. There were, in his view, two things that could spoil their efforts – drought, and a fall in the price of butter. As it happened, he had to contend with both these. Drought could cut production to almost nothing, yet the company had to maintain its overheads and buy forage at famine prices to keep the cattle and pigs alive. Two droughts in the '30s affected all the areas in which the company operated and there were others. The long fall on the London Butter Market meant that the R.P.D.C. had to take heavy losses on everything it consigned as it could never drop the price of milk in time to compensate. This was because it had to compete with the cheese factories which sold their produce locally. It managed to save something by building up its local sales of butter to about 40 tons a day at the peak, midwinter, period.

In spite of the difficulties, the River Plate Dairy Company enjoyed great prestige at this time in the eyes of the Board in London and Lovell & Christmas tried to set up a Canadian company, the Maple Valley Dairy Company, in the image of R.P.D.C. Experts from the Argentine commuted between Buenos Aires and Montreal. Harry Lovell became a member of the main Board and a member of the Maple Valley Board.

In spite of the understanding reached with Vestey's in 1930, the two companies found themselves drawn into increasing competition as the decade wore on. By 1938 the situation was such that neither Lovell & Christmas nor Vestey's was making a profit. The Chairman, William (III), was approached by Sir Edmond Vestey about an amalgamation of their interests in the Argentine dairy industry. The idea was not new. It had suggested itself quite naturally out of the arrangement made in 1930 and out of their joint control of La Euskara. It had been actually raised in 1934, but at that time the proposal went no further than discussions between the two companies. Harry Lovell had not felt able to support the fusion as he was already in the middle of an internal reorganisation.

When William (III) visited the Argentine in 1938, however, he found the R.P.D.C. directors more willing than previously to discuss a merger. Arrangements were made for the valuation of the companies concerned. Initially, the valuation was carried out by John May of Elowson and Wester and Harry Lovell. Understandably, they found it very difficult to agree on the value of each other's property.

Meanwhile, another loss was sustained in the June 1938 quarter and a memorandum making suggestions for more economical working was sent out from London. The negotiations dragged on and Harry Lovell left to take up his command in the army when war broke out in 1939. Heads of Agreement were not reached until March 1941. The arrangement made was that the River Plate Dairy Company and Elowson and Wester were to amalgamate, and the new group would be controlled on a 50-50 basis by Lovell & Christmas and Vestey's. Lovell & Christmas was to sell on commission all butter sent to the United Kingdom. All freight was to be offered to Vestey's Blue Star Line, and a proportion of the butter stored in the United Kingdom was to be placed with its Union Cold Storage Co. Price Waterhouse & Co. were to be appointed auditors and to be consulted on the formation of the new company. R.S. Beak of Vestey's was to be appointed President, Lt. Col. Harry Lovell, although on war service, was to be joint Vice-President with John May. The Heads of Agreement were implemented with slight changes, and amalgamation was a fact from 31 March 1941.

Harry Lovell returned to the Argentine to take up active duties as Vice-President in 1944. He had been demobilised in May of that year after being severely wounded. He may well have wondered if his war in the Western Desert was not more agreeable than his task as an executive director in the Argentine. He describes the post war period as 'quite the unhappiest period of my business life'.

One of the first things he discovered was that the R.P.D.C.'s fine herd of dual purpose Shorthorn cattle had been sold during his absence. It was a big herd, numbering thousands of beasts of all ages spread over several dairy farms. It had been the product of pedigree cattle imported at regular intervals from the United Kingdom. The cows were 'milked with the calf', the steers were fattened at different farms and sold direct to the *frigarificos* at baby beef prices. The best bulls were sold to the company's milk suppliers. Apart from the drought years, the cattle always gave a very good profit, as well as giving the company a stable supply of milk.

The sale of the herd was unfortunate in the light of the inflation which was gathering pace. Other dairy producers, such as Magnasco kept increasing their cattle and buying land. On top of this, there were many problems resulting from the amalgamation to be sorted out, but the real nightmare which became increasingly apparent was the political situation.

Argentinian politics had been uneasy enough in the pre-war period. In 1930, the radical leader, Dr. Irigoyen, had been overthrown in a *coup d'état* organised by the army. Although a man of reputed integrity and ability he had done little to stop inflation. He had introduced a minimum wage and raised railway rates sharply. To his credit, he had kept the Argentine out of the First World War. It was his overthrow that Harry Lovell witnessed on his arrival in the country in 1930. He was replaced by General Uribur, who was himself overthrown by another military coup in 1943. 1945 saw the rise of Colonel Peron and the beginning of real trouble for business interests.

Peron was backed by the insistent clamour of the workers and he stood for President as the self-proclaimed champion of the masses against the plutocracy and the United States of America. A general election was held in an atmosphere of turbulence and violence. Peron was regarded as a demi-god by his followers and he was instituted President in 1947. Afterwards he identified his opponents as 'all who are rich, those who defend the interest of foreign capitalistic trusts', adding for good measure that he would speak, 'with a firm voice on the day he ordered them to be hanged'.

The new President instituted a five year plan and decreed that after a company had provided for profits of 5% on the paid up capital, the remainder was to be used for the purchase of shares at par for the benefit of employees. Harry Lovell came to London in January 1947 and was welcomed by his colleagues. He told them of the difficulties he was valiantly trying to overcome. The following year, J.G. Elliott, who had succeeded to the Chairmanship of Lovell & Christmas on the death of William (III), visited the Argentine to help the company with its problems and to visit all sections of its operations. In November 1948, Harry Lovell relinquished his position as Vice-President and returned to England, having well and truly served the company's interests for many years in South America.

Peter Gomersall assumed responsibility for the Argentine business and visited Buenos Aires in November 1952 and again in 1956. On his return in January 1957 he recommended the setting up of two cheese plants at an estimated cost of two-and-a-half million pesos. The proposal was accepted and the plants were constructed.

Meanwhile, the political situation became even more difficult, and the effects of severe inflation were beginning to be felt. Urgent requests for additional finance were made in 1958. Once again Peter Gomersall went out to the Argentine. Next the Argentine government announced its intention of prohibiting the export of butter during the winter, and it was decided to sell two factories. In 1960 came a new government decree relating to the revaluation of properties and a tax payable on the new value.

The main interest of Lovell & Christmas had been its wish to obtain goods, and that of Vestey to obtain freight. With the developing political troubles neither of these objectives was easily fulfilled. In July 1960 the possibility of liquidating or selling the company was seriously considered. By 1961 it was only possible to arrange loans and cover currency risks at 19¼%. Negotiations for a disposal of the joint interest took place and a tentative offer of 700,000 pesos was accepted, but the deal did not materialise, presumably because of the financial instability in the Argentine.

Peter Gomersall had to make a report in July 1961 showing a loss of more than £100,000. In addition he had to announce that the British government had reduced the import quota on Argentinian butter. Two more factories were closed.

Conversations took place with Vestey's because it was thought that firm might be interested in acquiring the 50% interest held by Lovell & Christmas, as with its vast interests in South America and its large organisation on the spot it could be in a better position to cope with the problems.

Sir Rolande Wall met Mr. Ronald Vestey in Buenos Aires in July 1962 and as a result, Vestey's agreed to take over the interests of Lovell & Christmas and relieve it of its commitments in the Argentine. It was two months short of 23 years since Rolande Wall had sold the Maple Valley Dairy Company in Canada.

This is the lesson drawn from the Argentine by Peter Gomersall:

> A rather different story might have emerged if investments had been made in land and cattle and production concentrated on cheese rather than butter. Throughout the latter part of the period

> the Argentine was suffering from galloping inflation, in which conditions, solid assets in land and cattle, by appreciation, would have kept pace with inflation. Throughout this later period, the control of the River Plate Dairy Company was a joint responsibility of Lovell and Christmas and Vesteys.

The Argentine story is not wholly bleak for Lovell & Christmas did, in fact, make very useful profits out of the Argentine for many years. It had a 3% commission plus expenses on consignments of the greater part of the butter exported from that country during the first half of this century. Harry Lovell suggests that it made even more out of the River Plate Dairy Company than would appear from the R.P.D.C. balance sheets. After it became a wholly-owned subsidiary it was often more convenient to show the profit on the sales of the imported butter in the books of the parent company.

The quantity of butter received by Lovell & Christmas was substantial. No overall figures exist, although at one time in the '30s R.P.D.C. was making over 100 tons a day. There is no doubt that supplies from the Argentine were invaluable in keeping the parent company in its dominant trading position in the United Kingdom throughout nearly three generations.

## *III*

## *CANADA*

LOVELL & CHRISTMAS has been trading in Canada for the past 70 years. On the whole the company's activities in that country have been among the most rewarding in which it has been engaged. The success of Lovell & Christmas (Canada) Limited is largely the work of two men, R.M. Ballantyne and Gordon McLean, both of whom possessed great marketing ability, energy and resource.

Private letters reveal that a Canadian branch of Lovell & Christmas was set up in July 1896, but the first mention of it in the surviving London records is not until May 1898, when William Ware was appointed agent for Montreal, Belleville, Brockville and North New York. (This date is confirmed by Miss Bertha Dumbell who worked for the Canadian company for more than 50 years and acted as personal secretary to the three Presidents of the Company during that period. I am much indebted to her for the information she has given to me.) £3,000 was advanced to William Ware to enable him to set up the business and he was given a personal loan of £500.

Evidently things did not go too well because two years later the Board in London asked a leading London Chartered Accountant, E. Layton Bennett, to go to Montreal, prepare proper accounts and make a report. William Ware's employment was placed in abeyance pending the receipt of the report. When it reached London Ware was reinstated but he was forbidden to 'sell short' or to speculate, and he was ordered to send weekly stock figures to London.

The Chairman, John Cary Lovell was still not satisfied, and he decided to visit Canada and see for himself what was going on. In September 1900 he furnished himself with full powers to act on behalf of the Board and set out for Montreal via New York. He wrote a full account of the trip when he returned, and it is evident from this that he hardly rested by day or by night until he was laid low by a bad attack of lumbago. Even then he went on working, conducting interviews from his bed and in a Turkish bath.

John Cary sensed that something about Ware was wrong. As soon as he arrived in Montreal he began making enquiries, starting at the banks. Then, on the morning of 1 October 1900 he called on Ware without warning at his office. He found the agent hard at work. In spite of this he dismissed him on the spot 'because of his personal habits'. His enquiries in the town had revealed that Ware was consistently drunk during business hours and that on a trip to England 'his conduct on the voyage had been deplorable'.

The company was now without an agent in Canada. If the continuity of the business was to be preserved it was essential to find a replacement for Ware as quickly as possible, but this time it had to be someone absolutely reliable. The Chairman decided to make the appointment himself. Such a man, he was told, was R.M. Ballantyne of Toronto who was associated with his father, Thomas Ballantyne in a company called Stratford Knitting Mills. Without wasting a moment, John Cary made an appointment to have breakfast with Ballantyne in Toronto. Over the meal John Cary made his offer. The young Canadian hesitated. He was loathe to leave the family firm. Anyway he would have to consult his father who was away for a few days at Niagara Falls. If Ballantyne had not made up his mind, John Cary had. He was sure R.M. Ballantyne was the man to re-establish Lovell & Christmas's operation in Canada. Having made up his mind he was not the sort of man to tolerate delay and he immediately left for Niagara to see Thomas Ballantyne. He was joined there by R.M. Ballantyne, and the three men came to an agreement that R.M. should take over the branch at the beginning of December. In the meantime he was to pay regular visits to Montreal to see how the business was conducted.

It was after these hectic negotiations that John Cary went down with lumbago. Perhaps it was his illness which made him reconsider his abrupt treatment of William Ware, in any event, he listened to his pleas to be allowed to stay and serve under Ballantyne, provided he behaved himself. His work in Canada done, and his health improved, John Cary returned home.

Only a month later, in November, Ballantyne cabled to London 'Ware drunk continually – authority requested his immediate dismissal'. London agreed and paid Ware £600 (six months' salary) in lieu of notice.

The outstanding loan to him was 'to be left standing' and Ware was to repay it. The Minute caustically adds, 'if ever he is able to do so'.

Ballantyne wrote that there had been no unpleasantness when he told Ware to go. He himself was taking control at once, without waiting for the official commencement of his appointment. The agreement which he had made with John Cary Lovell gave him a salary of £600 a year, and a good proportion of the profits after Lovell & Christmas had charged 4% interest on the money invested in the business. At this time it consisted of buying cheese and butter from factories and producers and selling either in America, Canada or overseas. The branch also speculated in 'futures' and undertook general market work.

When Ballantyne took over the reins he found things were not as bad as they might have been. Ware, although not often sober, had always been a good buyer and judge of cheese. Even that stickler for quality, John Cary Lovell, could find no fault with his stocks when he had examined and tested them. Now, under Ballantyne's able leadership, the business began to expand. In April 1902 land to the value of £4,000 was purchased from Lord Strathcona and Mount Royal for the building of a warehouse and cold store in Montreal.

Ballantyne was given the title 'Managing Director of Canada' and a special arrangement was made concerning his dealings with Thos. Ballantyne & Sons and the Stratford company. Two years later, in April 1904, P.W. McLagan was appointed Joint Managing Director with Ballantyne. Profits continued to be satisfactory and supplies were regularly received in London. The confidence of the Board was amply demonstrated in 1910 when the two Managing Directors were given authority to borrow money for 'the Company's branch in Canada'. In the same year they were both entered on the voting list for the City of Montreal as 'representing Lovell & Christmas Ltd., of London, England'.

After the 1914-1918 War Ballantyne and McLagan suggested that the Canadian branch should be formed into a company. The Board of Lovell & Christmas approved the idea and asked them to 'formulate the new company at their convenience'. E. Layton Bennett, the man who had been sent to sort out William Ware in

1900, was consulted, and the two Canadian principals were invited to come and discuss the matter in London. In fact Ballantyne travelled to England alone. His journey was delayed by his own ill health and a local difficulty which had to be resolved. (The branch had accumulated a surplus stock of 10,000 boxes of cheese at a price which would mean a loss of £1 a box if they were sold at the current market price. It was considered advisable to go ahead with the sale because the Exchange showed every sign of deteriorating still further.)

Having supervised this unhappy operation, Ballantyne attended the board meeting of Lovell & Christmas which was held on 19 March 1920. It was decided to form a company in Canada with a capital of $1,000,000 of which $400,000 should be issued. All of it went to the parent company in payment for the business.

The first directors were R.M. Ballantyne (Chairman), P.W. McLagan, T.O. Hodge and J. Freeman. Lovell & Christmas's minute of 14 April 1920, reads: 'Resolved that the Company consent to Mr. R.M. Ballantyne incorporating a company in Canada with the name of Lovell & Christmas (Canada) and that a copy of this resolution certified as correct by the Secretary be forwarded to Mr. Ballantyne'. It is interesting to note that the auditors appointed in 1920, Riddell, Stead & Co., of Montreal have continued as such ever since.

There is no further mention of Canada in the London minutes until December 1923 when a profit of $81,000 was reported for the six months to September, and a loss of $25,000 for the month of October. No reason is given for this sudden deterioration. Earlier in the year McLagan had resigned from the company, and when William (III), the new Chairman of Lovell's, visited America and Canada he urged Ballantyne to strengthen his Board and approved the appointment of a Mr. Grieve as manager of the butter section.

The main reason for the Chairman's visit in 1923 was to accompany Mr. J.B. Wright of the New Zealand Co-operative Dairy Co. Ltd., following the appointment of Lovell & Christmas as its sole agents for America and Eastern Canada. Lovell & Christmas was to secure suitable premises in New York and appoint a responsible representative there. William (III) cabled back a proposition to form an American company, Lovell & Christmas (U.S.A.) Ltd. The idea was that Lovell & Christmas (Canada) should hold two thirds and an American firm with an established business, A.F. Lopez & Co.

should hold one third. He recommended Lopez as Managing Director as he had 'a good reputation as capable, hardworking, straightforward, and reliable'.

William (III) had been met in New York by R.M. Ballantyne and the amalgamation with Lopez was his idea. The company was formed in April 1923 with Ballantyne as President, Lopez Vice-President, Freeman and Grieve of Canada, and the Ministry of Food's resident accountant in New York, as directors. The man from the ministry, Mr. Kerr, was only to attend meetings and receive a nominal fee. The New Zealand Dairy Co. were very satisfied with the arrangement, and everything seemed well set for a good future. The first half year's profit was in the region of $12,000.

However, a few years later the United States' government decided to impose heavy import duties on butter and cheese, and it became impossible to operate the New York company at a profit. In June 1926 Montreal was instructed to close the New York office and appoint a local agent.

New Zealand butter was still sold in the United States through Lovell & Christmas in spite of the import duties. These sales were not always profitable. In 1934 Grieve made a contract with the Atlantic and Pacific Tea Company (A & P), one of the largest multiple shop concerns in the United States for 30,000 boxes of New Zealand butter. The arrangement was that the butter should be delivered at the rate of 1,000 boxes a day, five days a week. Although the butter was bought in New Zealand, the price paid for it by A & P was to be based on the closing price each day on the New York butter exchange.

Unfortunately the New York price was too low, and the contract began to involve Lovell & Christmas in heavy losses. The situation became so serious that the Board in London sent Rolande Wall to New York to try and retrieve the situation. After observing the future butter market and talking to the A & P broker he was able to adjust the contract and avoid further losses. The debacle led to the departure of Grieve from Lovell & Christmas (Canada).

Rolande Wall's problems in North America were not yet over. After leaving New York he went on to Montreal where Lovell & Christmas (Canada) was faltering after its early successes. Ballantyne had died in 1929, and John Freeman was now in charge.

Ballantyne's loss was proving to be a serious one and profits were falling, Rolande Wall was joined in Montreal by William (III) and the object of their visit was to see if Lovell & Christmas's fortunes in Canada could be restored by buying a dairy factory in Belleville and marketing packeted butter. The idea was to set up a company similar to the River Plate Dairy Company in the Argentine, and market the butter under a heavily advertised brand name similar to the successful *Golden Churn* line in Britain. The Canadian product was to be called *Maple Valley* butter and launched with a big advertising campaign.

Neither Freeman, William (III) nor Rolande Wall thought there was any prospect of profits and said so in a report which they submitted to London. The Chairman then sent to Canada an expert in butter packing from the River Plate Company to make another assessment. He came to London in August 1935 and strongly recommended the scheme. Although Rolande Wall still opposed the plan, the Board decided to go ahead. It cabled Canada to purchase the Belleville factory, and the Maple Valley Dairy Company Limited was constituted as a subsidiary with a nominal capital of $20,000. The venture ran into trouble right from the start, and within a year the Chairman, William (III), was in Canada trying to sort things out.

The main result of his visit was the appointment of Harry Lovell, the President of the River Plate Dairy Company, as a director of Lovell & Christmas (Canada) Ltd., and of the Maple Valley Dairy Co. How Harry was able to help the ailing Canadian company from the distant Argentine is uncertain. One of the problems William (III) mentioned on his return from Canada was the difficulty Maple Valley were having in obtaining supplies of butter.

Towards the end of 1936 two more creameries were purchased, one at Madoc and the other at Picton. The price paid for the latter was $15,000. This further investment failed to put the venture on its feet, and losses continued. Six months later a special letter was sent to Freeman expressing concern at the unfavourable results from Maple Valley. The whole situation in Canada had deteriorated badly in the six years since the death of R.M. Ballantyne. Freeman replied that there was a good chance of profits being earned in the next year or so. Meanwhile, Harry Lovell sent a costing expert from the Argentine, a Mr. Wilson, to see if there was any chance of reorganising the business on profitable lines.

Even if such a possibility existed, the directors in London now decided they had had enough. In December 1937 the Board, which had originally been so enthusiastic about the Maple Valley scheme, now decided that it could no longer support the continuing losses and resolved that the Maple Valley Dairy Co. should be liquidated. Selling the business proved to be easier said than done. The months dragged by; in spite of strenuous efforts by Freeman no buyer could be found. He was constantly pressed by London to try and obtain a bid.

In May 1939 the Board's patience ran out and it asked Rolande Wall to go to Canada and dispose of the business. Eventually an offer of $30,000 was accepted and the sale completed in September 1939.

Rolande Wall's summer in Canada in 1939 was as much a turning point for the fortunes of Lovell & Christmas in Canada as had been the visit by John Cary Lovell in 1900 which had ushered in the Ballantyne era 39 years earlier. The Board had decided to strengthen the direction of Lovell & Christmas (Canada) by the appointment of a co-director. With the sad Maple Valley episode behind it, the company badly needed a first class man to guide its recovery. Rolande Wall was entrusted with the task of finding him. He interviewed many applicants but none of them caught his eye. He had almost given up the search when he was telephoned by a friend of his in Toronto, Ronald Chisholm. Chisholm said he had found just the man for the job. And so it was that Gordon McLean came to Belleville where Rolande was finalising the sale of the Belleville factory.

> As soon as he walked into the room, Rolande Wall recalls, I was impressed and to John Freeman's horror offered him a salary and terms which we were offering to other applicants 10 to 15 years older. I was very nervous that when he saw the huge debit balances and losses he would refuse the job but it just put him on his mettle to fight the challenge.

On his return to London Rolande Wall said that this one appointment would justify his salary until he retired, and events have borne him out.

Gordon McLean is a practical trader with a pronounced flair for marketing and enormous energy. It is obvious that, although second in command, he galvanised the company in every respect. By June 1941 an entirely new type of reference to the Canadian company appeared in the London records. Following excellent results, a special bonus was to be awarded to Gordon McLean and John Freeman, who by this time was working with the Canadian government in charge of exports of cheese to the British Ministry of Food.

The good results were achieved despite the restrictions imposed on the cheese and butter trade at the outbreak of war. These restrictions made things very difficult for Lovell & Christmas who scrupulously avoided 'black market' dealings which were very prevalent at that time. It struggled along, running a legitimate business, and making up for the restrictions on trade with Britain by running a sizeable business with Bermuda and the British West Indies. (For a period of three years every pound of cheese shipped to Jamaica came from Lovell & Christmas).

The transformation in the financial position of Lovell & Christmas (Canada) is shown, better far than words can do, by the fact that on 1 July 1939 there was a balance sheet deficit of $269,000, and on 26 April 1969 there was a surplus of $577,712 after the payment of dividends of $1,867,000. The total includes the payment of 27½% on 13 June 1969. The first dividend was paid to the parent company for the year ending March 1949. In the 21 years from that date up to and including 1969 the company has paid 466¾% which makes a yearly average of 22.2%, or $88,800 a year.

The London Board in November 1944 decided to ask Gordon McLean to come and discuss post-war activities at a 'propitious time'. However, it was not until the spring of 1947 that he was able to come. He was warmly welcomed and congratulated by the directors on his 'recent cheese and meat transactions'. The main purpose of the meeting was to discuss the setting up of an office and establishing a representative in the U.S.A. After discussion it was resolved it was not a good time to appoint a resident representative because of the currency restrictions. Instead, the interests of the company would be best served by Gordon McLean's undertaking the task of securing supplies from the U.S.A. as long as it did not interfere with his Canadian duties. He thanked the directors for their confidence in him and said he would do his utmost.

McLean had already been active in the U.S.A. He had already sold one and a half million pounds of American cheese to the Ministry of Food. The following year he sold six million pounds.

He also arranged to supply eight million pounds of beef, but the transaction was never completed because the Chicago firm with which he made the deal was unable to complete it. McLean made arrangements with another firm, but in view of the circumstances, the Ministry of Food relieved Lovell & Christmas of their contract.

Initiatives taken by the Canadian company in the U.S.A. usually turned out better than that. On one occasion, the Chairman of the New Zealand Dairy Board, W. Marshall, was in Washington worrying about 457 tons of New Zealand cheese which had been turned down for technical reasons. McLean phoned him one Saturday morning, and purchased the lot. Within a week he sold the cheese in Montreal and Western Canada. The New Zealand Dairy Board was much impressed by the speed of the operation and has remained a firm friend of Lovell & Christmas (Canada) ever since.

Gordon McLean is a man who is always ready to chance his arm in the market. He once bought 10,000 New Zealand lambs with the idea of extending the business into meat. He had great difficulty in disposing of them because Lovell & Christmas was not a recognised meat dealer. He told Rolande Wall that he could not sleep at night until he had counted the 10,000 lambs one by one. By the time this arithmetic was complete only two hours of the night were left. The story illustrates Gordon McLean's humour, and the anxiety of a trader when things go wrong.

It is difficult to write the history of a trading company. Every day decisions have to be made to buy and sell at the right prices, staff have to be trained and kept enthusiastic, stocks have to be held in balance, decisions for forward purchases have to be made. Every day has its moments of exhilaration and depression and the results at the end of the year show if the interim judgments and actions have been good or bad.

The record of Lovell & Christmas (Canada) is one to be proud of. The firm has not only continued trading successfully and contributing much to the profits of London by its supplies, it has also become an acknowledged leader of the Canadian cheese trade. Its success continues under the spirited and dedicated direction of G. McLean, who became President of the company in 1961 when J. Freeman retired after 50 years' service to this important division of Lovell & Christmas.

# 8

## SVEND RUTZOU

THE STORY of Rutzou Ltd. is given a section of its own as it is typical of the development of the provision importing trade in England in the late 19th century, when first of all shipments would come from overseas to London; then a younger son of the shipper be sent to London to watch the sales, and later, if all went well, to open an office under the family name. That was what the young Svend Rutzou did.

Naturally as a Dane, Rutzou began with Danish produce, mainly butter and bacon, and he was fortunate enough to obtain the Dansk Andels egg agency. (Those of mature years will remember Dansk Andels as an outstanding Danish brand.) With this agency in his pocket Rutzou decided to go into the speculative European egg business with his brother Paul, who was an egg merchant in Copenhagen. More fortunes have probably been lost than have been made in this business. By 1925 Rutzou was in such difficulty that he approached Lovell's who agreed to take a majority shareholding in his firm, and guaranteed his bank account for £50,000. (No doubt in compensation he would have handed many, or most of his goods over to them for sale.) As part of this arrangement he formed his firm into a limited company, Rutzou Ltd., of which he became the Chairman. Lovell's guarantee continued until 1929 and was then raised to £75,000.

Svend Rutzou was a large, pleasant man with considerable powers of persuasion and in 1925 he induced Lovell's to take a majority interest in a company being formed by his friend P.J. Lassen to trade internationally in Roumanian eggs. Hoping to secure supplies of these eggs, Lovell's agreed to take a 75% interest in Lassen's private company and also guaranteed it for £25,000. The very next year the Roumanian firm was calling for extra money and by September 1926 loans had risen to more than £175,000.

Although uneasy, Lovell's Board did not seem unduly anxious about this hazardous business based in an Eastern European country. Peter J. Lassen (Roumania), as the firm was called, managed to repay some of the loans, but had to report a loss of £30,000 in 1927, when Lassen said that, without reorganisation, the company could no longer continue. At this juncture, Lovell & Christmas decided that it might be able to manage the business without Mr. Lassen and he was asked to resign. The firm was renamed Lovell & Christmas (Roumania) Ltd. The Board now discovered that the Roumanian egg packing stations were neither up-to-date nor very efficient. Losses mounted and within a few years had reached £70,000. Lovell's sent its Secretary to Roumania to dispose of the assets and the business was wound up.

Svend Rutzou hardly did Lovell's a favour by introducing it to his friend Peter Lassen. His own activities were certainly not as disastrous as his friend's, but neither were they wonderfully successful.

With Lovell's guarantee behind him, he became interested in Poland and in 1925 put up capital to finance a bacon factory at Radom. He was also regularly importing Polish eggs. During the glut season the eggs were pickled in Poland and brought over to England for sale in the Autumn, or else sold in Central Europe. In the same year he took a 50% interest in the Hardenburg bacon factory in Holland. The sales in London earned money, but the factory was unprofitable and was closed down prior to Hitler's War.

Whether because of unsuccessful speculations or because of the untimely arrival of the Depression, Rutzou's business did not prosper. In 1932 he was asked to retire while Lovell's contributed a very large sum to the credit of the profit and loss account. It was just before his departure that J.D. (Jack) Holgate was transferred from Lovell's to Rutzou. He relates that his presence was not greeted with pleasure. Knowing him and the state of the business, I am not surprised.

Svend Rutzou was succeeded as Chairman by W. Jones. Trade increased, but evidently the firm was not yet on an even keel, because in 1935 it made another application for financial help. Before judging it too harshly, the deplorable trading conditions of the early '30s must be taken into account. Jack Holgate says he had to sell Polish bacon for 3d. a lb. at about this time. With the market in such a state, he decided that the firm could not continue in the pig business in Budapest where also it had an interest.

His investigations revealed that the future there was uncertain. Rutzou had already advanced considerable sums of money, and in 1932 it was decided not to advance any more.

Jones retired in 1937 and Jack Holgate became Chairman. It was the turning point for the company. By 1939 it held good agencies in Denmark, Poland and other European countries, and the financial position was looking healthier. During the war directors of Rutzou and some members of the staff served with the Ministry of Food and with Trade Commodity Companies in executive positions, and Rutzou Ltd. acted as agent in the distribution of rationed food.

As soon as possible after the fighting was over, Rutzou regained its agencies in Denmark for bacon and eggs, in Holland for bacon, eggs and canned meats, in Poland for bacon, butter, eggs and canned foods and in the Argentine for butter. Other countries in Europe like Hungary and Roumania were so short of food they were unable to export. In recent years this situation has changed and business has been resumed.

The Polish business in particular has expanded, and nowadays Rutzou handles nearly every commodity from Poland which passes through the Provision Exchanges. Rutzou has its own selling offices in Manchester, Glasgow and Leeds, and is a member of the various provincial Provision Exchanges. The ill-starred trading of pre-war days has been left far behind, and there is no doubt that the change in the company's fortunes can be traced to the transfer of Jack Holgate from Smithfield to Tooley Street in 1931. His buoyant personality, sound judgment and restless energy have turned failure into success. In addition to his business undertakings, he is Chairman of the Provision Importers Association, and the Danish Bacon Agents Association. He takes a full part in the activities of the London Provision Exchange.

He would be the first to admit the help he has received from his colleagues, among them Mr. W.F. Betts, who was a director for 24 years and dealt mainly with eggs. John Holgate, son of the Chairman, was made a director of the company in 1961 after having been with the firm for 11 years, not counting the time spent at an English bacon factory and in Denmark learning the practical side of the bacon industry. Another who must be mentioned is W.A. Woolvett who had previously been with the company from

1928 to 1956, and returned as a director in 1963. He has twice been Chairman of the London Egg Exchange.

So often when firms are in poor shape they fade away. It is a pleasure to recount in some detail the story of one which is a real exception to the rule.

9

## THE MAKING OF FITCH LOVELL

THE PREVIOUS CHAPTERS on the history and enterprises of Lovell & Christmas depict a large, widely spread and increasingly prosperous concern. By the mid-1950s however, the firm had become vulnerable. Government financial policy also enabled mergers and take-overs easier. Lovell & Christmas lacked fluid capital, for it had expanded widely and, by the nature of its business, carried heavy stocks. Voting control had long since passed from the Board and the equity was held by many small shareholders. The firm seemed ripe for take-over and it was not long before some big fish were circling its West Smithfield headquarters.

As early as 1955 one of the leading merchant banks approached me through Hugh Fitch with the proposition that a consortium consisting of a) the merchant bank, b) an Australian company, c) Fitch, should make a bid over Lovell's head direct to its shareholders for all the ordinary shares, offering 24s. 6d. (compared with the market price of 14s. 6d.). As it happened Fitch had agreed only a few months before to participate with Lovell's on a 50-50 basis in a market company called Phillip's which operated in the Smithfield poultry pavilion. (Phillip's was a very small concern and, much to everyone's amusement, had six directors and only three staff.) Apart from this recent connection, Fitch had had a relationship with Lovell's for more than 75 years. We decided it would be wrong to make a bid without telling Lovell's directors in advance.

This was not at all what the merchant bank had in mind, but, despite our refusal, it continued to press and press the issue, preparing a number of alternative schemes. The Fitch Board however, persisted in its refusal to become involved and eventually the proposition was dropped.

Although opposed to a brutal take-over of this type, I had long realised that Fitch & Son and Lovell & Christmas had very similar assets and, even if a take-over were out of the question, an agreed merger could not be ruled out. Although Sir Rolande Wall and I discussed the possibility of such an amalgamation, for more than two years nothing happened except that Fitch and Lovell's became closer friends through their association in Phillip's; then, in the early months of 1958, it became obvious that Lovell's shares were being bought by other interests and that the take-over to which the company was so vulnerable was imminent.

In May, the first delicate, formal approaches were made between Fitch and Lovell & Christmas, with Sir Rolande Wall and I acting as intermediaries. Fitch was in a strong financial position, but a merger on the scale envisaged would endanger its cherished boardroom control. However, the Board agreed to allow negotiations to proceed. The Lovell & Christmas directors were also willing to negotiate, so, on 9 July 1958 Fitch's Chairman, Sir Graham Rowlandson, its Secretary, John Gilpin, and I met Sir Rolande and K.O.G. Huntley of Lovell's. We discovered that Lovell & Christmas had already received a firm offer of 37s. 6d. for its ordinary shares and that it had also been approached by two other organisations. Clearly, Fitch would have to move fast, both to achieve its own object and to enable Lovell's to avoid being swallowed by another firm and thus losing its identity. At this meeting we therefore decided to recommend our respective Boards to go ahead with the merger, which would be carried out by Fitch's making an offer for the ordinary shares of Lovell & Christmas and giving the necessary safeguards to Lovell's and its staff.

The first task was to deal with the public company which had already secretly purchased 18% of Lovell's equity. We finally extracted a promise from it that it would accept from Fitch any offer over 35s. for the shares it held. Another difficulty was presented by the Lovell & Christmas preference shareholders who had voting rights. Sir Rolande and I agreed to recommend to these shareholders that their shares should be replaced by a new issue of 6½% Fitch preference shares.

The question of the newly-merged company's name was happily settled by the combination of both former names in Fitch Lovell Ltd., a style which preserved the name of Lovell, which had a world wide reputation in the food trade. The name of Fitch & Son Ltd. was kept as a trading name to preserve the Royal Warrants held. It was resolved that Sir Rolande Wall and K.O.G. Huntley should be appointed directors of Fitch Lovell Ltd. and that R.E. Blanning and I should join the board of Lovell & Christmas. It was further decided to appoint three Vice-Chairmen of Fitch Lovell. These would also be Managing Directors, namely, Sir Rolande Wall, Norman F. Lambourne and I, A.C.A. Keevil, Clement (II), who had been attending board meetings for general instruction was also appointed a director.

An offer was sent to shareholders on 22 July 1958 for acceptance on 18 August of one Fitch Lovell 6½% £1 preference share for each L & C 6% £1 preference, and 27s. 6d. plus one F.L. ordinary share (underwritten at 10s.) for each L. & C. £1 ordinary stock unit. The offer was successful and Fitch Lovell Ltd. came into existence on 28 August 1958.

The comparative figures for the two companies at the time of the merger were:

| | *Fitch* | *L. & C.* |
|---|---|---|
| Net Profits 1957/58 | £629,000 | £325,000 |
| Turnover (approx.) | £14M | £49M |
| Net Assets | £3,062,100 | £3,027,000 |

In their new combination the two companies became one of the leading groups in the food trade. For Fitch, the merger confirmed its successful post-war policy. For Lovell & Christmas, the merger meant the preservation of the company's identity and structure within a group wholly sympathetic to its aims. At one step a company had been formed combining manufacturing, importing and agency, wholesaling and retailing.

The way was now open for further advances, and the newly organised company set to work with optimism and enthusiasm. A symbol of the new era was the opening in August 1958 at Strutton Ground in Westminster of the first supermarket in the group.

Fitch Lovell was now a national concern with its name prominently displayed in the High Streets throughout the country. We decided to give a press conference to announce the birth of the new group. Sir Rolande and I chaired the conference which had a marked effect on Fitch Lovell's public image. From then onwards we have always had widespread press publicity and very fair press comment throughout the country. Having launched the group we proceeded with the task of welding the two companies together. They both possessed strong traditions, and the integration might have proved difficult, but the reorganisation was as willing and happy as the negotiations had been. Credit for this must be given to Sir Rolande Wall, who was in a few years to become a much-esteemed Chairman of Fitch Lovell, and to K.O.G. Huntley, who would have become Chairman but for his sudden death in 1969.

The three of us who were Vice-Chairmen and principal executives in 1958 all saw the need to avoid becoming desk bound. We resolved to encourage a group spirit in our widely-dispersed company by constantly visiting the executives on the ground instead of asking them to come to head office. We felt that our presence would encourage the men in the front line and enable us to see for ourselves what was actually happening in the field.

In September 1958 Fitch Lovell, was organised into four divisions, Lovell & Christmas (under Sir Rolande Wall), and the three existing Fitch divisions which were: general provisions, bakery and timber.

General provisions, which were under my supervision, comprised Fitch & Son with its attendant small companies, Keevils' and the market companies, Bywaters, the meat retailers Layton and Burkett, Hale and Partners, the grocery retailers, Robsons of Bournemouth and Impey & Dyke. (Later in the year the small companies which revolved around Fitch & Son were all absorbed in it except for Fitch Export Ltd.) The bakery interests were under Norman F. Lambourne, and the timber companies under Graham Rowlandson. Financial direction was the responsibility of Graham Rowlandson and John Gilpin with me acting in an advisory capacity.

The policy agreed before the merger was to leave Lovell & Christmas to continue its own activities, but this meant that there were two chains of retail grocers in the group – Fitch's Hale & Partners, and Lovell's much larger World's Stores, and so quite early in the New Year, Hale & Partners was transferred to World's Stores.

There were other matters arising from the merger which required prompt attention. One was the question of Isaac Beer & Sons Ltd. (I.B.S.), the old-established, wholesale provision company specialising in bacon distribution, who owned bacon factories at Evesham and Downton. Beer's had been closely connected with Lovell's for more than 50 years and Lovell's owned about 27% of its ordinary shares. As Fitch had been trying for some time to increase its bacon interests we decided to try and acquire the balance of Beer's ordinary shares. This move was successful and, as part of our agreement, Beer's Chairman, Edward Shephard joined the Fitch Lovell Board. The development of Beer's is discussed later.

The other problem our new company now faced was finance. Fitch had operated with substantial bank balances for many years. Lovell & Christmas and Beer's, on the other hand, had overdrafts In the case of Lovell & Christmas, a substantial figure was involved, so by January 1959 our overall bank indebtedness amounted to some £1,300,000. It was obvious that additional finance would have to be raised.

It was decided to give a bonus of 1 in 1 'B' shares to ordinary 'B' shareholders and to make a rights issue of 2 for 3 'B' shares held at 6s., and this was done in May 1959. The issue was organised and made in our own head office under the supervision of K.O.G. Huntley and J. Gilpin. These two had also undertaken all the paperwork and registration involved in the L. & C. and I.B.S. mergers without recourse to merchant banks, and the skill with which they did this work was highly appreciated and almost incomprehensible to a new generation in these days when there is a compulsion to rush to specialists.

The issue of the 'B' shares was a success, and the capital of the company was raised to £3,000,000. The underwriting costs were 1½%, shared equally between Fenn & Crosthwaite our stockbrokers and Hart & Co. (now Samuel Montagu).

The shareholders in Fitch Lovell had risen to 8,000 and to ease the burden of the office work it was decided that the trading year should end in April instead of March and that the Annual General Meeting be held in September.

The growth of the company made it essential that a strict watch should be kept on capital spending, and all capital commitments in hand were submitted to the Board in January 1959, when they amounted to £1,370,000, with new plant for the bakery division taking the lion's share.

The growth of Fitch Lovell was in fact beginning to take on a momentum of its own. The exciting events of the previous year, far from exhausting the company, had begun a chain reaction. Four more propositions were under consideration early in 1959 and as time went by more and more companies came knocking on our door, eager to join the group. The acquisition of West (Butchers)

Ltd. made an important expansion to the meat division but most other applicants were unsuccessful. West's Chairman, David Galloway was invited by the President, Hugh Fitch, to join the Fitch Lovell Board on which he has served ever since.

Sir Graham Rowlandson resigned as Chairman in July 1959. Although he was a part-time Chairman with numerous interests in other fields he proved himself a good Chairman with sound judgment.

The directors did me the honour of asking me to take the chair. I was diffident because of my age. However, I had been closely involved in the expansion of the company for 14 years and knew the intricacies of our growing concern perhaps better than my colleagues and so I accepted. I felt that I would be able to keep expansion going, and I knew I could count on the close and warm support of my experienced and able colleagues.

I was able to mark the start of my term as Chairman by announcing in my report to the Annual General Meeting in September 1959, that the profits had exceeded one million pounds for the first time. It was a target that we had set ourselves five years before.

In keeping with our new policy of fostering public relations, a display of Fitch Lovell products was on view at the meeting. The rising interest in the company was shown by the presence for the first time of more than 100 shareholders. Another happy innovation was an invitation to the wives of directors and the Secretary to lunch after the meeting. It was felt that this would be a slight tribute to them for the patience they had shown at the repeated absences of their husbands on company business at home and abroad. This luncheon for the ladies has since become an annual event.

In spite of the good profit figure in 1959, we were disappointed with the results of I.B.S. and some of the smaller companies. The state of the timber division, for which Norman F. Lambourne had just taken over responsibility, was also disquieting. Finally it was decided that the division's problems could only be solved by bringing in new blood and, as related in the later chapter devoted to timber, we amalgamated with Machin & Kingsley, putting Alan R. Kingsley in charge of all our timber activities. Machin & Kingsley accepted in November 1959 the offer of 204,000 F.L. 'B' ordinary shares for their company. From then on the timber division stopped causing anxiety, (apart from a period in 1961 when Alan Kingsley was ill and the division found itself in serious difficulties after buying on a rising market, at which time we took the decision to liquidate the two timber companies which had been in the Group since before the war, K. Norman and d'Arcy Morrow, and trade only as Machin & Kingsley).

Two problems of finance arose in 1959. It was apparent that in spite of the issue made in January which raised the company's capital to three million pounds, Fitch Lovell was still under-capitalised. The 'B' shares which we had issued in January and at other times in the past had only one vote for every 48 shares. There was at this time widespread criticism of non-voting and partial voting shares, and, when we announced that we wanted to raise more capital, some finance houses told us that they were unwilling to underwrite for us a large issue of this type of share.

We were thus brought face to face with the second problem – loss of boardroom control if we issued more shares. Boardroom control was described by my good and revered friend the late Harold Wincott as 'valuable in a company's initial and probably most virile years to avoid take-over bids but not so important at a later stage when the easy raising of finance could be more important than retaining control'. Before we could proceed with the important step of widening the control of the company we had to consult the substantial minority interests in the Fitch Lovell subsidiaries for these minority shareholders held large numbers of Fitch Lovell ordinaries. At the time Fitch Lovell only held 50% of John Trent Ltd, 75% of Hale Home Bakeries and 74% of Keevil & Keevil Ltd.

Discussions with these shareholders were satisfactorily concluded and in July 1960 we issued 4,276,000 ordinary shares on a basis of 1 in 4, votes to be given to the 'B' shareholders. As compensation for their loss of voting control the ordinary shareholders were given one 6½% £1 preference share in the proportion of one preference share to 20 ordinary shares held. The applications for excess shares were enormous, and those applying for 3,000 shares received only 100.

We decided that it was no longer possible for all the registration work to be done at head office, and so it was placed in the hands of professional registrars, Amsdon, Cossart & Wells of Cannon Street, E.C.4. They were chosen by a committee of the Board in January 1960, and in the same month John Gilpin, the Secretary who had done so much work in registration, new issues and mergers, was elected to the Board on the proposal of K.O.G. Huntley.

While we consolidated our financial position, the momentum of growth continued unchecked. In 1960 there were no fewer than 12 propositions under consideration. We were particularly interested in a large hotel group and a Cash and Carry Wholesaling firm, the first time this business, which is now important to us, is mentioned in the records. In fact none of these negotiations came to anything and 1960 proved to be a period of consolidation rather than expansion. Lovell & Christmas however did take up an option to buy a 50% holding in N.V. Gevato, Meat Manufacturers of Driebergen in Holland. This proved to be an interesting investment leading to participation in the successful De Haan products and the eventual establishment of a meat canning factory in Lancashire.

In September 1960 I reported to the Annual General Meeting net profits before taxation of £1,172,000 after allowing the large figure of £460,000 for depreciation. On behalf of the shareholders, Edward du Cann, later the Rt. Hon. Edward du Cann, M.P. Minister of State, proposed the vote of thanks to the directors and staff. At this meeting we went one step further than with our display of products and provided samples for the shareholders to take away. We were somewhat astonished at the ardent manner in which some of them helped themselves.

September 1960 saw a big step forward in our retail meat division when we acquired the 100 meat and 30 provision shops of R. Gunner Ltd. The full story of this company is told in the chapter relating to meat retailing.

I became involved in many administrative problems early in 1961, a scheme to acquire preference shares in subsidiaries which were owned by outside shareholders, the formation of a property subsidiary, which has still to be activated, the transfer of our bank account from Coutts to the Westminster, the decision to enter the broiler poultry business, revaluation of the group's property and increasing trading difficulties in provisions wholesaling.

The burden of work during this period of rapid growth meant I became increasingly unable to carry out the visits to the trading companies which I had been in the habit of making and which I consider deserve the highest priority for the chief of any widely spread organisation. They are invaluable for gaining a real insight into what is really happening in the front line, and for assessing people at their job and creating a group spirit instead of a parochial one.

Rather than forego altogether the contacts which these visits afford, I decided to hold a series of small luncheon parties at the City Livery Club on the Thames Embankment for bright up and coming young executives, buyers, accountants and secretaries. I supplemented these gatherings with a fairly regular output of notes and memoranda which I sent to the various companies. In later years I learned that these efforts were more appreciated than I had any idea at the time. I have always tried to base the running of a business organisation on these wise words of Bob Gunner, the founder of R.Gunner Ltd.

> Good administration is vital, but once this is in motion and the accountancy is in good hands, always remember that the profits have to be earned in the shops and warehouses, and it is your privilege to be there and to give and obtain ideas and to be inspired by the imagination of youth. Without ideas and imagination and the right mentality to put them into practice a business will perish.

Fitch Lovell Ltd. was by now settling down to the life of a large corporation, not just a medium-sized business, and new problems were continually arising, of which the need for contacts between the Board and the executives was only one. Another pressing need was to control the growth of paper work, which proved to be easier said than done. People are always inclined to produce mountains of letters and memoranda in order to 'wave a flag' and show how much work they are doing.

Another chronic complaint of large organisations is the amount of time taken up in committees and sub-committees. I was always trying to cut back on them but without much success. Administration was particularly difficult in Fitch Lovell at this time because the head office was, to all intents and purposes, in two buildings some distance apart. The head office was officially at St. Martin's Lane, W.C.2., which was also the head office of the bakery group, but with the rapid growth of the provision and meat activity, the centre of activity was not in fact at St. Martin's Lane but at 1 West Smithfield E.C.1. This division of activities only worked because of the close co-operation and complete lack of jealousy among those concerned. The problem was solved when the St. Martin's Lane building was sold a few years later.

All these internal problems were minor compared with the need to establish contacts outside the group and outside the trade. The need for these contacts was becoming urgent. It was one more sign of the way the growth of the company into a national institution had changed the lives of those responsible. I was fortunate to know a number of people through other activities, particularly during the war, but even so my life tended to become a round of lunches with leading personalities in Whitehall, the finance houses, the Press and the heads of other companies. Added to this was the constant need to attend subsidiary company dinners and celebrations, all of which led to a lack of sufficient relaxation and exercise and a bad effect on the liver! I was naturally called upon to speak at many of these functions and for someone with an impulsive nature it was only too easy to say too much or to say the wrong thing and I was glad to be able to make use of a 'joke book' which I had painfully compiled over the years. It is easy to criticise these social occasions as the waste of a busy man's time, but there is no doubt that personal contacts in the right places are essential, and it is well to note that practically every merger in which Fitch Lovell has been concerned has come about directly through personal contacts and friendships.

These years, the early '60s, were a time of intense activity. The buildings at 1 West Smithfield were a hive of activity and the scene of continuous comings and goings. Directors were stretched to their limit in the affairs of the group and in the particular companies for which they were responsible. Some people say directors should get ulcers because it shows they are working hard, others that they should be fired if they do get them because it shows they are not up to the job. I do not know which argument is correct, but I do know that if ever Fitch Lovell directors should have got ulcers through hard work it was at this time. My own burden in trying to create a group spirit was eased magnificently by the unstinting efforts of the Vice-Chairmen and the other senior executives. All I lacked was time to do everything, and the only real burden I carried was the oncoming of age; both were handicaps in the important years of 1961 and 1962 when consolidation, grouping and expansion were all in full spate.

Consolidation and grouping were concentrated in the first of those two years and expansion in the second. Fitch Lovell grew faster in the 12 months leading up to the Annual General Meeting of September 1962 than at any time since 1958. Greens, the stores group joined us to give an added impetus to our decision to expand rapidly into supermarkets, and we entered large scale poultry production for the first time through W.D. Evans Golden Produce and the Golden Produce distributors, Henry Gillham. Our stake in the ham, sausage and pie manufacturing business was greatly strengthened by the purchase of the Dorset firm Millers, and we entered the fancy cheese and delicatessen fields through Auguste Noël and later L. Noël. All these exciting additions to the group are fully explained later.

The increasing scale and complexity of the group was mirrored by developments at Head Office. A group directory was published for the first time in 1962 showing the organisation of the group into divisions, and the name and telephone number of the executives in every company. The task of compiling the directory and of revising it was ably performed by D.J. Apps. David Galloway of West Layton came to Head Office to begin work on budget control and general liaison. The procedures which he began for presenting capital commitments and other statistical returns remain exactly the basis on which the more sophisticated information is presented to the Board today. With events moving so rapidly, Board meetings tended to become bogged down in the pressing needs of the various divisions, and so we formed a Chairman's Committee consisting of the Chairman and the Managing Directors to undertake special and urgent duties. It was the forerunner of the present Finance Committee.

With the company itself having to resort to special committees, budgetry control and a group director to keep track of itself, it is understandable that I find it more and more difficult to convey in this story the richness and breadth of the group's activities. Perhaps the best is to recall a few of the things written in the annual report for the 1962 Annual General Meeting.

1961/62 was reported to be an active and exciting year with turnover reaching a record £110 million. On the manufacturing side, that extensive building programme at Hales Home Bakeries at Clevedon had been completed and was coming into operation. Production of fresh cream cakes and 'bake at home' cakes had begun. We had purchased the 50% of John Trents, the original pre-war bakery company, which had been owned by outside interests and had created a new company, Hale-Trent Cakes. Lovell & Christmas's brands, *Blue Cap, Spam* and *Newforge* were all doing well, with *Newforge Chili Con Carne* and *De Haan*

*Tongues* particularly popular. Production of bacon, pies and sausages had advanced considerably. Supplies of English pigs had improved although the business continued to have its hazards because of changing government policies and 'duty free imports from certain European countries'.

I wrote that the year had been difficult for our first hand trade and in our overseas activities. Lovell & Christmas had finally decided to dispose of its interests in the Argentine, and H.J. Webb of Smithfield had been badly caught in the world slump in corned beef in which it specialised. Lovell & Christmas continued to do well in its wide importing agencies, particularly in dried fruits, and Fitch & Son (Export) continued satisfactorily in its ships' stores and entrepôt trade. A new warehouse for use at Southampton docks was nearly ready.

I was already having to report disappointment with W.D. Evans Golden Produce who had scarcely been with us a year, and as the chapter on poultry shows, it was some time before this firm settled down.

In the wholesale field I reported that the business was undergoing a transformation. Although there were 80,000 retail grocery outlets, 75% of the trade was passing through only 1,600 units. I. Beer & Sons still predominated as bacon specialists, and Fitch Home Trade and Wholesale Catering Services were doing well in their supply of hotels, hospitals and canteens. New premises were being constructed for it near Tooley Street.

My report on retailing said that the meat companies had had an excellent year and emphasised the big drive into supermarkets which followed the acquisition of Greens. We already operated 136 supermarkets and self-service stores.

I ended by saying 'throughout the Group there is a spirit of restless energy and enthusiasm which, coupled with our wide experience, permits us to face the future with every confidence'.

Not surprisingly, the great changes of the year were reflected in changes on the Board. Our policy of inviting the leaders of the subsidiaries on to the main Board brought in Sir William Beale of Greens, W.D. Evans from the new poultry business, and H. Boyes-Stubbs and F.F. Parker from the reorganised bakery companies. F.F. Parker's presence at Board meetings did not last long, for he decided to resign along with Norman F. Lambourne who left as Vice-Chairman and Managing Director in order to devote himself to a business of his own. His work ever since 1946 had been outstanding and had contributed greatly to the advance of Fitch Lovell. Edward Shephard also did not seek re-election as he wanted to retire after more than 50 years in the trade. Meanwhile R.E. Blanning had been appointed a Managing Director.

Hugh B. Fitch, the President died in February 1962 in his 89th year, a great loss to all who knew him. He was the first Chairman of the public company, from 1920 to 1953. He always disclaimed any commercial ability, saying that he relied on H.S. Rowlandson. From my close connection with him I can say that I found him a good judge of men who always knew what was going on and was always ready to intervene if things were not going the way he considered they should. He constantly encouraged those who had responsibility and stood by them in good times and bad. His distinguished appearance and charm of manner perhaps misled people into supposing he was a mere figurehead, but this was certainly not so. His keen interest in the company lasted right up to his death. I used to visit him every week in the last months and he insisted on being kept in close touch with the rapidly growing company and the welfare of the staff.

His presence was sorely missed at the Annual General Meeting in September 1962. In that year we decided that we had outgrown the *Great Eastern Hotel* where we had met for 40 years, and booked into the *Connaught Rooms* in Great Queen Street instead. It was just as well that we did, because 500 shareholders turned up, exactly five times as many as the year before. Cynics suggested that their presence was due more to the prospect of samples being handed out than to a sudden growth of interest in the company.

At the luncheon, which followed the meeting, Gordon McLean of Lovell & Christmas (Canada) was an honoured guest. It had been a momentous year for Lovell & Christmas. Not only had it taken the decision to leave the Argentine, but it had made a move which was in many ways more difficult. It had shifted its London warehousing and packing away from West Smithfield, where it had been for the best part of a century, to Erith in Kent. The firm had decided to move mainly because of the traffic congestion in central London. The property at Erith had a floor space of 108,000 square feet on a 3½ acre site. The cost of making the building suitable was heavy, but the saving in expenses was considerable and the new site gave much more scope for expansion than the cramped

34. E. Trevor Beer, C.B.E.
Director, Fitch Lovell Ltd.
from 1963; Deputy Chairman from 1970.

35. Clement Keevil, II
Director, Fitch Lovell Ltd.
from 1958

36. John Gilpin
Director, Fitch Lovell Ltd.
from 1960; Secretary 1959-62

37. E.M. Canevali
Director, Fitch Lovell Ltd.
from 1964

38. David Galloway, O.B.E., C.A.
Director, Fitch Lovell Ltd.
from 1959-71

39. I.P. McEwan, M.V.O., C.A.
Director, Fitch Lovell Ltd.
from 1969

40. K.O.G. Huntley, O.B.E., J.P.
Director, Fitch Lovell Ltd.
1959-69; Vice-Chairman 1969;
Died 1969

41. D.J. Apps, F.C.I.S., J.P.
Secretary, Fitch Lovell Ltd.
from 1962

42. The Chairman, Sir Ambrose Keevil, addressing the Annual General Meeting of Fitch Lovell Ltd., 1963

43. Cartoon of Sir Ambrose Keevil
'Men of London', 1961
reproduced by kind permission of *The Evening News*

buildings in West Smithfield and Hosier Lane. The Hosier Lane building was sold in January 1961 and the 99-year lease on the Erith property was signed in April. The move was completed by February 1962. The premises were inspected by the Lovell & Christmas Board on the 21st of that month and a Board Meeting was held afterwards at the *Black Prince Hotel* Bexley at which all connected with the difficult task of moving were congratulated on their excellent work. It was the end of an era, not only for Lovell & Christmas, but also for Smithfield, for the departure of Lovell's was followed by others, including Beer's, and it became clear that the days of Smithfield as the centre of the provision trade were over.

1962-63 was rather a contrast to the year which went before. There was a pause in the hectic expansion. In fact the only acquisitions apart from L. Noël which I have already mentioned, were the well known firm of Northern Ireland bacon curers, T. Forde & Co. Ltd., and J. & T.H. Staples Ltd., importers of caviare and other specialities.

Internally, there was plenty going on. At Head Office a big event was the decision to sell the St. Martin's Lane premises, which had been the registered office of Fitch and Fitch Lovell since 1929. The headquarters were concentrated at 1 West Smithfield. There were other important changes too. D.J. Apps was appointed Secretary. John Gilpin devoted himself to the supervision of the Fitch Home & Export Group and to financial matters. The 1962 accounts were selected by *The Accountant* as one of the 12 best prepared of the year and H.D.B. Laughlin was congratulated for the part he, as the Group Accountant, had played in this.

Other important developments at Head Office included the decision to commission a computer feasibility survey in April 1963, and in October 1962 we decided to rationalise all the charitable donations of the various companies by making a single covenant with the National Council of Social Services. With an eye to the future we began preparing in February 1963 a list of all the bright young men in the group, as a first step towards attracting and keeping men of the younger generation, the need for which was become more and more apparent.

From July 1962 onwards it was decided to stop holding the meetings and luncheons of the Board at the *Great Eastern Hotel*, where we had met for 40 years. We began to go to the *Butchers Hall* instead, which was considered more convenient. The change enabled directors to invite regularly leading personalities in finance, the press, and industry to luncheon, and many interesting discussions took place. It is interesting to note that on one particular day two future Lord Mayors of London were our guests. They were Sir Lionel Denny, G.B.E., M.C., and Sir Robert Bellinger, G.B.E., both of whom have connections with the food trade.

I have said that there were not many additions to the Group during this year, but this does not mean that nobody wanted to join us. The number of companies wishing to sell out to Fitch Lovell, which started soon after the Lovell & Christmas merger in 1958, continued and if anything increased. During one fourweek period in the autumn of 1962, no less than 24 companies approached us. All of these were turned down, for we were determined not to buy anything which was not absolutely right.

So it was that the most important new name to emerge this year was one given to companies that were already part of the group. This was Key Markets, the name chosen for the retail groceries chain which was formed by amalgamating World's Stores and Greens. It was to develop, as the name suggests, into a supermarket group, one of the finest in the South of England.

There were changes, once again, at Board level, although nothing like as many as there had been the year before. Norman Lambourne finally left us, and E. Trevor Beer, C.B.E., Chairman of I.B.S., was elected in January 1963 to take the place of Edward Shephard.

Then on 24 May 1963, I resigned as Chairman. It was the first meeting after the end of the trading year in which profits had, for the first time, topped two million pounds. I told the Board that I would be 70 in November and I felt the time had come to call a halt.

Sir Rolande Wall, M.C., was unanimously elected to succeed me. No one could possibly have had a more loyal and helpful colleague than Sir Rolande. Without his guidance and wisdom the achievements of the previous five years would have been impossible. As to my other colleagues, they were a splendid band of the highest integrity and capabilities. They were particularly forebearing about the things I did and the things I failed to do because of a volatile disposition.

It was a long way since I began in an old fashioned family business with profits of barely £2,000 a year. All the fluctuations over the years have shown me the truth of Ramsay Macdonald's words,

'If a long career has taught me anything, it is that it is never the right moment to take a painful decision'.

As far as the methods of chairmanship are concerned, I think it is hard to generalise, for no two chairmen work in the same way. One thing which is essential is the importance of ideas, and I always made a point of preparing ideas and thoughts for consideration at meetings of the Board. Free discussion, new policies and action did not always result from them, but at least the meetings were never dull. My main fault is that I am rather a lone wolf, perhaps because of my upbringing. Also I possibly came to high office too late in life.

I sometimes wonder if our company was tied too closely to the plan I had made 30 years before, at a relatively young age. The plan, for a widely based company comprising importing, wholesaling, manufacturing and retail divisions, which could have cold stores in common, was unusual in 1936 when I conceived it, although familiar nowadays. It was because I found that H.S. Rowlandson supported it that Keevil's had merged with Fitch. After the merger the plan was adopted as Fitch's policy and has been followed ever since. However, they say the true test of a chairman's work is the company's results in the six years after his retirement. If that is so I have no reason to be despondent, neither has Rolande Wall, nor R.E. Blanning.

I had intended to invite my brother Percy and one or two others who had been associated with me to be the sole guests at the lunch following the last meeting of the Board which I chaired, but W.D. Evans had invited two friends who were connected with a venture he was promoting in Italy. This spoiled my plans but enlivened the proceedings. One of Evans's guests was a most imposing figure, a Monsignor of the Roman Catholic Church, who was there because it was expected that the Vatican would be participating in Evans's scheme. I asked this personage how I should introduce him. 'Should I say, "Your Excellency", "Your Eminence", "Your Lordship", or what?' I enquired.

He replied in a distinct American accent, 'Call me Bill'.

My colleagues on the Board honoured me by presenting me with a portrait in oils by Edward Halliday, and the companies gave me a beautiful gift of silver pheasants. In addition I was asked to become President of the company.

So it was that, in spite of my resignation, I found myself writing the Annual Report for 1963 as President of Fitch Lovell. I wrote that profits had risen for the 10th year in succession, although our activities had been badly affected by the severe snows and frosts of the winter which had particularly disrupted food distribution by lorry which is a big part of our business. I said that the last year had been a year of reorganisation and told of my resignation and of the appointment of my successor.

I wrote that the new Hale-Trent cake name was fast becoming a national brand, and that Blue Cap, at their Gateacre factory outside Liverpool, were producing record quantities of *Spam* and *Chili Con Carne* in response to rising demand stimulated by extensive advertising campaigns. I noted that Blue Cap at Ditton Court in Kent had expended £100,000 during the year, and the factory was producing much larger quantities of Blue Cap frozen foods. The seven Lovell & Christmas packing units and the Blue Cap packet cheese plant were continuing satisfactorily. I recorded difficulties in poultry breeding and poultry packing and reported that Auguste Noël was regularly offering for sale 200 different types of cheese. I wrote that Keevil & Keevil had moved into the long-awaited new poultry market at Smithfield and that the wholesale division was 'full of confidence'.

The Annual General Meeting was attended by more than 700 shareholders plus guests and the Press. These A.G.M.s were beginning to be considered financial events of importance. Undoubtedly the refreshments, the samples (often referred to by the Press as 'hampers') and the large pictorial display have given the company splendid publicity and engendered a family feeling among shareholders, who have shown remarkable loyalty to the company. (By 1960 there were 10,000 shareholders; by 1965, 25,000.)

The new Chairman, Sir Rolande Wall, was immediately faced with a really tough year. The bakery division ran into trouble with its new automated plant and actually showed a trading loss instead of its usual big contribution to profits. Serious trouble came to light in the Evans Golden Produce poultry interests, and Evans' Italian scheme was found to be unsound. The steps taken to remedy this are recounted in the chapter on the poultry industry. The troubles at Hale-Trent affected the health of H. Boyes-Stubbs who did not seek re-election to the Board at the 1964 A.G.M.

There was more trouble to come. At a time when the development of supermarkets was at its height with 25 due to be opened, the stamp trading crisis broke, and the Board decided to withdraw from stamp trading in November 1963 in spite of the serious effect this was bound to have on some of our other retail profits. Key Markets were unfortunate enough to lose the valuable services of Sir William Beale about this time, when he resigned from the Board 'having decided to limit my business activities'. He was succeeded by David Galloway, who had always been a keen advocate of supermarkets.

Despite all these setbacks, Sir Rolande was able to announce profits only marginally lower than in the previous year. His report revealed that the group's property portfolio exceeded eight million pounds, and that the group had more than 14,000 employees throughout the world. He numbered their loyalty and efficiency among the group's greatest assets. He remarked that the group was sharing in the increasing demand for speciality products like continental cheese and cocktail cherries, and he saw the demand for caviare as a sign of the times. Fitch Export was benefiting in its ships' stores trade, from the increasing popularity of cruises. He revealed that Fitch Lovell companies supplied almost all the food for the Atlantic Survey based at South Georgia. His forecast for the future was fairly cautious. 'It is always difficult to prophesy results in the food industry, which is subject to wide market fluctuations and circumstances over which we have little control, but I see no reason why we should not continue to do well.' We did.

A happy event in May 1965 was the dedication on the 25th of that month of the Fitch Memorial Garden in the Churchyard of Saint Katherine Cree. It was given to the City of London by Marc F.B. Fitch. The garden was dedicated by the Bishop of London, the Rt. Rev. and Rt. Hon. R.W. Stopford, and opened to the public by the Lord Mayor of London Alderman Sir James Miller.

The inscription on the fountain in the garden reads:

> The Fitch Garden is dedicated to all those who work in the City and to the memory of James Fitch 1762-1818 who at Mid-summer 1784 opened his Cheesemonger's shop East of the Church of Saint Katherine Cree, his nephew George Fitch 1780-1842, and his direct descendants Frederick Fitch 1814-1909, Edwin Frederick Fitch C.C., 1839-1916, Stanley Fox Fitch 1867-1930 and Hugh Bernard Fitch C.C., 1873-1962, all citizens and Freemen of London and successive Principals of the firm now known as Fitch Lovell Ltd.

Among the prayers said at the ceremony I remember in particular: 'Lord, who hast taught that from those to whom much has been given much shall be demanded, look in mercy on those on whose shoulders rest the heavy burden of decision'.

The net profits for the year ending April 1965 were 10% up on the year before, and at the Annual General Meeting in September, it was announced that Group Sales' Turnover had reached £142 million, an average of 3s. 3d. a week for every household in the United Kingdom.

Soon after the A.G.M. Barrows Stores Ltd., the well known and high class Birmingham store was purchased, and later in the year our interests in Northern Ireland were strengthened by the happy addition of the old established bacon curers McElderry & Moffett Ltd.

The meetings of the Board now took place at 1 West Smithfield where a boardroom suite and directors' offices had been constructed on the second floor. The directors held a luncheon in the Board Room each month in addition to the monthly Board meeting luncheons and also other luncheons for various companies in the group. There were still quarterly meetings in the *Butchers' Hall*. On 25 March 1966. an Extraordinary General Meeting was held there in order to increase the capital of the company to £12 million.

A scrip issue of 3 F.L. ordinary shares for each 5 held was made and as a result the F.L. 2s. 6d. ordinary shares were consolidated into 4s. ordinary shares. In July 1966 Fitch Lovell (Insurances) Ltd. was formed to undertake the insurances of the various companies and such other business as they might obtain. D.J. Apps was the moving spirit, as he had been in the pension funds.

The Annual General Meeting was held on 23 September 1966 and Sir Rolande Wall retired as Chairman. It was most gratifying for him to be able to announce that profits for the year had reached the new record of £2,363,000 before tax. By this time it was estimated that the new Selective Employment Tax was costing the Company £365,000 a year. The prolonged seamen's strike had been an extra burden to be carried.

In his report to shareholders, Sir Rolande wrote:

> Since the last war, there have been vast changes in the trade and in our own company. Without the constant help and co-operation of my colleagues on the Board and in the companies, our Group

> could not have been raised to its present important level. During some forty-six years in the industry I have tried with them to help our work proceed happily and smoothly. No one could have had better or more loyal friends and I offer them my deep gratitude.

It is easy to see why he was held in affection and why he was esteemed greatly for his wise guidance and unselfish leadership.

He was succeeded in the chair by R.E. Blanning, and I can do no better than quote what Sir Rolande wrote of him:

> Our company is fortunate to have Mr. R.E. Blanning as its new chairman. He has been a Managing Director for five years and, more recently has been my deputy. He is well known throughout the food trade for his ability and sterling character and I feel sure that the company has a fine future under his guidance.

R.E. Blanning's duties in the Bacon and Pork Manufacturing Division were taken over with marked success by E. Trevor Beer.

In August 1967 the proposed scheme for the preference shares was implemented. £1,541,322 6½% preference shares were replaced by a similar amount of 7¼% unsecured loan stock 1992/2007 and the repayment of £142,301 6% and £100,000 5% preference shares. The purpose of this move was to simplify the administrative and tax structures.

During 1967 Marc Fitch retired and went to live abroad. His departure ended a family link with the Fitch company which had lasted for 183 years. Those of us who had been closely associated with him for a long time regretted very much the loss of one who was not only highly intelligent but a conscientious and able colleague at all times. The new Chairman appointed as his personal assistant Ian McEwan who was later appointed to the Board in 1969. His experience of administrative and accounting affairs filled a gap in the organisation and he has been able to render many services.

In spite of the heavy burden of Selective Employment Tax, the results to April 1967 showed another record both in profits and sales. Profits reached £2,383,298 before tax. In his report, R.E. Blanning said 25% of Canadian cheese brought into the United Kingdom was handled by Lovell & Christmas. Sales of *Newforge* fruit and vegetables were up 20% and were leading the rapidly-expanding market in canned new potatoes. Sales of prepacked bacon were on the increase, but that elusive fellow the English pig was on the decline again, and as a consequence losses in the bacon factories were reaching 40s. a pig. He gave the number of supermarkets in operation as 62 with another ten due to open the following year. He had a fair amount to say about Cash and Carry wholesaling which he said, 'will largely supersede the traditional Wholesaler'. He reported that C.C. Ryan (Wholesale Cash & Carry) Ltd. had joined the Group, and I.B.S. were experimenting with Cash and Carry as well as their Blue Riband scheme, which was a voluntary association of retailers.

The assets of Fitch Lovell at April 1967 had grown to nearly £22,500,000 of which no less than nine million pounds were in property.

R.E. Blanning continued to apply himself vigorously to the rationalisation of the group and to a firmer control of stocks and finance, and to an intensification of internal growth. His efforts were rewarded with an increase of nearly 29% in profits for the year ending April 1968. The only sad event was the serious illness of David Galloway who had to retire as Chairman of Key Markets soon after the Board had approved a five-year expansion plan. He was succeeded by Michael Brooke.

In his report to shareholders, R.E. Blanning mentioned the bad effect of the Foot and Mouth epidemic on the price of Pork meat for *Spam* and on the bacon curing factories and the retail meat companies, notwithstanding that the increased profits were partly brought about by improvements in bacon curing. He also revealed that Lovell & Christmas was packing 10% of the packed butter sold in the United Kingdom, and that better profits were being earned in the poultry business.

The improved profits had been achieved in spite of the heavy expenses foisted on the group by the government. Taxation now included Corporation Tax at 42½%.

Increasing trade and the fact that Fitch Lovell had been using large overdrafts caused the Board to consider raising extra long-term finance, and in August 1968 it issued 1 share in 8 to ordinary shareholders at 14s. The number of shares issued was 5,332,467.

As no Deputy or Vice Chairman had been appointed since R.E. Blanning vacated this position when he became Chairman, the Board resolved to appoint K.O.G. Huntley. One of the leading solicitors of those days, he had been a member of the Board for ten years, and although he had not been a full time director, the services he had rendered had been of the utmost value. Looking through the records I am impressed that whenever difficulties arose we turned to him. The many financial enterprises and mergers owe much to his wise professional competence and it was a sad loss when he died suddenly in December 1969. He would almost certainly have been the next Chairman of the company. John Betjeman writing of someone who had passed away once wrote – 'It's strange that those we miss the most are those we take for granted'. The same could be said of Oliver Huntley, for he was one of those who tend to be taken for granted, but when the waters became deep one turned unconsciously to him to steer the boat to shore.

R.E. Blanning's reports for 1969 and 1970 stress the continuing trend of the group into food manufacture, processing and packaging, he had the great satisfaction to report profits in 1970 exceeding £3,500,000, an increase of about 50% since he assumed the chairmanship.

A hydrostatic cooker was installed at the Gateacre meat canning plant of Lovell & Christmas, and the Manchester cheese factory moved there after a compulsory purchase order. A new cheese factory was set up at Erith, and the Chairman reported further advances in butter packing. After extensive modernisation and a move to a new factory in East Kilbride in Scotland, Lovell & Christmas were by 1970, packing 12% of the total U.K. production of packed butter under brand names which included *Country Life* (English), *Scottish Pride, Kerrygold* (Irish) *Fernleaf* (New Zealand) and *Kangaroo* (Australian). The largest-ever advertising campaign for *Spam* was launched, and exports of *Spam* were started to Australia, Hales Cakes increased their sales and moved steadily into a position of greater prominence and recognition.

This brings me to the end of the group's development to 1970. As its activities have grown more widespread, it has become more and more difficult to cover adequately everything that has happened. I hope to remedy this in the following chapters which deal in greater detail with the different divisions.

## 10

## THE KEEVILS AND HORSES AND POULTRY

NICHOLAS DE KEVILLY of Camelay, a village of Somerset in 1260, is the first name in records of this old Wiltshire family. The direct male line is traceable back to 1330. They were nearly all yeoman farmers and as such lived within a radius through the centuries of about 20 miles, so it has been comparatively simple through Baptismal records to trace their ancestry.

They were a quiet lot. None of them seems to have been put in prison, the pillory or the stocks, and there is no record of the early Keevils holding any public office, although armorial bearings were granted in the 16th century to one Thomas Keevill. For his crest he chose a horse's head. If that denoted a particular interest in horses, then it is an interest which has survived down the centuries to modern times. They do not appear to have occupied Keevil Manor or owned the village of Keevil, although certain lands in the Keevil parish belonged to them in the 15th century. Unlike the Lovells in the next county, the Keevils are not recorded as taking part in civil wars, rebellions against the crown or intrigues at court. They were a steady family, and with that steadiness came respect as they grew into one of the leading families in the farming and trading community of the West Country. There was a great deal of intermarriage with other well known local families. Keevil girls married into the Pococks, one of whom, Sir Sydney Pocock, was a noted Liberal politician; into the Frowds who founded the firm of Lilleywhites and Frowd, into the Burnetts who were leaders in the West Country cloth trade and into the Longs. The best known member of this famous Wiltshire family was the Rt. Hon. Walter Long, later Viscount Long, who served in various Tory governments in the latter part of the 19th century and during the First World War. He was considered seriously for the post of Conservative leader in 1910 and would probably have been chosen had it not been for the influence of the industrial interest in the party which preferred Bonar Law.

I think it will be sufficient for present purposes to start with my great-great-great-grandfather, Richard Keevil, who was born in 1710 and died in March 1770. He was a Master Thatcher employing 100 men and left £18,000 on his death, a very large sum indeed in those days.

One of the beneficiaries presumably was his fifth son, also called Richard, who was my great-great-grandfather. He was born in 1737 and was almost certainly the first member of the family to secede from the Church of England in the religious revival and revolt against the Established Church which swept through the West Country in the mid-18th century.

The family became Independents and then Particular Baptists. Richard Keevil (II) and his wife and children would have been baptised by immersion in a flowing river. His example was soon followed by his relations. Many of the numerous members of a prolific family became preachers in Independent chapels throughout Wiltshire and Somerset. They must have been men and women of a determined character, for at that time dissenters were still subject to legal restrictions and social ostracism.

One of Richard Keevil (II)'s sons was called Job, he was my great-grandfather. He lived to the age of 92. He and a brother both left £18,000 – which would be worth at least seven times that figure now. Job Keevil had 12 children, and one of them was my grandfather Peter. He was born in 1807. It is quite something to be able to say that one's grandfather was born 163 years ago.

Peter Keevil was a much loved man. When I was young, I was told many stories about his kindness, unfailing good temper and charitable acts. My mother and others said, 'He was the kindest man we ever knew'. Someone wrote a small book about him called *The Happy Wiltshire Farmer*, and copies of it are still in existence. He was a staunch Independent and the leader of the Baptist faith in his district. Like the others, he was baptised in the open river. His tomb is to be found in a family vault in the Baptist churchyard at North Bradley. Many other members of the family are buried there too. He was educated at Taunton, where my father and eldest brother Percy were also educated.

A good farmer and a prominent member of the Taunton Corn Exchange, in about 1850 he increased the wages of his men from

8s. to 9s. a week, much to the fury of the other farmers in the area who accused him of being sentimental and refused to speak to him. He is said to have died from a heart attack while running to catch a train. Certain of his descendants also have the habit of hurrying at the last moment to arrive in time for their appointments.

Peter Keevil married twice. The names of his wives and children read like extracts from the Bible. His first wife was called Karen Happoch after the wife of Job, their three sons were called Enoch, Noah and Job. His second wife was called Mary, and he had 11 more children by her. Their first four sons were called Peter, James, John and Joshua. My father, the 11th of the 14 children, was named Clement. He was no doubt called after the Clement in one of St. Paul's letters, where he mentions a list of people and adds 'and Clement also'.

Obviously employment could not be found for all the members of this large family. The first to leave home was Job. He came to London and founded the wholesale provision firm of Keevil & Best in Cowcross Street, Smithfield. It is reported to have been the leading firm about 1850 at the time when the Lovells first came up from Somerset. Job Keevil is said to have dressed immaculately and driven the smartest horse and trap in town.

Peter (II), the eldest son by the second marriage, came to London some years later and began the firm which became known as Peter Keevil & Sons Ltd. It is remembered by very many in the Trade today as the largest purely wholesale firm of provision merchants in the Southern Counties. Following the death of his brother Job, Peter acquired the firm of Keevil & Best and also some years later George Bowles, Nicholls & Co. Ltd. Peter Keevil's became prominent manufacturers of margarine at their Western Margarine Co. Ltd. After 70 years' trading, and the death of Peter and his two eldest sons, the business was sold to Garfield Weston by Peter's remaining son, Frank. It had become a public company in 1947. The name was changed to Food Securities Ltd. and still operates under that style.

Like all the family, Peter (II) was passionately fond of horses and farming, and as he prospered he bred horses and farmed on a large scale. For this reason he was delighted when his younger brother Clement also decided to come to London in 1866. Clement, then barely 16 already had a reputation as a judge of horses. It may have been that which earned him a reputation as the brightest of the family. Apparently when my father left home he was told to be sure to look after Peter because he was slow and not too clever. If there are any who remember Peter (II) this advice will raise a smile. He was a veritable giant in his industry, almost if not quite on a par with John Lovell.

The two brothers came to an understanding that, although they would trade separately, Clement should not enter the provision trade. Instead he was to concentrate on poultry and meat. Even at the end of his life he was unwilling to enter the bacon trade in competition with his brother except on a small scale.

Clement launched out on his own in 1872 by opening a store in Brixton. It was on the main Brighton Road near the railway bridge, where there is a branch of Boots the chemist now. He used to buy goods in the Central Markets and was almost immediately spotted as a young man of unusual alertness. Frederick Dean, a wholesale poultry and game dealer asked him to come into partnership. Dean's firm had been established in the Old Newgate Market in 1794. Clement, only 23 or 24, agreed. He left his business in the care of his manager, Thomas Weston, after having owned it for only two years. However, instead of devoting all his time to the business, he could not keep away from Shire Horses, a hobby which became almost an obsession with him. It gave him intense happiness all his life, but it hindered the complete commercial success which he was so well equipped to have attained.

He married my mother, Emma Louisa Long about this time. She was the daughter of Richard (Penruddoch) Long, and they had 12 children. I was the last, born some seven years after the 11th.

Only two of us are still living, the other being my sister Elsie who lives in Saskatoon, Canada. (She married for the third time at the age of about 80.) Apart from myself, I think my father's favourite was Roland. (He went to Canada with some horses of my father and stayed there. He took up painting when he was approaching 70 – with some considerable success for pictures of his are in the Canadian Academy. Others can be seen in the Beaverbrook collection, and Princess Margaret also bought one or two.)

Another of my brothers, Archie, followed Roland to Canada with the ambition of becoming a preacher. Even as a boy he used to preach to the poultry from the top of a hen-coop. Eventually he did find his way into the Church and became Bishop for all Canada of the Reformed Episcopal Church. (The tributes paid to him on his death were all full of his kindly nature and willingness to help all those in need. A memorial book containing his hymns and poems was published by his many friends.) Another brother, Norman, was an actuary with the General Accident Insurance Corporation at Perth in Scotland.

Among my numerous cousins, I would like to mention Captain Cecil Keevil, the son of my uncle Richard, the favourite brother of my father. Cecil fought in the Boer War and then came back to his death in the First World War. He was killed when his aeroplane was the only one sent up against a Zeppelin over St. Paul's Cathedral. His sister Gladys Richford was one of the original Suffragettes, her membership number in the movement was 20. She had extraordinary good looks and when she rose to heckle Winston Churchill about 1909, he said, 'I don't like being interrupted, but it is not so bad when one is heckled by a beautiful lady'.

Commander John Keevil, D.S.O., was another distinguished cousin. He became a naval historian and the Secretary to the British Medical Society. His comparatively early death was a great loss to the literary world.

Like most Victorians, my father was a stern disciplinarian, but he was so pleased with my arrival after such a long time that he allocated a special cow to provide milk for me, and he is reputed to have said, 'I have made all my children afraid of me but this one will love me'. As I grew up I became his inseparable companion. Even when I was only seven or eight we would spend long hours together with the stud books of the Shire Horse Society and the Hackney Horse Society. He would boast that I knew more about pedigrees than he did. Earlier still I would ride on the cross bar at the rear of his tricycle, and when he went to Horse Shows I would sit astride his shoulders, although I could see little because of his tall felt top hat. This spoiling could have harmed me, but for the discipline imposed on me by the older members of the family.

Clement had farms and breeding establishments at Penge in Kent, at New Malden in Surrey, Leighton Buzzard in Bedfordshire and Little Horkesly on the Suffolk borders where he died in 1925. My mother did not share his enthusiasm for farming, and so for 20 years his home was situated at Watford and Harold Wood, half way between the farm at Leighton Buzzard and Horkesly and the City.

In spite of his interest in the horses, my father made a point of always being in Smithfield not later than 6 o'clock. On a typical working day, he would leave home at 4.30 or 5 o'clock in the morning in order to reach the City on time. Then, the morning business done, he would leave for his farm about 10 a.m. and return home about 8.30 p.m. I would wait for him and watch him write notes to his farm bailiff whom he had left only an hour before Then I would run and catch the 9.15 p.m. post. My father would eat and be in bed by 9.45 p.m. It was a hard routine with little time for relaxation or social life, but he never seemed to tire.

Frederick Dean soon faded out of the business. Clement found that he could not run the firm on his own and find time for his horses, and so he persuaded Thomas Weston to become his partner. By this time Tom Weston had bought the store which he managed for Clement but agreed to come to Smithfield and join him. For 25 years the firm traded as Keevil & Weston. Weston was a first class salesman, and Clement with his engaging personality was adept at attracting large consignments from the farms to which he travelled frequently. The business was mainly the selling of poultry, game, eggs and pigs from the English countryside.

Clement's austere religious upbringing had instilled in him the virtue of honesty, and as time went on he became increasingly unhappy about the method used generally at that time of charging 5% commission on sales. He was aware, as he wrote up his daily commission sale return, that frequently the goods of two or three farmers would be sold together. The quality of the produce might vary considerably; although the buyer might pay a higher price for one consignment than another, the commission would be worked out on the whole sale. Consequently the money paid to the farmer who had sent the superior goods would be lessened by being bulked with the inferior.

The system also encouraged unscrupulous traders to write down a higher price than was actually made and calculate their commission on that. If the market was falling, there was no way that the consigner could detect this. The same trick could be worked on a rising market.

Clement decided he would try a different method entirely. He began to pay the farmers 'net prices' which would be fair to the senders and give him a reasonable profit. It meant that they had to trust him more, but it protected them against the snags of pure commission selling. Keevils still operate in this way, and it has become a common practice in the trade.

Market business in the closing years of the 19th century was brisk but the working hours were short. Work began at 5 o'clock in the morning. All sales made by 8 o'clock had to have commission accounts completed and the cheques ready for posting by 9 o'clock. Cheques for sales made before midday had to be ready for dispatch by 1.30 p.m. The salesmen would leave at 1 o'clock and the office would close at 2. Clement had the business carefully organised, he divided it into eight departments under a manager, and he was insistent that each manager had an understudy. He must have been a good judge of men, because several of his employees became leading figures in the trade when they began businesses of their own. I can remember Ernest Russell of Russell Woodhouse Ltd., Joseph Richards, Chairman of R. Gunner Ltd., Frank Pinnock of the Northlight Egg Co. Ltd., Charles Rodgers of Sumeray & Rodgers Ltd., L. Hewitt of Gracey Bros. and many others.

They were good days in the market then. Who will say that the men who lived and worked either as employers or employed in the latter days of the 19th century in Smithfield were not happier in many ways than we are now? For the salesman, the early mornings and the hectic hours of trading were compensated by the comparatively short hours. Many of them took up sport in the afternoons, provided that is, that they could resist the delights of the Smithfield public houses which were open from midnight and all the time that the market was trading. Many notable athletes came from Smithfield. I can remember, among Keevil's staff, Harry Blackstaffe, six times the winner of the Diamond Sculls, and Gus Hodges, a cycling champion.

It was an attractive pattern of living for the employers too, and profits for the successful came relatively easily. So it was that few of them troubled to expand their businesses outside the market. Their complacency contrasts strangely with the energy of men in other parts of the food trade, like John Lovell, William Vestey, Thomas Borthwick and John Sainsbury who all founded vast companies.

The firm of Keevil & Weston, at any rate prospered well within the confines of the market. By 1900 it was generally considered to be one of the two or three largest in the wholesale poultry and game trade. Clement and his partner, however, were never on intimate

44. Clement Keevil, I, 1851-1925

# NOTICE.

1. No Smoking allowed on or about the premises, Farm buildings or Stock-yards.

2. A place for everything and every-thing in its place.

3. Untidyness means waste, waste brings want.

4. Take care of other people's property as if your own.

5. Do not put off till to-morrow what should be done to-day.

6. A stitch in time saves nine.

7. Do it now!

8. Do not to-day what to-morrow you will wish you had not done.

9. Waste not, want not.

CLEMENT KEEVIL.

45. Instructions issued by Clement Keevil, I, in 1900

46. E. White, A.C.A. Keevil, C.E. Nokes
Directors of Keevil & Keevil Ltd.

47. Keevil's destroyed premises:
the Smithfield fire, 1958

48. Offices and Warehouse: Keevil & Keevil Ltd.,
57/59 Charterhouse Street, London, E.C.

49. Modern Poultry Packing Station:
J.H. Brown Abbotshay Ltd.

terms. He treated Tom Weston as very much the junior, but Weston looked upon himself as the mainstay of the business.

One reason for this, perhaps, was Clement's continuing involvement with his horses, which were known wherever Shire horses were bred. Edward VII bought horses from him, and the Duke of Albany personally visited the stud. Stallions were sold to the Argentine, America, Canada and all over Europe. He was one of the founders of the Van Horse Parade in Regent's Park which is still held in 1970. In his day there were many hundreds of entries to the Parade, but now only a few remain, although more entries have been attracted in recent years.

Several famous horses were bred in his stables or passed through them, some of their names still appear in present day records, for example – Blagdon Benefactor, Lockinge Blagdon, Fen Champion and Lady Harold.

He was one of the first in the country to realise the potential of the Freisian breed of cattle, and I believe he was one of the founders of the British Friesian Society. He was a great believer in good pastureland and insisted that there should be lots of clover in his meadows. Some 30 years after his death, a well-known landowner said to me, 'I have never seen such splendid fields as your father had'.

Clement was popular with his fellow traders at Smithfield. He led a successful battle against the Corporation of London which was trying to move the poultry merchants into a different part of the market. In 1888, when he was 37, some 200 merchants and salesmen nominated him to stand for election to the Common Council and represent their interests, among them were John Cary Lovell, Isaac Beer, Henry Gillham and John Bidwell. The roll of firms supporting Clement 83 years ago is an indicator of the pace of change in the food industry. Only about a dozen of them are still in business, and half of those are part of the Fitch Lovell Group.

Clement's programme was on the side of progress. He wanted electric light brought to the City, the construction of a new vegetable market, improved railway facilities at Smithfield and an equitable manner of dealing with the water rate. However he found he did not really enjoy the Common Council, the Guildhall and the Mansion House. In spite of his overwhelming majority he retired after three years and did not stand again.

The business, meanwhile, was changing. With the coming of refrigeration, poultry imports rose sharply, whereas before they had come mainly from France and Italy, they came before the turn of the century from Canada, America, and particularly from Russia. Clement, with his conservative love of English produce and the English countryside disapproved of the new import trade but Tom Weston saw to it that the firm had a fair share.

Weston died rather suddenly in 1908. It was something my father was not prepared for. He had always hoped my brother Roland would come into the business, but he had sent Roland on a trip to Canada with an outstanding stallion which he was showing at an exhibition in Toronto. Roland liked the country and decided to stay there.

For the time being, there was nothing for it but for Clement to manage on his own. With a heavy heart he sold all his horses at a time when his stud was at its peak, and determined to give his time to the business.

Fortunately my brother, C. Percy Keevil wished to marry at the time and was willing to settle down in London. He was living then in Manchester but he agreed to come South if my father would offer him a partnership. This he did. He offered Percy three sevenths of the business, provided he paid for his share of the assets plus three years' profits as goodwill. This was the normal arrangement in those days, and I became a partner 12 years later on the same terms. My father lent Percy the necessary money at 5% and allowed him £400 a year until the money was repaid.

Ever since he left school, where he had distinguished himself in mathematics, C. Percy Keevil had only two ambitions – success in business and success in the cricket field. He certainly achieved the first. Even before his return to London in 1910 at the age of 33, he had already done well in the silk industry. He was anxious to take over the office and administration of the family business, but Clement Keevil would have none of it. 'You have to learn to buy, sell, and make a profit', he said, 'my office is well run. Those in charge have been there twenty years. You keep away from them and learn how to make money'.

Ironically, only a few years later it was discovered that the three senior clerks had embezzled more than £6,000 by keeping duplicate ledgers and cash books. (This is the equivalent of about £30,000 today.) My brother was then given a free hand in the office!

In the meantime, he had shown that he possessed real ability as a merchant, and within a year of his arrival business had increased noticeably.

In 1911 the *Meat Trades Journal* wrote a special article on Clement Keevil headed 'Men we meet at Market'. It mentions the building of a cold store, and the sale of 50,000 Russian chickens to a West End store. The store was Harrods and the quantity was enormous for the time, although it sounds almost routine in these days of mass-produced broiler chickens.

I mentioned earlier that my father was not keen on foreign produce or on the import trade. One country he did enjoy doing business with was France. We imported a large number of French turkeys at the time, and we also sent them certain grades of Russian poultry for which there was no demand in England. I think his liking of France was partly the result of his interest in the French Percheron breed of heavy horse.

One night during my school holidays he came home from visiting his brother-in-law, the Rev. E. Heath Brown who was the English representative of the French Protestant Churches presided over by the famous Pasteur Saillens, known as the French Spurgeon. To my surprise my father announced that my uncle was arranging for me to go to Paris at the end of the next school term and study French. I was to stay at the home of Saillens' daughter. It was not only his liking of French horses which prompted my father to send me to Paris, he also always regretted his own lack of knowledge of foreign languages and was determined that I should not suffer this disadvantage. Whatever the reason was, I cannot be sufficiently thankful to him. As well as increasing enormously my outlook and education I also met in Paris the lady who is now my wife.

On my return from Paris I entered the firm. I began as an office boy, at £1 a week (high wages at that time and showing favouritism), but I was soon permitted to arrange the prices of foreign exchange.

Payments were made promptly to European countries as soon as goods were sold, and it was essential to buy foreign currency at the lowest price – even 1/16 of a penny made a difference – to increase profit. The first firm I remember dealing with in the money market was Singer & Friedlander. I remember Samuel Montagu too. They were very helpful, particularly a Mr. Weinberg. I used to think it great fun to try half a dozen houses to find the lowest rate.

I thought nothing of fixing a rate three or six months in advance. To me the hour by hour fluctuations in the price of money was no different from the fluctuations in the price of chickens in the poultry market. I was still in my late teens when I was playing this game of almost high finance. That is why, I suppose, I have never been able to understand the bright boys in the modern banking world who are afraid of the operation of a floating pound.

Gradually, however, I began to become more involved in the real business of buying and selling in the Market. Each morning I used to buy quantities of game and small Russian chicken for export to the Continent. It was a good merchanting education, but I cannot remember making much profit. Then my father put me in charge of the New Zealand and Australian meat section in place of a charming but usually inebriated Scotsman. I was just 19. I began in a rising market, helped by purchases already made for future delivery of many thousands of New Zealand lambs. Soon I had increased the trade. Everyone was high in my praise and I thought I was a budding genius. I continued to buy heavily on the rising market as everyone told me lambs would be short. The inevitable happened; the market collapsed and the sorry loss was more than £2,000, a lot of money in those days. All my father said to me was, 'I hesitated about sending you to a University, it would have cost about the same, but I expect this experience will have done you as much good as Oxford or Cambridge'. Whether he was right or not I do not know, but I still shudder when I see young and enthusiastic people following a short and rising market.

By this time the name of the business had been changed to Keevil & Keevil because my brother had become a partner. Always very much an autocrat, my father refused to allow the firm to become a Limited Company. He used to say, 'People confide their goods to me. I like their trust and wish to be responsible personally for any debts which I could not be in a company with limited liability'.

It never occurred to the traders in the great distributing markets of London before the First World War that the markets could diminish in importance, and so when Keevils' decided to expand they decided to do so by acquiring tenancies in Leadenhall and Billingsgate. They took over an ailing business in Leadenhall Market, but the venture was not a great success and the tenancy was sold after a couple of years. No suitable opportunity occurred in Billingsgate.

The only way the firm became involved in ventures outside the world of the markets was through its efforts to recover bad debts, which were one of the big problems in those days. Although every invoice was scrutinised by the partners themselves, a month rarely passed without two or three customers being in difficulties. The firm tried to run the businesses of defaulters on several occasions. Keevils sometimes managed to put them on their feet and enable them to pay their debts, but I cannot remember any real successes with this policy. Once we took over a restaurant in Soho and renamed it the KK Restaurant. I think it must have been in 1911. One of my jobs was to pay regular visits to the place, inspect the books and try to find out if the staff were honest. No profits were made and happily the restaurant was sold. As far as I can remember, the manager bought it and altered the name. I was never much good as a caterer, and I did not do very well when I tried my hand as a waiter either! Still, it gave me a little more experience. One thing I learnt was to look with suspicion on the practice of taking over firms who owe money and become unable to meet their commitments.

Suddenly, the Great War was upon us. Like so many of my friends I could not volunteer for the army quickly enough. I left behind my meat departments without adequate management just at a time when they were improving nicely. I see from the record that they gained some notoriety after my departure for selling large quantities of Australian sheep at 2½d. per lb. and River Plate lambs at 5d. a lb., or about 12s. 6d. each.

My brother Percy always suffered from a duodenal ulcer, and about 1916 or 1917 he collapsed in the market with a perforation. No doubt he would have died but for the timely intervention of Dr. Westerman, a noted City character who carried on a practice for about 50 years in Snow Hill.

My father continued trading as best he could under the mild government control of those days, then six months later Percy was back. At once he began a wholesale business in canned goods, one of the few items practically free from direction. The end of the war found me in Netley Hospital recovering from wounds. Meanwhile I had got married, and so I made an application for immediate demobilisation. It was granted without delay on a temporary basis. The actual termination of my service was delayed until 1921.

Percy and I were so anxious to proceed with building the business again that I took only a few days leave before joining him. In the last years of the war my father had bought another farm at Horkesly near Colchester and was taking a much less active part in the business. He had begun building another stud of Shire horses to which he gave suitable wartime names – Blagdon Shrapnel, Blagdon Howitzer, Blagdon Barrage, Blagdon Nordenfeldt and so on. He loved these beasts so much that he hardly realised that the day of the heavy horse was over. With tears in his eyes five or six years later he had to have all his stallions castrated, and they ended their days as cart horses. It was a tragic fate for these noble animals, but the cost of keeping them in stud was prohibitive when no one wanted their progeny.

My mother died a year or two after the armistice and my father moved permanently to Horkesly. After that we saw very little of him at Smithfield.

The price of poultry was still controlled, and because of this, practically none were sent on commission. Apart from French and Irish turkeys at Christmas, there were as yet no imports from Europe, and so we decided to build up a wholesale provision business. As I have said, we had a gentleman's agreement about provisions with my uncle Peter. We told him of our intentions and he said he did not object. We were able to obtain the services of several useful people demobilised from the Services and so we formed a useful team.

We expanded in other ways too in this period. In 1921, I think it was, we bought a public house and also a coffee house next door to Lovell & Christmas. The address was 23-24 King Street, now Smithfield Street. We converted these into small warehouses. They were completely destroyed during Hitler's War. (The new buildings constructed on the site are now occupied by Payne & Son.) At about the same time, my brother arranged to take over the manager and travellers of a canned goods firm which had closed down in the post-war slump. From this date onwards the provision departments gradually improved, although their progress fluctuated somewhat.

On decontrol, we decided not to enter the meat trade seriously because the rest of the business was progressing rapidly. As far as poultry was concerned. I was responsible for imports from France, Italy and Canada. Keevils' had not been leading importers from these countries in pre-war days, but it was not long before we were among the two or three most important. I do not claim credit for this achievement for myself. Percy, and through him, the firm, had a reputation for complete honesty in trading, and he was known and respected throughout the country. He was able to effect sales during my absence abroad to obtain supplies. Our success was entirely due to a team effort.

I was proud of my efforts in the Normandy goose trade, however. Before the war Lovell & Christmas had a virtual monopoly of it, and I can remember going with my father to call on John Cary Lovell to purchase 50 cases at a time. By the 1920s, however, Lovell's was not so active in Normandy and it was an exhilarating moment when I managed to persuade its shipper to transfer his allegiance to us.

Talking of geese brings me naturally to turkeys. There are many still alive who remember the great turkey slump of Christmas 1923. 1920, 1921 and 1922 had all been excellent years, and so in the autumn of 1923 buyers flocked abroad to buy the birds. Prices opened in excess of 3s. a lb. Everyone was sure the market must rise, but Percy sent me a telegram in November when I was buying on the Continent. It read, 'Be careful. Someone will have a headache before Christmas'. As so often, his judgment was right. Prices tumbled from 3s. to 4d. a lb. Even at this price the turkeys could not all be sold. No refrigerated wagons were used in those days and tens of thousands of birds had to be destroyed.

After this catastrophe, Edward Freeman of J.J. Freeman Ltd., called a meeting of importers to try and obtain agreement about maximum buying prices. There were about 50 of us, if I remember aright. Surprisingly everyone agreed the unusual unanimity having been encouraged by the severity of the losses all were nursing. A loose type of association was formed, and, as I was the youngest, I was appointed secretary. Later in the year I was sent to France to spy out the prospects for the forthcoming season. I remember that I was due to return on a certain day to report to a specially convened meeting. I arranged to come back by air, but air travel was uncertain as well as a little dangerous in those days 45 years ago. My plane was caught up in storms and the meeting had to be disbanded. In spite of this early setback, the pricing arrangements worked reasonably well and went on right up to the outbreak of war in 1939. The association became known as the 'Hopeful Club' but by the end the number of importers had shrunk from 50 to a dozen.

Talking of turkeys reminds me of another incident in the French Christmas trade which ended in a High Court action. One morning during Christmas week in 1922 I was in the warehouse at King Street, when the manager of Mory & Co., the transport agents came in, accompanied by a woman heavily veiled in black as though she was in deep mourning. Mory's man said the woman had lost her husband suddenly and that he had exported, via Mory, a large number of turkeys to London, and as she knew no one, she had come to ask Mory to find a buyer. More out of sympathy than need I bought them. The woman asked if she could have payment then and there, as she wished to return and bury her husband. My father happened to come into the warehouse at that moment, and I asked him if he would see to the payment. This he did, even to the extent of taking the woman to the bank and making sure the cheque was cashed. The turkeys were delivered and sold, if my memory is reliable, either to the Army & Navy Stores or the Civil Service Stores.

A month later a friend, who was an importer came to see me and said he was taking an action against me for stealing his property, namely the turkeys for which he had paid against railway receipt in France. The woman had drawn her money from her bank against railway receipt, caught the night train to London and sold the turkeys a second time to us. The importer took the action against both Keevils and/or Mory. We won eventually, but not without help from Holman Gregory K.C., later the Recorder of London. I was sorry for the importer, but the episode showed the need for extreme caution in opening credits.

My father died suddenly in 1925 from a perforated duodenal ulcer. Ulcers are something of a family complaint. Under the rules of partnership, there had to be a stock-taking the next day, and accounts had to be prepared within a fortnight, so that his two sevenths share could be divided between Percy and me on the basis of payment of assets plus three years goodwill. This meant finding a large sum of money very quickly in cash. It was far more than I possessed – the profits of the previous years had been good. My father-in-law stepped into the breach and lent me the money at 6½%. I was able to repay it in less than four years, but only by cutting my personal expenses to an absolute minimum.

My father's will is typical of the way responsible people dealt with their estates at that time. The money was to be divided between his many children. The shares allocated to any unmarried daughters were to be invested on their behalf in Government stock yielding not less than 5%. My eldest sister died at the age of 88, some 40 years later. The war Loan purchased at £100 was sold for £36 and the cost of living had risen three times.

My father's death was the end of an era. We marked the new order by immediately forming a limited company. In spite of the difficult trading conditions into which we were heading, the new company did very well and doubled its profits within four years. The good results were due to a large degree to the friendship, almost the partnership, between Percy and Stephen Siratsky of Fitch & Son. It was also due to a wise policy of non-speculation in an era of increasing world supplies and falling prices. Even during the worst years of the international slump the returns improved. They reached their peak in 1932, and hard though it is to believe, the trading profits were higher than 25 years later in spite of inflation. In fact we were surprised to see published figures of large public companies in the trade comparing badly with our own. In 1939 when the Ministry of Food assembled figures on the poultry industry for its war-time organisation, Keevils' sales' turnover was the highest in both the home and the imported trades.

The Christmas trade naturally was very important in the poultry business. We were buying turkeys further and further afield. Apart from France and Italy, they were coming from Hungary, Jugoslavia, Roumania and Canada. At the height of the Christmas rush there might be as many as 30 railway trucks carrying 100,000 turkeys rolling towards London from Central Europe at the same time. It was a hazardous business for these trucks were uninsulated. They were made of wood and cooled only by a tray of ice which would be put into each truck at the start of its six day journey. Similar arrangements were made for poultry from the South of France, which was four days' journey away. We were entirely in the hands of the weather. Any form of delay could be disastrous. I remember one year nine trucks with 3,000 turkeys in them were derailed. The entire consignment was seized by the authorities as unfit for human consumption. Not surprisingly, we found it hard to keep our eyes off the weathercock on the market tower, hoping to find it pointing North or East. We lost business of course if supplies failed to arrive in good condition, but the risks of the pre-war markets were carried mainly by the shippers. Percy Keevil insisted that he was a commission salesman and rarely speculated.

It was in Percy's nature to follow a policy of safety first, but I think the Depression caused us all to have a defensive outlook, In fact at one point a plan was evolved to form a joint public company with other firms at all levels in the trade. There was support for the plan in the financial world, but the firms we approached were nervous of the outlook and apprehensive of the possibility of war, and so the plan was shelved.

By this time, around 1936, both Percy and I were beginning to feel that we had had enough of the market. He wanted to take up farming, and I was offered the chance of representing two safe constituencies to become a Member of Parliament. Accordingly, we approached Lovell & Christmas and asked them if they were interested in buying our firm. Our reception from J.G. Elliott was not encouraging. We tried another friend and put the same proposition to him, but once again without success. We even thought seriously of going public by ourselves, and a draft prospectus was prepared. All ideas like these were quickly stopped by the approach of war.

I was Chairman of the Co-ordination Committee of the Provision Exchanges of the United Kingdom and the information available to me forced me to the conclusion that war was inevitable and unlikely to be long delayed. I realised that the Munich agreement in 1938 which was welcomed by the ordinary folk of Great Britain could only put off hostilities for a short time. The war scare at the time of the Munich crisis could readily have sent food prices up sharply, but the President of the Board of Trade asked me to obtain a gentleman's agreement that prices would be frozen. The Trade played its part magnificently.

The Government in the shape of the Food (Defence Places) Department wrote a letter to me as Chairman of the National Provisions (Defence) Committee thanking us for the good example we set as this extract shows. 'As you are aware, the agreement was followed by similar agreements in a large number of other trades, and this proved of real national value.' The letter was published in *The Grocer* in October 1938.

The National Provision (Defence) Committee was eventually superceded by the wartime arrangements which were proceeding space. One of these was the Ministry of Food's London Area Committee (Provisions & Grocery). I assumed the Chairmanship of it and later of the committee with responsibilities for the East and South East areas of England. The main function of these committees was to ensure continuity of supplies in the event of the destruction of the warehouses and buildings of the wholesale provisions and grocery trades. The duties became very hectic during the heavy bombing of London. All the firms in the heavily populated areas were asked to make alternative arrangements to carry on their businesses if they were bombed out. Keevil's, like the others, prepared depots outside London.

In my wartime administration job, which I held until I was appointed to a Command by the Army in 1942, I was given as secretaries first Farrant Gillham of Henry Gillham and later Dudley Game. I was glad to leave the Ministry because I was by temperament a most unsuitable civil servant.

The streams of paperwork and the delays before decisions were reached were naturally foreign to someone brought up and trained as I had been. I was much more at home with the quick decisions needed during air raids. I was succeeded by G.R. Bradfield, the Chairman of Bishops Stores and of Harvey Bradfield Ltd., a good friend and probably more suitable than I.

While I was Chairman, I organised the Trade Association to control imported poultry and rabbits, helped by my brother Percy and I. Graul of the Ministry of Food, a man who was never appreciated as he should have been, in my opinion. Percy was Chairman of the new organisation, but Alan Sainsbury (now Lord Sainsbury) was anxious to have the position. He persuaded my brother, who hated taking chairs or public speaking, to relinquish the chair in his favour. The change was not greeted with universal approval in the trade because there was some doubt as to whether J. Sainsbury's were really importers. However he proved a first class Chairman.

Keevils' suffered a great deal of bomb damage. Nos. 23 and 24 King Street were destroyed. Nos. 228 and 229 Central Market were reduced to a mass of rubble and 36 Snow Hill was badly damaged. Yet with the indomitable spirit of the old yeomen of England, Percy refused to be shifted from Smithfield where he had traded for so long. In fact he defied orders from the Ministry of Food to move. The fact that the orders were given and signed by me did not make the slightest difference to him.

Percy and the Market Superintendent, Ernest Hornsby used to do firewatching together, and some important buildings were saved by their vigilance on more than one occasion. The other members of staff who had not been called up for active service also took their turns at firewatching. One of them, Mears, was killed when a V.2. rocket burst nearby.

As the war and the wartime controls dragged on, the profits of Keevils' suffered. Once again Percy and I began to feel that we had had enough, and again we talked about selling the business. I spoke about this to J.T. Clayton, a director of Fitch & Son and the Secretary of our Wartime Wholesale Group. Accordingly, I went to see H.S. Rowlandson immediately after the war. We could see no point in soldiering on with the business, at that time. Percy had four daughters and no sons, and I had no idea that my son would want to enter the business.

H.S. Rowlandson was quite co-operative and an agreement was reached for Fitch to buy a majority interest. I found that their provisions side was hardly of the same calibre as ours, although they had made good profits from their other interests. Under the deal we made, about half Keevils' profits were to remain with Percy and me. In fact it was a favourable bargain for Fitch because from 1946 Keevils' profits began to improve and in only a few years they reached £100,000. I had no complaints, because I was able to purchase Fitch shares at a low price and in due course they showed large profits. Also I was given the challenge of wider responsibilities, for I was asked to join the Fitch Board and take over responsibility for the bulk of their provision companies.

I was soon to be proved wrong in my fears that no other member of the family would come into the firm. My son Clement II who had married during the war decided not to go back to Oxford and asked to come into the business. Naturally we could not refuse him, but as he had no business experience we decided to place him under the stern discipline of my brother. Then my son-in-law, John Gilpin asked if he could join us. As he had a penchant for mathematics we placed him in the office. They have both, in different ways, proved their worth. They have always shown their loyalty and have never taken advantage of the fact that they are related to me.

John Gilpin was soon spotted by H.S. Rowlandson, and he asked us to release him to be the Secretary of Fitch & Son Ltd. He then came entirely under H.S.R. and learned a great deal from that shrewd and intelligent man.

The years immediately after the end of the war were taken up with fitting in the men demobilised from the forces, rebuilding, as far as permits allowed, the bomb-damaged premises and trying to extend the business outside the controlled commodities. A large number of pre-war records had been destroyed, and there was a big task to be done in putting the firm in the right shape to face decontrol when it finally came.

To start with the main office was temporarily situated in the upper storey of market stalls to which Percy had moved on the destruction of 228 and 229. It was obvious in 1946 that we should not be able to rebuild 23 and 24 King Street, so we decided to buy the lease of 55 Charterhouse Street from Peek Bros & Winch. The lease was a short one, but the freeholders, the City of London, granted us a new lease of 60 years with the kind help of Ernest Hornsby. The whole of the main building and most of the outbuildings were badly damaged by constant bombing and fires and the next problem was to obtain a building licence.

We approached the great American firm, Armours, and offered to let them use the top two floors as offices. They agreed and exercised influence through American channels to obtain the necessary permits. Almost certainly we would not have obtained them without the help of Armours. The rebuilding and the conversion of the upper floors into offices took nearly two years.

The work was slightly delayed by a discovery made by the builders. While they were excavating in the yard adjoining the railway lines, they came upon large numbers of skeletons. Almost certainly, they had uncovered some 17th-century plague pits. The bones, disturbed after resting tranquilly for 300 years, had to be carefully moved away under the supervision of the Church. According to one theory, a tributuary of the Fleet River ran past the Charterhouse in those days, and it was the custom at that time to bury plague victims in the banks of rivers.

My brother Percy decided to retire in 1953, the year following his 75th birthday. The previous Christmas was the first time since the war that Christmas turkeys had been decontrolled, and his handling of the market was classic. Turkeys opened at nearly 7s. a lb., with Irish exports easily the dominant factor. During the years of control, the Irish exporters had sent their turkeys to the government war-time Association. In this year of decontrol they continued to send them to the importers who had been members of the Association in the same proportion as they had been allocated during control. The wartime allocations had been based on pre-war sales figures certified by the Ministry of Food. As Keevil's had the largest pre-war sales, they received the biggest share. Percy Keevil judged that the market must fall, and so he opened his sales at 6s. a lb., about 9d. under the price of the market. Once again he was right. Within ten days the market price fell to 4s. a lb. Percy had made a good proportion of his sales at 6s. when the rest of the market were trying to get higher prices, and so when the accounts were summarised, his average price was far and away the best in the country.

It was a splendid exit for a man who, although a 'lone bird' was the best judge of the market in his day. In fact he was recognised as one of the two outstanding figures of the trade in Europe. How he would have done today, in the entirely different and much larger trade, it is impossible to say, but in his day he was supreme. As a trader he was a safe man. He seemed to scent bad markets and was never afraid to follow his own opinion, regardless of others. He was exceptionally good at figures, and exercised a tight control over the office. While he was working he talked about nothing but business. In many ways he was a difficult man to work with, secretive and obstinate. Away from business he was quite different, generous and a lover of all sport. As a principal of a medium-sized business he was outstanding, but he was nervous of expanding outside his own metier which he knew so well.

On his retirement, he signed an agreement to remain as an 'advisor' but he insisted on the inclusion of an unusual clause: '. . . he would advise when requested so to do, but even then, only when he wished to do so . . .'. In the event, nothing could keep him away from Smithfield, and he came regularly until he was 89 years of age.

The partial retirement of Percy, my own increasing involvement in Fitch made a great deal of extra work and responsibility fall on my son Clement II. Things were made still more difficult by the death or retirement of the men who had been in charge of departments before the war. They were good reliable men, like Charles Bamfield, who had died, and W. Whitear who retired about this time after many years of good service. One man I remember in particular was W. Portiway, in charge of the bacon departments since 1930. His health was failing and he died several years later. All these men were in the provision section. In the poultry section, Albert Stocker and George Whapshott had gone. All the records have gone too, I am afraid, and so I cannot give the exact dates.

Clement II realised that it was urgently necessary to obtain fresh blood of high calibre. So in the early '50s, an old established firm in Leadenhall, Sprigens & Co., was purchased from Charles Nokes who was at once made a director. He has since been Clement's right hand. He is a man of considerable charm, with a great capacity for work. He is a first class salesman and a man of the highest integrity, and he has served the company well and loyally ever since he joined it.

At this point, Keevils' was well placed to hold its leading position in the traditional poultry business based at Smithfield. It had moved into the rebuilt premises at 55 Charterhouse Street and was back in 36 Snow Hill. In 1954 Keevils' was able to re-occupy its old premises in the war-damaged poultry market, numbers, 228, 229, 230 and 231. In addition there had been some useful diversification. Keevils' formed a joint company with Elkes Biscuits Ltd., which operated most satisfactorily for some years until it was wound up at the request of Elkes.

Then on the decontrol of meat, Keevils' formed a company with Frank Wallis, which was called Keevil & Wallis Ltd., for the sale of pig meat. It was not a large company but it was never a source of difficulty and from its various stalls in the market provided a profit to the parent company during the 15 years of its existence.

Even the labour difficulties at Smithfield in the late 1940s had been overcome. Keevils' had never had a strike up to that time, but they were caught up for a week in the wave of labour unrest which swept Smithfield. In fact troops were sent into our premises in Charterhouse Street, to ensure the distribution of rationed food. It was amusing to be told by the pickets, 'You know we don't want to strike, but what can we do? You will forgive us Guv'nor'.

Even in the General Strike of 1926, all the staff had turned up and accompanied those of us who went to the docks to obtain our goods. I recollect that in that strike with the exception of one or two rough journeys, not without danger, the atmosphere at the docks and wharves was reasonable and quiet.

Yet however well Keevils' were prepared to do business in the old way, it soon became clear that the old way was gone never to return. Far reaching changes were taking place in both branches of the firm's business – provisions, wholesaling and poultry.

In wholesaling, as we have already seen, self-service stores and supermarkets were radically altering the old pattern of trade, and distribution was moving more and more away from Smithfield.

The changes in the poultry trade were to be even more startling. Intensive culture methods were beginning to spread from America. The emphasis began to swing rapidly from importing to home production on a scale unimaginable before the war. Although the size of the new industry was impossible to forecast in those days, the methods had been foreseen in the late 1930s by Percy Keevil and his friend Siratsky. They conducted some small experiments with frozen eviscerated chicken, but without any success. Like so many pioneers they did not reap the reward of their ideas.

As for the speed at which home poultry production proceeded the statistics speak for themselves. The number of turkeys produced yearly in Britain has increased from one million to nine million, and the elaborate import trade in turkeys which absorbed so much of my energy before the war, has ceased. Even more startling has been the increase in the production of chickens, which has become the most dynamic growth sector of British agriculture. Production of broiler chickens has shot up from five million in 1953 to an astonishing 230 million birds in 1968. The retail price of a roasting chicken was 5s. 6d. a lb. in 1953. By 1968 it had fallen to 2s. 4d. a lb. – a remarkable fact in an age of inflation. Consumption of poultry meat was as follows.

| | *per capita* |
|---|---|
| 1955 | 6.4 lb. |
| 1960 | 11.5 lb. |
| 1965 | 16.4 lb. |
| 1970 | 23.1 lb. |
| 1971 (Estimated – reduction due to fowl pest) | 23.0 lb. |

The growth of the poultry industry and the growth of supermarkets were not unconnected, for practically all the poultry is eviscerated and packed in standard bags and dispatched, frozen, direct from the producers to the multiple shops and supermarkets, by-passing to a large extent the great markets like Smithfield.

The markets have become simply centres for surplus supplies and for fresh poultry. Even so, the growth of the poultry trade has been so fast that the quantity handled by Smithfield is still twice what it was before the war. The market at Smithfield still has a big effect on prices, which bears out the theory that it is the surplus which dictates the price of the whole.

Clearly these dramatic changes could not go unacknowledged by Keevils' if it was to maintain its position in the trade. Clement II saw that if the poultry was largely going to by-pass the wholesalers it was essential to become involved in production, and so in 1958 we set up a packing station at Abbotshay in Hertfordshire. It depended on growers for its supplies, unlike the poultry plants of today with their hatcheries, broiler houses, deep freeze cold stores and insulated vans for delivery. However, it was a beginning. It served, and still serves, as a useful source of supplies, and it was the prototype from which emerged the important poultry operations of Fitch Lovell today.

As things turned out, Keevils' did not become the vehicle for Fitch Lovell's poultry production, although the new business is under the direction of Clement II. I will explain how that happened but first I must finish the story of Keevils', which has remained primarily a market company.

As a market company, its history is interwoven with the history of the market itself, and so I cannot proceed without mentioning the story of the most memorable event in the history of Smithfield. On the night of 22 January 1958, the whole of the Poultry and General markets, carefully rebuilt after the war, were destroyed by fire. Considerable gallantry was shown in salvaging books and stocks and within three days business was resumed. Keevils' were fortunate in having warehouses nearby and also the use of other market premises in the Fitch Group. Less fortunate traders displaced by the fire were allowed to share the stalls of competitors in an adjoining market known as The Village. Obviously this was only an emergency concession, and it was clear that something else would have to be done.

I was asked to convene a meeting of the displaced traders. It was held in our offices in Charterhouse Street, and it was decided to try and find a bombed site and ask the Corporation of London to put up a temporary market.

The Corporation agreed to this plan, and with commendable speed, leased a bombed site at the corner of Hosier Lane and Smithfield Street which had been occupied by I. Beer before the war. They quickly built the temporary market which became the home of the poultry trade until the burned down buildings could be rebuilt. The Corporation were determined to erect a new and modern market and they pressed on at great cost with the construction of the fine new market which stands today. I have particular reason to remember the opening by the Lord Mayor on 5 July 1963 because while I was attending the ceremony, my car, which I had been told to park in Hosier Lane, was towed away by the police and put in a car pound!

In spite of the fire, and the difficulties of trading in a temporary market, Keevils' continued to place its faith in Smithfield. It bought from Fitch & Son the stalls of H.J. Webb & Co., which it found most useful since the space it was allocated in the new market was less than that it had before. Keevils' duck trade is now carried on at Webbs under W. Worton, and is the most important in London and maintains the lead established by Tom Weston 70 years ago. Keevils' also trades in bacon through Webbs and sales of that commodity are doing extremely well.

During the last five or six years, Keevils' has had a stern struggle to maintain its business in changing circumstances. It can be said that it has been reasonably successful – more so than many of its competitors. Ted White who is in charge of the provision department has been made a Director and has carried out his duties with energy and with success. He still retains, for example, the export order for eggs for the British Army of the Rhine. In the poultry department, the old hands have helped Charles Nokes loyally and well.

It is difficult to say what the future will hold. A market firm can keep expenses lower than a traditional wholesaler. In spite of the change, Smithfield remains an important centre, and opportunities occur far more readily in markets than in the carpeted offices of executives. It could be argued that only firms which are owner directed and controlled are in a position to seize the opportunities which arise. The fact remains that the return of capital employed by Keevils' is very high compared with most of the firms in the food trade. If and when Britain joins the Common Market, there should be still more openings, for Keevils' still retains good contacts in all the countries which make up the European Economic Community. It could be a chance to attract young men into the trade once more.

I have now told the story of Keevils' up to the present time. I only wish I could mention more of the men and women who have contributed so much to the business in the 97 years since Clement Keevil first went into partnership with Frederick Dean. However among them I remember Arthur Cox, George Sexton, Harry Dacombe, W. Blake, Frank East, Arkell, Charlie Elliott, Ted Cole and the remarkable Miss Masters who in 1917 was probably the first woman to work full time in Smithfield Market. Later she left to marry and become Mayoress of Ilford.

I may have finished the story of Keevils', but the most exciting chapter in the tale of Fitch Lovell and the poultry industry is still to come. From the beginnings at Abbotshay, Fitch Lovell have become substantial producers of poultry.

The decision to enter this field in a large way was not taken until 1961 when Fitch Lovell acquired by an issue of shares, a firm called W.D. Evans Golden Produce Co. Ltd. Pressure to enter broiler production was strong and it was felt developing Abbotshay would take too long. This new company was really two concerns which had very recently amalgamated. The W.D. Evans side ran chicken hatcheries, and Golden Produce was basically a poultry producing plant with broiler houses. The company, which had only been floated the year before, had already achieved an enviable profit record.

Initially, the existing management continued to run the business. W.D. Evans was mainly engaged in breeding and hatching a commercial strain of pullets known as the Maxi. His company owned six hatcheries, and aimed at a nationwide distribution of his pullets. He was also a pioneer in egg production by contract. Evans joined the Fitch Lovell Board, and initially, all went well. The Maxi won the highest prizes at many national laying trials. Then, within a year of his joining Fitch Lovell, things began to go wrong. Newer and still more productive strains of bird began to appear from America in competition with the Maxi.

Evans, who was a man of much energy, initiative, and optimism, began to look overseas, and he formed a company in Italy which was supposed to be backed by the Vatican. The idea was to invest in poultry production in the depressed areas of Southern Italy. The concern was called Maxilay Italiana and through it Evans hoped to double his company's exports of chicks and eggs. The Fitch Lovell Board were only asked to make a small investment and guarantee a bank overdraft which was insurable, and so it agreed. The venture, which became known as Val Basento never prospered, and it was found to have no written agreement with the Vatican, and so it was decided not to support it with further finance. A final settlement of the Val Basento affair was only reached in 1966, through the untiring efforts of K.O.G. Huntley and E.T. Bur. Another company, which Evans tried to set up in Holland, also failed, and in January 1965, he resigned from the Board.

It was Evans's resignation which led to Clement II's taking responsibility for the Evans concern. It was not long before he found himself with the worries of the Golden Produce side of the business as well.

Golden Produce began in a boat yard at Lymington in Hampshire. It was started by a Mr. and Mrs. Calcutt shortly after the new methods of rearing and processing broiler chickens had reached the country from America. They began by persuading local people to build broiler houses on their land. When the birds were ready, they were sent to Golden Produce for processing and sale on a profit-sharing basis. When production reached 20,000 birds a week, they formed a joint selling company with Henry Gillham Ltd. of Smithfield on a 50-50 basis, called Gillham Golden Produce. It was at this stage that the Calcutts decided to begin rearing day-old chicks themselves and so they decided to merge with W.D. Evans who had always wanted to expand into the table poultry industry.

For some time after Evans's resignation, the Calcutts remained in charge of Golden Produce, but eventually they decided to retire, and so it was that Clement II assumed responsibility for the business which he ran under managers helped by Farrant Gillham of Golden Produce. Sadly, Calcutt did not live to enjoy his retirement. He was killed shortly afterwards in a motoring accident.

Clement II soon became dissatisfied with the results and administration of Golden Produce, and it was decided to call in C.E.M. Hardie (now Sir Charles) to do an investigation and institute really up-to-date methods of costing and accounting.

With the financial side of the business sorted out, Clement and Farrant Gillham turned their attention to the product itself. It was becoming clear that the Maxi bird in which W.D. Evans had invested so heavily, was not holding its own against the international competition. The amount of finance needed to undertake further research and improve the Maxi strain was great and it was decided that it would be better to leave this field altogether and concentrate on producing table poultry. The W.D. Evans hatcheries were kept going, however, producing broiler chicks for Golden Produce. It was a further step towards the fully integrated unit. By this time in the mid 1960s, production was reaching 100,000 birds a week.

The next step was to look at the independent producers who were still supplying fully grown birds for processing. The profit-sharing scheme was unsatisfactory, and so it was decided that the best thing to do was to buy them all out. By this time the aim was total vertical integration, which was furthered by the purchase of a minority interest in a leading manufacturer of foodstuff. About the same time a new hatchery company was formed with a breeding flock farm concern.

Meanwhile, Henry Gillham Ltd. had found itself in an anomalous position, owning half the Golden Produce marketing company. Gillham Golden Produce. Farrant Gillham, the Chairman, agreed that Fitch Lovell should buy a majority interest in the company, and Farrant Gillham became the director responsible for the Golden Produce plant.

I must just pause in this story of modern expansion to write a little about Gillham's, because it is an old Smithfield family closely connected with the Keevils' through their West Country origins. Henry Gillham was the son of a Somerset farmer and he decided that it would be more profitable to sell meat than to rear it. He actually went to Chicago to learn how it was done and then set up in Smithfield in 1881, relying on consignments from relatives and friends in Devon and Somerset. In the early 1890s his nephew, Henry II joined him and 20 years later, around 1911, Henry I sold the business to him and returned to Taunton where he bred prize cattle with considerable success. Farrant Gillham writes, 'When Clement Keevil Senior heard of the exhorbitant price his old friend had charged for the business he went down to Taunton and shamed the old man into reducing the price by £2,000!'

Henry II's health was poor, and he was away from the business for long periods. In spite of this, the firm did reasonably well in their two market stalls. Henry died in 1936, and Farrant took over the business at the early age of 25. He was the youngest tenant in

Smithfield. In 1939 the firm acquired another stall, but all three were destroyed the following year during a bombing raid in September 1940. The business moved, and three weeks later was burnt out by incendiary bombs. As I have said, Farrant became my part-time Secretary at the London Area Office of the Ministry of Food. His cheerful personality and conscientious work were a great help to me in those turbulent and dangerous days. He was asked to join Brigadier General Young in the London and Eastern Area office, which he did to my regret. He was called to the colours in 1941, having formed his firm into a private limited company.

When the market was re-opened in 1954, Gillham's moved back to its old position where it had an excellent block of five stalls with good cold stores. When the market was burned down in 1958, Gillham's went into the temporary market, and moved back into its present premises when the new Poultry Market was opened in 1963. Thus Henry Gillham Ltd. has only spent 11 of the past 31 years in its own premises. I point this out so that present and future generations may know of the spirit which overcomes seemingly insurmountable difficulties. Almost every record has been destroyed. An old wage book from 1892 survives with a laconic note against one name: 'left – embezzled badly'. One highlight of the firm – they won the Smithfield Football cup in 1939, but only because they played their window cleaner, who was an excellent goal keeper.

Gillham's had a 50% interest in J.H. Brown Ltd. a poultry growing and processing company with two factories, one in Norfolk and one in Essex, and it became evident that for complete freedom of action, Fitch Lovell should acquire the balance of the shares in Henry Gillham and the 50% in J.H. Brown, and this was done in 1967. This move brought Fitch Lovell's poultry sales to well over 300,000 birds a week.

Since then, the company has built a new oven-ready plant in Essex, which, when opened, was the most up-to-date in the country. Clement II and his excellent young team must be congratulated for the work they have done and the initiative they have shown. The broiler industry has far outpaced any other aspect of British farming over the past 15 years. It has its own particular hazards due to quick production and fluctuating sales price – it is an industry for young men and there is still room for growth both in this country and overseas.

More than any other part of the Fitch Lovell story, the history of the poultry trade illustrates the main theme of this book, how families mainly in market trade on a small scale grew up and joined together to form a vital part of the modern food industry.

## 11

# ISAAC BEER AND HIS SONS

THERE IS NO NAME which is more closely interwoven with that of Fitch Lovell than Isaac Beer. Isaac Beer appears in the 1856 books of Christmas and Lovell as a customer, and the two firms were soon to become keen competitors in the Ostend trade. Time and again their paths have run together until in 1959 Isaac Beer and Sons Ltd. became part of the Fitch Lovell group.

The story of Isaac Beer goes back to early 19th-century Canterbury and is a tale of a business built up in the face of adversity. 30 years ago A. Ernest Beer wrote a memoir for his family which ended with the words, '. . . it is possible it may interest some others who still believe that there is sentiment, even romance in commerce'. He called the narrative *Isaac Beer and His Sons.* It is an apt title because through most of the history of the firm of Isaac Beer the family has paid a dominant part.

The Beers are of old Kentish stock although the names of Huguenots Chartier and Thorel, who settled in Canterbury after being expelled from France, appear in the family tree. Isaac Beer the founder of the firm, was born in 1818, the son of James Beer, who traded wholesale and retail in provisions and groceries in St. George's Street, Canterbury. For some years, Isaac worked for his father. His abilities must have been outstanding even at this early time, for he managed to persuade someone to lend him £300 to begin his own business.

He is reputed to have begun with only one assistant, a bedroom, one or two chairs and a lard barrel as a table. Resources were so scarce that he had to do all his own cooking. Yet such was the strength of his personality that he managed to do something which was almost unheard of in those days. He courted, and became engaged to, a Miss Mount, the daughter of one of the local landed gentry. The fact that Isaac was in trade was bad enough, but worse, his business was struggling and only recently established. However, he was determined and eventually her parents were reconciled to the match and Beer and Miss Mount were married in 1848.

Isaac soon found Canterbury too small for his activities, and two years later, at the age of 32, he moved nearer London and set up in Deptford, Ernest Beer says Isaac's wife helped 'at the desk' which suggests it was a retail business. She must have been frequently absent from the shop, for children arrived with Victorian regularity. In 10 years, six sons were born. It was hard to obtain good milk in those days, and so Isaac bought a cow for the benefit of the children. He began to sell the surplus to his neighbours. However, he had no licence and he soon came into conflict with the authorities. Once again he got his way, winning the right to trade in milk, and he decided to set up in the dairy business in earnest. He turned his stables into a cowhouse, bought 12 cows and began employing roundsmen. The new venture prospered and he bought Hatcham Manor Farm at New Cross and kept 50 cows.

Isaac Beer seemed to be set fair to make his fortune, but just as everything seemed to be going so well, he was struck two blows which would have been more than enough to crush a man who lacked his relentless determination. First, his highly prized dairy herd was afflicted with cattle plague and had to be destroyed. Then, in 1858 his beloved wife died. Courageously, Isaac battled on.

Luckily the Deptford shop continued to prosper and he was able to support his motherless family. In 1862 he married again and had a further five children by his second wife. Eight years later, she too died. Once again Isaac Beer was left to cope alone, only this time there were even more mouths to feed. Misfortune acted as a spur to greater effort. He decided to begin trading in rabbits and pigs from the Low Countries and in a short time was one of the leaders in the Ostend trade. This made it necessary for him to move nearer the centre of London and he established himself in Southwark Bridge Road where he had a large warehouse, bacon stoves, and stables. This is the first time bacon is mentioned. It was to become a staple part of the business, as the firm have been leading distributors of bacon for the past 100 years. The Ostend trade went so well that during the '60s Isaac sent one of his sons to Belgium to take charge of an exporting house which he had formed there.

The business was now prospering and, following the example of John Cary Lovell and the others of his time, Isaac Beer stopped living over the business and moved out to the then fashionable suburbs. He bought a house first in Peckham and later in Clapham.

The trade in Ostend pigs kept growing, and he decided the time had come to put the seal of success upon his business by moving to the hub of the London provision trade – Smithfield. Fired with enthusiasm for the idea, he bought a site in 1885 opposite the new Poultry Market at 15 King Street, and threw all his energy into the construction of a new building. It was designed with flats over the business area as Isaac had decided he had seen enough of the suburbs, when the building was completed he moved into the flats on the upper storey with his sons and daughters and a housekeeper.

The King Street building had absorbed not only Isaac Beer's enthusiasm, but also a large part of his capital, and when his business was caught in the slump of 1890 he found himself in financial difficulties. His sons who had been with him in the business had to leave to take up other positions, except for Charles, the eldest boy of his second family.

At this low point in his fortunes, and when he was more than 70 years of age, he decided to marry his housekeeper, who became his third wife. He worked early and late with his old determination, in order to rebuild his business. He asked his son Ernest, also of his second family, to rejoin the firm. Ernest, who was now working in a firm of china and pottery makers agreed. By this time Isaac was 76 and failing in health. It was now that John Cary Lovell came to his assistance. It was thought better for Isaac to retire, which he did in 1894, and Charles and Ernest took over the business, backed by their good friend John Cary and began making good the adverse balance and retrieving the family fortunes. Before Isaac died in 1901 he had the satisfaction of seeing his old business revived and his good name restored.

Ernest wrote of him,

> . . . he was a typical Victorian, all through his life a hard worker and resolute fighter. Although outwardly austere, he had always the interests of his large family at heart, gave them a comfortable home and a good education. My brother Charles and I had the advantage of five years at the Merchant Taylors School and subsequently the opportunity to study foreign languages in Germany and France, for which I can never be sufficiently grateful.

When Charles and Ernest took over the business they concentrated on the Belgian trade, and also on Danish bacon and American box goods. (These were preserved meats and bacon which were shipped from the U.S.A. in large boxes.) They built new bacon stoves and engaged more employees. Ernest wrote,

> . . . we toiled early and late, living on the premises. Six o'clock in the morning saw us often at the docks, supervising the unloading, weighing and dispatch of the goods from abroad, and at eleven p.m. we would be locking up the stables after the last van had returned from its journey and the horses had been put away. Seventy hours a week was then a common average for both masters and men.

The hard work and close attention to detail paid. Business increased. The horses were moved to new stables in Clerkenwell to make more room at King Street. The brothers bought warehouses in Hosier Lane and Cock Lane. (They acquired an unusual bit of the history of London when they bought the Cock Lane premises, of which more in the next chapter.)

All through this period, Lovell and Christmas had helped the Beers with financial guarantees, and when the business was formed into a limited liability company in 1918, they took up a portion of the equity. By this time Beer's was established as one of the foremost, perhaps the foremost, of the wholesale distributors of bacon in London and the leaders in the Ostend Trade.

One of the secrets of the revival of Isaac Beer & Sons Ltd. at this time was the very close relationship between Charles and Ernest. As well as being brothers, they were bosom friends and it was a terrible shock to Ernest when Charles died suddenly in 1924.

It must have been only a year before his death that I made the acquaintance of Charles on the cross channel steamer from Ostend to Dover. I was young, inexperienced and shy at the prospect of meeting the well known Charles Beer, but I had no need to fear. He was a charming man and immediately asked me to have dinner with him on the ship. My first thoughts were, 'What a large man and what a large moustache'. There are some people whose warmth of personality puts one immediately at ease. Charles Beer was such a person. I shall never forget the five hours I spent with him during what turned out to be a rather stormy crossing. Nor will I forget his cheerfulness and his fatherly attitude to me, or the way he ordered Burgundy for us, insisting that it was the best drink in the world. I soon realised how it was that he was so successful in gaining and keeping the confidence of his shippers, his customers and his staff. After this meeting he continued to show an interest in me, and offered me both help and advice in the remaining months of his life. His sudden death came as a shock and left a big gap.

Ernest was now the only director of the company and he immediately set about appointing senior members of the staff to the Board. Ernest had a very different temperament from his brother, but he was highly intelligent, quick moving and exceedingly kind. I treasure a letter he wrote me in 1929 in which he thanked me in the most flattering terms for some service I had been able to render him during the hectic Christmas trade of that year. I. Beer's business continued to grow and a depot was opened at Norwich equipped with facilities for bacon smoking and with storage space for all kinds of provisions. A motor delivery service was established to cover the eastern counties.

A few years later the government of the day decided to restrict imports of bacon in order to increase home production. Beer's decided to enter the manufacturing stage of the bacon trade. In 1933 it took a controlling interest in a Wiltshire bacon factory at Downton which needed capital. It quickly bought the balance of the shares and began a programme of modernisation. The latest Danish machinery was installed and chilling and curing rooms were constructed. Beer's also established a branch depot in the vicinity to supply the South and South West with provisions.

In the same year, the private company of I. Beer and Sons Ltd. was changed into a public limited liability company with its shares quoted on the Stock Exchange.

Ernest Beer had a splendid team around him in those pre-war days. I remember particularly John Smith, an outstanding salesman who died very suddenly to the great sorrow of the community at Smithfield and beyond. Other members of the team of whom I have memories were Arthur Mummery, Gilbert Trevers and William Punchard the father of Alan Punchard who is now a senior partner in Hallett's, the Fitch Lovell accountants.

One man who came up through the firm in those days was Edward Shephard. He excelled as a buyer in the widely fluctuating markets before the war and was always seeking fresh fields to conquer. He was a dynamic man and became a leading figure among the Wiltshire Bacon Curers and eventually was elected Chairman of the National

Committee of the Provision Trade. He was a forthright speaker and the trade is in his debt for his efforts during and after the war. On his retirement in 1963 he became for a period the Chairman of the British Bacon Curers' Federation. He is now able to spend much of his time with the flowers and trees he knows and loves so well.

E. Trevor Beer, Ernest's son, joined the firm in the year Charles Beer died, and is today Chairman of the company, a director of Fitch Lovell and in addition has responsibilities for Fitch Lovell's entire bacon curing and manufacturing activities. Like other members of his family, Trevor had the sorrow to lose his wife at an early age, but in due time he had the good fortune to meet and marry the charming lady who has done so much to create for him and the family another extremely happy home. On the outbreak of war, he was called up. His war record was distinguished. He attained the rank of Group Captain in the R.A.F. and was appointed a C.B.E. for his services. He is and has been always a loyal and valued colleague.

Writing about Edward Shephard and Trevor and the war has led me ahead of my account of the firm, for it was before the war in 1938 that Ernest Beer retired after a disagreement with the rest of the Board. He had wanted to merge the firm with Geo. Bowles Nicholls & Co. Ltd. but he was unable to obtain the unanimous approval of the Board. He was about 80 by this time and he decided to sell his shares in the company to Lovells and retire. Edward Shephard succeeded him in October 1938.

Beer's suffered badly from enemy bombing during the war. The building erected by Isaac Beer in King Street, which had been its headquarters for more than 50 years was completely destroyed, and with it all the firm's historic records. Its warehouses and bacon stoves in Hosier Lane and Cock Lane were badly damaged, yet it managed to carry on working from the depots set up outside London. Once again its old friends Lovell and Christmas were able to help.

Beer's, Lovell's and Lovell's subsidiary Phillips and Vanderhaege had formed an emergency joint company on the outbreak of war and set up outlying depots in case London was so heavily bombed that distribution from the centre was impossible. This had been done on the instructions of the government which was worried about the effect of bombing on the distribution of food in London and the other centres of population. As it turned out, the fears were entirely justified. The bombing of Smithfield, the centre of the wholesale provision trade and the capital's main meat market, was little short of catastrophic.

If it had not been for the emergency depots there would undoubtedly have been severe dislocation of supplies. The name of the Beer-Lovell emergency company was Beer, Phillips, Lovell Ltd. and the plan was that B.P.L. would take over if any, or all of the three companies' operations were disrupted. It certainly proved its worth on the night of 10 May 1941, when Beer's King Street premises were hit by high explosive and incendiary bombs. The warehouses and stores were largely destroyed yet because of B.P.L. distribution went on almost unchecked.

Beer's troubles were not over. In April 1942 its Norwich depot was destroyed. Yet once again, such was the energy and virility of the company in those wartime days, that new premises were found within 24 hours and distribution continued without a break. The B.P.L. Company, having proved its value, was liquidated in 1948.

But first I must record how Beer's narrowly escaped yet another war loss. Before the war it had acquired a controlling interest in G.M. Truss which was one of the two main agents for Lithuanian bacon. A few months before the outbreak of hostilities the Lithuanian government decided that it would market its own bacon, and so it paid Truss substantial compensation for the loss of the agency. Soon afterwards the Lithuanian bacon factories were destroyed in the German invasion. Then Lithuania became part of the Soviet Union, and no Lithuanian bacon has been shipped to the United Kingdom for the past 30 years.

As the war ended, E. Trevor Beer and the other serving members of the staff rejoined the company as soon as they were demobilised. A period of rapid expansion followed, helped by the good profits coming from Beer's bacon factories in the days of control and semi-control. Beer's acquired Alfred Mason & Co. Ltd. of Leicester in 1945 in order to develop its wholesale business in the Midlands. A number of small wholesale firms found themselves at the end of the war either without premises because of the bombing, or else with elderly principals without succession. Naturally these firms were looking round for someone to buy their businesses from them. Two who joined I. Beer at this time were Sevens Dray & Co. and Chennells of Eastbourne. Whitlock Bros., one of the old established

Smithfield firms, whose partners were well known characters on the Provision Exchange, had all their business property obliterated by enemy action. They had managed to carry on by sharing the premises of a fellow trader, but after the war, they too came to Beer's and merged with them. F.G.B. Whitlock later joined Beer's Board and rendered excellent service until his retirement this year. With his departure, yet another of the old provision families of London has no representative in the trade.

Beer's saw that the home bacon industry was going to become more important and obtained a controlling interest in another English manufacturer, Collins Bros. of Evesham.

When the Fitch Lovell Group was formed in 1958, it was only natural that I. Beer should become part of it in view of the close association between Beer's and Lovell & Christmas, and in fact it joined Fitch Lovell in 1959.

Lovell's already held 27% of the ordinary shares. It was thought desirable by Fitch Lovell that the consideration for the purchase should be in a new class of non-voting or partial voting shares so as not, at that stage, to alter the board control of the parent company. The negotiations were not entirely straightforward because news of the impending bid leaked out to the market, something which had not happened during the merger with Lovell & Christmas or any other acquisitions by Fitch Lovell. Shares in Beer's – universally known as I.B.S. – moved up sharply on the Stock Exchange.

Negotiations continued and an offer was made to I.B.S. shareholders on 5 November 1958 of seven new 'B' shares for three I.B.S. ordinary shares. Altogether 999,999 of the new shares were issued in exchange for 428,571 I.B.S. shares.

An arrangement was made with Fenn & Crosthwaite (Hugh Robinson) who undertook to purchase any shares not accepted for an underwriting fee. As part of the agreement, Edward Shephard was invited to become a member of the F.L. Board. He retired in August 1963 after completing 50 years of service and Trevor Beer succeeded him asChairman. Trevor also took his place on the Fitch Lovell Board.

In the final report of I.B.S. as a separate company issued with the 1960 Fitch Lovell report, Edward Shephard complained of the shortage of English pigs and of the problems for the bacon industry caused by the government's participation in the European Free Trade Area. The report lists seven companies belonging to the 'Ibson

Group' – I. Beer & Sons Ltd., A. Mason & Co. Ltd. of Leicester, A.E. Chennell Ltd. of Eastbourne, all these three being in wholesale distribution. The bacon and meat product factories are listed as Collins Bros. (Evesham) Ltd., Collins Bros. (South Wilts) Ltd., and Sussex Canners Ltd., Brighton, and an egg packing station at King's Lynn is mentioned – Woods Sadds' Eggs Ltd.

In spite of the financial security of belonging to Fitch Lovell, these were not easy years for I. Beer. The post-war years of good profits and growth were followed by a time of intense competition and upheaval in the wholesale provisions business, which is not over yet. Smithfield, having never really recovered from the devastation of the war, was becoming less and less of a centre. Privately owned retailers, particularly in the South of England were unable to compete against the multiple chains and the new supermarkets rising in every quarter. Among the retailers going out of business were old established customers of Beer's. The new supermarkets were tending to cut out the wholesaler and deal direct with manufacturers. Meanwhile the wholesale food trade is following the example of the retail trade and, limping behind, is going into supermarketing. The same pressures have driven it there – the heavy cost of transport, rising overhead expenses and reduced profits in an era of standardisation and pre-packaging. The wholesalers call it 'Cash and Carry' trading, but all it amounts to is wholesale supermarketing.

It is some 10 years since I advocated this trading in a memorandum to Fitch Lovell, but it is only in the last year or so that Beer's and the others have taken up the challenge. The first 'Cash and Carry' unit was opened in July 1968. It is easy to write that it should have been earlier, but a company with a large and widespread organisation and hundreds of employees who have loyally supported if for a long period cannot move as quickly as firms which have no such structure or responsibilities.

Soon after this move into 'Cash and Carry' Beer's made an even bigger decision. It decided to leave Smithfield, where it had maintained its headquarters for 80 years. Apart from the declining importance of the area, the traffic and labour difficulties all played their part in the decision. I. Beer was a real part of the old Smithfield scene and its departure was a sad event, but there was no prospect of rebuilding its old premises, and even if there had been, it would probably have been unwise. The firm left in

50. The first shop of
Isaac Beer, 1850

51. I. Beer & Sons
premises at
15 King Street, 1924

52. I. Beer & Sons' stables in the 19th century

53. The Smithfield warehouse of I. Beer & Sons Ltd., blitzed in 1941

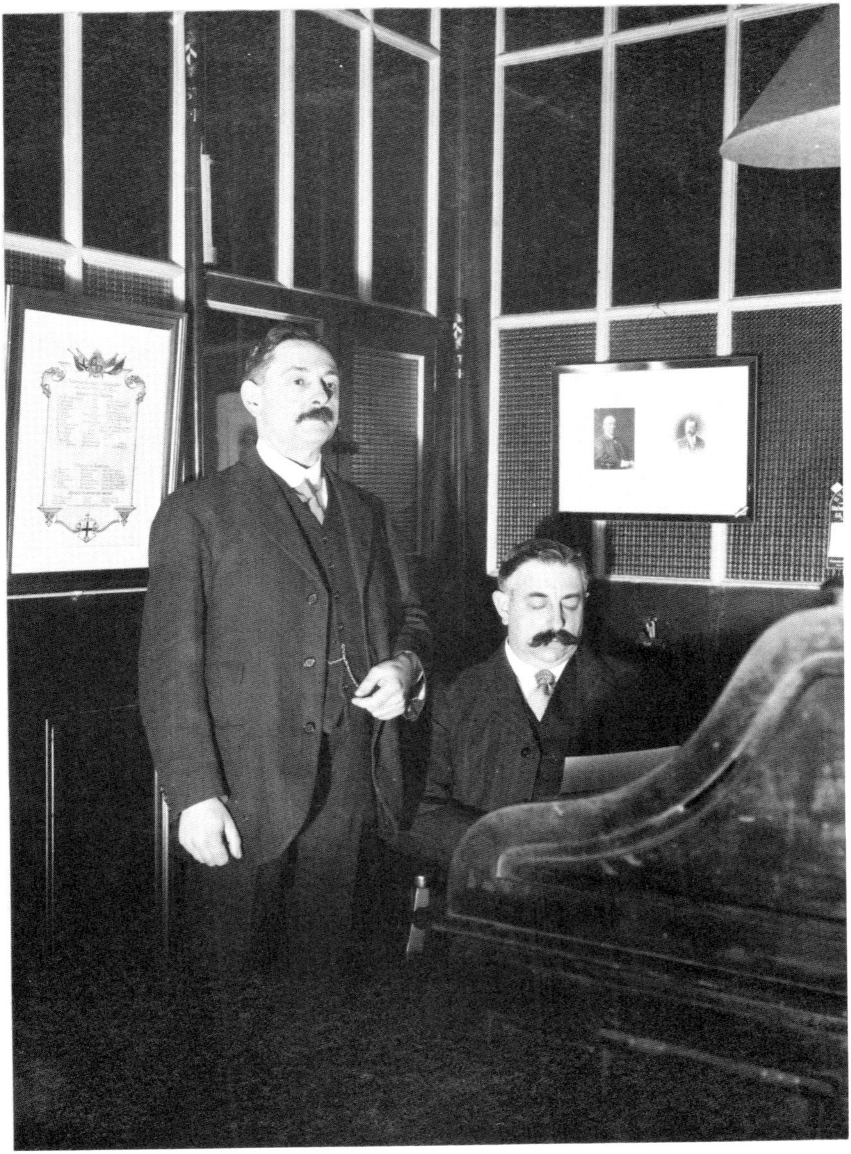

54. Charles and Ernest Beer, 1912

55. I. Beer & Sons Ltd.: transport in the early 1920s

56. I. Beer & Sons Ltd.: modern transport

November 1969. Its main warehousing and distribution centre was moved to Hainault in Essex and later to Norfolk and its offices and headquarters to Bury St. Edmunds in Suffolk.

Meanwhile, Geoffrey, the son of E. Trevor Beer, has joined the company. He is the fourth generation of the family to come into the firm. He has been very active and is now in charge of the wholesale operations since his father has assumed the big and responsible job of supervising the Fitch Lovell bacon and meat manufacturing activities.

Thus another old and esteemed firm has moved from the Smithfield scene. The changes which time imposes on people and firms are sometimes sad, but responding to challenges has been part of the firm's history, so I do not fear for its future.

---

### *THE BEERS OF YESTERYEAR – A RHYME*

They began each morn as the first streaks of dawn
Pierced the night clouds with arrows of light
And hard they worked in a crazed sort of way
All day and on to the night.

The first to arrive were the rabbits at five
Which were finished long afore eight,
And workers whose part meant a half seven start
Were thought to be rather late.

We'd be well in a fix if by quarter to six
The pigs hadn't come to the door
Where 'Greenwood' and 'Benzie' in almost a frenzie
Would restlessly pace the floor.

When I began as quite a young man
Things moved at a fright'ning pace.
The firm seemed to be a strange world to me
With giants all over the place.

There was 'Trevor' and 'Webby' and 'Freddie' and 'Dick'
And the governor was 'E.B.' you know,
You'd recognise 'John' by his eighteen odd ston
And 'Shep' by straw hat and bow.

There was hustle and bustle and shouting and noise
Enough to 'waken the dead
I stood there aghast as 'Ben' walked past
Six fore-ends perched on his head.

I think of the morn when Geoffrey was born
Of the posters announcing the news
'Beers Bacon Builds Bonny Boy Babies'
A slogan the Danes could well use.

The old house was haunted or so it was said
When you slept there strange noises you'd hear
And one dark night with no-one in sight
'Ren' watched all his sheets disappear.

This then was the firm where we all served our term
Without much L.S. or D.
But change each year brings, and we all know that 'fings
Ain't now what they used to be'.

So here's to the Beers of those yesteryears
The foundations they laid don't decay
And may we inherit the turbulent spirit
That gave us the Beers of today.

*S.G. Mead.*

*Mr. Mead is an employee of I. Beer & Sons, and has been with the Company for over 40 years.*

12

## THE COCK LANE GHOST

IN THE LAST CHAPTER I wrote that Isaac Beer's bought some of the history of London when it purchased its warehouses in Cock Lane at the turn of the century. It shares this history with Lovell & Christmas who bought *The Wheatsheaf* public house and numbers 22 to 30 Cock Lane in 1935. Apart from bricks and mortar, what the two companies obtained for their money was the Cock Lane Ghost. The haunting of Cock Lane is remembered by few today but 200 years ago it was a sensation, the talk of the town for an entire season. For weeks and months revelation succeeded revelation. Scandal was piled upon scandal, just like a play. In fact the easiest way to tell the story is to begin, like a play, with the Dramatis Personae. The drama had a distinguished cast:

| | |
|---|---|
| Francis Lynes | alias 'Scratching Fanny' the Principal Ghost. |
| William Kent | lived with Frances Lynes. Accused by 'Scratching Fanny' of murdering her. |
| Elizabeth Lynes | William Kent's wife and another ghost |
| Ann Lynes | Sister to Frances and Elizabeth. |
| Carrots | Esther Carlisle, William Kent's servant. |
| Richard Parsons | Clerk at St. Sepulchre's Holborn. |
| Elizabeth Parsons | The younger daughter of Richard Parsons through whom 'Scratching Fanny' communicated. |
| Mary Fraser | A servant and interpreter of the ghost. |

| | |
|---|---|
| Rev. Stephen Aldrich | Rector of St. Bartholomew, Smithfield and lecturer at St. Sepulchre's. |
| James Franzen | Landlord of *The Wheatsheaf.* |
| Rev. John Moore | Rector of St. John's Clerkenwell, who buried Frances and headed the Committee of Enquiry. |
| Dr. Samuel Johnson | The famous writer who made the report of the Committee. |
| Lord Mansfield | The Lord Chief Justice who conducted the trial. |
| Horace Walpole | Son of the Prime Minister, Sir Robert Walpole. |

The year is 1761. James Fitch, the real founder of Fitch Lovell, was nothing but a boy on his father's farm at Great Dunmow. None of the other firms which grew up into Fitch Lovell had even been thought of. But Cock Lane ran, in those days, just as it does now in a straight line from Snow Hill to West Smithfield. Today it is a quiet backwater, lined with tall warehouses. Part of it has not been rebuilt since the bomb damage of the last war. But in the mid-18th century, Smithfield was a densely populated quarter of the City and Cock Lane would have been teeming with life centred on its inn *The Wheatsheaf.*

There were three reasons why the appearance of a ghost in this insignificant alley should have excited such interest. Unlike so many other apparitions, the Cock Lane ghost seemed to be really authentic. Dozens of people, including clergymen were to see, or rather hear, the ghost. Secondly, Scratching Fanny was one of the few ghosts, apparently, venturing back in search of revenge. Neither Press nor public could resist the story of the woman who returned from the grave to accuse her lover of murdering her with poison as she lay sick with the smallpox. The manner of her return was equally irrestible, as she delivered her weird and frightening message through a series of sinister knocks and scratches.

The third factor in making the Cock Lane ghost a 'cause célèbre' was the involvement of Methodism. The Methodists, who were making great strides at this time, were known to be believers in spirits. People seeking to discredit them tried to accuse the Methodists under their great leader John Wesley, of sponsoring the ghost in their own interests.

So it was that London, and many of the leading figures of the day found their attention caught by the extraordinary stories coming out of Smithfield, Dr. Johnson, David Garrick, Horace Walpole, William Hogarth and even the Duke of York were to become implicated.

The story begins far from London in the Norfolk countryside, where a certain William Kent owned an inn and a Post Office. He married a girl called Elizabeth Lynes, but unfortunately she died in childbirth. The child too, died soon afterwards, and the desolate William, by all accounts a most affectionate and kindly man, turned to his wife's sister Frances, or Fanny, for consolation. However, her family objected strongly to the couple living together, and so William made a special journey to London to seek the best legal advice. The counsel to whom he presented his case confirmed what he already knew. In the eyes of the Church and under the law as it then stood, William Kent and Frances Lynes could never marry. The fact that Elizabeth's child had survived her, even for a short time, was an insurmountable barrier.

William broke the news to Fanny. By this time the couple were deeply in love and they decided that it was unthinkable to separate. It was also impossible to continue living in Norfolk where everyone knew them, and so they decided to move to Greenwich and tell everyone there that they were man and wife. As proof of their intention to form a permanent partnership, they made wills in each other's favour. After committing her soul to Almighty God, and her body to the earth, Fanny made bequests of 2s. 6d. to her five brothers and sisters and left the rest of her property to William Kent at his 'absolute disposal'. As a mark of love and trust, she appointed him her sole executor, and he did the same for her.

Fanny's family were furious at what they considered the couple's sinful behaviour. They made no attempt to conceal the matter. A sister of Fanny's, living in Pall Mall, called Ann, was particularly outraged and out-spoken. William and Fanny soon left Greenwich; it is not known whether they were driven out by the spiteful tongue of Ann. This time the unhappy pair decided to take shelter in the anonymity of the City itself. First of all, William tried to buy a house, but he was unsuccessful and they had to be content with lodgings near the Mansion House. Almost certainly their landlord found out about their condition, for William was forced to lend him £20, a transaction which has the smell of blackmail. Once again, William and Fanny were on the road.

So it was that our story wound its way towards Smithfield. One morning at early prayers in October 1759, Richard Parsons, the clerk of St. Sepulchre's Church, Holborn, noticed a genteel couple standing at the back and showed them into a pew. St. Sepulchre's is known to all members of the Smithfield Community. Both John Lovell and Clement Keevil, it is reputed, were church-wardens. It stands opposite the Old Newgate Prison and the Old Newgate Market. Today the Old Bailey is its nearest neighbour, just across the road.

After the service, the couple introduced themselves to Richard Parsons as Mr. and Mrs. William Kent. They thanked him for the service and mentioned that they were in search of lodgings, and told him how they had lodged near Mansion House, and about the loan of £20, and how they had to arrest their former landlord to get it back.

Parsons was most sympathetic. As luck would have it, he himself had lodgings to let, just round the corner in Cock Lane. At once the couple went to view them and quickly came to terms.

The house was number 20, occupied today by J. Lidstone, the builders. It was a plain fronted house, three stories high with a room on each floor, connected by a winding staircase. Parsons lived there with his wife and two daughters, the elder named Elizabeth. They must have had to squeeze up to make room for the Kents, but the two families seemed to rub along quite well in spite of the cramped quarters. The Kents were quiet and accommodating and both families were delighted by the news that Fanny was expecting a baby.

The Kents were well pleased with their lodgings and brought with them their red-haired servant Esther Carlisle, who was known to everyone as 'Carrots'. It seemed as if they were safe at last far from the prying eyes and wagging tongues of Fanny's family, and under the protection of Richard Parsons, who was known as a 'a very drunken fellow but otherwise of a respectable character as befitted the Clerk of St. Sepulchre'.

However, once again the rumours began to circulate. It was whispered around Smithfield that the new couple lodging at Parsons' in Cock Lane were not married and never could be married because she was the sister of his deceased wife. Soon after these rumours began, Richard Parsons borrowed £12 from William Kent. It was agreed that the loan should be repaid at £1 a month. It is not known whether the loan was made on the same unpleasant basis as Kent's advance to his last landlord. At all events, he made no attempt to leave Cock Lane, and some months later he felt secure enough to go away from London on business, leaving Fanny behind. Fanny asked if Elizabeth Parsons, then aged 10, could sleep with her to keep her company. Mrs. Parsons agreed and Elizabeth moved into the Kent's bedroom.

A few days later, Fanny complained to Mrs. Parsons that she had been disturbed by the most violent noises in the night. Mrs. Parsons could not understand it. She thought the noises might have been coming from the cobbler who worked next door. However, on the following Sunday the noise was so loud that Fanny jumped out of bed and ran into Mrs. Parsons and asked her if the shoemaker worked on Sundays. 'Of course not', was the reply. Fanny took Mrs. Parsons upstairs to listen, and she, too, heard the strange sounds. An investigation was immediately set on foot and a local Minister of Religion came to listen, but unfortunately he died before he could make his report. Nevertheless news of the haunting got out and was known at *The Wheatsheaf* and probably further afield as well.

William, now back from his business trip, began to quarrel with Parsons. Parsons refused to pay back the money he had borrowed, either because he was spending all his money on drink, or simply because he knew Kent was unmarried and thought he was in his power. William Kent put the matter into the hands of his attorney, just as he had done when his landlord at the Mansion House had refused to repay him. He had already made an arrangement to take a house off Red Lion Street, within a few yards of the present premises of Auguste Noël.

By now, Fanny was eight months pregnant. This house was not far from St. John's (St. John's Street is the home of West Layton). The rector there was an acquaintance of the Kents, the Rev. Stephen Aldrich by name. He was a very orthodox priest, not at all like the incumbent at St. Sepulchre's, the Rev. John Moore. Although a man of the highest integrity, Moore was much inclined to Methodism. Although the house off Red Lion Street was not quite ready, William Kent decided that they had stayed long enough at the Parsons, and he decided to leave anyway.

In January 1760, they went and lodged temporarily with a local jeweller. It was there that Fanny was suddenly taken very ill. Her doctor, Cooper by name, ordered her to be 'blooded' and provided a nurse for her. It was decided that the best thing to do was to put Fanny into a coach and move her straight away to the house off Red Lion Street. The next day Dr. Cooper called with an apothecary, James Jones of Soho. They diagnosed that Fanny had smallpox. The news of her illness and the quarrel about the money with Parsons spread through the neighbourhood and her sickness was interpreted by many as a visitation by God on sinners. The good folk of Smithfield and Holborn followed the course of the illness with a more than neighbourly interest. Fanny became very weak, and the Rev. Stephen Aldrich waited on her and tried to assure her there would be forgiveness for what she and William had done. In fact he assured her their deed would not even be considered a sin a hundred years thence. He was not far out. The Deceased Wife's Sister Act was repealed in 1902.

Fanny died on 2 February 1760. William Kent, overcome with grief, ordered the undertaker 'to make as good a coffin as he could, both lined and covered . . .'. He ordered no name to be put on it, as he feared prosecution if he gave Fanny his own name. Nevertheless, he registered the burial in the name of Kent 'being determined she should suffer no reproach whatever might be the result'. He was clearly apprehensive about the consequences, for he invited Fanny's sister Ann to come and see the body. His enemies were to state that the coffin was already screwed down before she came. This he denied vehemently. The body was laid to rest in the vaults of St. John's, Clerkenwell.

While she was lying ill, something happened in Cock Lane which revived the story about the haunting of number 20. James Franzen, the landlord of *The Wheatsheaf* called on the Parsons. Richard was out, so he sat with Mrs. Parsons and her daughter. Strange noises were heard which sounded to Franzen like 'knuckles against the wainscot', Mrs. Parsons told him that they heard the sounds every night. Franzen was terrified and began to run out of the house. As he opened the door, 'he saw something pass by him in white, seemingly in a sheet, that shot past and went upstairs'. Afterwards he said light from the figure threw a beam through the window and lit the clock in a schoolroom nearby.

By this time, Franzen was thoroughly shaken. He rushed home and sat by his kitchen fire, too frightened to go to bed. As he sat there, a knock came on his door. If such a thing were possible, he was even more terrified, for he thought it was the ghost coming for him. But when the door opened it was Richard Parsons. He too was in a state of terror.

'Give me the largest brandy you have', he shouted.

'Why, what is the matter?' asked Franzen.

'Oh Franzen', said Parsons, 'I have just seen the ghost'.

'So have I', groaned Franzen, 'what is the meaning of it?'

Parsons said he thought the ghost was almost certainly the restless spirit of Elizabeth, the first wife of William Kent who had come to warn him and Fanny that they were living in sin.

About this time Richard Parsons's daughter Elizabeth began to suffer from convulsive fits. The noises and knockings continued.

In such a tight, crowded community, such things could not be kept secret, and more and more people began coming to Cock Lane to hear the ghost for themselves. The lodger who had taken the Kents' place in the house refused to stay. Parsons called in a carpenter, Bateman Griffiths, and told him to take down the wainscotting. Nothing was found, so Griffiths nailed it back. The only possible answer seemed to be that the noises were coming from some supernatural power. Richard Parsons, the clerk of St. Sepulchre, naturally turned to Rev. John Moore. Moore was most interested.

It must be remembered that the Methodists, or Wesleyans, were believers in ghosts and spiritual apparitions. John Wesley himself is said to have believed and repeated stories of apparitions, witchcraft and possession by spirits. In fact there was even a ghost in Wesley's own family. His mother Emily Wesley had been puzzled by groans and knockings in various parts of her house, and she came to the conclusion that it must be a ghost. The spirit became a bit of a nuisance, and eventually, the Rev. Samuel Wesley, John's father, called the ghost into his study and rebuked it as 'a deaf and dumb devil'. The ghost was reputed to converse with the old clergyman, communicating with him through a series of knocks. The Wesleys' ghost became known as 'Old Jeffrey'.

Now John Moore was a priest of the Church of England, but, as I have said, he was most sympathetic to Methodism, and probably knew all about 'Old Jeffrey'. No doubt he was not at all surprised when he went round to the house in Cock Lane, to hear the scratchings and knockings louder than ever. From then on he became deeply involved in the interpretation of the mystery.

He and Parsons decided to do what Samuel Wesley had done, and persuade the ghost to answer questions and identify itself 'knock by knock'. They came to an agreement that if the ghost replied with a single knock, it would mean 'yes' and a double knock would mean 'no'.

At first the knocks, scratches and moans seemed to come from different parts of the house. Now, under the careful scrutiny of Moore and Parsons, they began to be exclusively associated with Elizabeth Parsons who was now aged 11. The sounds followed her wherever she went. They were especially prevalent when Elizabeth and her younger sister were in bed. John Moore was most persistent in his efforts to find out the reason for the visitations and before long, by questions and knocking replies, he was informed that the ghost seen by James Franzen when Fanny was dying was indeed the spirit of Kent's first wife. This much Richard Parsons had already guessed. The startling new fact to emerge was that the dead wife had returned to give warning that William Kent was about to poison Fanny. It was further revealed that the knockings and other sounds heard since Fanny's death were from her own spirit which had returned to say that she had been poisoned two hours before she died and that she was now seeking for justice.

The story of the Cock Lane ghost spread through London and Ann Lynes, Fanny's sister in Pall Mall came forward to say that she had been 'deprived of the pleasure of seeing her dear sister's body as it was screwed down some time before she came to the house'. This statement strengthened the suspicion of foul play.

Religiously, the Rev. John Moore was in favour of taking the ghost on trust, but in view of the seriousness of the allegation made by it against poor William Kent, he felt it was necessary to have the support of fellow clergymen. Among those who were called in was the Rev. Thomas Broughton, the Secretary of the Society for Promoting Christian Knowledge and an early Methodist. He visited Cock Lane on 5 January and left convinced of the authenticity of the ghost. By now, not only the existence of the ghost, but the charges against William Kent were becoming widely known.

Inevitably the newspapers got hold of the story, and the *Public Ledger*, a well known journal at the time, was the first to publish an account of the whole proceedings. It advised people who were interested in the ghost to contact Moore. One of the paper's readers who did was Kent himself. Although he knew that the accusations against him were false, he did not know whether to believe in the spirit. Moore said he did not think Kent was a murderer. He suggested that Kent had better come to a seance with Fanny, and certain questions were duly prepared. That same evening, 12 January, Kent and Moore went to Cock Lane, accompanied by Dr. Cooper and Mr. Jones the apothecary, the two men who had attended Fanny during her fatal illness.

It was William Kent's first visit to Cock Lane since he had left almost exactly a year before after the quarrel with Parsons and before Fanny fell ill. The party entered the house and went upstairs. Elizabeth Parsons was publicly undressed and put to bed with her little sister. The bed was placed in the middle of the room, and the company sat all around it. The room was in darkness. The part of interrogater was taken by one Mary Fraser, an elderly servant who had taken to interpreting the spirit regularly. They waited in silence. After a time the knocking began. Then Mary Fraser began her cross-examination.

'Are you the wife of Mr. Kent?' 'No' (two knocks)
'Did you die by poisoining?' 'Yes' (one knock)
'How long did you live after receiving it?'
'Three hours' (three knocks)
'Did Carrots [Kent's servant] know of you being poisoned?'
'Yes'
'Should Mr. Kent be taken up?' 'Yes'.

Then to the consternation of William Kent, one of the audience said 'Kent, ask the Ghost if you shall be hanged'. The answer came 'Yes' in one knock.

Kent cried out, 'Thou art a lying spirit, thou art not the ghost of my Fanny. She would never have said such a thing'. But although he said the ghost was not that of Fanny, he clearly believed, as Moore did, that 20 Cock Lane was haunted by something.

After this episode the ghost became notorious. Large crowds filled Cock Lane. When it became widely known that the ghost followed Elizabeth Parsons wherever she went, the girl became a celebrity.

Two nights after Kent's visit to Cock Lane, Elizabeth stayed the night at a neighbour's house and two noblemen came to hear the noises. One of them was the Earl of Dartmouth, a Methodist sympathiser. His companion was probably Horace Walpole, now the Earl of Orford since the death of his father, the Prime Minister, Robert Walpole. He was known by this time to be taking an interest in Scratching Fanny.

Now that Society was beginning to take up the ghost, three more newspapers carried the story of the extraordinary happenings in Smithfield. Accounts appeared in the *St. James Gazette*, the *London Chronicle* and *Lloyds Evening Post* during the following fortnight. Still bigger crowds filled Cock Lane, and the narrow streets round about were jammed with the coaches of fashionable people come to see for themselves what it was all about. For the people of Smithfield itself the novelty was beginning to wear off, and they were becoming tired of being continually pestered for information. James Franzen offered a ready welcome to inquirers at *The Wheatsheaf*, however, and his business began to prosper.

William Kent attended another seance on 18 January and took with him his friend the Rev. Stephen Aldrich of St. John's, Clerkenwell, who had buried Fanny, and also Mr. Jones the apothecary. The ghost vehemently repeated the accusations against Kent, and called for the servant Carrots to confirm what it had said.

Carrots had moved to a new situation after Fanny's death, but the industrious James Franzen found her and brought her to Cock Lane for a seance. Carrots was unperturbed and when told that her dear mistress, just before dying had said she was being poisoned, the servant replied, 'Nonsense, she could not speak for four days'. William Kent arrived at the house the same evening, very late, with several others, including Franzen and the Secretary of the S.P.C.K. the Rev. Thomas Broughton. The room, the staircase, and the street were all crowded. At the end of the session the Ghost caused yet another sensation by stating, through the usual code of knocks, that if Carrots and her master were carried before a magistrate, they would both confess to the murder. At this point there was a bustling sound in the wings. The faithful Carrots, unable to contain herself any longer, rose to her feet and pushed her way forward. Calmly, she asked, 'Are you my mistress?' 'Yes', came the reply. 'Are you angry with me madam?' Carrots demanded. 'Yes'. 'Then madam', Carrots exploded, 'you may be ashamed of yourself, for I never hurt you in my life'.

The outburst sent a ripple of alarm down the stairs and out into the street. The crowd, most of whom had just come to stare, felt the presence of something sinister, something for which they hadn't bargained, and they began to melt away. James Franzen was left in the bedroom with only the child and Mary Fraser. He was too frightened to move. The seance went on until four in the morning, with the implacable Mary Fraser continuing to ask her questions. Finally Franzen stumbled back to *The Wheatsheaf*. Afterwards he claimed that the ghost followed and terrified him and his wife in their bedchamber.

Further seances were held in Hosier Lane as well as Cock Lane. Elizabeth's fits became more frequent. The ghost became the talking point of the whole of London. At times it seemed as though the whole of London had come to Smithfield.

The public were divided as to whether the ghost was real or a fraud. Either way, the situation was intolerable for William Kent. At this point he was advised to do something which he should have done considerably earlier. He was told to institute an action for conspiracy against the Rev. John Moore and Richard Parsons.

His friend the Rev. Stephen Aldrich, whom he went to once more for advice, said he thought that the affair had gone beyond the point where a law suit could stop it. In his view, nothing less than a public inquiry would suffice. The only authority who could enquire into what had become a public scandal in the City was the Lord Mayor Sir Samuel Fludyer. He was petitioned and on 23 January he agreed to hear the case. He was, however, very cautious. A predecessor in office had fallen into grave difficulties with ghostly imposters on two occasions. Sir Samuel said he did not intend 'to stir much in it'. He refused to issue a warrant for murder against William Kent, or against Moore and Parsons for conspiracy. Instead he gave directions for the inquiry to be held by a committee at the house of the Rev. Stephen Aldrich, and 'that neither trouble nor expense be spared in detecting the truth'.

The inquiry was becoming overdue. Public interest in the ghost was turning to hysteria. Young ladies at a boarding school at 37 King Street refused to go upstairs, or to sleep when they were in bed. The building, incidentally, would have been where the Poultry Market now stands. It was also probably the first premises of Lovell & Christmas.

The credulous and the frivolous, according to the newspapers, continued to gather in Cock Lane. One wrote, 'the clergy, the laity, the nobility and the commonalty continue their nightly attendance on the invisible agent'. The presence of the commonalty and the laity is understandable, it was the involvement of the clergy and the nobility which made the Cock Lane affair so extraordinary.

The nobility were particularly assiduous in their patronage of the spirit. Horace Walpole wrote on 29 January,

> We set out from the opera, the Duke of York, Lady Northumberland, Lady Mary Coke, Lord Hertford and I, all in one hackney carriage and drove to the spot. It rained torrents but the lane was full of mob and the house so full we could not get in – at last it was discovered the Duke of York was present and the company squeezed themselves into one another's pockets to make room for us.
>
> The house was wretchedly small and miserable, we tumbled over the bed of the child to whom the ghost comes, and whom they are murdering by inches in such insufferable heat and stench. We stayed until an hour after one.

The British Museum has in its possession two superb drawings or cartoons by Hogarth and Field dating from this period which show the credulity of the English over the events in Cock Lane. Also in the Museum is the original of a Broadside Ballad entitled *Cock Lane Humbug 1762.* The intelligentsia, at least, were not deceived.

Meanwhile, the Rev. Stephen Aldrich was laying his plans for what he hoped would be the unmasking of the ghost. In consultation with Lord Dartmouth he formed a formidable Committee of Inquiry. They chose Mrs. Oakes, matron of a lying-in-hospital, Dr. John Douglas, a well known exposer of imposters, a physician Dr. John Macaulay, a Captain Williamson who was so determined to expose the ghost that he had already attended seances with a loaded pistol and stick. Last, but not least, was that famous enemy of humbug, Dr. Samuel Johnson.

Aldrich's plan, to which the Committee agreed, was this. The child was to be put to bed by trustworthy women. When the knocking began, the ghost was to be asked to accompany William Kent to the vaults of St. John's, Clerkenwell, and to knock on Fanny's coffin. The time and place were to be kept secret. Dr. Johnson was asked to act as secretary to the committee and draw up the report. He wrote that they entered the girl's bedroom at 10 o'clock on the appointed evening. Elizabeth had already been put to bed in accordance with the Committee's instructions. The Committee solemnly waited for an hour for the arrival of the ghost, but they heard nothing. Then they went downstairs and interrogated

Richard Parsons who denied, in the strongest possible terms, any knowledge of fraud.

Then they decided to proceed to the vault of St. John's to see if the spirit would overcome its unaccustomed bout of coyness and knock on the coffin. But once again, nothing happened. Even when William Kent went down into the vault, together with the committee members, there was silence.

Dr. Johnson ends his report with these words: 'It is the opinion of the whole assembly that the child has some art of making or counterfeiting particular noises and that there is no evidence of higher causes'.

Armed with this unequivocal statement from such a distinguished committee, William Kent went to see the Rev. John Moore and asked him to make an affidavit accepting the findings of the inquiry 'to put a stop to the affair and clear up his reputation and character to the world'.

But Moore refused. Even if Kent had not murdered Fanny, he asserted, the visitation was plainly a judgment on him for having lived in sin with her. And so the seances went on. When the ghost was taxed with its refusal to knock on Fanny's coffin, it indicated that the body was not there. In the face of this new slander, there was nothing for it but to open the coffin. On 25 February William Kent, Stephen Aldrich, the undertaker, the Clerk and the Sexton to the Parish descended into the vault. The undertaker identified the coffin, the only one without a plate or inscription, and opened it before Kent and the other witnesses, and, according to a contemporary account, 'a very shocking sight it was'.

At last, the spirit had been definitely and categorically proved wrong. Meanwhile, Kent took steps to have an affidavit signed by Dr. Cooper and others concerning Fanny's illness and death. But what really did for the ghost were the efforts of a Mr. Missiter. Not satisfied that the Committee of Inquiry had done enough to discover the truth he persuaded Richard Parsons 10 days before the opening of the coffin, to allow Elizabeth to sleep at his house.

Parsons agreed, and so Elizabeth was taken to his house in Covent Garden. For four nights the scratchings and knocks went on. Then for the next two nights she was made to sleep spreadeagled in a kind of hammock with her hands and feet fastened. There were no knockings. Then she was told that she had only one night left to prove her innocence. Unless the ghost was heard, she, her mother and her father would all be sent to Newgate Prison. This time, however, her hands and feet were not tied. She was left alone in the room, but she was observed throughout the night through a peephole. Presently she was seen getting out of bed and taking out of a hiding place in the chimney a piece of board, about four inches by six. She climbed back into bed, and soon afterwards the knockings began again.

In the morning, the child strenuously denied all knowledge of the piece of wood. But when the bed was searched, it was found.

As so often, public opinion changed almost overnight, and swung behind Kent. The Cock Lane Ghost became a figure of fun. David Garrick, John Beard and Samuel Foote all introduced satirical plays at their various theatres. The King and Queen attended at least one of them.

But it was by no means the end of the affair as far as the promoters of the ghost were concerned. The Rev. John Moore, Richard Parsons, Mary Fraser and one Richard James were all put into the dock on a charge of conspiracy. James turned out to be a tradesman who had been responsible for the articles which appeared in many of the newspapers. He was a kind of 18th-century public relations' officer.

On the day of the trial, the court was full to overflowing. Among the witnesses were James Franzen, Carrots, and the doctor and apothecary who had attended Fanny. A large number of credulous people who swore the ghost existed appeared for the defendants.

According to Horace Walpole, the Rev. John Moore gave a letter to the Lord Chief Justice, who was trying the case, from the Archbishop of Canterbury interceding on behalf of Richard Parsons. Walpole says the Lord Chief Justice put the letter in his pocket unopened saying it could not possibly refer to the case.

The trial lasted from ten in the morning to half past nine at night. The Lord Chief Justice took an hour and a half to sum up, the jury 15 minutes to reach their verdict of guilty. Two other people were tried the following Monday for 'publishing against Kent in a newspaper' and fined £50 each. The conspirators were not brought up for sentence until some time later in the hope that they would pay damages to Kent. Six months later they had all failed to make satisfaction and so they were all committed to the King's Bench Prison on 27 January 1762 to await sentence at the end of the law term. A few days later Moore and James appeared in court

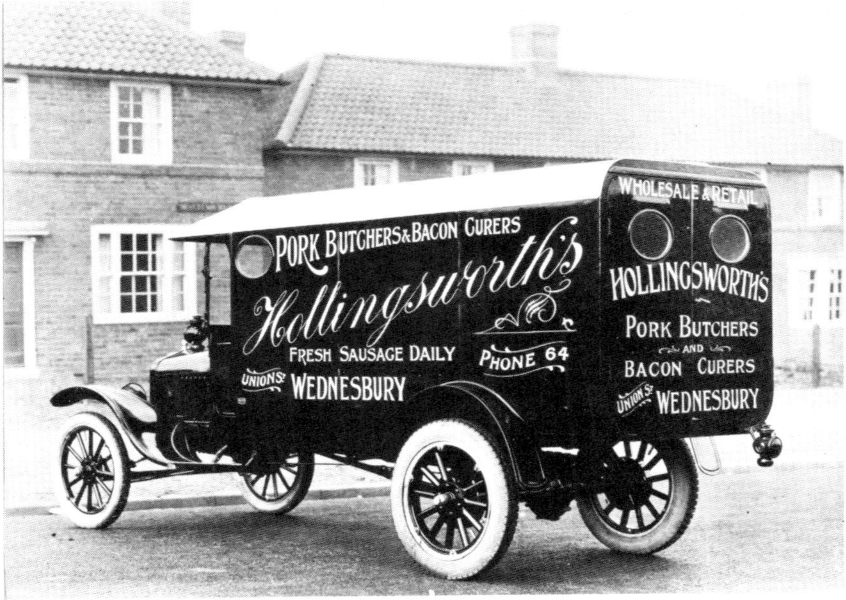


57. Hollingsworth's early motor transport

58. Roberts & Birch modern transport

59 and 60. Bacon preparation department: old and new

61. S.K. Gathard,
Joint Managing Director,
Bywater-Hollingsworth Ltd.
from 1970

62. Miller's modern factory

63. F.F. Parker
Managing Director
Hale Trent Cakes Ltd.
from 1965

64. G.S. Salmon
Joint Managing Director,
Hale Trent Cakes Ltd.
from 1965

65. Hale Trent factory at Clevedon

again and it was announced that they had paid Kent £588. They were dismissed and reprimanded by Mr. Justice Wilmot.

That was on the 11 February. The following day, Richard Parsons was sentenced to two years' imprisonment and ordered to stand in the pillory three times. His wife was sent down for a year, and Mary Fraser for six months. Mr. Justice Wilmot, according to a contemporary account, 'in a speech most excellently adapted to the occasion, expiated on the indignity of such an imposture'.

Yet Richard Parsons went on protesting his innocence and there were many still prepared to believe him in spite of everything. When he stood in the pillory for the first time on 16 March he was very kindly treated and a fair sized collection was taken for him. The same thing happened when he stood in the pillory at the Royal Exchange and at Charing Cross.

Before you pour scorn on their credulity, consider a strange sequel to this tale. 70 years later, Fanny's coffin was opened again by the artist, J.W. Archer, who said he found the body of a good looking woman, well preserved and with no sign of smallpox.

The vaults of St. John's were cleared in 1860, so no one will ever know.

Cock Lane today stands almost unchanged but I. Beer's lorries are too big to rumble down it, *The Wheatsheaf* has been demolished to make way for Lovell & Christmas, King Street and its school pulled down to provide space for a Poultry Market and the remainder demolished by Hitler's bombs, Hosier Lane is still busy, St. Sepulchre's still stands in its ancient beauty on Holborn Viaduct and St. John's, Clerkenwell serenely looks down on the activities of Auguste Noël and West Layton.

Perhaps the spirit of the Rev. John Moore and his clerk wander unseen about the Church in the same way as they wandered in person when William Kent and his Fanny attended the early morning prayers and took their lodgings in Cock Lane over 200 years ago.

## 13

### FROM CHOCOLATES TO COVENT GARDEN

I WENT to Covent Garden recently to visit Edwin Bevington Ltd., the newest member of our group. As I wandered fascinated through the market pavilions, past Smirke's Opera House and down the shabby streets where so much of the fruit and vegetables are sold, I could not help wondering why we, of London, so rarely visit these quarters which are surely of the most interesting in our capital city.

It is a pity that youngsters studying for their 'O' and 'A' level examinations in geography cannot go and have a practical lesson seeing strawberries from Mexico, Tanzania and New Zealand, avocado pears from Israel and South Africa, oranges from Brazil, pineapples from Kenya, aubergines from France, grapes from Greece and Italy, tomatoes from Bulgaria, grapefruit from Cyprus, Jamaica and Israel, figs from Turkey, apricots from Hungary, Spain and South Africa and so on. They would learn more than from text books.

I found Bevington's very like the market firms to which I have been accustomed. The alertness of the salesmen, the wide variety of goods, the continuous bustle of lorries, trucks and porters made the visit for me both exciting and rewarding.

Covent Garden, in many ways, is old-fashioned and the business of most firms very personal. This may be inevitable as the shippers of perishable overseas produce rely on the knowledge of, and need to have confidence in, their agents and representatives, as indeed do the customers.

There are still a good number of firms whose principals are at their posts by half-past four every morning ready to assess the market and make their sales – Bevington's is one of these firms.

Their day is long because it is seldom that they are able to leave until late in the afternoon.

Nowadays there is a tendency for the heads of some of the larger firms to arrive at breakfast time and leave the early morning business to salesmen, but the 'old timers' do not think they are as efficient or as well placed to achieve worthwhile results.

Bevington's, who have an outstanding reputation for integrity and straight dealing, was founded by Edwin Bevington, the present chairman, nearly three quarters of a century ago. He will soon be 90 years old but his intelligence is not abated; he is still an active and sprightly man.

Edwin Bevington's father was employed at Rowntrees of York, at a time when their staff consisted of a handful of people. Rowntrees decided they would try and sell their cocoa and chocolates in London and sent young Bevington, as their first representative, to try and open up the trade.

He evidently did well as he was able to send his son, Edwin, to Belgium, knowing that a thorough knowledge of French would stand him in good stead later in business.

When Edwin returned, his father gave him a newspaper and told him to read the advertisements and find himself a job. This he did with a Spanish grape importer in Gracechurch Street, E.C., at 10s. 6d. a week.

It was not long before the Spaniard went back to Spain and, recognising the abilities of the young man, he introduced him to a Spanish orange importer who engaged him at the same rate of 10s. 6d. a week.

The importer evidently liked Edwin because when he retired and returned to Spain he took the young man with him and after a short while booked him a berth on a coaster going to Almeira. It was not a very good boat and the sleeping bunks were full of fleas and such, so Edwin spent the night on deck with the various animals who were on the same voyage.

Spain, at this time, some 70 years ago, was very different from the Spain of today, but there were more opportunities for business and Edwin arranged to represent and sell for a Spanish shipper. He came back to London and founded his business.

Two years later there was a series of very bad frosts in Spain and the shippers were ruined. Edwin Bevington was left with £80 with which he began trading on his own account. He earned £40 the first month but the market fell, he lost nearly everything and was left with £6.

A broker in Monument Street, E.C. saw that he was an able young man and financed him, as a result of which he spent 30 years in the Monument Street area building up his business before moving to Covent Garden.

During this time, and while he was still very young, a Belgian representative offered him a post with a high salary in Antwerp for six months. Edwin took his brother into partnership to look after the business and crossed the Channel.

When he returned to London he received, almost at once, a telegram from the Belgian – 'Meet me in Paris'. He went without delay and his friend said, 'I will give you £8,000 and, if necessary, more if you will join me'. The reply was definite: 'Thank you but I intend to make a business of my own'.

Steadily and surely, helped no doubt by Edwin's knowledge of French and Spanish, the firm grew and prospered. It was formed into a limited liability company and two sons, Wilfred and J.M. joined their parent and have proved worthy members of a distinguished commercial family. The company was strengthened some years ago by the arrival of G. LeFlay who had obtained much experience in Boro' Market.

Today the connections spread wherever fruit and vegetables are produced or shipped, and growers, representatives and shippers consign their goods to them in confidence.

Edwin, now approaching his tenth decade, still comes regularly to Covent Garden and he writes, 'Our business is done, apart from foreign contracts, entirely by word of mouth and this is the way I like it'.

The success of Edwin Bevington Ltd. is summed up in these words of confidence.

14

## THE PIG AND HIS PRODUCTS

THE SUCCESS of the bakeries and the uncertain future facing the wholesale trade in the early 1950s turned the thoughts of Fitch to the wisdom of increasing its manufacturing capacity. Its association with Keevils' in Smithfield and with the profitable retail meat company of Layton and Burkett channelled those thoughts towards the bacon curing industry. Neither Fitch, nor Lovell & Christmas had previously been deeply involved in this field and so, as far as the Fitch Lovell Group is concerned, the now extensive bacon division is a new development.

As usual Fitch followed its policy of buying established businesses rather than starting a new one from scratch. One firm, Bywaters', dates back well over 100 years, and the other three, Collins Bros., Millers and Roberts & Birch have all been in business for more than a generation. I will touch on the background of these four firms and explain how they came into the group.

At first Fitch found it difficult to gain an entry into the bacon and cooked meat trade. Wartime controls were still in force and even the least efficient firms could make good profits and so naturally were reluctant to sell. Several small businesses were investigated, but the directors decided that buying a small concern lacking strong management and needing investment, would simply be buying trouble for the future.

Then Collins Bros. of Evesham approached us, this was just the kind of well-established medium-sized firm we were after and negotiations were nearly completed when Beer's came to an agreement with the Collins family to acquire a majority interest. It was naturally a disappointment at the time, but in due course Collins' was to find its way into the group when Beer's itself became a member.

After this false start Fitch continued its search and at last its patience was rewarded when, in November 1953, it was introduced through Charles Clores' Investment Registry to Bywaters', a well-known Midland company whose bacon, sausages, cooked meats, hams and pies were well-known over a wide area. In addition it owned some 30 retail shops in which its products were sold, and also delivered to other retailers and to hotels. Negotiations were carried out as quickly as possible, as time was not on our side, and agreement was reached in principle on 6 January 1954.

It was an important day, not only because it was the birth of the bacon division, but also because it brought into the company a man who was later to become Chairman of Fitch Lovell. That man was R.E. Blanning. Little did either of us realise what the future held for him as we hastily initialled the Heads of Agreement outside a Birmingham railway station with three minutes to spare before the train left for London.

Bywaters' has had a rather chequered history. Its early records have not been preserved and much of my information about the first years of the company's history comes from a Mrs. Lee, the daughter of a C.H. Twigg who once owned the business.

According to Mrs. Lee, the Bywater Pork Pie, the first and most famous of the firm's products, dates back to 1833, when the original Bywater family was living in Ludgate Hill, Birmingham. The original Mr. Bywater was a baker, and the family lived over his shop. It was Mrs. Bywater who began making the pies in her own kitchen for sale in the shop. The Bywaters had a large family of eight or nine children. One of them, Mary, continued making the pies after her parents died. She had left her mark on the business, for the 'M' in M. Bywater & Co. Ltd. stands for Mary. She had two nieces who lived with her and helped the now growing business. (They were the Misses Sanders, although most people referred to them as the Misses Bywater.) No doubt it is they who appeared in advertisements published by the company years ago as, 'The two maiden ladies who made the pork pies and sold them from their front room converted into a shop'. A delightful water-colour painting of the original shop by Paul Bradden still exists and shows the name *M. Bywater* over the door.

Mary Bywater died around 1887, some 40 years after making her first pie and her two nieces carried on until the elder died in

December 1894 or 1895. By this time the quality of the pies was appreciated over a wide area and the business had extended considerably when it was bought by Mr. Twigg, an old friend of the family. The old premises soon became too small for the increasing trade and an adjoining building was acquired. Mrs. Lee tells me that the business passed to A.D. Wimbush Ltd., the well-known bakers and confectioners, on the death of her father in 1914. There are no records to confirm this date, but the firm definitely owned Bywaters' by 1920, when the elder son of A.D. Wimbush (also A.D.) was in charge of the small factory at Small Heath a few hundred yards away from its present site, to which it moved some time before 1925.

Wimbush and his son did not altogether agree with each other in the running of the business, and their differences only ended when the father gave Bywaters' to his son, who in his turn severed his connections with the Wimbush bakeries.

Meanwhile the Bywaters' business was growing. Sales spread throughout the Midlands. In 1930 R.E. Blanning was engaged, at the age of 21, to improve the retail side of the business. In 1935 the business was incorporated as a limited liability company under the name of M. Bywater & Co. Ltd. The capital was £40,000 £1 preference shares and £40,000 ordinary shares (160,000 of 5s. each). A.D. Wimbush (II) owned all the ordinary shares.

A public quotation for the shares was obtained in 1936 and R.E. Blanning was appointed a director although only 27 years old. The three directors were A.D. Wimbush (II), B.T. Davies, Managing Director, and R.E. Blanning. Wimbush, the Chairman, sold his entire holding to the public, a move he must have regretted, because the following year, after the ordinary dividend had been passed, a shareholders' committee was formed, and on their advice both Wimbush and Davies were promptly removed from the Board, R.E. Blanning remained and ran the business with the shareholders' nominees until 1939. Meanwhile, there was litigation between Wimbush and the shareholders, with the courts finally coming down in favour of the former Chairman.

When the case was over, the company was reconstructed with A.D. Wimbush (II) and R.E. Blanning as controlling directors. Business increased in all directions. In 1952 the capital was raised to £120,000. A.D. Wimbush (II) was anxious to retire and that was the reason for Fitch's acquiring a controlling interest, with

R.E. Blanning remaining as Managing Director. It is noticeable that through all the vicissitudes of the previous 20 years R.E. Blanning had stayed on the Board, a tribute to the confidence he engendered in those with whom he worked.

For some years Bywaters' had had plans for extending its factory. This project finally came to fruition in April 1958, when the new premises – modernised and brought up to date – were opened by the Chairman of the Pig Industry Development Authority in the presence of a distinguished gathering which included the Deputy-Secretary of the Ministry of Agriculture, and the Vice-Chairman of the National Farmers' Union.

On the day of the opening R.E. Blanning was elected Chairman of Bywaters', a fitting recognition of his loyal and tireless efforts. The new factory, at the time possibly the most modern in Europe, was largely devised by him. He had been impressed by his visits to Denmark, Sweden and Holland and was desirous of improving the standards in British factories. The English Bacon Industry is indebted to him in many ways as he has served it unremittedly for years as Chairman of the Midland Curers and Vice-Chairman of the National Federation.

Five years passed before Fitch Lovell's bacon interests were extended any further. The next step, when it came, was a by-product of the merger with Beer's, which was itself the natural consequence of the merger between Fitch and Lovell & Christmas. Lovell's had a substantial shareholding in IBS, and IBS in turn, owned Collins Bros. the Evesham bacon curer which had almost been bought by Fitch. IBS also owned the South Wilts. Bacon Factory at Downton in Wiltshire. This factory was later closed as the area was adequately served by Millers of Poole – of whom more later.

The history of Collins' is even more turbulent than that of Bywaters'. The firm was founded in the early part of this century by two brothers, William and Frank Collins who owned a butcher's shop in Evesham High Street which, after a while, was enlarged to provide slaughtering facilities. The brothers began to make sausages and cooked meats. In 1929 they expanded into the curing of Wiltshire bacon and equipped a bakery where they made pies. They bought a factory in Mill Street which had been used for vegetable and fruit canning, and moved the slaughtery there.

In 1941 the successful partnership was incorporated as a private company with William, Frank and his son J.F. Collins as directors. J.F. Collins was appointed Managing Director. Towards the end of the war, however, serious discord arose between the three men over the running of the business. Their disagreements became so heated that the family doctor was asked to be on hand during board meetings in case one of them had a stroke! Their differences proved irreconcilable. Obviously the situation could not continue, so it was decided to sell the business. The family could not even agree on the sale, however. At the last minute William Collins and his daughter refused to proceed. The other two shareholders, Frank and his son took them to court to make them do what, it was claimed, they had already agreed to. They lost what on the face of it was a cast-iron case. The company was back in the unsatisfactory position of having its shareholders and directors at loggerheads.

A solution had to be found. A few months later the auditors suggested that Beer's should be asked to run the factory. The family agreed. Beer's were approached and agreed to do this. In 1954, Frank and J.F. Collins decided that they had had enough. They sold their shares to Beer's and severed their connection with the company. V.E. Shephard of Beer's was appointed Managing Director of the company which continued to do well for a few years, but profits began to decline as competition increased with the decontrol of meat. However, its reputation for high quality products, particularly meat pies, was maintained.

V.E. Shephard retired as Managing Director in 1969, Collins' then entered into close association, under new management, with Roberts & Birch, the fourth main bacon firm to join Fitch Lovell. Since then results have improved considerably, which makes one feel that the true potential of Collins' had never been realised before.

I hope it continues to do well, for Collins' is a valued part of the pleasant agricultural community of Evesham. In fact many of the staff own small market gardens, a fact which creates labour problems at the factory at certain times of the year! The company has made one notable contribution to the amenities of the town. At one time it owned the lock and weir in the River Avon adjacent to the factory. The river drove a turbine under the factory which supplied it with electric power. When this was no longer required, the company made a gift of the lock and weir to the Lower Avon Navigation Trust which has repaired the weir and put the lock in good order so that the river is now navigable for pleasure boats as far as Tewkesbury, and gives happiness to many hundreds of holiday makers during the summer.

For the third stage in the development of the bacon group we must leave the Midlands where Fitch Lovell had established a strong base for further advance, and go down to Poole in Dorset. It was a part of the country with which we were already familiar, because in 1955, the retailers, Robsons of Bournemouth, had joined the group. From our visits to Robsons, we realised that sales of pies and sausages in South West England were dominated by W.L. Miller of Poole. We also knew that several national manufacturers were anxious to buy the firm. Fred Miller, an outstandingly intelligent, capable and independent man, was standing out against their blandishments.

By coincidence. I got to know Fred Miller. We soon became friends and later I had the pleasure of meeting his brother and sisters. I suggested that he might be happier selling to Fitch Lovell than to any of the other companies who had approached him, but he was still not anxious to sell. However, being a fair minded man he felt that I should put my proposition to the other members of the family who owned large interests in the business. Fred said he preferred not to be present when I did this.

The family conference was a pleasant affair. They were not adverse to the idea of a sale, but they would not come to a decision without Fred. Eventually his reluctance was overcome and Heads of Agreement were drawn up. He has not regretted the decision. In April 1970 he wrote that the merger, 'has turned out to be a very happy association'. We, for our part, have been very happy with Fred Miller and with Miller's. Completion of the sale took place in February 1962. The consideration was 31 Fitch Lovell 6½% pref. for 25 Miller 7½% pref. and 6 F.L. ordinaries for one Miller £1 ordinary.

The Miller story starts 95 years ago. As with Bywaters' and Collins', the business began as a retail shop. It was situated at 104 High Street, Poole, and sold pork, bacon and groceries. However, it was not a Miller who opened the shop, but a Mr. Harris. 15 years later, he engaged Fred Miller's father, W.L. Miller as a first hand. In 1897 Harris suddenly decided to sell up and emigrate to Canada, and offered the business to W.L. Miller. Not surprisingly, the young first hand did not have the necessary capital. However, his father-in-law, a master baker by the name of Gallop, came to the rescue and loaned him the money. That Harris should have offered the shop to him, and that his father-in-law should have lent him the money shows that two men at any rate were confident that he would make a success of the business.

They were proved right. W.L. Miller and his wife Rose worked hard and the business increased so profitably that before long they had paid back every penny of the loan. They established a reputation for pork and pork sausages. There is an old photograph which shows the shop bearing the sign *W.L. Miller, Pork Butcher*. Underneath are written the words 'The noted house for sausages and fine pork. Pork selected from the best dairies. Home cured hams a speciality'. How different from modern advertising techniques! More than anything else, this simple, direct message tells of the close relationship which existed between the proprietor of a business like Miller's and the customers.

W.L. Miller did so well that he was able to send his four sons and two daughters to be educated at the Church Grammar School. F. Lionel Miller – Fred – was the second son. He left school at the age of 16 and went into engineering, an interest which he still keeps 40 years later as Chairman of Coolmotor Limited. When Fred was 21 his father asked him to join the firm. The year was 1924. W.L. Miller had decided to start wholesaling and wholesaling meant deliveries.

In the 1920s there was a lot to be said for putting this side of the business in the hands of someone who knew what went on under the bonnet of a lorry; so Fred set out in a newly acquired Bullnose Morris selling his father's sausages to the shops in Bournemouth and Poole. He must have been a first-class salesman, for his journeys soon began to take him to ever-widening areas in Dorset and Hampshire. Soon more vans and salesmen had to be employed.

The father and son formed the business into a limited company in 1936. About the same time they bought some land at Sterte, near Poole, and began in 1937, to erect a factory on the site. Business boomed, and it was extended in 1939, but the outbreak of war later that year put an end to any hope of further progress. It was only with the ending of meat rationing 14 years later that any advance could be made.

Meanwhile, in 1944, the firm's founder, W.L. Miller, had died, and Fred became Chairman and Managing Director. Two of his brothers, Leslie and John inherited shares from their father and became non-executive directors.

Fred Miller wasted no time as meat rationing came to an end. A new meat department, cold stores and bakery were built. An up-to-date abattoir was added and live pigs were bought direct from the farmers in Dorset and Hampshire. Gradually Miller's products began to dominate the region. The reasons for their success are not hard to find. Miller's scored through the drive of its Chairman, its concentration of sales within a small area, its excellent delivery organisation and the high and consistent quality of its goods made in a model factory in a delightful setting.

After the merger with Fitch Lovell the direction remained in the hands of Fred Miller. On top of the work he has done there, he has provided valuable help and guidance to other companies in the group.

I have so often told of firms growing from humble beginnings until it reaches the front rank of its industry, that perhaps I have made the achievement sound routine. But of course it is far from that. For every firm that makes the transition there are hundreds which do not. The achievements of the successful few are no accident. They are the result of countless decisions correctly taken, of solid integrity coupled with the unceasing urge to improve and advance. To these qualities Miller's have added humanity towards a large and increasing staff. It is fashionable to scoff at paternalism these days, but I am sure that in some respects we are poorer without it.

The broad outline of Fitch's bacon division was completed in March 1965, when the important Midland firm of Roberts & Birch joined the Group. R.E. Blanning of Bywaters, who had been the Director responsible for the division for some years, had been looking at this firm for a long time because he felt its geographical position at Burton, and its factory potential would strengthen his division considerably. Roberts & Birch shareholders were given three Fitch Lovell ordinary shares and 12s. 6d. in cash for every 10s. 2s. 6d. stock unit of Roberts & Birch.

Negotiations with Roberts & Birch had in fact begun five years before, but they had been broken off because of doubts by Fitch Lovell about management succession. Later, however, Roberts & Birch appointed J. Fisher as Production Manager. He is a superb technician with energy and imagination, and he made the improvements which enabled Roberts & Birch and Fitch Lovell to come to terms.

Once again, the story goes back to a small pork butcher's shop started by A.J. Roberts in 1857 at 10 High Street, the block of shops in front of the Burton Market Hall, within a stone's throw of old Burton Abbey, where the monks had first brewed Burton Ales from the local gypsum waters.

From the start, Roberts slaughtered pigs on the premises, and there was a gate at the side of the shop through which the pigs used to come. Some were brought in farm wagons, and others were unloaded at the Railway Cattle Dock and walked down Cat Street (later renamed Station Street).

For some years the shop continued as a small family business, building up a name for good quality pork, home-cured bacon, pork pies and sausages. A.J. Roberts was not seriously interested in expansion and devoted much of his time to civic affairs, becoming Mayor of Burton and an alderman. It was not until the arrival of John Henry Birch that things began to move. He joined Roberts in the early years of this century. He came from Newhall as his father had moved to Hawkins Lane where he worked as a cobbler. John had spent a short time as a clerk at the old Salt's Brewery in the High Street. He very quickly adapted himself to his new work with Roberts, becoming proficient not only in the clerical side but the practical side of the trade as well. He realised the firm's growth potential and despite the misgivings of the ageing alderman, acquired in April 1923, the present factory at Mosley Street, and the staff, consisting of about 30 employees, moved there. One of the most successful products was the *Rangemore Sausage* which is still popular today. It resulted from a visit to Burton by King Edward VII. He stayed at Lord Burton's home, Rangemore, and the firm sent up the specially made sausages to the royal table.

Several of the men who started at Mosley Street in 1923 are still there doing part-time work for the company. The factory was originally a tannery, and thus had large cellars, which were converted for curing. (In fact when John Birch bought the factory it was being used for making toys.)

Times were very difficult in 1923, and for the first 12 months the venture was at great risk. Hours in the factory were long and everyone turned his hand to the job of the moment, whether it was slaughtering, making sausages, cutting, manufacturing pork pies or cellar work. In those days a man was glad to be in work, and John Birch set an example by working from six in the morning to seven or eight at night, when he would begin dealing with his correspondence to catch the night mail at 9 p.m. There were from 100 to 250 killings a week in those days. The slaughtering was done on Mondays, Tuesdays and Wednesdays. Apart from sausages, pies and bacon, the firm were selling pork loins, dry-salted cured shoulder bellies known as *Robirch Specials* and a gradually increasing number of York Hams. As business picked up, the staff increased, although it was still small – about 50 men.

During the General Strike of 1926 a soup kitchen was opened in Mosley Street and another in Swadlincote for the destitute families of the South Derbyshire miners who were on strike. Roberts & Birch supplied large quantities of bones to make the soup.

When the strike was over, the firm, now becoming widely known as 'Robirch', began to forge ahead. It was supplying fresh meat to the Lancashire seaside towns and was a leader in the Midlands shoulder belly trade, while Robirch York Hams were becoming famous. Robirch products were reaching an ever wider market, and much publicity attended the exporting of regular shipments of *Rangemore* sausages, which went by the ton to Port Said and to Spinney's of Haifa. York Hams were despatched as far away as Rangoon packed in oat husks and metal cases.

The shadow hanging over the trade in the 1920s was competition from the Continent, especially from Denmark. The governments of the day felt it was worth flooding the home market with Danish bacon in order to be able to sell British manufactured goods in Denmark.

The English bacon trade responded by forming protective associations to make sure its voice was heard. These led to the establishment of official marketing boards for bacon and pigs. John Birch was active in the Midlands Bacon Curers' Association, and soon became a member of the Bacon Marketing Board. His colleagues were Ernest Marsh, Tom Hollingsworth and John (later Sir John) Bodinnar.

His solution to the problems facing the industry was to learn as much as possible from the Danes and to try and adopt their methods. He visited bacon factories in Copenhagen in 1930 to gain an inside knowledge of their curing methods, and promptly began equipping a £30,000 plant on the Danish pattern. He engaged experienced curers and a technical adviser, and curing began in 1931. The new cure was a success. Killings rose to 1,300 a week. All this development was paid for from current liquid cash resources. After the initial flotation of the limited company in 1928, no more money was raised. It was the era of development by private enterprise backed by know-how, energy and industry, with no room for passengers in management, office or factory.

Competition with the Danes remained fierce. For Robirch, as for the whole bacon trade, the '30s were a period of education, particularly in the type of pig needed if English bacon was to compete successfully. The trade continued to respond by building up marketing schemes and fighting for the level of imports to be controlled.

Problems of a different sort faced Robirch in 1939 with the outbreak of war and the imposition of wartime controls. A large cold store was immediately built and handed to the Ministry of Food for storing meat and bacon. Production of bacon continued under control and the company's ingenuity was stretched to the limit in the search for substitutes for scarce supplies of fresh meat. Food was manufactured using raw materials like whale meat and soya bean.

Just before the war ended, the company suffered a great blow in the loss of its pioneer and builder John Henry Birch, J.P. who died early in 1945. He was succeeded by his son Arthur John.

The company continued as a Ministry of Food production unit until the ending of controls. Robirch concentrated on building up its retail strength and in the early '50s controlled a chain of 30 shops in towns throughout the Midlands. Decontrol brought new problems for the company and it found itself struggling to maintain profitability. It was not until the early '60s, when J. Fisher joined the firm, that Robirch resumed its upward climb.

Strenuous efforts were made to develop the production of sausages, pork pies, cooked hams and cooked meats for sale in the home market. Modern machinery was installed and there were big alterations in packaging. Intricate machines were brought in for wrapping, sealing and coding with production dates. Transport methods were changing too. Pigs began arriving more and more by road in new double-tier cattle wagons direct to the factory from the farm. The whole selling system was changed on the advice of management consultants and Robirch adopted the modern van-salesman method. It was in the midst of all these developments that the agreement was reached with Fitch Lovell.

J. Fisher writes,

> Possibly this was the great turning point in the Company's history. It had developed and become a well organised production unit with very great potential which the Fitch Lovell directors quickly realised and turned to rapidly increasing through-put of high quality goods, particularly the new pre-packed bacon, boiling joints, pork pies and pastries, sausages and many other manufactured goods.

At this point, with four strong companies in the division, R.E. Blanning left to become Chairman of Fitch Lovell, in the knowledge that the original Fitch objective set out soon after the war to develop a viable interest in the bacon industry, was well and truly underway.

He was succeeded by E. Trevor Beer, who had considerable experience both with I. Beer & Sons and in Denmark. The delicate question now arose as to whether it was desirable for the four companies to continue producing independently a wide range of products each under its own brand name. Quite apart from the natural reluctance of the firms to give up either their names or any part of their traditional output, there was the problem of customer loyalty to these old established brands. Trevor Beer applied himself to this difficult question with energy and tact. Production was reorganised so that, while Miller's continued to produce a wide range of goods, Bywaters' concentrated on bacon, Collin's on ham, and Robirch on the so-called 'small goods'. A standard label was designed with the Miller's name on it in the South and Bywaters' & Robirch in the Midlands and North. Collins' sadly disappeared as a brand name. Fears that these changes might lead to loss of business proved unfounded.

The second main development of recent years had been the gradual closure of the retail shops owned by the factories in the group. It used to be a sound practice for bacon curers to own shops which acted as guaranteed outlets for their products, but in the supermarket era these shops, which are mostly small, have become less important.

A further development which took place in 1970 was the purchase of the goodwill and many of the fixed assets of Hollingsworth. Tom Hollingsworth, a great Midlands character, had sold his busi-

66. George Beale, 1865-1953
An outstanding pioneer of the
Multiple Trade

WHAT THE BUTLER SAW

67. Worlds Stores, 1952
Reproduced by kind permission
of the *Punch* Proprietors

68. Worlds Stores old shop
at Wells, 1932

69. M.C. Brooke
Chairman of Key Markets
from 1968

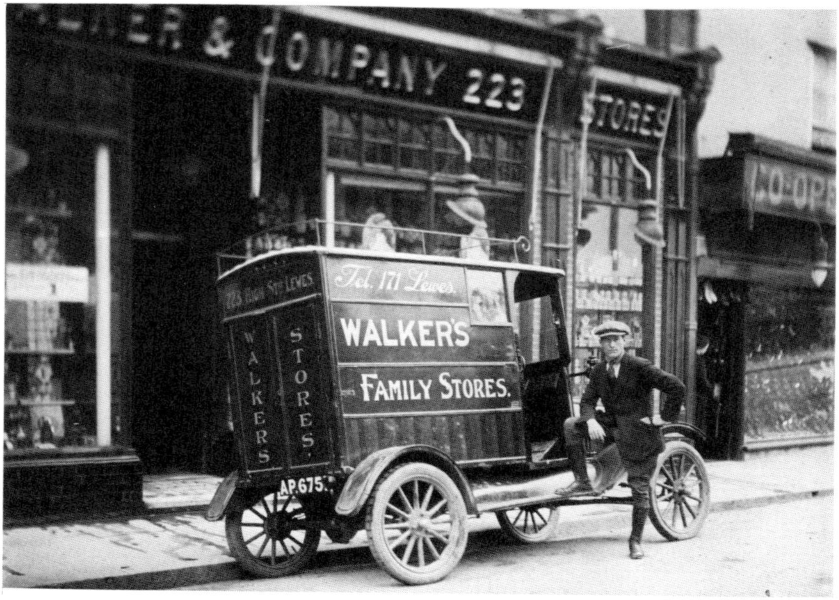


70. Walker's Stores: early shop and motor van

71. Modern supermarket at Isleworth:
Key Markets Ltd.

72. T.M. Cox
Chairman, West Layton Ltd.
1960-1970

73. Joseph Richards,
Chairman and Managing Director,
R. Gunner Ltd., 1957-60

74. C.J.N. Couture
Chairman and Managing Director,
R. Gunner Ltd., 1960-69

75. War-time mobile shop operated by R. Gunner Ltd.

76. Modern butcher's shop of R. Gunner Ltd.

77. Modern butcher's shop of West Layton Ltd. (left)

78. Presentation of awards to promising apprentices of West Layton Ltd. by Sir Ambrose Keevil, 1962

ness a few years earlier to a national company with widely diversified interests, but eventually this company, decided to streamline its activities and consequently Hollingsworth's factory found itself part of the Imperial Tobacco Company who, in its turn, approached Fitch Lovell, as it did not consider bacon curing likely to become part of its activities.

The trading side of Hollingsworth was transferred to Bywaters' and Peter Hollingsworth had become a joint Managing Director with S.K. Gathard. The name of the company has been changed to Bywater-Hollingsworth.

So, the position at the time of writing is that Fitch Lovell have a wide band of factories in the Midlands and a strong concern in the South and South West and is poised to leap forward as it fully realises the potential of the division which has already become one of the most important parts of the group.

The North Irish firm T. McElderry of McElderry & Moffett Ltd. and the Ulster firm Thomas Forde & Co. Ltd., are also bacon and by-product manufacturers and although for administrative reasons they are not part of the division, they work in close conjunction with it.

Details of these companies can be found under the divisions which administer them: McElderry under Lovell & Christmas and Forde under Fitch Home and Export.

## 15

## THE BAKERY GROUP

THE FIRMS WHICH grew into what is now the bakery group played a vital role in the development of Fitch Lovell, for it was the profits from bakery more than from any other source, which primed the rapid growth of Fitch & Son Ltd. in the 1940s and early 1950s.

The story begins, however, two decades before that, with a firm called George Partridge & Co. Ltd. in which Fitch had an interest. It was described in the 1920 prospectus as 'bakers' sundriesmen'. It sounds dull, but actually, its business was rather unusual. The firm was managed by C.S. Johnston, a man with a flair for invention. He was importing glycerinated egg yolks in barrels from China and imported albumen, and he had found a way to reconstitute the two into eggs for the bakery trade.

He was anxious to find a small bakery to experiment with this product in the manufacture of cakes. He talked about this project to H.S. Rowlandson, and in 1927 the two men bought a small bakery in North London owned by a man called Mehrtens. This was a private venture on the part of H.S.R., and Fitch was not involved. When I say Mehrtens was a small bakery, you will understand this as it operated from beneath the railway arches at Holloway. Johnston and Rowlandson each owned half the company. They changed the name from Mehrtens into Electricakes Ltd., a scarcely more appealing title to our ears, though no doubt it sounded very modern in those days.

A few years later, Fitch & Son purchased half the equity, and the name Electricakes was dropped in favour of the sober sounding title John Trent Ltd. All this time the firm was in fact still being run by the original Mr. Mehrtens who remained through all the changes as General Manager. With the participation of Fitch, the bakery began the first of a series of moves which have taken it to various parts of London and finally to Somerset.

The first move was to Knotts Green, E.10, where a travelling oven was installed. Trade increased, and the firm took over a leather factory in Skelton's Lane, Beaumont Road, Leyton. However, although sales were booming, the company had failed to do its sums. It discovered that it was working flat out for nothing. The losses began to build up, and in 1933 it became clear that it urgently needed to recruit an expert to organise a proper costing system. The sales supervisor, George Cook said he had a friend with considerable experience in costing which he had gained in the jute industry, first in Dundee and later in the Far East. His name was G.S. Macdonald. George Cook said he was willing to come and work for John Trent.

The introduction was accepted, and Macdonald soon had his nose in the books. What he discovered was even worse than everyone had feared. H.S. Rowlandson came down to Leyton at once, very worried about the £25,000 loan which Fitch had advanced to the company. He said he would have to close the bakery and salvage what he could to pay back Fitch.

The Fitch Lovell bakery story might have ended there, had it not been for Macdonald. He pleaded with Rowlandson to give him a chance. He was sure that under the right sort of control the bakery could be made to pay. Rowlandson was persuaded, and in a very short time, Macdonald was proved right. By 1939, John Trent had extended its bakery activities to include preserving jam, and the firm was well and soundly on its feet. Just prior to the war H.S. Rowlandson's son-in-law, Norman E.F. Lambourne who had been working in his family's Birmingham firm was persuaded to come south and take over the sales side of John Trent.

During the war, Trent's received very large allocations of sugar from the Ministry of Food, based on the quantities it had been using before the war, and the company forged ahead.

In 1941, Fitch's bakery group took a big step forward when Fitch & Son bought 65% of Hales Home Bakery (Clevedon) Ltd. of Clevedon in Somerset. After the sale the name was changed to Hales Home Bakeries Ltd. The firm had been built up by a Bristol baker called Frank Hale.

The story goes that Frank Hale had a small baker's shop at Staple Hill, Bristol where he specialised in lardy cakes. Apparently his health was delicate, and his doctor advised him to move out from Bristol to the countryside. Accordingly, he took a little baker's shop in the village of East Clevedon. (I'm not sure of the date, but I believe it was 1928. The shop still stands in front of the modern Hales factory.) No sooner had he arrived, however, when the flour market had one of its major slumps. Frank Hale decided that this was a good opportunity to expand. Buying large quantities of flour at rock bottom prices, he started making 1 lb. cakes and selling them wholesale. They appeared in the shops at 6d. each. He called the new product *Hale's Farmhouse Cake*, and the name soon became well known far beyond the village of Clevedon.

Frank Hale engaged salesmen and opened depots at Swindon and Totton. Sales of the cakes spread throughout the West Country. He turned the business into a limited company in 1933. It continued to grow, but Frank was always frail and was relying on his son to succeed him. However, his son announced that he intended to become a doctor. During the war Frank became very ill, and at this point, the representative of a Business Transfer Agent in London happened to be passing through Clevedon on his way to the West Country for a holiday. He decided to call in, and as a result of this visit, he introduced Frank Hale to Fitch & Son.

Soon after the sale, Frank Hale had to go into hospital for an operation from which he did not recover. *Hale's Farmhouse Cake*, on which the fortunes of the company had been based, died with him. After the war it was difficult to get the right ingredients of the right quality, and so the line had to be dropped. Instead a new cake was launched, called *Mother's Cake* because the recipe for it came from Norman Lambourne's mother. He had moved down to Clevedon on demobilisation to take over the direction of Hale's, leaving G.S. Macdonald in charge at Leyton. Unfortunately Hale's were attacked by Ranks, the flour people who claimed that *Mother's Cake* infringed their registered trade mark *Mother's Pride* flour. The lawyers advised that it would probably be more expensive to defend an action than to surrender, and so the name was changed to *Grannie's Cake*. Even to use this name, Hale's had to enter an agreement with Meredith & Drew Ltd., who owned the trade mark *Granny's Cookies*, that they would not make cakes and Hales would not make biscuits under the name *Granny's* or *Grannies*. After the problems with the name had been sorted out, the new cake became even more popular than the farmhouse cake had been, and it is now one of the best selling cakes in the South West and Midlands.

The mention of Meredith & Drew leads us to the Far Famed Cake Co. Ltd. Meredith's was rationalising some of its activities just after the war, and wanted to sell its bakery in Poplar, East London which dated back to the 1880s. Rowlandson came to terms with it, and John Trent bought the company in January 1946.

By this time, Fitch's bakery group had become extensive, and a bakery committee had been set up to co-ordinate the activities of the various bakeries. D.J. Apps who had been an audit clerk in the accountants who did John Trent's audit before the war, joined John Trent as Office Manager and became secretary of the bakery committee. New machinery was installed at Far Famed, and many improvements were carried out at Hale's. The profits of the bakery group rose steadily.

Norman Lambourne had a long standing ambition to begin a bread-baking plant. By this time the group was also running a number of retail shops which would provide an outlet for it, and so the bakery committee decided to build a small plant for the production of just enough wrapped bread to supply the retail shops. After some time, Norman Lambourne found a site at West Drayton, near London Airport which was suitable for a much larger operation, and the bakery committee agreed to give the go-ahead for a plant capable of processing 1,000 sacks of flour a week (a sack of flour produces approximately 220 quartern loaves). An expert in the automatic manufacture of bread, F.F. Parker joined Trents, through whom the project was being launched. (Parker's family firm, Parkers Bakeries Ltd., had been sold and he was unhappy in the giant corporation which had purchased it.)

The bread plant began production in 1953, and within 18 months it was making a profit, a tremendous achievement by Norman Lambourne and F.F. Parker. The target production figure of 1,000 sacks of flour a week was reached in May 1957. Although Trent's was responsible for the bread operation, the product was sold under the name of Hales Bread. It was becoming so successful that it was beginning to worry the national manufacturers, and several of them made approaches. In the end an offer was received from Joseph Rank Ltd. which the Boards of Fitch & Son and John Trent felt they could not refuse.

It was the end, after barely six years, of one of the most successful ventures in the Fitch Lovell story. The sale was important for another reason. It stimulated Fitch's already strong cash reserves and smoothed the financial path for the imminent merger with Lovell & Christmas.

The success of the bread venture was tempered slightly by the failure of another project. At a time when bakery profits were at their peak, a largish group of retail bakers shops trading as Crisps Bakeries was purchased, but Fitch's bakery division was essentially manufacturing and lacked anyone with retail experience, and the new company never made profits. Instead it simply dissipated the energies of the executives, and after a few years it was decided to sell its various branches and liquidate the company.

Meanwhile G.S. Macdonald, the man who had saved the existence of the bakery group back in the '30s, had retired, and Norman Lambourne took over responsibility for the group. He was almost immediately faced with a sharp deterioration in the cake trade, but with his energy and imagination he surmounted the many problems in a year or two. Things were particularly difficult because the problems in the cake business coincided with the need to provide heavy investments for the bread plant.

After this difficulty had been overcome, the bakery group continued to expand its activities. Its products have been featured several times in the Fitch Lovell annual reports. One picture shows a Hale's van with the caption 'Hale's Cakes are carried fresh from Clevedon to over 10,000 shops a week in the West, Midlands and North'. (This was a reference to the policy of direct overnight delivery from the factory which had replaced the old network of depots which both Hale's and Trent's set up, from Okehampton and Bridgend to Sheffield in the North, Mildenhall in the East and Ashford and Burgess Hill in the South.) Another picture shows the automatic swiss roll plants at Clevedon with the caption 'Swiss Rolls are produced by the mile'. There are pictures of the four acre extension of Hale's factory at Clevedon and of the new automatic machinery there and at John Trent and Far Famed. Others show mass production of *Grannie's Cake*, a biscuit plant automatically coupled with a chocolate enrober, and an automatic plant making 9,000 jam tarts an hour at Leyton.

The factory alterations, new buildings and the installation of the most modern machinery kept the whole bakery group fully occupied and they were glad to retain the services of F.F. Parker after the sale of the bread bakery.

Soon after Fitch's merger with Lovell & Christmas a number of smaller companies which were a relic of the Fitch days were sold off to enable the bakery group to concentrate on its main activities. They included firms making jam, sweets, crystallised cherries and one small factory making dog biscuits. (The dog biscuit company was called Chorbo Foods Ltd. The biscuits could not compete against the nationally advertised brands. However the biscuits were exceptionally favoured by dogs, and had the finance been available to advertise the product and develop the company it might well have been a success.)

In 1962 the group was disturbed by the resignation of Norman Lambourne. For a long time he had the ambition to own a company of his own, and when the opportunity arose to acquire Kunzle in his home town of Birmingham he decided to go ahead and achieve his life long desire. F.F. Parker who had been so closely associated with him decided to go too. Both men were much missed. H. Boyes Stubbs who had been in charge of Hale's took over the general direction of the bakery group at the suggestion of Norman Lambourne, and Sir Rolande Wall consented to become Chairman in addition to his many other duties. Unfortunately, the cake trade now entered another of its cyclical difficulties and H. Boyes Stubbs had serious problems to contend with almost from the day he took over. Worse still, his health began to suffer to such an extent that he had to retire.

Meanwhile Sir Rolande, who by 1963 had assumed the Chairmanship of Fitch Lovell, had appointed as his personnel assistant, Norman Damerell, whom he had known during the war when he was at the Ministry of Food. Norman Damerell had a long experience of the bakery trade, and the company was fortunate that he was available to take over the group. It did not make a profit in 1964, which was an unlucky beginning for Norman Damerell, but he and his team steadily improved things. They were greatly helped by the return of F.F. Parker. At Far Famed, Gordon Salmon was doing great work and gradually the position improved until they have now regained their old level of profitability and indeed surpassed it.

The holdings of the Rowlandson family in John Trent had been acquired by Fitch Lovell before the departure of Norman Lambourne and as a further step in re-organisation, Hale's and Trent's were merged in March 1965 into Hale-Trent (Holdings) Ltd., with Fitch Lovell owning 83% of the equity. The Trent premises in East London were sold and Trent's moved down to Clevedon. Far Famed remain at Poplar and much of its output goes direct to Woolworths.

There exists a fine imaginative spirit in the group from which Sir Rolande has now retired and Norman Damerell has taken the chair. It is meeting the changing competition of these days with every confidence. One should never forget that it was the bakery group which was the foundation of the success of Fitch Lovell Ltd.

# 16

## FROM SMALL SHOPS TO KEY SUPERMARKETS

THE NEXT TWO chapters are devoted to Key Markets, the Fitch Lovell supermarket operation, and the retail butcher's chain, West Gunner.

Key Markets, one of the most progressive supermarket firms in the South of England, is the offspring of a marriage in 1961 between two old established multiples, World's Stores, largely a Lovell & Christmas interest, and Green's Stores a chain mainly concentrated in Essex. Over the years these firms have themselves absorbed a number of other groups. It is in the nature of a chain store company that all its branches should bear the same name, and thus many of the names of original branches are completely forgotten outside the trade, and no doubt World's and Green's will follow them. However, they were both successful in their day, and their origins are interesting. Green's in particular was closely associated with the pioneers of multiple stores.

World's Stores was in the Fitch Lovell family first. Once more the Luftwaffe must be blamed for lack of information about a company's early history. The head office in Trinity Street, London, was bombed in 1940. Officially, World's Stores was founded in 1906, although Lovell & Christmas did not become involved in it until 1919. However, according to a Mr. Inkpen, who was an employee of the company for over 40 years and rose to the rank of inspector, the history of World's Stores goes back well into the 19th century, and the firm was founded by none other than John Cary Lovell himself. Inkpen says the shops were first opened as a result of a quarrel between John Cary and Frank Beer, one of the sons of Isaac Beer, who was the buyer for the Home & Colonial Stores, which, at that time, was the largest of the new multiple chains.

Apparently, John Cary depended very much on Frank Beer's orders for cheese. As we know, John Cary had provided some much needed assistance for Frank's father. This friendly arrangement suddenly came to an end, when, for reasons which are unknown, Frank Beer stopped ordering his cheese from Lovell & Christmas. John Cary Lovell was not the sort of man to take this lying down. Impetuously he declared that he would open his own chain of shops. He engaged a man, Robert Cobley of the Star Tea Co. and told him to open as many shops as he could. John Cary said that he would provide finance. 23 shops were opened. They were very small, selling about eight lines only.

At this point, John Lovell settled his differences with Frank Beer and gave up his plan to rival the Home & Colonial. He told Cobley to open no more shops and sold the chain to S. Frost & Co. Whatever the authenticity of this attractive tale, there is no doubt that shops bearing the name World's Tea Stores were in existence in 1893. The 1906 date officially regarded as the date of foundation and celebrated in a golden jubilee in 1956, is in fact the year in which the firm was formed into a limited liability company under the name of the World's Stores Ltd.

In 1906 it was operating 71 branches with an average turnover of £60 a week. Inkpen writes that managers were paid 30s. a week, which does not sound so little when compared with the prices of the groceries they sold. Lard was 3d. a lb., margarine 4d., cheese 5d., and butter 10d. Inkpen's memory cannot have been far out, because there is a wages' book in existence which goes back to 1919. In that year a manager received the princely sum of £2 a week. In the same book, National Health contributions are recorded in 1921 as 7d. per man per week, 4d. was paid by the employee and 3d. by the firm.

World's Stores was active in the South and West of England. By 1914 the number of branches had increased to 114, and the chain grew even bigger when the 23 shops of Walker's Stores were absorbed in 1916. (Walker's was based on Henley-on-Thames, and some of its shops were quite large. An early price list shows hundreds of lines of patent medicine, china and hardware, presumably the firm's main business.) for some years after this merger the company was known as World's and Walker's Stores Ltd.

Lovell & Christmas began buying shares in 1919. In November of that year it purchased 17,000 at 20s. each from S. Frost & Co. In June 1921 it bought 70,000 shares from the Investment Alliance Ltd. for £80,000. It is not clear from the records exactly when control of the company passed to Lovell's. It must have continued buying shares in considerable quantities for in 1924 it refused an offer by the North Europe Trust Co. who offered to buy 422,712 shares at 25s. each. Lovell's presumably owned all these at the time. Almost certainly they constituted a controlling interest.

Many branches were added in the 1920s and at one time the number reached 200. However, complaints were made at Lovell & Christmas Board Meetings of the low return on capital employed. Henry Frost, the Chairman of S. Frost & Co. Ltd. an outstanding figure in the retail trade, was asked to become Chairman and Managing Director in 1928. Mr. Webster, who had been in charge of the chain for many years, retired. Henry Frost quickly set to work. He closed uneconomic branches, modernised others and quickly earned the thanks and congratulations of Lovell & Christmas. In 1933 he gave six months' notice of retirement as he was being appointed Managing Director of Allied Suppliers Ltd. to which he was selling his own shares in the family company of S. Frost & Co. Ltd.

During the Second World War, the offices of the company had to move out to Henley when Trinity Street was destroyed. Many of the branches were damaged in the bombing and six were completely destroyed.

After the war, Alan Elliott and his brother Dennis, sons of the Chairman of Lovell & Christmas, took over the management of the company. They had to face the difficulties of the post-war period, the repairing of damaged branches and re-staffing in a period when the pattern of trade was changing fast. However, they were able to report in 1956 that the number of branches was larger than ever and prospects were excellent. In particular, they had built up an outstanding reputation as bacon retailers. By 1957 profits had topped £200,000. Many of the shops were being converted into self-service.

When Lovell & Christmas merged with Fitch & Son in the following year, World's Stores absorbed the retail group which Fitch & Son had been building up since 1957 called Hale & Partners. Many of these had been converted into self-service shops, and they had one supermarket at Strutton Ground in Westminster. It was the first in the Group and it opened in August 1958. Reg Harrison, now with Lovell & Christmas, was the driving force behind Hale & Partners, aided by his brother William and John Gilpin. On the merger, Reg Harrison became a director of World's Stores.

Meanwhile, under the dynamic leadership of Tesco, supermarkets were spreading rapidly through the towns of Britain, and it became clear that Fitch Lovell would have to move quickly if it was to have a share of this new type of trading. It was considered advisable to buy into supermarkets by acquiring a group which had already progressed further along the supermarket road than World's Stores had, and so in 1961, the firm acquired the share capital of Green's of Ilford.

Arthur William Green the founder of Green's began trading as a grocer at 86 High Road, Ilford, in 1895. The business grew and in 1921 he turned it into a private limited liability company with a capital of £50,000. By 1929, there were 33 shops, including a paint and hardware store and two drapery stores, one at Upminster and the other at Corbetts Tey. Green took corner sites and operated sub-post offices wherever he could. It remained a family type of business, with credit given, a delivery service and licences to sell wine and spirits.

It was at this point that Green's came to the notice of the remarkable George Beale. He was in his middle 60s by this time, but behind him lay a lifetime of involvement in the phenomenal growth of multiple stores in Britain. He had opened up the North-east of England for the Maypole Dairy Company, rising to Chief Inspector at the age of 36. When Maypole went public in 1898 he could see little hope of promotion and decided to begin on his own, paying £30 for the 'ingoing' of his first shop in Newcastle and another £3 to have it cleaned. By 1916 his company which he called the Meadow Dairy Company had 400 shops and George Beale moved his headquarters to London.

The rapid growth of this and other multiple shops was largely due to the margarine manufacturers who financed them in rather the same way that John Lovell financed the butter producers in New Zealand, Australia and the Argentine. The reason for their interest is not hard to find. Margarine, which was only invented in 1869, encountered strong sales resistance in traditional shops. By financing the expansion of the multiples the manufacturers were creating outlets for their product. By 1900 the multiples were selling 50% of the margarine manufacturers' output.

Beale's backer was Van den Bergh, now part and parcel of the modern Unilever group. In 1927 Beale and Van den Bergh's gained virtual control of Lipton's, the Company which, under Sir Thomas Lipton, had started the multiple ball rolling. Events moved quickly, and in 1929, the two main margarine groups Jurgen's and Van den Bergh's got together under the name of Unilever, and their extensive interests in the multiples made a merger in that field only a matter of time. In fact it took place in the same year. Lipton's, Home & Colonial, Maypole, and Meadow came together under the name Allied Suppliers. George Beale became Vice Chairman, one of his sons, Tom, became Managing Director of Meadow, and another, Roy, was Managing Director of Lipton's.

Inevitably, one is led to ask why such a man should be interested in a comparatively small concern like Green's. The answer, I think, is that George Beale could not bear the thought of being involved in a concern over which he had little direct control. It was this desire for independence which had led him to quit Maypole to start his own company 30 years before. Now he resigned again, and took his sons with him. He bought Green's and sold it to his sons for the price he paid – £54,000 – in order to ensure that they too would own the company they worked for.

The two brothers were joined by the third son William, just down from Pembroke College, Cambridge, and the three of them began the hard job of expanding Green's. George Beale stayed on the Board and happily watched the success of his sons. Most of his still considerable energy went into a farm of 1,000 acres to which he had retired. The young Beales had been well trained, and they followed the classic techniques of the leading multiples, trading for cash, selling fast-moving lines and expanding wherever new sites at low rents could be found. No shop was more than 50 miles from the warehouse, in fact for many years, 25 miles was the limit. The branches were often only half a mile apart. Growth was closely linked with the pre-war building boom in Essex, which remained the main area of operation.

Many freeholds were bought for £1,000 or £1,500. It was proved that a shop taking £60 a week could be profitable if the overheads were low enough. In the 10 years preceding the war the chain grew from 33 stores to 125. The Beales were opening shops at the rate of nearly one a month. The rapid rate of expansion created great opportunities for the staff. Many who began as errand boys about this time hold important positions in Key Markets today. During the war many girls stepped up to become manageresses and did splendidly.

Although, during the war, Essex was in the flight path of the German bombers and no fewer than 90 shops were damaged in the bombing, there was a splendid *esprit de corps* in the company. Somehow all the damaged shops managed to be back in business within 24 hours of the bombs falling. Even the company officials enrolled themselves into repair squads to help clear up the damage before returning to their desks at Head Office. A special welfare committee kept in touch with all the members of the staff in the forces and made sure that their jobs were waiting for them when they were demobilised.

William Beale was released to join NAAFI. After training he went to West Africa to be in charge of facilities for troops in Sierra Leone, Gambia, Gold Coast (Ghana) and Nigeria. Two years later he was posted to the 21st Army Group to help plan NAAFI's part in the invasion of the Continent. He quickly became NAAFI's Number One in Europe, responsible for an area stretching from Normandy to Berlin and for a business with a turnover of one million pounds a week. Under his control were breweries, bakeries, biscuit factories, ice cream and mineral water plants as well as clubs, cafes and shops. He was given an O.B.E. for his services. This work, while extremely important to his country, was also valuable experience for William Beale and for Green's.

After the war the company began to diversify away from the Essex area. In 1945 it bought George Lunts & Co. of Liverpool who owned 90 shops and two bakeries. The company was built up and eventually sold to our good friend Webster of Wright's Biscuits Ltd. Unfortunately much of the profit on the sale of Lunts' was lost by an unhappy adventure into ice cream at Lytham St. Annes. Green's bought the Cremado Ice Cream Company in 1948, while sweet rationing was still in force. The product was sold from stalls along the Golden Mile at Blackpool and to a lesser extent in Green's own shops. Eventually Cremado was sold to Eldorado showing a loss of £80,000. As William Beale writes: 'A man should stick to his own last'.

About this time fears began to grow that the Labour Government might nationalise distribution. In order to protect themselves against this possibility, the ever adventurous Beale brothers decided to open up in Rhodesia. They began with a three point plan: to grow beef, to grow tobacco, and to open stores for the natives. Almost certainly they spent too much time, energy and money on the Rhodesian project between 1949 and 1953, and the main business began to suffer. As William Beale says, 'we had not learnt the lesson of Cremado Ice Cream'. Roy Beale decided to stay in Southern Rhodesia and he purchased the Rhodesian interests from his brothers. Tom, the other brother, had already retired from active participation, and so William was left to run Green's in England on his own. While the company's sights had been set on Africa, the multiple grocers at home had been making rapid strides and Green's was falling behind in the race, especially as self-service stores were beginning to appear in the high streets. Green's first excursion into this new trade was a failure. The shop, which was at Barkingside, had to be converted back into counter service. In spite of this set-back, most of the branches were made semi-self service over the next few years and several shops were converted into full self-service.

William Beale, with his son Richard, visited America in 1958 to attend a National Cash Register seminar. They were so inspired by what they heard that they stayed up most of the night to produce a plan for the future of Green's. After long discussion they wrote down four points on the back of an envelope; to send senior managers to America over the following six months, to open a super-market, to obtain 'know-how' in meat retailing and fresh produce, and to do this quickly by taking over a company.

Not long afterwards, William Beale met George Dyson, who owned 20 shops. 13 of them were grocery and provisions stores, seven meat shops. He also had a supermarket at Enfield and another due to be opened. A deal was made and Green's paid Dyson his asking price of £500,000 for the business. A new company, Green & Dyson Ltd. was formed as a wholly-owned subsidiary of Green's Stores Ltd. With the newly acquired skills of the Dyson group and George Dyson's own flair for property, the policy of opening supermarkets as quickly as possible went ahead successfully. A five year development plan was drawn up. Meanwhile, in 1958, Green's Stores had become a public company with an Authorised Capital of £500,000.

A profitable experiment was made in 1959 which pointed clearly the direction in which food retailing was heading. A discount store was opened in a disused cinema at Southend in which Green's held the food concession. There were misgivings in the trade about the project, but right from the start the aisles were jammed with people. All the supervisors had to be called in during the night to restock the gondolas.

While supervising the recovery of Green's, of which he had become Chairman in 1951, William Beale somehow found time to return to NAAFI. He became its Chairman in 1953 and steered it through a difficult period when the staff was contracting from 20,000 to 12,000. The shops were changing into supermarkets. Meanwhile 'Char and wods' canteens were being made into clubs and small department stores were being opened for the families of service men in Germany. William Beale was knighted in 1956 for his many services, an honour which everyone knew to be deserved. He was strongly supported during this busy time by C.E.M. (now Sir Charles) Hardie who joined the Board of Green's in 1953. Hardie is one of the leading accountants in the City of London and is now Chairman of Fitch Lovell.

Sir William Beale became Chairman of the National Multiple Grocers in 1961 and during his two years in office organised the trade against stamp trading with the help of Lord Sainsbury and Malcolm Cooper. Stamp trading had spread through the U.S.A. like wildfire, and the brake upon it here was the result of their efforts.

Then in November 1961 came the offer by Fitch Lovell for the share capital of Green's. It was accepted by the shareholders. They received one Fitch Lovell 6½% preference for one Green & Dyson preference, and two F.L. ordinary shares for each G & D ordinary. Sir William Beale was invited to join the Fitch Lovell Board as a Managing Director. At the time Green's profits were £222,828.

Immediately, the big task began of fusing Green's with World's Stores. At first a Management Committee from the two companies was set up, then the following year their separate identities were merged under the new company Key Markets Ltd. There were now no fewer than 400 branches to be managed. The many difficulties

79. Ludovic Noël,
Founder of L. Noël & Sons,
1837-1901

80. Auguste V.A. Noël,
1875-1952

81. E.V. Noël,
Chairman, L. Noël & Sons Ltd.
1952-1971

82. N. Ouwehand and M.P.E. Delaporte,
Joint Managing Directors, Auguste Noël Ltd. from 1965

83 and 84. Auguste Noël Ltd.:
Warehouse, old and new

86. L. Noël and Sons Ltd.:
premises at Soho Works, S.E.5

85. L. Noël & Sons:

*Reproduced from* THE SUNDAY TIMES, 5.9.43.

87. Site of Machin & Kingsley premises in Aldersgate Street, E.C.1. after bombing in 1943

88. Norman B. Machin, Chairman and Managing Director, Machin & Kinglsey Ltd. from 1963

89. Alan R. Kingsley, President, Machin & Kingsley Ltd. from 1963

90 and 91. Modern plywood and building boards

were gradually overcome. The closure of uneconomic shops proceeded steadily and a long term plan for supermarkets was agreed. Distribution was centred round warehouses in Essex. In fact, the new company took shape much more quickly than we had a right to expect.

In 1964, with the groundwork completed, Sir William Beale retired and was succeeded by David Galloway who had come into Fitch Lovell through West (Butchers) Ltd. He was a strong believer in supermarkets, and on his initiative West's had opened a supermarket at Walton-on-Thames many years before. He had the assistance of Michael Brooke, Peter Williams, Gerald Fuller, Richard Beale, Reg Sharp and others from World's and Green's, and proceeded to shape them into a closely knit and enthusiastic team.

Unfortunately, in 1968 he became seriously ill and had to relinquish the Chair. His four years had been a period of intense activity, with the creation of new supermarkets, the training of staff, the implementation of new buying systems and warehousing. Computers had been installed to cope with the vast increase in the size of the business. All this had placed great strains on David Galloway and his executives. Michael Brooke, who had been Vice-Chairman, succeeded him. He had a lifelong experience of the food trade. Under his direction Key Markets continue to advance and have achieved an enviable reputation. The stores have a definite image of their own, with meat, fresh produce and delicatessen as prominent features, just as Sir William and Richard Beale envisaged when they wrote their ideas down on the back of an envelope 13 years before. As supermarkets become still larger, Key Markets are now diversifying into many types of goods outside food. By 1969 the number of supermarkets had shot up to 80, in addition there are 150 self-service and counter service shops – a big change compared with the 400 smaller shops in 1962.

Alan Elliott who managed World's Stores after the war still remains a director of Key Markets. His particular knowledge of property made the Fitch Lovell directors turn to him when they needed someone to supervise the Fitch Lovell properties, the portfolio of leaseholds and freeholds having risen to nine million pounds.

The problems facing Key Markets in 1970, with individual rents of £15,000 a year and upwards for stores of 7,500 sq. ft. and fitting out expenses of perhaps £45,000 are rather different from those facing the multiple pioneers in the 1890s when rents were 10s. a week and fitting out expenses were £70. The possibilities too are greater with turnovers of which George Beale could not have even dreamed. The skills needed are different too. The buyer in the old days had to be a judge of quality and grade. He had no cold store to preserve his perishable produce. Today almost everything is packaged and graded, and most of the selling has already been done through national advertising before the goods reach the supermarket. The challenge now is to preserve and develop the individuality of Key Markets. Without this special image the supermarkets will become nothing but giant stalls selling standardised goods. This state of affairs could lead to price cutting on a scale unknown even in the inter-war years.

Just as men like George Beale and John Lovell rose far above the ordinary through their personality and imagination, it is expected that Key Markets will surmount whatever problems may lie ahead.

## 17

### WEST GUNNER

THE FITCH LOVELL meat division, now known as West Gunner, can have pride and satisfaction in the outstanding reputation its shops enjoy today and in the steady contribution which it has made to the group's profits over the years. The decision by Fitch & Son to go into meat retailing was taken soon after the war, at about the time we decided to develop our manufacturing interests and retail groceries.

With my Smithfield experience I took a special interest in the meat retailing project right from the start. Although it was agreed that Fitch should be in retailing, I was not particularly happy about retail groceries. I could remember only too clearly the poor record of the cut-price multiple grocers before the war. In 1947, of course, it was too soon to forsee the supermarket explosion. When I voiced these fears to business agents they pressed me to enter meat retailing because, they said, it was a business of craftsmen and as such must survive and even expand. The advocates of a new supermarket industry, on the other hand, were loud in their conviction that the local butcher's shop would virtually disappear within 10 years because housewives would want to do all their shopping in one shop, the supermarket, where they would be happy to buy prepacked meat.

Neither of these forecasts have proved correct. In spite of competition from the supermarkets, the butchers have survived surprisingly well, although the optimistic forecasts of the late '40s have not been fulfilled. The retail meat trade can hardly be described as a growth industry now, but one can only be pleased we bought, in 1950, seven shops in London trading under the name of Layton & Burkett.

I have to admit that I have come to a firm whose origins were obscure but I know the Burketts were a family who had been in the meat trade right back into the 19th century, and that in 1950, the business was owned by a Lawrence Crisp.

The shops were considered to be among the best in London. Crisp had inherited the shops from his father, but had not inherited his father's interest in butchery. (This may have been his father's fault, for he appears to have spent more time teaching his son about wine than about cutting meat. Crisp had been trained from an early age to be a connoisseur of Burgundy. He told me his father used to blindfold him and give him wine to taste. He would have no dinner unless he could tell the district from which it came. In spite of this parental persuasion he grew up with austere habits and an indifference to wine which bordered on dislike.) He was a man of ample means, and was not compelled to rely on the shops for his living, and so he approached a business agent by the name of Whiles, well known to me, who negotiated the sale.

We were very satisfied with the results of Layton & Burkett and after a year or so we decided to buy some more meat shops. This time we were looking for 15 or 20, and more important, we were looking for someone who would be able to take over the management of the new chain, as we were finding it hard enough supervising seven shops in a field with which we were unfamiliar, although we were fortunate to have the help of James Brannan. He was the senior man at Layton & Burkett, always cheerful and hardworking, and had a thorough knowledge of his trade. He gave loyal and valuable service right up to his retirement in 1970.

I used to go to the market fairly regularly at this time, and so knew the leading buyers in the Home Counties area. One man who had particularly impressed me was T.M. Cox who had four flourishing branches in East London and Essex. He was not enthusiastic when I mentioned the idea of merging with us because he did not think the group which would result would be big enough. We were thinking bigger too, so I began to look around again, and approached Bernard Thompson who had 10 shops in the North London area with good turnovers and profits. Then began the delicate task of simultaneously persuading Bernard Thompson and T.M. Cox to sell and getting Cox to agree to manage the new group. I was successful and by 1953 Layton & Burkett had grown to 22 branches with T.M. Cox as Managing Director.

The headquarters now were moved to some spare offices belonging to Keevils' in Charterhouse Street, and T.M. Cox applied himself with imagination to fusing the various units into one concern. He was a perfectionist particularly in display, purchasing and shop fitting; the shops were gradually developed and have become outstanding in London for their quality and presentation. They well deserve the description 'Butchers of Distinction'. T.M. Cox is an unusual man in many ways. He was brought up in the trade and knows it thoroughly. His wife was a Miss Cornell, her father founded the well-known meat traders John Best Ltd. Cox's father was an outstanding character in the food contracting business.

By 1958 Layton & Burkett had grown to 49 shops, mainly by the acquisition of new businesses, among them a firm called Edgley's. Layton was strongly placed to expand into a much larger scale of operations, and in 1959 Fitch Lovell merged it with West Butchers Ltd., a public company with 80 branches, which Fitch had acquired in a share exchange. West's had been founded by James Preston, who, in 1894, inherited his father's shop at No. 1 Charlton Road, Somers Town. Another branch of the family owned Preston's dairy, a few doors away, where, it is rumoured, they had close connections with the family who founded the great Sainsbury business.

James Preston was one of the outstanding figures of the meat trade. He is still remembered by many today. He was tall, extremely good-looking, immaculate in dress and manner. He wore a fresh flower in his buttonhole every morning. A pair of bright and dashing hackney horses would take him to market and round his shops. He was known by everyone in the trade as Gentleman Jim. I remember selling him a long line of sheep in 1912. They were for collection at 5.30 a.m. Unfortunately they were delayed for a quarter of an hour. As far as I remember there had been a transport strike. The minutes slipped by and James Preston waited. Then he turned to me and said coldly but courteously, 'Young fellow, I cancel my order. You are 15 minutes late. Everything I want has to be exactly as arranged. I will give you a rest from orders until you learn to be punctual'.

By the end of the First World War his business had grown considerably. The Charlton Road shop remains the number one shop of West Layton to this day. In 1918 the business was formed into a private company under the name of West Butchers Ltd. The name was taken from West Smithfield where the Head Office was situated in the Lovell & Christmas building. The capital in 1918 was £30,000. It was increased to £100,000 in 1921 and to £200,000 in 1934 when the £1 ordinary shares were subdivided into 5s. units.

At this time West became a public company and Mr. J.T. Greenwood was elected Chairman on the retirement of James Preston. David Galloway, who was Chairman of West's at the time of the merger with Fitch Lovell, joined the company as Secretary the following year. He joined the Board in 1941, became Managing Director in 1948 and Chairman in 1950. Throughout its history, West's had always been a profitable company, keeping abreast of the times and gradually increasing the number of its branches. Its maximum pre-acquisition profit was reached in 1956, when it was more than £100,000. The number of branches was brought up to 80 by the purchase of Parish & Sumerfield who operated in Dagenham and Essex, and Baldwin Bros. in suburban Surrey.

A medium sized company with many valuable freehold properties is clearly vulnerable to a takeover bid. In June 1959, Fitch Lovell learned that definite approaches were being made by financiers.

We decided that West's would go well with Layton & Burkett to make a fine retail division, Accordingly we made an approach to our friend David Galloway. Terms and conditions of a merger were agreed without too much delay. Then outside operations on the Stock Exchange drove West's shares up from 17s. 6d. to 24s. 6d. At the same time there was a decline in the value of Fitch Lovell shares. As the transaction was to be on a share exchange basis, the run up to completion day was exciting and very difficult. We were forced to advance the terms of our offer to 13 F.L. shares for four West shares. The deal worked out satisfactorily in the end and the offer was made unconditional in July 1959.

The integration of West's and L & B was directed by David Galloway and T.M. Cox. It is always a difficult process, but in this case it was done without too much dislocation. The new company became known as West Layton and took as its headquarters a new building in St. John Street, E.C.1 which West's was already building for itself before the merger. (As I have mentioned, West's had originally been at West Smithfield. The office which I have used for the past 12 years was used by West's Chairman for many years, and David Galloway when he was their Secretary worked in the adjoining office now used by Miss Harmer.) Not long after the merger, David Galloway moved back into 1 West Smithfield to take on new responsibilities with Fitch Lovell's Head Office, and T.M. Cox was left in charge of West Layton.

David Galloway was interested in supermarkets. In fact West's had opened one while he was Chairman, thus he was able to play a large part in the development of Key Markets. Under T.M. Cox, West Layton have continued to develop as high class meat retailers and also specialists in delicatessen.

The Gunner side of the Fitch Lovell meat division had quite different origins, although the founding father Bob Gunner was, like Gentleman Jim Preston of West's, a great character at Smithfield. Being characters was about all they had in common. Where Preston was tall and elegant, Bob Gunner was rotund. While Gentleman Jim sported a flower in his buttonhole, Bob Gunner was recognised everywhere by the small cap which he wore on his head. He was a superb trader, a keen businessman who rose from simple beginnings to the heights of the trade and never allowed himself to be spoiled by the riches he acquired or the power he wielded. He remained a practical man in every way, and particularly I remember him for the help he gave to young men. Although his firm became successful in the meat trade, he actually began trading in cheese. He opened his first shop at 138 Essex Road, Islington about 1903. It was an old-fashioned cheesemonger's in which he also sold ham and hogmeats. In the rooms above this shop his son Ernest Gunner was born. Half a long egg-case served as his first cot.

It was not long before Bob opened a second shop in Chapel Street, Islington, then another sprang up in London Fields, and another in Essex Road, and another outside London at Cricklewood. In fact trade increased so fast that in 10 years he was able to open a warehouse and offices at 28 Cowcross Street. He began packing tea there as well as the bulk buying of commodities for his shops. He wanted to buy bacon at first hand, but was cold-shouldered by the Home & Foreign Produce Exchange – now the London Provision Exchange. As it happened, the Exchange was also making difficulties for a young Dane called Charles Hansen who was to found the Danish Bacon Company. The story goes that the first order given to the DBC came from Bob Gunner.

During the First World War, anti-German feeling ran high and among those who suffered from it were German Pork butchers of whom there were quite a number in London. Many of their shops were damaged and their windows smashed. One of them called Wenninger could not bear to endure these humiliations and R. Gunner agreed to buy his business. So it was that Bob Gunner entered the retail meat trade.

As the years went by butchers' shops and provisions' shops were opened in equal numbers. In about 1928 Gunner began building a warehouse and factory in Lever Street. Today the premises house the factory of Highland Food Products who make small goods – sausages, pies and so on – for West Layton and R. Gunner. To give some idea of the size of the business in the mid-'20s, Dutch porker pigs, which Bob Gunner always favoured, would be allocated to each shop every Friday morning on a basis of never less than 100. Bob Gunner is known to have bought as many as 1,000 at one bidding.

When Ernest Gunner entered the business he was sent to Germany to learn how to make sausages. When he came back, he organised sausage production centrally, first at the large London Fields branch and then at Lever Street. Previously each shop had made its own sausages. Ernest Gunner remembers that, at London Fields, one ton of linked sausages had to be hanging on gambrels behind the counter for the retail trade of the shop before the sausage-making machinery was stopped for breakfast at nine o'clock.

In 1926, when an embargo was placed on Dutch Pork, Ernest Gunner joined forces with the son of a Dutch bacon curer from Dordricht and together they slaughtered, cut and pickled pork which they shipped to England listed as bacon. It sold like hot cakes. It is said that half the window beds in the Gunner shops were filled with pickled pork cuts. Eventually, however, the Government tightened the definition of bacon. The trade was finished and Ernest came home.

There was a bacon shortage in 1932 and 1933 and so Gunner's opened its own bacon factory at Letchworth to make sure of supplies. During Hitler's War, Lever Street was set on fire, but the firm was fortunate that only one branch was destroyed in the air raids. In 1950 Gunner's expanded into Canada. It took over a bacon factory at Hamilton and in 1961 built a new factory at Burlington.

In England, expansion began as soon as possible after the war. Walter Holland & Sons Ltd., pie manufacturers of Baxenden near

Manchester, was taken into the company and in 1947 Bob Gunner decided the time had come to issue shares to the public and these were very well received by investors.

There was an abrupt change of direction after the death of Bob Gunner a short time later. Ernest had become more and more involved in the Canadian venture and manufacturing interests, and he decided to concentrate on them. He came to an arrangement with Joseph Richards of Joseph Richards (Butchers) Ltd. whereby control of the Gunner retail business passed to Richards and the Canadian and manufacturing interests remained with Ernest Gunner and the Holland family. As it was the retail business which was to join the Fitch Lovell Group, the Gunner family with Ernest at its head now disappear from our story.

Before I relate how the Gunner retail business joined Fitch Lovell, I must just write a little about Joseph Richards, for he and his family have close connections with Keevils'. The Richards were an old Bermondsey family. I can just remember Joe's father, a large good-tempered man who eyed his son with some apprehension, for Joe was a sailor, an aggressive, impetuous but able man, who would obviously not be content forever with the life of a simple seafarer.

Actually I knew his brother much better. George worked in the Wholesale Meat Department at Keevils' in the years before the First World War. He was a mentor and guide to me when I took over the department at a time when I was little more than a boy. His one failing was a love of gambling amounting to an obsession. It was George Richards who took over from me when I went into the army in 1914. It was George who persuaded Joseph, on one of his rare spells at home, to leave the sea and come and work for Keevil. I think he started in 1913. He did not stay long. Like me, he went off to the war. On his return in 1919 he put his savings, about £100, into a shop in Tower Bridge Road. He was shrewd, hardworking and progressive. In due course he was joined by his nephew Charles Couture, who was as calm and reliable as Joe was hot-headed. Their business flourished. Eventually they bought the small but excellent firm of Chalk & Cox. By 1955 profits had reached £100,000, although they still had fewer than 40 branches. By this time Joe was well able to indulge in his hobby, flyfishing. In fact it was in 1953, 40 years after he first joined Keevils', that I was his guest at the Flyfishers Club, of which he was a most respected member.

Joe suffered badly with a duodenal ulcer and often took long trips abroad, leaving Charlie Couture in charge at home. When he was particularly depressed by this ulcer he would come to see me to discuss a merger with Fitch & Son. We talked intermittently for some years, but our discussions did not come to anything. It was not until 1960, when the Richards business had been swollen by the addition of the 118 Gunner shops, that Joe Richards decided that he did not want to be involved in his advancing years with such a large concern. He approached us again and we offered four of our ordinary shares for 15 Gunner shares plus 1s. cash per share. The offer was accepted by the shareholders in August 1960. Joe Richards became President and Charles Couture the Chairman. There was an interchange of directors between West Layton and R. Gunner. A Meat Committee was set up to co-ordinate the activities of the two companies and later the foundations were laid for a wholly merged company under the name of West Gunner. The expectation was that the two companies would grow together and that they would work closely with the meat section of Key Markets. In fact this has not happened, possibly because of changes at Fitch Lovell Board level.

I believe that integration should not be too long delayed, even if such a move means disregarding personalities. Of course, integration is easier to talk about than to achieve, and often when five is added to five the result is less than 10. Possibly West Layton and R. Gunner would not have done so well as one integrated company. There is no doubt that they have progressed well down their separate paths and produced excellent results. Nevertheless I remain convinced that in circumstances like these, the time does come when integration becomes necessary for the health and future of the companies concerned.

The last thing I want to do however is to detract from the solid achievements of the two companies in the 11 years since Gunner's joined the meat division. New shops have been acquired, old ones have been modernised and refitted. Schools have been opened to train young men in the craft of butchery. Great advances have been made in refrigeration, both in the design of cold storage chambers and in refrigerated counters. The two companies have successfully created a chain of modern stores out of their old meat retail shops. They are recognised as outstanding in the trade.

In spite of the separate identities of the two concerns, co-ordination has been good. The most notable example of it is the common food manufacturing company, Highland Food Products, which makes pies, sausages and so on. In fact the Consumer Association's magazine *Which?* rated Highland's ordinary sausages as the best of their type made in the country.

I wish I had more space to write about all the people who have made the meat division such a success, but they have the satisfaction of knowing that their services have been appreciated to the full. Many of the men I knew and worked with are now following me into retirement. Charles Couture retired in 1969, and L.W. Digby, who was first appointed to the Board of West's in 1948, retired in 1970. Ever since the formation of West Layton he has been its invaluable second-in-command. He is a man of imagination with the vital practical experience so necessary in the trade. No history of the meat division would be complete without special mention of him. He is a man blessed with charm and powers of leadership.

Another colourful character who retired in 1970 was James Brannan, known throughout Smithfield and beyond as Jim. As a buyer, shrewd but most popular, he has always been in a class by himself. I have known him and enjoyed his happy personality for more than 40 years. I have never failed to be impressed by his cheerfulness and his capacity for work. For more than a generation his normal hour of rising was 3 a.m. As he drove through the West End on his way to market, the ladies of the street used to greet him with a cheery 'Good morning Jim' all down Piccadilly and Shaftesbury Avenue.

Now only the old warrior T.M. Cox is left to direct his younger staff at West Layton and his retirement too is not far distant. At R. Gunner, Laurie Couture is in charge, surrounded by loyal henchmen.

Somehow I feel this brief chapter does not convey an adequate picture of our meat business, of the countless day-to-day decisions and efforts needed to administer a large number of retail shops, of the problems of looking after a staff numbering more than 1,000, of buying highly perishable products on fluctuating markets to which supplies must come from far flung points of production, of choosing the right sites for new shops, and of organising construction and maintenance work at the high level required, and most of all, of the dedication needed to keep the confidence of the public.

All these things the meat division has done and done well. For Fitch Lovell, meat retailing has been a successful and rewarding venture which has added materially to the prestige and profitability of the company.

## 18

# THE NOËLS

TODAY THERE ARE TWO Noël companies in the Fitch Lovell Group, Auguste Noël Ltd., importers and factors of continental and home-produced cheese, and L. Noël & Sons Ltd., importers and manufacturers of cocktail cherries, sauces and other speciality foods.

The Noël family shares with the Beers the distinction of triumphing over adversity with determination and integrity. As their name suggests, the Noëls trace their origins to France, where, in the first half of the 19th century, Théophile Noël was engaged in the drapery business in Normandy. In 1858 one of his sons, Ludovic Noël, applied for a passport to England, just as Svend Rutzou had done.

Unlike Rutzou, Ludovic Noël did not bring his father's trade to England, but opened a food shop and, at the age of 23, began trading under his own name. Almost certainly he specialised from the start in French butter and cheese, the chief products of the area from which he came. He is reputed to have been the first importer of Camembert and Rocquefort cheeses. In the 1860s he extended his business to all kinds of provisions and the importation and bottling of French wines. Like so many of his countrymen, he settled in Soho, where his first shop was in Little Newport Street. Although now most of them seem to be Italian or Greek, there are still such shops in that area, which has changed so much in other respects.

In 1866 the business moved to 48 Old Compton Street and the following year to 43 Frith Street where Ludovic Noël was looked after by his youngest sister who had joined him from France. During the years that followed he met his wife, Susannah, an English girl from Norwich. Three sons were born at Frith Street.

Meanwhile Ludovic's reputation was growing. The British Dairy Farmers' Association, formed in 1876, awarded him a large number of gold, silver and bronze medals for his French, Swiss and Italian cheeses. He received royal warrants from Napoleon III and the King of Portugal. He became one of the first members of the London Chamber of Commerce when it was founded in 1882.

The business was now becoming too big for the rather cramped premises in Frith Street, and so in 1886 Ludovic moved to 7 Soho Square next door to the so-called 'Burfords Panorama' (which was acquired in 1891 for the French Protestant Church, opened by the Bishop of London in 1893). Here, three more sons and a daughter were born.

Even in the bigger building in Soho Square, the business was still not on a very large scale, but it must have been prosperous as two of Ludovic Noël's sons went to University College School then situated in Gower Street, where I and H.D.B. Laughlin, the Group Accountant of Fitch Lovell, also were educated.

It was at Soho Square that Ludovic Noël began manufacturing and bottling. Jams, under the name of *Martinache* sold well, and the brand was also used for a large range of imported goods, including sardines. (I think that Martinache was a relative of the family as there is a letter from him describing the conditions in Paris during the siege in 1870. He writes that the ration was 30 grammes of horse meat a day and he describes how the people were driven to eat dog soup and rats.)

As the business developed Ludovic Noël began to take on office staff. One clerk John Stevenson remained with the firm for 30 years and served as Company Secretary for 17 years. (He was the father of Frances Stevenson who was Lloyd George's secretary for many years and eventually married him. She is now the Dowager Countess Lloyd George.)

The offices which Stevenson occupied in the early years were rather Dickensian. Two clerks sat on high stools at a long bench taking orders for two warehousemen who packed them up for delivery by bicycle or tricycle to customers from Shepherds Bush to London Bridge. The strong smell of French cheese was everywhere. (There was no refrigeration in those days, of course.) It is still recounted that once a consignment of *Pont l'Eveque* was delayed, and when it arrived the odour was almost insupportable.

Nevertheless, Ludovic was determined to save as much of it as possible, and so he told his men to start unwrapping the cheeses. Bravely they did as he said. Yet the struggle was too much even for these battle-hardened troops and they were overcome. Determined not to give up, Ludovic sent out for a bottle of brandy and stood by plying the men with glasses of it to revive them. At last, fortified in this way, they were able to complete the job.

When the American canned goods trade developed in the 1890s Noël's decided to take part in it and opened an office in St. George's House, Eastcheap, under the direction of Eugene, the second son. Business increased rapidly and the firm took a 99-year lease on Clink Wharf, Southwark. On the adjoining land it built a factory to which it intended to transfer most of the work being done in Soho Square. (The wharf was actually the site of the old Clink Prison from which the use of the word 'clink' as a popular term for prison was derived.)

Unfortunately, before the factory was completed, Eugene Noël died suddenly, and the whole responsibility for directing the project fell on the shoulders of Auguste Noël, the third son, who was only 24. (The eldest son named Ludovic after his father, had decided to return to France.) Auguste later married the daughter of the family doctor living in Soho Square.

At this point, in 1900 the head of the firm, Ludovic senior, decided to turn Noël's into a limited company with himself as chairman and his wife and Auguste as directors. The new company operated from the premises at 7 Soho Square, which gave delivery service to West End stores and restaurants, an office in Edinburgh to deal with the Scottish trade, and the factory at Clink Wharf. The factory had three main departments, the kitchen department, for the production of potted meats, soups, anchovies, galantines and such like, the bottling department for capers, gherkins, and olives, and the jam department for jams, ginger and fruits in syrup.

Though Ludovic Noël unfortunately died in 1901, only a year after he had formed the company, Auguste succeeded his father as chairman and business continued to be good. The firm excelled in seeking out the exotic delicacies increasingly demanded by fashionable Edwardian society and began to import Foie Gras, quails, larks and cockscombs. It appointed agents in South Africa, Canada, and India. All the time the reputation of L. Noël & Sons Ltd. continued to grow. There were more gold medals from the

Franco-British exhibition at the White City in 1908, and from other exhibitions, as far away as Cape Town. An extension was built to the factory in 1910, the jubilee of the firm's foundation, to meet the ever-increasing demand for its products.

In the years immediately after the death of the founder, his widow was the only other director besides the new Chairman, Auguste. In order to strengthen the direction, Edouard was elected a director in 1912 on the occasion of his marriage. E.V. Noël, the present chairman of L. Noël & Sons Ltd. joined the firm in 1908. Edouard and E.V. were the youngest of Ludovic's eight sons. In fact three of their brothers were already serving in the firm before they were born. After service in the office and at Clink Wharf E.V. left for Perigueux in France to learn about preserving foods with the firm of La Forest.

His absence from the firm was longer than he intended, for while he was in France, the war broke out. In fact by coincidence he was staying with his eldest brother, Ludovic, in Paris at the time. They both received telegrams calling them to the colours at the same time, E.V. to the British Army and Ludovic to the Franch Army. Both E.V. and Edouard were called to the 3rd. Bn. The Royal Fusiliers, in which they both held commissions. Auguste, just returned from a business trip to Canada, was now left to run the business.

Looking back, I think the period just before and during the war was the heyday of L. Noël & Sons Ltd. as it was constituted in those days. Naturally the war made supplies more difficult to obtain and Auguste had no difficulty in disposing of whatever was available.

Meanwhile both Edouard and E.V. were wounded at Neuve Chapelle in 1915, and E.V. was again a casualty on the Somme. They were both seconded to the Royal Flying Corps. E.V. celebrated the end of the war by getting married and becoming a director. However, the two officers returned to conditions very different from the Edwardian prosperity which they had left four years before and Noël's ran into serious difficulties as the post-war boom came to an end. The company had overbought heavily during the war on the rising canned goods market. In addition, it became clear, as competition increased that the Clink Wharf operation in a factory built on six floors, was uneconomic.

92. Fitch & Son: old transport

93. Fitch & Son (Export) Ltd.: Van, 1930s

94. Fitch & Son: premises at London Bridge

95. R.G.J. Evans,
Managing Director,
Fitch & Son Ltd. from 1966

96. Robson & Sons: stores, 1910

97. Robson's Bournemouth Central Cash and Carry, 1970

Although on the friendliest tersm, the brothers could not agree on the best way out of their difficulties. Edouard and E.V. wanted to sell Clink Wharf and build a new factory outside London, but Auguste and the family cash creditors would not agree. So it was that Auguste decided to leave the family firm and set up on his own.

He took premises near Marble Arch, and, under the style of Auguste Noël began to import foreign cheeses. He used to wear a straw hat and a grey coat, according to one of my sources, and he was known as 'Mr. Cheese'. Today the company he founded is one of the two largest in the trade. That explains why there are two Noël companies. How they both came to join the Fitch Lovell Group I will explain later.

After the departure of Auguste, the other brothers and their mother did not, in fact, sell the Clink Wharf factory. Instead they continued trading from it, and their business in speciality foods continued quite well until it was struck by three heavy blows. In 1926 the factory was shut down and picketed in the General Strike. The adverse effect on Noël's trade was considerable. Then the next year Susannah Noël, the widow of the founder, died at the age of 75. She had been a director for 23 years, and Chairman since Auguste resigned. On her death, the estate had to be wound up, placing yet another strain on the company's liquidity. The final straw, however, was the depreciation in value of the pound in 1931 following the decision to leave the gold standard. The cost of imports, which formed an important part of the business, rose sharply. It was a sad moment for a firm which had won so many gold medals and held royal warrants from kings and emperors. The directors decided in 1931, in order to safeguard their creditors, to go into voluntary liquidation and continue trading under a Liquidator. The creditors were paid 15s. in the pound with another 1s. 9d. later, and it was hoped that the sale of Clink Wharf and the factory would provide enough to pay 20s. in the pound. Unfortunately however, the Depression intervened, and the premises had to be sold for a very small amount.

The difficulties which the firm now found itself seem to me to have had three causes, first, over-expansion, secondly the death of Eugene, the brother who was in charge of the building of the factory and who might have been able to run it more profitably had he lived. Thirdly Noël's suffered from heavy overhead expenses (exceedingly difficult to avoid in a business where orders might be only five or six small items). The records of the period have almost all been lost, but it is not improbable that, had they followed John Cary Lovell's advice,'Cut your losses and remain in the market', and sold the factory earlier, they could have built reserves to meet the slump. It is easy, however, to be wise after the event.

A firm with less determination might have gone out of business in the situation which faced Noël's in 1931. However, it decided to soldier on, and in order to keep going, came to an arrangement with Harry Peck & Co. Ltd. under which financial control passed to Peck's, but Noël's continued to trade under its own name, with Edouard in charge of production and E.V. responsible for sales. Edouard and E.V. set to work to repay their debts and rebuild their business. Freed from financial restrictions and heavy overheads the company began to advance again. It began to import raw cherries and started marketing the famous *Noël Cocktail Cherries*.

Then in 1937 with the assistance of Auguste, the brothers discharged their debts in full. The final dividend was received by the creditors on the day of the 100th anniversary of the birth of the founder. (I must record in passing that in the following year a young lady, Miss Hilda Camp, who had joined the company in 1929 became Secretary. She is still with the company and has rendered wonderful service.) E.V. himself had acted as Secretary until 1932, having sat for the C.I.S. in 1921. The association with Harry Peck continued happily and during Hitler's war the company progressed very considerably.

In 1946 Peck's indicated that it would be willing to dispose of the shares it held in Noël's. Edouard and E.V. naturally were anxious to have control back in the family, and they acquired the shares with the assistance of Auguste, who returned to the family company as Chairman, with E.V. as Vice-Chairman. His own company, Auguste Noël Ltd. continued to operate separately.

For some years after Peck's sold its interests back, Noël's continued to share its premises, but eventually Peck's needed the room and so Noël's acquired another speciality foods concern, G. Sheldrake & Co. Ltd. and moved into its factory in Coburg Road, S.E.5 which it still occupies. The factory was renamed 'Soho Works', the name borne by all Noël's premises since they left the West End. The company advanced steadily in its new home. Auguste died in 1952, well respected and with a fine record. E.V. was elected Chairman and his wife Eve became a member of the Board. Soon afterwards, Edouard retired from active duties, although he remained a director until 1962. As for E.V. he is still Chairman of L. Noël & Sons Ltd. A special ceremony was held in 1968 to mark his 60 years' service to the company and his 50 years as a director. The many tributes paid at that time showed the esteem and affection in which this great gentleman is held.

With E.V. safely installed in the chair of L. Noël, I must go back now and trace the fortunes of Auguste Noël Ltd. This firm did not become a limited company until 1950, when it was still operating from small premises near Marble Arch, but its business in continental cheese was substantial. After the death of Auguste in 1952, the directors left in charge were G. Murad and Marcel Delaporte who were joined later by Nick Ouwehand who came from V. Draper Ltd. Murad resigned in 1963, leaving the direction to his two young and able colleagues.

A policy of more vigorous expansion was adopted after Auguste's death. The demand for Continental cheese has developed rapidly in recent years, perhaps because of the holidays abroad enjoyed by hundreds of thousands of people who never travelled far from home in the old days. As business increased, the firm moved to Turnmill Street in the vicinity of Smithfield in 1957. These premises too proved insufficient and a site was bought nearby where the most modern fancy cheese warehouse in the country was built with up-to-date refrigerated store rooms. Today Auguste Noël's green vans cover the South, Midlands and the North from its London headquarters and regional depots.

Auguste Noël joined the Fitch Lovell Group in 1962, and the last nine years have seen a happy and profitable association. I cannot speak too highly of Marcel Delaporte and Nick Ouwehand now recognised as leaders of their trade. They enjoy the confidence of the principal Continental shippers, their customers and their staff.

I still have not explained how both the Noël companies came under the Fitch Lovell umbrella. It happened like this. There was a certain amount of publicity in the Press about the merger with Auguste Noël, and E.V. Noël wrote to the trade papers to make clear that the firm referred to was not L. Noël & Sons Ltd. I wrote to him saying I hoped the news of the merger with Auguste Noël Ltd. would do no harm to his company. I also suggested that perhaps he might care for us to meet.

We did meet and found many common interests, both inside and outside our commerical activities. We agreed that it would benefit all of us if L. Noël & Sons Ltd. also joined the Fitch Lovell Group and this fusion took place the following year. The consideration was 14 Fitch Lovell ordinary shares plus 3⅓ F.L. 6½% preference shares for every 5 Noël ordinary shares, and one F.L. 6½% preference for each Noël 5% preference.

So after more than 40 years apart, the two Noël firms finally came together under the aegis of Fitch Lovell. No doubt Ludovic Noël would have been pleased. Perhaps he would have been surprised too at the progress the businesses have made since he sold his first cheese in a single room in Soho over 100 years before.

## 19

# TIMBER

TIDY MINDS may wonder why a food composite like Fitch Lovell should be involved in the importing and wholesale of such an inedible product as timber, but readers of this story will be aware that trading conditions in wholesale food became deplorable in 1930s. World production was rising, prices were falling and profits were nearly impossible to earn. At that time food wholesaling comprised virtually the whole of the business of Fitch & Son.

H.S. Rowlandson became convinced, as the '20s advanced, that there was little future in the provision trade, and so decided to diversify, first his own personal interests, and then those of Fitch. One field he guided the firm into was, as we have seen, the bakery business. The other was timber. It became for him something more than a mere hedge against possible losses in provisions. It had a peculiar fascination for him. In particular he used to go personally to Finland to buy timber, and I remember his telling me how delightful these trips were.

In 1929 he persuaded Fitch & Son to take a 50% interest in Plywood Industries Ltd. and a little later 50% of a company called Nachman Kramer & Sons Ltd. was purchased. The investment in the two concerns was £50,000. As with H.S.R.'s bakery venture, the beginnings were inauspicious. But whereas the bakeries soon picked up and progressed more or less steadily thereafter, the timber interests gave trouble continually. Within five years £20,000 had to be transferred out of the main reserves of Fitch to cover their losses.

In 1930 the premises of Nachman Kramer in Tabernacle Street were destroyed by fire. Things were so bad at the time that the company was already being liquidated. Far from being the final straw, the fire turned out to be a help. The freeholders of the site did not realise that Kramer's had not renounced the lease, and began to rebuild without Kramer's consent. Legal action was taken and the freeholders had to pay substantial damages.

Fitch & Son did not continue its association with either Nachman Kramer or Plywood Industries. Instead it consolidated its interest in a new company set up by Nachman Kramer's brother Norman. He called his company K. Norman Ltd. to avoid confusion with his brother's firm. K. Norman built up a good name in the plywood trade although profits were still hard to come by. In addition it had a subsidiary at Slough called Balbow Ltd. which made veneered panels. In 1938 K. Norman entered into association with E. d'Arcy Morrow. He was an outstanding trader and even if K. Norman could not make profits, Morrow did.

Norman's was appointed Importing Agents for the Government during the war, which assured its profits to the time controls would end. Within three years of the lifting of controls, K. Norman was again in trouble. (The firm was being run by E.C. Griffiths, who had originally been engaged as Secretary and Office Manager, and previously had been an audit clerk in a firm of accountants. Looking back one realises it was clearly unfair to expect a man with his background to run a difficult marketing company.) The difference between its profits and those of d'Arcy Morrow was marked. Unfortunately E. d'Arcy Morrow, who had never been a robust man, became seriously ill in 1954 and died. The timber section never recovered from his loss. It was operated by conscientious men with strict accountancy control, but it could not prosper. Even the drive of Norman Lambourne who took charge of the section later did not make up for the lack of a man, like d'Arcy Morrow, who really knew how to buy and sell timber on the volatile and highly speculative markets which were a feature of the plywood trade. Office control over market operations often meant buying and selling at the wrong times. During this time I remember visiting Verney Wharf which was owned by the timber section and being disturbed by its condition and the general lack of control.

It was clear to us that something had to be done. It happened that in 1957 Keevils' had leased a warehouse with offices in Charterhouse Street to the well respected timber and hardboard merchants, Machin & Kingsley. Their Vice-Chairman, Alan Kingsley, had been a friend of mine for years and he was also known to other directors of Fitch. We thought it would be a good idea to try and persuade him to join the Fitch Group and take charge of the timber division. At the same time we would acquire the ordinary shares of Machin & Kingsley. Agreement was eventually reached and the company came into the group in December 1959. We were all optimistic that with an expert like Alan Kingsley in charge the troubles of the timber division would at last be over.

For a time all indeed went well, but unfortunately Alan Kingsley became ill in 1961. In his absence excessive buying on a rising market resulted in serious losses, so Fitch decided to cease trading in K. Norman and d'Arcy Morrow and for their businesses to be absorbed by Machin & Kingsley.

Machin & Kingsley was only a medium-sized firm, but its position was different from that of the other two companies. Not only did it have strong direction from the families who had started the business, but right from the start it was well diversified.

The firm had been founded in 1886, when P.J. Machin and Alfred Kingsley began to trade as paper merchants with offices in the City. They must have been able and energetic, because before long they were importing strawboard for box making and book binding from Holland. This soon became a major part of their business. At the turn of the century they became engaged in textiles and certain cotton materials. The original partners were joined by their sons Bertram and Cecil Machin, and Eric and Alan Kingsley. During the First World War, they all volunteered for the Services, and sad to relate, Bertram and Eric did not return.

Kingsley Senior died in 1919 and Machin Senior the following year, leaving Cecil and Alan in control of the business. They became directors of the limited company which was formed in 1920.

Their offices were in Hare Court, Aldersgate Street, on the site of a Dissenters' chapel which had been built in 1706. The ground floor and basement of the chapel were still there. (The deeds of the site go back to the time of William and Mary, and the company possesses an indenture dated 1792.)

Machin & Kingsley began importing plywood in 1920, when it was still a new material. Alan devoted his energies to this trade and did much to make plywood the high class product it is now. Cecil looked after the paper and board business and maintained the close association with the Dutch manufacturers which his father had enjoyed. His son Norman entered the business about 1930 and assisted Alan Kingsley in plywood. Norman Machin is now the company's Chairman. About this time, Alan began to take an interest in wallboards. They were then a somewhat primitive product, as plywood had been 15 years before, but Alan Kingsley saw their future and began to trade in them. Today wallboards form a major part of the company's activities, and have become widely-used as high-quality building material.

Meanwhile in 1933, Norman Machin took charge of a Manchester factory which the firm had opened for the production of veneered panels for the furniture trade. It did well until war-time trade restrictions forced its closure. Most of the staff of Machin & Kingsley served in the forces. Robert Cherry, who had been with the company since boyhood and who was appointed a director in 1965, was appointed an M.B.E. for his services in the Middle East. Unfortunately, Machin & Kingsley is another of the long list of Fitch Lovell companies which lost its headquarters during the war. The historic Hare Court building was completely razed. Machin & Kingsley moved out to temporary offices in Chislehurst where Cecil, Alan and the remaining staff continued to operate the business under great difficulties.

After the war, Norman Machin was made a director and his brother Roy began as sales' representative for paper and board in London. The firm moved back to offices in Old Jewry, E.C.3, staff were demobilised and the business gradually returned to normal. Cecil Machin and Alan Kingsley resumed their work on trade associations and helped the industry as a whole to settle down after the war. Alan became President of both the Plywood and the Wallboard Associations. His son Brian joined the company in 1948 after National Service. He and Roy Machin were elected directors in 1950. Brian did very well, particularly on the building side, and everyone was sorry when he decided to resign from the firm eight years later. However we all admired his reasons for going. He had decided to take Holy Orders in the Church of England.

Meanwhile the company pressed on with its long standing policy of diversification. In 1952 it began to distribute insulating material manufactured by Fibreglass Ltd. of St. Helen's. At first this new business was administered by the wallboard department, but it grew so fast that it soon became a separate department and now forms a major part of the firm's business, and Machin & Kingsley claim to be one of the largest stockists and distributors of Fibreboard Structural Insulation materials in the United Kingdom. Its warehouses hold more than half a million square feet of insulation materials. Once again the firm foresaw the potential of a new material, as it had done with plywood and wallboard before the war.

The lease on the offices in Old Jewry was a short one, and they were due for demolition in 1956. However I was able to let Machin & Kingsley part of Keevils' premises and the firm still occupies these offices in Charterhouse Street. In addition, it has taken over some space in the Fitch Lovell building at 1 West Smithfield. After the firm's merger with Fitch Lovell, Cecil Machin became President and occupied an office at West Smithfield until 1963. (He died a couple of years later at the age of 77. He was in the company for no less than 59 years and left behind him a reputation for upright conduct and industry second to none.)

Alan Kingsley followed him as President and the Chairmanship devolved on Norman Machin. Alan Kingsley has always been recognised as one of the characters of the plywood and wallboard trade. He was a great mixer and a shrewd if speculative trader, respected by those who knew him. I remember someone's saying, 'If everyone was like Alan Kingsley there would be no troubles in the world'.

The new Chairman, Norman Machin, is a different type of man, but one of those to whom the high compliment can be given, 'the more you know him, the more you respect and like him'. He has proved an excellent Chairman, maintaining the high traditions of the company and assisting in the firm's considerable recent advances.

One of the most significant of these advances has been in the Midlands. A.E. Farrell, the wallboard manager there, had built up turnover to such an extent that the company decided to build its own office and warehouse accommodation in Birmingham. It was the first time it had ever constructed its own premises and the venture has proved most successful. The Manager of the wallboard department, Robert Cherry, was elected a director in 1965. Apart from the Fitch Lovell nominee, he was the first director who was not a member of the Machin and Kingsley families. His sterling work and unusual sales ability fully justified this honour.

The only other director not bearing the family names up to this time was Christopher Cotterell, a nephew of Alan Kingsley who joined the firm after serving in Korea. He began on the sales side of the Building Department, and made such progress that he became a member of the Board in 1960. His abilities augur well for the future of the company. Machin & Kingsley have been fortunate to have a secretary such as Watson for many years. The trade is intricate and he has acted – as is the case of most medium-sized companies – as Accountant as well as Secretary.

In 1966 a large main depot for the London area was opened at Barking. The stocks of all departments are housed there under one roof. This increased capacity relieved the pressure of demand caused by the rapid increase in the use of modular and prefabricated structures in the building industry.

Business in boxmaking board, display board and wrapping papers has also boomed, partly through increased sales within the Fitch Lovell Group. Now a packaging division has been formed. Another important development has been into silk screen printing display board. Machin & Kingsley entered into a successful arrangement with a factory at Mitcham to market this product, and in 1969 bought the factory.

Since Machin & Kingsley joined the Fitch Lovell Group its turnover has increased three and a half times and its profit more than four times. This in itself justifies the decision taken when the old timber division was struggling to stay in a business far removed from the mainstream of the group's activities.

Nor has this growth been achieved at the expense of staff relations. As so often in a family concern, these have remained excellent. A quarter of the 60 members of the staff have been with the company for more than 20 years. The President can boast of an association lasting no less than 56 years. Leonard Watson the excellent secretary and office manager, and Robert Cherry have both been with Machin's for 40 years, and there are four others with the same length of service. It is a proud record, and this loyal and highly specialised staff can be proud of their achievements in manufacturing and selling plywood, cardboard, papers, display board, building board, fibreglass and other materials. As far as the group is concerned, it has now left far behind the old speculative plywood trade which absorbed much of Fitch & Son's capital and concern in days gone by.

# 20

## FITCH HOME AND EXPORT

WE APPROACH THE END of the story to 1970. It remains for me to describe the important activities of the Home and Export division, which is an umbrella organisation for a number of the smaller companies and for the general wholesaling activities carried out by Fitch before the Fitch Lovell merger, and which were then virtually the whole of Fitch's provision business. Not that the Home and Export division is inconsiderable. In fact under the supervision of John Gilpin the director responsible, the division shows the best return on capital in the entire group and contributes materially to overall profits. One reason for this is that the companies within the division are medium-sized, and it is possible for the executives responsible to supervise their capital expenditure and operations in detail and for John Gilpin to make sure that each unit stands well and truly on its own feet, and to find out at an early stage if things are likely to go wrong. But the key to the division's success lies in its obtaining executive managers of high calibre who can be given a large measure of autonomy, men of real trading ability who can take quick decisions and supervise their own administration and so do not burden their companies with elaborate office organisation. Their reward is that they are able to see the results of their own efforts, and maintain the closest relations with their staff. To run one of these small companies can be a very gratifying job, provided one is not unnecessarily worried by Head Office.

The division was not formed in its present shape until 1961, although of course many of its activities go back to the earliest days of Fitch & Son and inevitably, much included in this chapter will have already been touched upon earlier.

If I begin with the Export rather than the Home side of the business, it is because Fitch Export Ltd. was one of the pillars of Fitch & Son before the war and the earliest formed limited liability company. It goes back to the turn of the century, and was almost certainly started by John Baker, the van driver who rose to the Vice-Chairman of the company. Exactly when and why he began the Fitch Export department is unknown, indeed much of the history of Fitch Export would have remained unknown but for Fred Lee who managed to unearth old papers for me. From these it is clear that by 1905 the Export department had its own profit and loss account and balance sheet.

Quite possibly John Baker thought of the idea of exporting provisions to the distant parts of the globe while driving his van to the docks, or else during his earlier days as a sailor. The vans of Fitch & Son would go to the docks to collect imported supplies and Baker's imagination may have been fired with the idea of putting things into ships as well as taking them out. No doubt he was encouraged by Edwin Fitch, the senior partner at that time and an untiring and energetic man. By 1905 the firm had branches at the London Docks, Liverpool and Southampton. The Export department concentrated on shipping the high class provisions for which Fitch & Son were so well known at home. Before long it took the next logical step of making further use of its branches to provision ships, and today the provisioning of ships has grown to be as important as the exporting trade in itself.

The business rapidly went ahead. The Export department was formed into a Private Limited Liability Company in 1906 with an issued capital of £50,000. Two years later it opened its own Head Office at Coronation Street, Lloyds Avenue, E.C. The net profits for the year were about £6,000. Fitch Export Ltd. did business in China, India, the Falkland Islands, Gibraltar, Malta and East and West Africa. Sales in these distant lands were promoted by agents who used to travel once a year, spending up to six months abroad, representing other trading companies as well.

I have found a card issued to a Mr. Guid for a journey by him to South Africa in 1901. That was the time of the Boer War, and quite possibly he went after orders from Officers' Messes – the sort of business in which Fitch & Son delighted in those days. The elaborately worded card bears the words 'Contractors to H.M. Government' and of course the feathers of the Prince of Wales, whose Royal Warrant Fitch & Son held, and the leopard head which was the Fitch & Son trade mark, taken from the armorial bearings of the Fitch family. It was, in fact, the card of a firm admirably qualified for the task of supplying home comforts to the guardians of the far flung outposts of empire. Another card of the same period, printed in the same flamboyant style, declares 'Presented by E.A. Crawford, Manager'. This was the same Ernie Crawford who was with Fitch for more than 60 years and succeeded to the direction of Fitch Export when John Baker retired.

I have also come across a beautiful folder of the same period called the 'Shipping and Export Folder' which shows the services which the company could provide. Fitch, it informs, are 'Exporters of High Class Provisions to the Chief Markets throughout the World'. There are photographs of the leopard's head on the back and pictures of 'Royal' Hams. Sides of bacon are well photographed, but the type of bacon and the conformation of the pigs would not be acceptable today. No doubt they were much appreciated at the time.

Still expanding, Fitch Export opened a depot at Bristol in 1913, and joined forces in 1914 with Thomas Drabble of Tooley Street and with Baronoff-Sieffert of St. Petersberg to develop trade with Russia. Because of the war and the Russian Revolution nothing came of this scheme, although Drabble, Baronoff & Sieffert, continued after the war as a vehicle for the operations of Stephen Siratsky (see p. 20). In 1914 the net profit of Fitch Export had risen to £15,000 – (£75,000 at least in modern terms) the major part of Fitch's profits.

Between the wars Fitch Export became involved in a company in Rangoon called Barnett's Cold Stores Ltd. The records show that Fitch invested £2,283 in order to acquire 49% of the company. The purpose of the venture was to increase exports to Burma. When the scheme was proposed it was estimated that exports would amount to £5,000 per annum, which would be a reasonable investment taking into account freight rebates and dividends from Barnett's. As things turned out the forecast was optimistic. Between 1930 and 1935 shipments from Fitch averaged only £3,500 a year. Freight rebates averaged £57, and only two dividends were received. (A good photograph survives of the premises in Rangoon of Barnett's Cold Stores Ltd., showing a large retail provision stores. There is no sign of a cold store and no mention of it in the accounts.)

All the records were lost and the premises were damaged during the Japanese occupation of Burma but the damage must have slight since Barnett's were only given £450 out of the £10 million allocated by the British Government to U.K. business interests in Burma which had suffered in the war. Afterwards business in Burma became virtually impossible and Fred Lee did a first class job in disposing of Fitch's interest there.

Meanwhile the emphasis of the business gradually changed from export to ships' stores for although traditional lines, like *Special Hams* and *Old English Cheese* were sent to the Falkland Islands, the Malay States, Gibraltar, Malta and the Virgin Islands, there has, in general been a decline in demand for such things abroad. Nowadays also manufacturers in the United Kingdom and producers abroad tend to send their goods direct to the points of consumption. But on the ships' stores side, the leading shipping lines continue to place their orders with Fitch Export. For years, the firm supplied provisions for the *Queen Mary* and *Queen Elizabeth* and today provisions the *Queen Elizabeth II.*

E.A. Crawford who directed Fitch Export for many years eventually gave way to A.H. Jones who saw the company through the difficult days of the war and the years of control. Sadly he was in charge in 1947, the first year since the formation of Fitch Export that it made a loss. He retired in 1951 and was succeeded by Fred Lee, a most capable man with a thorough knowledge of the shipping world who had spent many years with Ruddins (Liverpool) Ltd. He has guided the company with such efficiency that today it is probably better based that at any time in its history. It still operates from London Docks, Liverpool and Southampton, where new premises had to be built because the old ones were utterly destroyed during the war. The staff is small and notable for its length of service. A recent count at Southampton revealed that three members had 150 years' service between them.

Talk of Fitch Export naturally leads to Fitch Home, which is the original Fitch & Son and trades as such. It was, of course, the kernel of Fitch's business at one time, and much of its story has already been told. The business was the sale of high class provisions mainly to hotels and clubs, but the profit record in the years after the war was lamentable. When the Home and Export division was formed in 1961, Fitch Home moved into the neighbourhood of Tooley Street together with Wholesale Catering Services, which had come into the division as the result of an agreement with Allied Suppliers Ltd. By this time the Home division had left behind the poor record of pre-war and the dismal record of the post-war years, and, once established near Tooley Street, the two companies continued to do even better by concentrating on hotel and catering customers and leaving the field of general wholesaling. The man responsible for the success of these companies is R.G.J. Evans. It has been a hard struggle in a competitive climate and he has watched the steady decline of many rival firms. No praise is high enough for what he and the others responsible have achieved; their results are now among the best in the whole Fitch Lovell group.

Evans also supervises Impey & Dyke Ltd., a firm of traditional wholesalers specialising in bacon, who operate from Redcross Way. Despite the competition from cash and carry wholesalers, Impey & Dyke has kept its business and maintained a reasonable level of profitability. It is one of the oldest firms in the trade. In pre-war days Impey himself was a well known character and his daughter Madeleine was private secretary to Sir Rolande Wall for many years.

Also under R.G.J. is the Southwark Bacon Drying Company. It is the only one of its kind left in London, and smokes bacon for a variety of wholesalers and supermarkets. I have always expected this company to become redundant, but it continues to provide a service needed by many. The smoke of generations is embedded in the walls of its premises, reminding me of pictures of London in the earliest Victorian days. S.P. Walpole, the manager, is considered by many to be the outstanding cricketer of the provision trade. He has regularly made 1,000 runs a season in the highest class of club cricket.

Moving away from London, Robsons' of Bournemouth is another company in Fitch's Home division. It is a firm of hotel suppliers, retailers, and now cash and carry wholesalers. This business was purchased in 1955 for two reasons: to shift Fitch's distribution away from the London area, and to increase the property content of its investments. Ironically, much of Robsons' property has been sold for sums approaching the cost of the shares. The firm is an old established one, and part of the life of Bournemouth for generations. When the local papers printed special editions to mark Queen Victoria's Diamond Jubilee in 1897, Robsons' took more space than any of the other local firms. Its advertisements show pictures of its coffee roasting room, the rice and spice store, the stockroom for brushes, the tea blending room and various retail shops. There are also some rather tired-looking horses and dusty vans above a caption reading 'Vans for prompt despatch and careful delivery'.

Henry Robson came from Whitby in Yorkshire and in 1886 opened a small shop in the Triangle at Bournemouth. It was not long before he expanded all over the town and began to serve the large hotels. He was a public spirited man and became a town councillor, an alderman and a J.P. He was Captain of the Fire Brigade, twice Mayor of Bournemouth and was Deputy Lieutenant of Hampshire, a particular honour for a man without military service (normally this much prized appointment only goes to men with at least ten years' military service behind them). Henry Robson ran his firm for 50 years. He was succeeded by his son Archie who was also an alderman of the borough. Archie was followed by A.H. Abbott. He too was an alderman of Bournemouth. I remember Abbott with particular pleasure. These men were admirably helped by S.W. Cook who died recently, and whose shrewdness and care some of us will always remember. For the past ten years C. Cockcroft has been the firm's General Manager and has guided it out of its old fashioned ways into modern paths. The small retail shops are disappearing and the wholesaling is now done from a fine modern depot mainly devoted to Cash and Carry and is developing fast. Cockcroft ably assisted by Leighton Jones and many others, deserves the highest praise for his company's steady and sure advance.

Robsons' is not the only firm to be brought into the division in recent years. The two Noël companies and Machin & Kingsley have already been mentioned. A few years ago also the small Collins Catering Company was formed to undertake catering work, and in 1964 Thomas Forde of Bangor in Northern Ireland was added and also J. & T.H. Staples Ltd. Forde's specialises in *Ulster Rolls* and *Belfast Hams*, and is the leader in the industry. Staples' is well known for its caviare, Foie Gras and catering packs of high quality canned goods. It has the entry into the most exclusive firms in the metropolis. Once based in Soho the firm has been known to me for years through connections with the Chandler family of Smithfield.

I also knew the firm's charming and able manager, W.J. Vaughan, for many years. I had been somewhat surprised to find the offices and warehouses of this rather austere firm situated between a striptease club and a betting shop, and when the lease ran out, John Gilpin decided to move Staples to Sidcup. I thought him mistaken in leaving the West End, but in fact Staples' trade has increased considerably since this move.

Another recent member of Fitch's Home division is Austen & Griffin Ltd., formed about 1950 to do maintenance work and shopfitting for the Hale and Partners' retail chain. The standard of its work is much appreciated by high class chain stores and its order book is generally full. Sometimes one hears that the firm's prices are too high, but never that its workmanship is poor. It is run in detail by its Managing Director, E.L. Bradly, who personally draws up plans, prepares estimates, buys the materials and supervises the work. It has never borrowed money and generally returns a profit 80 times its original capital.

The latest member of the Home & Export division is the firm of C.C. Ryan of Sidcup who joined the group in 1969. Its activities are mainly Cash & Carry wholesaling. It is a cheerful enterprising firm run profitably under Mr. & Mrs. John Robins, who were the proprietors before the merger, and who now seem to work even harder than before.

There are more than 15 companies in Fitch's present Home and Export division – more than enough for one man to supervise – their success can be shown by the fact the profits have more than trebled in recent years, and that practically all the capital for expansion has come from within.

If blame is apportioned when enterprises go wrong, proper credit must be given when they succeed, and thus John Gilpin and his close colleagues deserve warm praise on the excellent record of the Home and Export Division.

# 21

## 1970/71 – A SUMMARY

THE NUMBER of changes which can take place during one year in an organisation the size of Fitch Lovell is surprising – particularly in personnel.

R.E. Blanning finished his agreed term of chairmanship at the Annual General Meeting in September, but consented to remain on the Board. As will have been realised, from the main story, his chairmanship was distinguished and he handed over the company in splendid shape when it had achieved record sales and record profits.

He was succeeded by Sir Charles Hardie, one of the best known men in modern British industry and one whose activities cover a very wide field. His first year as Chairman witnessed an upsurge in profits and in his review, now in print, he pays handsome tributes to his predecessor and the staff, not only for their efforts but for the general state of the company.

As Sir Charles is unable, owing to his other commitments, to spend all his time with Fitch Lovell he appointed E. Trevor Beer to be Deputy Chairman, or as he calls him in a happy phrase 'my link man'. Consequently most of the day to day work has fallen on E.T.B. who has proved, as was expected, most assiduous and untiring in his efforts.

E.L. Bradly, the Managing Director of Austen & Griffin, died suddenly in 1970. He was a founder member of his company and almost entirely responsible for its success. He was succeeded by his right hand man, Pieter Sanders.

N.W. Damerell, Chairman of Hale Trent Cakes Ltd. also passed away unexpectedly. He joined Fitch Lovell in 1963 as Personal Assistant to Sir Rolande Wall, with whom he had been closely associated in the Ministry of Food during the Second World War. He had a lifelong experience of the bakery trade and when that group was reorganised in 1964 Fitch Lovell were fortunate to have him step into the vacancy. A quiet modest man respected and esteemed by all who knew him, his loss was keenly felt. R.E. Blanning consented to act as Chairman in his place, the day-to-day running of the company resting, as hitherto, on the shoulders of the two tried stalwarts of the division, F.F. Parker and G.S. Salmon, the joint Managing Directors.

E.A. Noël, for 50 years a director of L. Noël & Sons Ltd., died in July 1971 soon after the retirement of E.V. Noël, his brother, from his Chairmanship of 19 years. E.V. was appointed Honorary President as a token of appreciation of his 63 years' service in the company. His wife Mrs. E.M. Noël also resigned as a director at the same time as her husband. R.E. Miles, the son-in-law of E.V. has assumed the chairmanship and one of his first acts has been to acquire the business of Pannett & Neden, Herb & Spice Packers, who were established in 1868.

W. Whitear, for many years the manager of Keevils' dairy produce and canned goods departments, who had retired after some 40 years' service, was knocked over by a passing motor car near his home and died after a stay of two months in hospital, during which time he did not fully recover his senses.

Other leading personalities who are happily still with us, but who have reached the age of honorable retirement are much missed – it is difficult to envisage some of their companies without them.

T.M. Cox, the incomparable and formidable T.M.C., one of the great characters of the meat trade has at last called it a day. In spite of indifferent health, bravely borne, he guided the West Layton company from small beginnings to its unique position in the retail meat trade. People said he slept but rarely and used to spend the night hours inspecting shops in a different area every night. He had a touch of genius and of course the eccentricities which go with genius – many stories will be told of him in the future.

Clement Keevil (II) has taken over the chairmanship of the meat division, and a new director L.D. Randall has taken over the day to day supervision of both West Layton and Gunner. He was not previously in the meat trade and began at a time of great difficulty in the trade, but already things are looking better all round and the steps towards a merger into West/Gunner are steadily going ahead, congratulations are due to him and all concerned.

Fred Lee of Fitch Export also retired in May 1971. Fred was a Liverpool man, an astute trader, a loyal and completely trustworthy General Manager. When he took over the Export and Ships' Stores trade some 25 years ago, the company was not making a profit; today it is doing extremely well. He has been succeeded as Managing Director by R.A. Murrant and J.R.K. Smart of Southampton (of Rugby Football Fame) and B. Turk have been appointed directors of the division. Turk has been with Fitch since 1946 and on the administrative side has done a plethora of jobs in many companies, in fact he has been almost a personal assistant to John Gilpin, and is always ready for more work.

Then there is Jack Holgate of Rutzou who has also retired. Those who have read the chapter on Svend Rutzou will appreciate something of what he has done. He was, and is, one of the outstanding characters of Tooley Street and the London Provision Exchange. Long may he live, not only to enlighten the golf course but the lives of his old friends of whom I am very glad to be one. He has been elected President of Rutzou Ltd., a fitting reorganisation of his services and has been succeeded as Managing Director by his son John.

There have been several moves into new premises during the year, such as that of Carter's – the fruit and vegetable section of Fitch Export – which had moved from Wharf Road E.11 to a new temporary warehouse built adjacent to the Export buildings at West Ferry Road.

The Bacon division made an important acquisition when it acquired the business of Tom Hollingsworth. This has now been merged with Bywaters' of Birmingham, and the company operates as Bywater-Hollingsworth.

This brings me to something which seems to have become almost a habit, as Bywater-Hollingsworth, like I. Beer's and West Layton, have asked me to become Honorary President on my retirement from Bywaters' board, bringing me to '4 not out'! The honour is agreeable, the work very slight and the one job in the world from which one cannot be dismissed.

An important newcomer to the family has been George A. Cannon who was elected to the Board of Fitch Lovell in May 1971. He was previously the chairman of Food Securities Ltd. – formerly Peter Keevil & Sons Ltd. – so I feel a close affinity with him. His responsibilities will be mainly in the retail interests of the group as well as Cash and Carry.

Fitch Lovell (Insurances) Ltd. has really established itself during the past year. This company is a testimonial of the resource and initiative of the ubiquitous Denis Apps, its Chairman, who always seems to have time to take on duties extra to his Secretaryship of Fitch Lovell. The group, as well as this particular company, owe him much for his devoted work over many years.

I. Beer has been busy reorganising much of its business into Cash and Carry wholesaling and the beginning of new branches in this direction. Miller's of Poole have opened one new depot and two more are due to be opened shortly. An interesting innovation at Hale's of Clevedon is the installation of a 'live' storage system which will keep perishable stock on the move in proper rotation, speed up the through-put and reduce wastage, handling and cost. Rutzou Ltd. has acquired the company of G.N. Truss & Co. Ltd., Polish bacon agents, old friends of the group and closely allied to I. Beer's in pre-war days.

*The Fitch Lovell News*, under the editorship of D.J. Apps (another of his jobs) has now materialised. Two lively numbers have been published and it is proposed to circulate four a year. In its April edition the journal mentions, *inter alia*, that Pieter Sanders, the general manager of Austen & Griffin has won a world championship at Basle, Switzerland for his canaries, also that Mary Rand used to work for the group. It does not mention Anita Lonsborough, the Olympic swimmer, formerly with R. Gunner, or the renowned Michael Caine once reputedly employed in Lovell's butter factory.

It is hoped *The Fitch Lovell News* will continue to flourish and keep the many thousands of members in our group abreast of our 'business' news, and also of the doings and achievements of our members in other fields.

A sadder note is struck in the two bomb explosions in Northern Ireland which badly damaged the buildings of Thos. Forde. These occurred within a fortnight. The rapid reparis of the first damage was a credit to all concerned. The pity was that the second explosion caused almost the same destruction as the first. Fortunately the production lines were not affected, so that business continued, in spite of the wreckage, as though nothing had occurred.

Lovell & Christmas moved its cheese factory to Erith in December 1970 and went on to shift operations at the end of the following month, the Erith business has become of outstanding interest in the locality and the Mayor of the Borough paid a visit in June 1971 to show his appreciation. J.T. Woods, who has done so well at Erith, was appointed to the L. & C. board in June 1971. The Board is now composed of youngish men, full of vitality, which augurs well for the firm's future.

The Far Famed Cake Company has built a new despatch department and extended its production areas, the total additional floor space being about 9,000 sq. ft.

Key Markets has continued its expansion and is carrying out its long term plan, and also as part of its re-organisation has vacated its Garretts Green warehouse. P. Firmston-Williams has resigned his position as a Senior Director and there have been other changes consequent on a reconstruction of Head Office operations.

Roberts & Birch has opened a new depot at Caldicot to supply the Bristol/Newport area. It has also now depots in operation at Amersham, Barnsley and Bridgend.

A familiar and much esteemed figure will be greatly missed when David Galloway retires from the Fitch Lovell Board of Directors in September 1971. Apart from his abilities and his experience as an accountant he will be remembered for a long time because of his public relations work and for the excellence of his relations with the staff who worked with him and under his Chairmanship.

This chapter is a brief summary of the year since the Fitch Lovell story was written and cannot begin to mention all the everyday activities, the decisions taken and the advances made. It cannot mention all the staff who have died or give the names of all who have retired after long service. It is satisfactory, however, to think they are provided for in their retirement, as indeed in many cases have their dependants.

Fitch Lovell still thinks of their staff as human beings and although it expects a full day's work for a full day's pay feels a sense of responsibility for each of them. Modernists can call this Paternalism if they wish, but they cannot say it is bad.

Shareholders at our annual general meeting must have been tired of hearing me say, 'Our biggest assets are not shown in our balance sheet, they are the 14,000 men and women who, all day and every day, carry out their duties to the best of their abilities in the interest of our Company'.

22

## ODD MEMORIES AT EVENTIME

THESE ODD MEMORIES are confined to the growth of an industrial enterprise as this book is not an autobiography.

I feel it strange that it is not the famous or the outstanding personalities one remembers with most affection but the ordinary men and women, some of whom – especially 50 years ago or more – had little education and rough manners but who served their companies with loyalty and devotion, as indeed they served my family and me.

The care and protection they gave me, an impossible and probably bumptious young man, because I was the youngest son of the 'old guv'nor', is something I can never forget, nor the amount of hard knowledge of a different world I learned as we drank mugs of steaming coffee or tea at five o'clock on winter's mornings in the blasting cold of Smithfield.

One I remember particularly was responsible for my breakfast, and for laying the table for our mid-day meal, in an upstairs room approached by an iron staircase, at 2 p.m. and bringing the food, hot and steaming from the *Old Cock Tavern* next door. He was insistent that for a growing lad (as he called me) it was essential to have a pound of rump steak each day.

Many things were altered by the First World War, the younger staff were dispersed, many of them never came back from Flanders or Gallipoli and others shifted to different occupations.

Never do I cease to wonder at the patriotism shown in 1914 and the early years of the war. The bulk of the population was not well treated, wages were very low and life was terribly hard. I doubt if in the so-called affluent society and the welfare state of today, the response for volunteers for war would equal the million who answered Kitchener's call.

Perhaps the 60,000 casualties on the first day of the Somme in 1916 and the terrible slaughter at Passendaele in 1917 changed more than anything else the attitude of the masses, who always seem to pay the price. Perhaps it was the unemployment and disillusion of the after-war years of those who had been promised a 'land fit for heroes'.

The almost Puritan strictness of the pre-1914 days seems unbelievable today; if a man was more than five minutes late he was sent home and a day's pay forfeited. There was no overtime, working days were long, and holidays at the most were one week after some years' service. No smoking was allowed until late in the afternoon, some 10 hours after beginning the day. All the same, beer was not much more than 1d. a glass and 10 Players cigarettes cost 2½d. or five Woodbines a 1d., and entrance to the Arsenal Football Ground was 4d., but I seem to remember as much hearty laughter, not to mention bawdy jokes, and as many smiling faces and as much willingness to help, as I find now. The days were long – especially Fridays when the Market closed at 4.0 p.m., and Saturdays when it was open for retail until 10.0 p.m.

Looking back there was a lot of unnecessary waste of time. I remember when the large American companies bought stalls on Smithfield and to everyone's surprise closed for business on Friday at noon and did not open on Saturday. This was a revolution but in 10 years their example was followed by most British firms.

I cannot remember my father driving his own horse and trap to market, but I can remember many others doing so, and the men who used to get a meagre living looking after the horses whilst the drivers were doing their buying in the market. Some of the turnouts were very smart as butchers were always inclined to be flash.

After the First War in 1919 and the succeeding years we began to build up a new staff, and for 25 years or more most of us worked together, close friendships were formed with every grade, we knew their families and, on the whole, their troubles, problems and triumphs were ours. Not many of these friends are left now, but their doings remain with me.

I remember well one of the problems on the inter-war years was 'bad debts' and it was always a practice on Saturday mornings for my brother Percy and me to scan every invoice and until this was done the office staff was not permitted to leave. To ensure they did not, their pay was withheld until all the statements were approved.

Eventually everything progressed, and we managed to finish on Fridays at about 7 p.m. It is strange today to think of the heads of a growing business perusing and passing up to 1,000 accounts a week – but so it was.

I remember with affection and gratitude those who schooled and taught me something about merchanting. This art, because it is an art, cannot be learned from books or hearsay. Much can be acquired by constant companionship and close watching of those who are truly successful, but practice and the making of mistakes are even more necessary. The quality of judgment remains a vital prerequisite.

One of my earliest memories of Smithfield goes back to 1908. This was the year my father, Clement (I) took Percy into partnership and gave all the staff a dinner in the *Holborn Restaurant*. I was also invited, as from my earliest days my father intended I should come into the business. Such was the power of his personality that I accepted his intention as fact, and never, even in my mind, doubted this is what I had to do.

The *Holborn Restaurant*, and its associate *Frascati's* a few hundred yards away, were a centre for business and masonic gatherings in those days. Decorated with much gilt and a plethora of red plush furnishing and red curtains, it gave more pleasure to the Victorians and Edwardians than it would to the modern generation; all the same the buildings had more character than the glass and concrete faceless buildings now erected on their sites.

My memory of the dinner was my surprise that people could eat and drink so much, and my petrification when my father said, 'My youngest son on leave from school will now speak – one day he will be your chief'. Words just would not come, and the tears were very near. After what seemed an interminable time I stuttered 'Thank you very much. I wish you good luck!' The applause from the gathering, who had well drunk, was possibly the greatest I have ever received.

As the evening wore on, my father, I think, sang a song, or I may be mixing this with the songs he sang at the Harvest Suppers on his farm. He had a big voice and no idea of music, and the result was generally to reduce his audience to silent stupification. When he had finished, one of the guests, a heavy man with a heavy moustache walked – or rather lurched up to him – 'Guv'nor', he said, 'I've had a great evening, but I shall not be in the market at five tomorrow, I shall be late'. 'Right', replied my father, 'don't come at all, you're sacked'. The evening continued merrily.

When I reported for business in 1910, my father told me he had had a contract with his barber since 1881, which enabled him to be shaved, his hair and side whiskers cut and his moustache trimmed, as often as he wished for 1s. 6d. (7½p) per month, to be paid even if he did not have anything done. This arrangement lasted until his death in 1925.

The only similar arrangement I ever had was with 'Blackie' the market shoeblack to whom I paid 1s. a week for many years, plus a small turkey at Christmas, for the cleaning of my shoes or boots every day. He became a trusted friend, and never have my shoes shone so brightly as when Blackie rubbed them with his shabby cloth, hissing the while like an old time groom.

My brother, Percy, inculcated the necessity of a knowledge of accountancy and the close supervision of costing: this did not come too difficult for one most of whose family imagined themselves mathematicians.

The early '20s witnessed an expansion of our business, both buying and selling, to the continent of Europe and to America; which involved the purchase of foreign currency. As there was no one else to do this I had to undertake the task; looking back it was enjoyable, exciting and splendid training as nearly all currencies fluctuated from day to day.

When the First World War ended the French franc was 25 to the £1, the Italian lire the same, today the French franc has depreciated 50 times, the Italian lire about 70 times. This fall was not steady and regular, but a rise and fall from week to week. Everyone knows what happened to the German Mark which was 20 to the £1 in 1914 and how within 20 years it was necessary to have a suitcase, with million mark notes, to pay for a meal. This depreciation of currency in Germany was surely a main cause of Hitler's rise to power and of his war. Lenin may well have been right when he said that the easiest way to revolution was by inflation and destroying a nation's currency.

The first firm I dealt with was Singer & Friedlander, then Ullman's, then Samuel Montagu. Our policy was to cover the currency as soon as a purchase or sale was made, even if the delivery was several months ahead. This was seemingly safe but I remember sometimes that when goods arrived, say three months late and the value of the £1 had strengthened, competitors who had not covered were able to undersell us.

The £1 in 1918 was worth nominally $4.78; by 1920 it had fallen to $3, it rose erratically to $4.50 in 1923, fell to $4 in 1921 and regained its old value of $4.80 in 1925. The Bretten Woods agreement in 1944 fixed it at $4, today in 1971 it is about $2.50. The £ is once more a floating currency, we do not know if this will continue – if it does a fresh element will be brought into merchanting again.

I have cited the above figures to give some ideas of the problems facing international trading in earlier years.

Particularly do I remember the fairness of a French Court of Justice in the 1920s. We had made an advance in French francs to a shipper in French turkeys, I cannot recall the exact amount but probably £5,000 to £6,000. The shipper refused to pay, stating he had sold them at a firm price. We took the matter to Court, I believe at Bourges, the case took well over a year to come up, during which time the franc had deteriorated. The judge not only awarded us the case but an additional payment of 50% in francs to compensate for the fall in value of the currency.

My memory of my brother Percy in earlier days was of his extreme secrecy and it took me a year or two to find out how he controlled the family business. He had a number of small black books which he studied each week, a list of these could be interesting and perhaps instructive to young people running family businesses. They may be surprised at the detail supervised at a time when the business was growing rapidly. The following were the little black books which were passed and initialled weekly.

1. Electric light and heat consumption.
2. Trunk calls (time taken on each).
3. Petrol used and list of journeys (car and lorries).
4. Weekly expenses each department departmentalised.
5. Turnover of each salesman and traveller.
6. Animal book (showing exact number of birds of different kinds received during week, also cases, etc. of provision items).
7. (A larger book) Customers' book, containing all customers showing if they had purchased during week.
8. Senders' book (similar to Customers' book) showing if they had consigned that week.

9. Details of Petty Cash payments during week.
10. Forward Purchase book.
11. Departmental details of weekly sales and profits.
12. Cold store book with stocks and movement.

and there were other books.

All these 'little black books' were prepared by one clerk, they were in addition to the books and ledgers as kept normally by all reputable firms.

There are three things I remember well. The ledger clerks were not allowed to go home until the ledgers were balanced and every day the stock of each department had to be taken and any discrepancy reported.

Even in my father's time none of the family ever left the premises, even for half an hour – without saying we were going out and where we were going.

It was always a matter of honour that one of the family was the last to leave after all the staff had gone. On the rare occasions when we all left, the Office Manager was placed in charge.

Of course the staff rarely exceeded 60 or 70 and the actual weekly sales were of the order of about 3,000 separate items. The market sales staff generally left by 2 p.m. (having begun at 5 a.m.) so the difficulties of carrying out the routine were not too great.

It always seemed to me the office staff had the worst of any bargain. They were very badly housed, sitting mainly on high stools at high desks in dingy offices. They had their meals on their desks and their hours were from about 6 a.m. or 7 a.m. to 5 p.m. or 6 p.m. and Saturdays to the time they balanced their books, generally about 1 p.m.

Conditions were no worse with us than elsewhere, and many of the staff stayed during most, if not all, of their working life.

Conditions definitely improved in the 1930s, but clerical workers always found it difficult to obtain jobs. I remember that whenever we advertised for a ledger or stock clerk (in the *Daily Telegraph*) it was usual to have more than 400 applications. These facts give a gloomy picture, but as I have written earlier there was plenty of laughter and fun in those days, and time was somehow found for games and hobbies.

I remember in pre-1914 days, and all the time of my youth, that we always carried our gold coins in little pig skin purses, with slots for one golden sovereign and a smaller one for our 10s. coins. The only bank notes were the large elaborately printed £5 notes which still I remember nostalgically.

A poignant memory is of the rather sudden death of my father, Clement (I), in 1925. The firm ceased business at breakfast time, and although he had not been active in business for many years, all the staff attended the funeral, taken in coaches, with many of their wives, and a multitude of other people. I remember my sister Mabel saying to me, 'You have lost your best friend now'. The years showed how right she was! His life is summed up by the words of St. Paul, engraved on his tombstone, 'I have fought a good fight'.

It was about this time, perhaps earlier, that I began to wonder if the detailed work and restricted activities of a medium-sized firm would satisfy me in spite of the good profits we were enjoying. Of course, the growth of the business widened one's horizon and the appointment, at too early an age as I realise now, to government committees and trade committees partially compensated, but the urge to put into practice new ideas and methods was insistent. I remember the elation when we bought an old public house and an adjoining coffee shop in King Street (now Smithfield Street) next to Lovell & Christmas, and converted them into small warehouses, and a little later when we took a long lease of 36 Snow Hill – now demolished and part of a new building.

All these beginnings of expansion were good, but it was not long before we were in the midst of the depression of the late '20s and early '30s. The defensive spirit was uppermost, as is only natural in times of retreat, and the failures of wholesale and retail customers were a constant worry. This defensive attitude affected the outlook and was probably the cause of my schemes in the mid-'30s, and the reason for the basis on which Fitch Lovell's expansion was formed in later years.

One memory everyone must keep who lived in the '20s is the General Strike. The nation's life stopped at a stroke, but resilient as always, ways and means began to be found.

On a Sunday morning the telephone rang and I was told there were, I think, 150 cases of French eggs at the Wharf and if we could obtain lorries not on strike there was a fair chance we could obtain delivery. This was done by finding a man and his sons who drove their own lorries. In those days, 1926, cases contained 1440 eggs, and weighed 2 cwt. each; therefore the weight would be about 15 tons.

We drove to the docks – as on other occasions – and were given small hammers so that if the strikers tried to climb into the lorry we could hammer their fingers.

On this occasion as on others there was little trouble at the docks, when we returned to Smithfield, the market police opened the large iron gates. A friend and customer was passing by and we persuaded him to come and help us.

The lorries drew into the market and I drove my own car, in which I had picked up my brother Percy en route. Manoeuvring inside the narrow aisles of the market I backed my car, knocked my brother over, spraining his ankle and his wrist. This left only my 'press-ganged' friend and me to deal with the 2 cwt. cases. Balancing them with help on my back, the top protruding beyond my head and the bottom on a level with the calves of my legs. I found it not so difficult as one would imagine, and in a couple of hours we completed the job, the 250,000 or so eggs were most acceptable to Londoners the next morning.

A memory relating to another strike has always remained, a union porter and shop steward, a big rather fierce man, came up and demanded I should do something and do it quickly. 'You had better see my brother', I said. 'No I shan't, I have too much respect for him' he replied. 'Why?' I asked. 'Well, I have known him for 25 years and his tie is always properly tied and his coat properly buttoned up'. The reasons for respect are indeed strange, but I think there is a lesson here.

The hectic fortnights before Christmas in the inter-war years, with inadequate refrigeration, are naturally full of memories, but one stands out from the others. It had been a full and busy day from 5 a.m. and was nearing 8 p.m. I was rather impatient because the Stock Clerk had not come to take stock and let us go home. He was a sober, excellent clerk with one drawback – he could not stand the Office Manager.

It must have been nearly nine o'clock when he came into the warehouse with a knife in his hand. He came up to me, a strange glassy look in his eyes, and spoke very deliberately, 'I am sorry, Sir, but I have been looking everywhere for X [the Office Manager] I want to kill him. Please excuse me'. Brandishing his knife he ran off. Our stock was not taken that night.

The Office Manager was found hiding behind the stacks in the stationary room. The Stock Clerk was back at duty the next morning at 6 a.m., full of apologies, saying he had been persuaded to drink several whiskies, a thing he never did at work. He remained with us for another 25 years, and became as excellent an Office Manager as he had been a Stock Clerk.

The acute Depression coupled with the desire to help British agriculture caused the government to intervene in the importation of certain food, noticeably bacon. An overall figure for imports was fixed in order to help the British Pig Breeders. It was found the amount of imports permitted did not meet the demand and I was deputed in November 1936 to lead a National deputation of the Provision and Produce Exchanges, and the Federation of Retailers.

The President of the Board of Trade, Rt. Hon. Walter Runciman (Lord Runciman), The Minister of Agriculture, Rt. Hon. W.S. Morrison, who, according to the press release

> received a Deputation representing all sections of the bacon distribution trade of the country. The deputation asked that the total permitted supplies of 10,800,000 cwts. of bacon should be increased by 10% and that an Advisory Committee should be set up to keep in constant touch with the Board of Trade and the Ministry of Agriculture on all matters affecting the industry . . .

My memory of this important meeting was of the coldness and aloofness of the Ministers. They did not seem to be well acquainted with the problem, or care much about it, and their prepared replies were non-commital and unencouraging.

However, the imports were duly increased, an Advisory Committee was set up, and still exists, 35 years later. The general attitude of Ministers to Industry has greatly changed today, one suspects many of the problems of the inter-war years arose because the governments of that time were too distant from the people and the trades that really mattered.

Some years previously I had presented a case to the then Minister of Agriculture (Walter Elliot) on behalf of the National Poultry Council, and its concern with the low price of eggs and poultry. I must have presented the case badly because Walter Elliot intervened before I had finished and demolished one by one all my arguments and told me next time to have a better brief before my colleagues and I wasted so much ministerial time. I must have been bad, because Walter Elliot was a kindly man, full of humour – he did not show it to me that morning!

The rise of Hitler and the possibility of a second world war caused us, I recollect, to become inward thinking. The years leading to Munich in 1938 were disturbing, business was difficult, public and home life was shadowed by the approaching tragedy. More and more I became involved with outside matters, and more than a year before the outbreak of war a few of us, who were so-called leaders of the food industry, were summoned to Whitehall and told to arrange certain emergency measures in case war should break out.

I was appointed Chairman of the National Defence (Foods) Committee, which was a temporary committee to arrange defence measures. There was a feeling of nervousness throughout the country, especially when the Prime Minister made his various air flights to Germany before Munich.

The government was afraid that food prices would rise during this period of acute apprehension and the Board of Trade asked me as Chairman of the Co-ordinating Committee of the Provision and Produce Exchanges of the U.K. to take steps to arrange a voluntary standstill of prices until the results of the Prime Minister's various talks with Hitler were known.

In August 1938 the idea of controlling prices was anathema to traders. However, without too much difficulty, agreement was reached with all the Exchanges in the U.K. and the Retail Trade, with the result that a veritable standstill was achieved for nearly a month.

The President of the Board of Trade, the Rt. Hon. Oliver Stanley, who, but for his untimely death a few years later, might well have become Prime Minister, wrote to me on 6 October 1938,

> I am writing to express my sincere thanks for your work during the recent crisis in connection with the organisation of the distribution of provisions throughout the United Kingdom. I feel very much indebted to you not only for your personal efforts, . . . but also for the way in which you obtained the co-operation of provisions importers throughout the country.

This letter, with a covering note from me as Defence Chairman, appeared in the trade and national papers. At the time it seemed all part of the day's work, but looking back over the years it was surely a bigger triumph than one realised. Thus memory reminds me it is often the ordinary jobs which are the most important.

Memories of the next year are numerous and varied, almost all connected with preparations for war and are best told elsewhere; gradually we came to the tense moment in September 1939 when the strained and disillusioned voice of Neville Chamberlain was heard over the radio, 'We shall fight against evil things, brute force, bad faith, injustice, oppression and persecution'. War had come again to Britain.

I had got rather 'out of step' with the Ministry of Food in the months before the war, probably my fault for over-ebulliance in dealing with the Civil Service, and I doubted an appointment, so I was more than gratified when Mr. Feavearyear (afterwards Sir Albert) asked me to take over the Chairmanship of the London Area for the trade three days before the declaration. I could not envisage myself in Whitehall and have grateful memories of Gordon Lovell, and the placing of a suite of offices at my disposal right in the middle of the Smithfield area.

When the Germans began their intensive air war on London, among the first places to be destroyed in the immediate neighbourhood were Keevils' and I. Beer's warehouse and the other premises in King Street, and shortly afterwards a large part of the Poultry Market. The emergency arrangements worked well, and Keevils' moved into different sites in the Market and Charterhouse Street, where they still are.

Later, under continual bombing, the overall London position became almost disastrous, but somehow we pulled through. I remember Lord Woolton, the Minister of Food, coming down to see me and his astonishment that firms could carry out their vital business under such conditions of wreckage.

London were fortunate during the 'blitz' period in having as their Divisional Food Officer a great old warrior, General Sir Julian Young, who later was placed in charge of the Eastern and the whole of the South Eastern areas of England. He asked me to be chairman of these areas for Provisions and Groceries. My memories are pleasant because there was little to do as the bombing had largely subsided and the trade had become organised.

Never very happy and certainly not very good as a Civil Servant – unpaid at that – I remember how pleased I was to be appointed to a Military Command in 1942. J.R.P. Postlewaite, who had succeeded 'Skinny Young' wrote far too kindly about me in his book *I Look Back*, stating on one occasion when there was an exodus northwards and roads were crammed with vehicles and bombed out refugees that his emergency feeding arrangements could not cope and that we 'solved the difficulties by some means which appeared to me at the time to be almost miraculous', and later, on my retirement, 'Colonel Ambrose Keevil who had steered the wholesale ship through the first two years of war . . . tendered his resignation. The Ministry owed him much; London also owed him much'.

All these praises were appreciated but I remember how much nearer John Masefield came to the truth – because it is really the men in the front line who bore the brunt and the bloody burden.

> Not the bemedalled Commander, beloved of the throne,
> Riding cock-horse to parade when the bugles are blown
> But the lads who carried the koppie and cannot be known.

My post-war memories consist mainly of trying to fit the returning soldiers into positions which suited them. Six years had changed boys into men, and juniors into seniors.

A most unpleasant recollection is of the first strike which Keevil's had had in over 100 years of existence, and the feeling of bitterness and disillusion which this engendered. Strikes in the Smithfield area were widespread after the end of the war, and troops had to be called in to help with food distribution. I had little doubt at the time, and no doubt now that these strikes were fomented by agitators – the result probably of communist infiltration in the armed services. This influence seems to have declined of recent years and we have suffered no serious labour troubles for a long, long, time.

The years following the war are fully dealt with in the chapters Fitch to Fitch Lovell and the Making of Fitch Lovell. My memories of these years are of incessant work, happy enthusiasm and, in a way, the implementation of one's ideas. I was also busily engaged in many activities outside Industry which I believe is the right thing to avoid staleness.

The decontrol of many imports, including turkeys, took place in the early '50s and I set out on a pilgrimage to the Centre, the South West of France and the country bordering the Pyrenees in the Gers, Tarn and the Garonne to trace our old exporting friends.

One day I arrived at a village in the department of Gers to call on an old sender. He was a cheerful man not renowned for his sobriety, during the war he had died – I am sure Louis (as I will call him) was a leader of the local Resistance. His daughter and son-in-law, who lived in the same house as their father had lived, insisted I should stay and feed with them. Louis's old wife was still alive but rather quiet, and like all grandmothers in the region sat in the corner of the room near the fire with a little table for herself, with black dress and white cap. The Gers is the country of real Foie Gras and very strong Pernod, and we began a magnificent meal with happiness, but Grandmère was still silent.

Those who knew this part of France will remember that the ground floors of most houses are of earth, families live in the same house for a 100 years and the earth becomes hard as wood and very shiny. We had finished the meal and the ceremony of making the coffee had begun when Grandmère stood and held up her arm. Turning to her son-in-law she said, 'Go and find a spade and a fork and bring them here'. He did so. 'Now', she said, pointing to a place on the floor, 'dig and dig hard. Louis and I lived in this house for nearly two generations. The night we were married we buried there a bottle of Armagnac. It is now 50 years. Dig it up for Monsieur Keevil the great friend of Louis, and we will all drink to his memory and their friendship.' The oil lamp flickered on the table, the dust-covered bottle was brought forward, Grandmère, her children and grandchildren and I all drank to Louis – to General de Gaulle and the Roi d'Angleterre. Grandmère and I then drank together. She sat down and went to sleep and I went out to the waiting motor car. The moon was brilliant, the Pyrenees were glistening white in the distance. What a night – what a tribute – what a memory!

As one grows older inevitably friends and colleagues die, some of them leave a big gap and many memories. It would not be right to mention any by name because in their different ways they all enriched my life.

I have always found it difficult to accept gracefully a presentation, mainly I think because of the surprise at receiving it and realising, without hypocrisy, that probably someone else should have had it. The gifts I received on my retirement at the age of 70 from Fitch Lovell, and on my golden wedding anniversary are still precious and appreciated far more than I can write.

These jottings of various memories have purposely omitted, whenever possible, the mention of any names, but three deaths in recent years cannot be forgotten. Ted Coles, a porter and warehouseman for 40 years at Keevils', deaf as a door post, rough, strong, loyal, with a good brain, a close friend indeed. His fear was that he would not draw a pension because he was too old when a pension scheme was introduced. He did not draw one as he was killed instantly in a motor accident a few months before the time of his retirement.

Another is that of Oliver Huntley when, in 1970, he had just reached a point in his brilliant career from which he could have surged forward. A sudden illness intervened and he died almost at once, and the two positions on which he had set his heart, the Presidency of the Law Society and the Chairmanship of Fitch Lovell, had to be filled by others. He has left a gap difficult to fill in the Law, in Industry and in the lives of his friends.

Lastly my brother Percy, who did not quite reach his 93rd birthday. I remember the cricket we played together, and the rowing on the river Thames over 60 years ago, and in later times the close association with him in business for 50 years. My fear of his efficiency and his all-seeing eye, his punctuality, his capacity for work, his forthrightness, his austerity, coupled with my admiration for his judgment of fluctuating markets, his sudden bursts of generosity and kindness, all remain with me together with surprise at his shyness.

His last years were not very happy. He lived by himself in one room in a Nursing Home. It seemed sad that after his unremitting toil, the wealth and honours which he had truly earned, that the death of his wife and the absence of a home should have left him somewhat lonely. His four daughters constantly visited him and he spoke with much appreciation of them; all the same it seemed a strange finish to a life such as his.

Scanning this chapter, I note the memories are nearly all of distant days, that no mention is made of the captains of industry and the distinguished people who have crossed my path. Perhaps they were not so amusing or so human as the lads who worked in Smithfield and Tooley Street. Still there is not very much one can write about fitted carpets and air-conditioned offices, or about lunches at the *Savoy Grill*, the *Ritz* or the *Dorchester*, or long receptions or short cocktail parties.

Many board meetings and committees are well described by the Persian poet '. . . and heard great argument about it and about, but evermore came out by the same door as in I went'.

Mergers and takeovers can be exciting but they only differ in degree from normal types of trading. The personalities and their powers may be greater, but fundamentally there is little difference.

Looking back, life in business has been fascinating and exacting, and the standard of honesty at all levels extremely high, the millions of pounds sterling of goods bought and sold each week in Fitch Lovell are nearly all sold by word of mouth, and without contract, and so it has been all my life.

Although everyone we meet affects our lives – as indeed we do ourselves with each person we meet – there are some people who have had a big influence and who have largely shaped one. There are others whose loyalty and help over the years has always been a source of wonderment.

Throughout the story of Fitch Lovell and these odd memories there is hardly a mention of the female sex. Perhaps because they seldom occupy the positions of power, but without them and all their support, help and influence, we would have achieved nothing. So I thank them all – wives, fellow workers, personal secretaries, housekeepers and all – asking them to accept this tribute as entirely sincere.

Some day perhaps I will write of those whose lives have been interwoven with mine, from Blackie (the Smithfield shoe-black) to captains of industry, from market van men to great scholars, from salesmen to philanthropists, from Trade Union leaders to Prime Ministers, but however I may write of them and their qualities, the words of the Hebrew prophet Micah, written over 2,600 years ago are insistent – 'What doth the Lord require of thee but to do justly and to love mercy and to walk humbly with thy God'.

## APPENDIX I

### *BIBLIOGRAPHY*

Anglo American Council on Productivity, *Retailing*
Beer, A. Ernest, *Isaac Beer & His Sons*
Boswell, Jones, *J.S. 100 The Story of Sainsburys*
Boyd-Orr, Lord, *Food. The White Man's Dilemma*
Centenary Number, *The Grocer 1862-1962*
Crawford, Sir William, *The People's Food*
Ellis, Aytoun, *300 years on London's River*
Fitch, M.F.B., *Notes on the Fitch Family*
Fitch & Son Ltd., *Minutes* 1920-1958
Fitch Lovell Ltd., *Minutes* 1958-1970
Gerrard, Frank, *The Book of the Meat Trade,* Vol. 1
Gerrard, Frank, *The Book of the Meat Trade,* Vol. 2
Goodall, J.A., *Antecessors of James Fitch, Citizen of London*
Grant, Douglas, *The Cock Lane Ghost*
*Hays News* 1967, *The London Provision Exchange*
Heath, Barron, *Some Account of The Grocers' Company*
Jones, P., *The Poulters of London*
Kent, William, *An Encyclopaedia of London*
Kingham, G.C., *Our first 100 years*
Lloyd, E.M.H., *Experiments in State Control*
Lovell & Christmas Ltd., *Minutes* 1896-1969
Lovell, Edward & Spencer, *Lovell*
Lovell, Lt. Col. H.O., *Argentine notes*
Mari, Eric de, *London's River*
Mathias, Peter, *Retailing Revolution*
Noël, E.V., *Noël*
N.Z. Co-op Dairy Company, *The Empire's Dairy Farm*
Pearse, Arthur, *The History of the Butchers' Company*
Peterson, P.J., *Pioneering under the Southern Cross*
Postlethwaite, J.R.P., *Stock Book*
Twigg, C.O., *The Market Clock*
Wilsher Peter, *The Pound in your Pocket 1870-1970*

*also*

Various Memoranda, Manuscripts, Indentures, Price Lits, Correspondence, legal documents etc. etc. dating back over 100 years.

# APPENDIX II

*SHAREHOLDERS – 1947/1970*

| Year | 5% Pref. | 6% Pref. | 6½% Pref. | 7¼% Loan Stock | Ordinary | Total |
|---|---|---|---|---|---|---|
| 1947 | | 130 | | | 356 | 486 |
| 1948 | | 125 | | | 396 | 521 |
| 1949 | | 130 | | | 412 | 542 |
| 1950 | | 126 | | | 418 | 544 |
| 1951 | 314 | 124 | | | 464 | 902 |
| 1955 | 363 | 139 | | | 1,010 | 1,512 |
| 1958 | 322 | 141 | | | 1,383 | 1,846 |
| 1960 | 310 | 140 | 2,260 | | 7,300 | 10,010 |
| 1965 | 231 | 144 | 4,359 | | 20,934 | 25,668 |
| 1970 | – | – | 63 | 3,152 | 21,333 | 24,548 |

## APPENDIX III

*GROUP PROGRESS REPORT 1951-1970*

| Year Ended | Trading Profit £ | Net Profit Before Tax £ | Fixed Assets £ | Reserves £ | Ordinary Dividend £ |
|---|---|---|---|---|---|
| 1951 | 465,600 | 445,900 | 740,700 | 638,500 | |
| 1952 | 461,700 | 435,600 | 917,200 | 894,700 | 30,200 |
| 1953 | 447,900 | 417,000 | 1,012,200 | 976,400 | 45,900 |
| 1954 | 264,400 | 210,000 | 1,223,100 | 983,400 | 38,500 |
| 1955 | 462,300 | 364,400 | 1,447,400 | 1,074,000 | 45,000 |
| 1956 | 592,000 | 481,100 | 1,733,800 | 1,304,700 | 51,800 |
| 1957 | 657,800 | 510,000 | 2,092,000 | 1,195,500 | 57,500 |
| 1958 | 835,700 | 629,800 | 2,357,400 | 1,354,200 | 63,300 |
| 1959 | 1,545,100 | 1,019,900 | 5,565,100 | 3,199,700 | 105,200 |
| 1960 | 1,813,900 | 1,172,200 | 6,773,200 | 3,964,500 | 196,400 |
| 1961 | 2,145,200 | 1,416,700 | 9,677,900 | 5,724,900 | 265,700 |
| 1962 | 2,917,900 | 1,873,700 | 16,318,500 | 9,633,900 | 341,100 |
| 1963 | 3,129,600 | 2,076,100 | 17,991,800 | 10,106,400 | 431,700 |
| 1964 | 3,180,800 | 2,001,800 | 19,435,200 | 10,677,900 | 431,700 |
| 1965 | 3,635,200 | 2,209,400 | 20,006,300 | 10,873,600 | 466,700 |
| 1966 | 3,760,900 | 2,363,500 | 20,948,700 | 8,412,300 | 554,800 |
| 1967 | 3,914,700 | 2,383,300 | 21,176,000 | 8,893,300 | 848,400 |
| 1968 | 4,769,600 | 3,213,100 | 21,793,100 | 9,816,500 | 883,100 |
| 1969 | 4,902,900 | 3,405,400 | 22,617,600 | 13,282,900 | 1,028,000 |
| *1970 | 5,392,600 | 3,619,600 | 23,736,300 | 14,018,900 | 1,199,800 |
| 1971 | 6,236,000 | 4,440,000 | 24,805,000 | 15,177,000 | 1,440,000 |

* Extended period.

NOTE: The above figures are taken from the published Accounts for Fitch Lovell Ltd. to 1970. The published Accounts for 1971 were on a new format. The figures shown above for 1971 have been adjusted to be comparable with all other years quoted.

# APPENDIX IV

## *SHARE CAPITAL*

### *Capitalisation & Rights Issues (since 1946)*

| | | |
|---|---|---|
| 1946 | June | Rights: 1 for 3 10s. Ordinary Shares @ 20s. |
| 1947 | May | 10s. shares converted into 2s. 6d. Ordinary Stock Units. |
| 1949 | July | Bonus: 2 for every 5 2s. 6d. Ordinary Stock Units. |
| 1950 | Aug. | Bonus: 1 £5% Pref. for every 22.5 Ordinary 2s. 6d. |
| 1951 | July | Bonus: 1 £5% Pref. for every 22.5 Ordinary 2s. 6d. |
| | Nov. | Rights: 2 for every 5 Ordinary held @ 10s. |
| 1955 | Nov. | Rights: 1 for every 4 Ordinary held @ 10s. |
| 1956 | Nov. | Bonus: 1 Ordinary for each Ordinary held. |
| 1959 | May | Bonus: 1 'B' Ordinary for each Ordinary of 'B' Ord. held. |
| | May | Rights: 2 'B' Ordinary for each 3 Ord. or 'B' Ord. held @ 6s. |
| 1960 | June | Bonus: One £1 6½% Pref. for every 20 Ord. held (equalisation voting rights of 'B' shares which were converted into Ordinary). |
| | June | Rights: 1 Ordinary for every 4 Ordinary held @ 7s. 8d. |
| 1962 | | Bonus: 1 Ordinary for every 10 Ordinary held. |
| 1964 | | Bonus: 1 Ordinary for every 5 Ordinary held. |
| 1966 | | Bonus: 3 Ordinary 5 Ordinary held to consolidate 2s. 6d. Ord. into 4s. Ord. |
| 1968 | | Rights: 1 Ordinary for every 8 Ord. held @ 14s. |

NOTE: No shares in Fitch & Son Ltd. were sold in 1945, neither on nor off the Stock Exchange; the nominal price quoted was 7s. 6d. to 10s. for 1 ordinary share of 10s.

Anyone purchasing 100 shares at the beginning of 1946 (say for £50), and who had kept all their script bonus shares and taken up and kept their rights issues, would have had slightly more than 15,000 shares in June 1970.

## APPENDIX V

*DIRECTORS AND SECRETARIES OF FITCH LOVELL LIMITED*

**Directors**

| | | |
|---|---|---|
| Beale, Sir William F., O.B.E. | 1961-1963 | Appointed O.B.E. 1945. Created Knight Bachelor 1956 |
| Beer, E. Trevor, C.B.E. | 1963- | Deputy Chairman 1970- App. C.B.E. (1946) O.B.E. (1942) |
| Blanning, R.E. | 1958- | Deputy Chairman & Managing Director 1962-1966. Chairman 1967-1970. |
| Boyes Stubbs, H. | 1962-1964 | |
| Canevali, E.M. | 1964- | |
| Cannon, G.A. | 1971- | |
| Evans, W.D. | 1961-1965 | |
| Fitch, H.B., C.C. | 1958-1961 | President 1959-1961 |
| Fitch, M.F.B. | 1958-1967 | |
| Galloway, D., O.B.E., C.A. | 1959-1971 | App. O.B.E. 1959 |
| Gilpin, John | 1960- | |
| Hardie, Sir Charles, C.B.E., F.C.A. | 1970- | Deputy Chairman 1969-70 Chairman 1970- cre. Knight Bachelor 1970 app. C.B.E. 1963 (O.B.E. 1943). Officer U.S. Legion of Merit 1944 |
| Huntley, K.O.G., O.B.E. | 1959-1969 | App. Vice-Chairman 1969 (deceased 1970) App. O.B.E. 1944. App. Officer in the Order of Orange Nassau 1954. |
| Keevil, Sir Ambrose, K.B.E., M.C., D.L. | 1958-1969 | Chairman & Managing Director 1959-63. President 1963-1969. Hon. President 1969- App. K.B.E. 1962 (C.B.E. |

| | | |
|---|---|---|
| | | 1944. B.E. 1918). cre. Knight Bachelor 1952. awarded Military Cross 1917. Bar to M.C. 1918. app. Chevalier of the Ordre de Merite Agricole 1939. app. Chevalier Legion of Honour 1957. |
| Keevil, A.C.A. | 1958- | |
| Lambourne, N.F. | 1958-1963 | Vice Chairman & Managing Director 1958-1962 |
| McEwan, I.P., M.V.O., C.A. | 1969- | App. M.V.O. 1945 |
| Parker, F.F. | 1962 | |
| Rowlandson, Sir Graham, M.B.E., J.P., F.C.A. | 1958-1959 | Chairman 1958-1959. App. M.B.E. 1943. cre. Knight Bachelor 1956 |
| Wall, Sir Rolande, M.C. | 1958-1969 | Vice Chairman & Managing Director 1958-1962. Chairman & Managing Director 1963-1966. cre. Knight Bachelor 1946. awarded Military Cross 1917. |

**Secretaries**

| | |
|---|---|
| Apps, D.J., F.C.I.S., J.P. | 1962- |
| Gilpin, John | 1959-1962 |

# APPENDIX VI

*ROYAL WARRANTS*
*held by Fitch & Son Ltd.*

| Date | By Whom Granted | To Whom Granted |
|---|---|---|
| 2 March 1863 | H.R.H. Edward, Prince of Wales (who became Edward VII) | Frederick Fitch |
| 4 Dec. 1888 | H.M. Queen Victoria | William Bellamy (Bellamy Bros.) (later of Fitch & Son Ltd.) |
| 20 Feb. 1897 | H.R.H. Edward, Prince of Wales (who became Edward VII) | Robert Bellamy and William Bellamy. (Bellamy Bros.) (later of Fitch & Son Ltd.) |
| 29 July 1901 | H.M. Edward VII | William Bellamy (Bellamy Bros.) (later of Fitch & Son Ltd.) |
| 30 July 1901 | H.M. Edward VII | Edwin Frederick Fitch (Fitch & Son Ltd.) |
| 27 May 1907 | H.M. King Alfonso of Spain | Bellamy Bros. |
| 10 Dec. 1910 | H.M. King George V | Fitch & Son Ltd. |
| 17 July 1922 | H.M. the Dowager Queen Alexandra | Hugh Bernard Fitch. Edwin F. Ashelford. (Fitch & Son Ltd.) |
| 1 Jan. 1936 | H.R.H. Edward, Prince of Wales (who became Edward VIII) | Hugh Bernard Fitch (Fitch & Son Ltd.) |
| 1 July 1940 | H.M. King George VI | Marcus Felix Brudenell Fitch. (Fitch & Son Ltd.) |
| 15 July 1955 | H.M. Queen Elizabeth II | Marcus Felix Brudenell Fitch. (Fitch & Son Ltd.) |
| 1 June 1967 | H.M. Queen Elizabeth II | John Gilpin (Fitch & Son Ltd.) |

# APPENDIX VII

## *THE FITCH SUCCESSION FROM NOTES LEFT BY H.S. ROWLANDSON*

The firm of Fitch & Son was founded in 1784 by James Fitch, and established in Leadenhall Street. James Fitch was the third son of George Fitch of Clopton Hall, Gt. Dunmow, who died July 1st 1799.

James Fitch took his brother William into partnership who died in April 1801.

James Fitch took his nephew George Fitch into partnership in 1812, which Articles are still in existence.

Subsequently James Fitch died and George Fitch took his brother Thomas Fitch into partnership – they removed in 1828 to premises in Bishopsgate, then known as No. 66, and later renumbered 99.

There were financial difficulties in 1828 and Charles, a cousin of George and Thomas, left.

The firm again suspended payment in 1832 and Thomas returned and re-opened in Leadenhall Street opposite Balleter Street.

Thomas Fitch retired from the partnership in 1836, in whose stead George Fitch took his son Frederick into partnership and traded for a time as George Fitch & Son.

George Fitch retired 24th June 1841, and Frederick Fitch carried on alone for the next twenty years.

Frederick Fitch then took his son Edwin Frederick Fitch into partnership which partnership remained until 1880, when Frederick Fitch retired and Edwin Frederick Fitch was the sole partner.

Edwin Frederick Fitch took his son Stanley Fox Fitch into partnership in 1890, and no further changes were made until 1906, when the Export Department was turned into a private Limited Company under the title of Fitch & Son, Export, Limited, to be followed, in 1907, by the Home Department also being turned into a private Company, under the title of Fitch & Son Limited. These two Companies continued their separate existence until 1920, when the present public Company, FITCH & SON LIMITED, combining the two Companies, was formed, Mr. Hugh B. Fitch becoming the Chairman.

At the end of December 1929, after having been established at the Bishopsgate premises for 101 years, the Head Office of the Company was removed to 80/81 St. Martin's Lane, W.C.2.

Marcus F.B. Fitch, son of Hugh B. Fitch, was elected a Director of the Company on the 12th March, 1930.

---

P.S. The Green Livery, brass buttons and hackney horse vans of Fitch were one of the sights of London in the mid-19th century and later.

# APPENDIX VIII – *THE LOVELLS AND CHRISTMASES INVOLVED WITH LOVELL & CHRISTMAS*

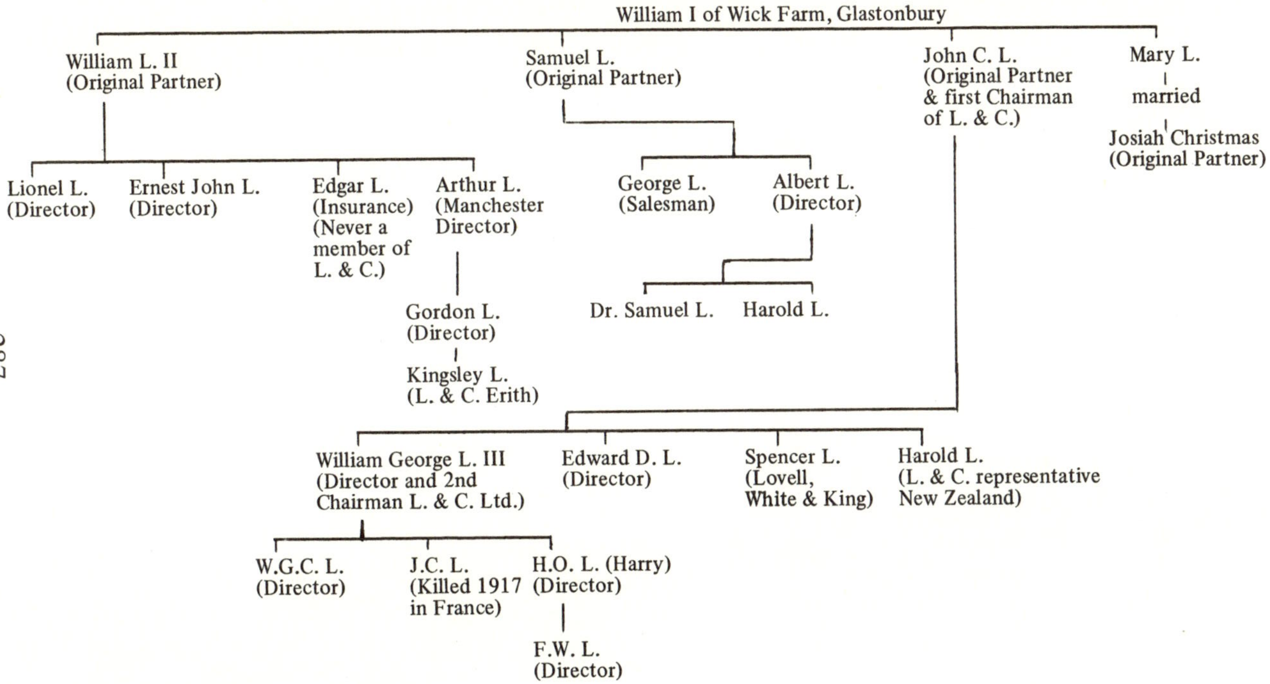


NOTE: Edgar Lovell was the founder of Lloyds of London; Spencer Lovell, the founder of Lovell, White & King (Solicitors); Sidney Lovell, the founder of Popham, Lyon & Co. of the Stock Exchange.

## APPENDIX IX – *THE BALANCE SHEET OF*

| | | | | |
|---|---|---|---|---|
| 1856 Dec. 31 | To Creditors | 5 | | 4431 6 8 |
| 1852 Nov. | Capital of | | | |
| | Chas. Christmas | 1 | 100 | |
| | Wm. Lovell | 2 | 100 | 200 |
| | Profit Nett | | | 2176 13 6 |
| | C Christmas | | 1088 6 9 | |
| | W Lovell | | 1088 6 9 | |
| | | | 2176 13 6 | |
| 4467 8 9 | | | | |
| 73 3 6 | | | | |
| 4540 12 3 | | | | |
| 4431 6 8 | | | | |
| 109 5 7 | Surplus divisible between partners | | | |
| | | | | 6808 0 2 |
| | To C. Christmas | | 36 11 9 | |
| | W. Lovell | | 36 11 9 | 73 3 6 |

This is the Balance Sheet referred to in the memorandum of settlement between us

Charles Christmas

William Lovell Junr

| | | | | |
|---|---|---|---|---|
| | By Debtors Good | 9 | | 4046 13 1 |
| | Doubtl. & Bad | 5 | 334 14 10 | |
| | " Coles | | 113 14 11 | |
| | advance on Cheese | | | |
| | Less Cheese Sold | | 89 1 4 | 24 14 7 |
| | By Bills receivable viz | | | |
| | Vize | | 13 14 3 | |
| | Corney | | 47 6 8 | 61 0 11 |
| | " Stock on hand | | | |
| | Cheese, See book | | 142 5 6 | |
| | Butter | 87 | 5 | 147 5 6 |
| | " Cash at Bankers | | 177 14 8 | |
| | " " in hand say | | 10 | 187 14 8 |
| OCB 179 | " " Balc unaccount for | | 1193 18 5 | |
| | | | | 4467 8 9 |
| | " Chs. Christmas | 1 | | 1380 5 8 |
| | " Wm. Lovell | 2 | | 960 5 9 |
| | | | | 6808 0 2 |
| | " Cary advance on Cheese | | | 34 10 - |
| | " W. Lovell carting | | | 19 12 6 |
| | " Cash balc ascertained | | 12 1 - | |
| | less estimate above | | 10 - - | 2 1 - |
| | " Maynard allowed | | | 17 - - |
| | | | | 73 3 6 |

# APPENDIX X

## *LETTER FROM CHARLES CHRISTMAS TO WILLIAM LOVELL 1857*

Dear Sir,

On the settlement of our Copartnership transactions and the execution of the Releases between us it was understood that in the event of our recovering a sum equal to £250 from Mr. Charles Crowther our late Clerk out of the debt he owes to our late Firm that I should out of my half thereof allow you the Sum of £50 the Rent of the Premises at No. 40 Snow Hill.

On my part therefore I do hereby undertake to you in consideration of the Mutual Release and discharge of our Copartnership Accounts which has been signed by me this day that if the said Sum of £250 is recovered from the said Charles Crowther that I will then allow you the Sum of £50 out of my share of it in pursuance of the above agreement between us.

Yours truly

Chas Christmas

## APPENDIX XI

*AN INDENTURE TO ROBSON OF BOURNEMOUTH, 1912*

THIS INDENTURE made the 3 day of April
one thousand nine hundred and twelve
WITNESSETH that Irving John Curtis
of Wimbourne
in the County of Dorset
Son of John Curtis
Wedboro
Wimbourne
by and with the consent and approbation of his father
testified by his executing these Presents, doth put
himself Apprentice to Henry Robson
of The Triangle Bournemouth
in the county of Hants.
to learn the Art, Trade or Business of Grocery &
Provision Dealer
and with him after the manner of an Apprentice to serve
from the 22nd day of June 1912 until
the full end and term of three years from thence next following, fully to be complet and ended. During which term the said Apprentice his Master faithfully shall serve, his secrets keep, and his lawful commands obey:- he shall do no damage to his said Master or his Goods, nor suffer it to be done by others, but shall forthwith give notice to his said Master of the same, when necessary:- he shall not waste the Goods of his said Master, nor lend them unlawfully to any; nor shall he do any act whereby his said Master may sustain any loss, with his own Goods or others during the said term:- without Licence of the said Master, he shall neither buy nor sell during his Apprenticeship; nor shall he absent himself from his said Master's service day or night unlawfully; but in all things as a faithful Apprentice shall behave himself towards his said Master and others, during the said term. And the said Henry Robson
shall instruct his said Apprentice in the Art,

Trade or Business of Grover & Provision dealer which he useth by the best means in his power shall teach and instruct or cause to be taught and instructed:- the said Henry Robson will pay the said Apprentice the Wages following – that is to say

| | | |
|---|---|---|
| 5/- for week during the 1st year | ) | except in case of serious |
| | ) | illness or other cause |
| 6/- " " " " 2nd " | ) | necessitating his absence |
| | ) | from business for more |
| 7/- " " " " 3rd " | ) | than one week at one |
| | ) | time. |

These presents shall be handed over to the said I.J. Curtis on the completion of the said term, with a Certificate of such service endorsed thereon. AND for the true performance of all and every of the said Covenants and Agreements the said Parties bind themselves by these Presents. IN WITNESS whereof the said parties have hereunto set their hands and Seals the day and year first above written.

| | | |
|---|---|---|
| Signed, Sealed and Delivered | ) | |
| in the presence of | ) | I.J. Curtis |
| | ) | |
| Edward Brown | ) | John Curtis |
| 111 Alma Rd | ) | |
| Bournemouth | ) | Henry Robson |
| | ) | |
| | ) | |

# APPENDIX XII

## *APPRENTICESHIP DUTIES WORLDS STORES LIMITED*

# First Year

### FIRST SIX MONTHS

1. Clean Scales, Panels of Counters, Assisting in keeping Warehouses tidy, Clean Windows, etc., and wait on Window Dresser.

2. Fill up all fixtures and face up from reserve stock properly, and ticket at correct prices.

3. PAPER.

   CUT UP IN PROPER SIZES. ALL BROWN PAPER.

   FILL UP HOOKS IN SHOP WITH BAGS, Etc., FOR THE WEEK.

   KEEP PAPER ROOM AND FITTINGS TIDY.

4. TAUGHT THE WAY TO :—

   FLAT WRAP—Cokernut, Fruit, Cereals, Sugar, Rice, Coffee and Spices, Tuck Sugar, etc., properly.

   Open bag, fill, weigh, and wrap any stock.

   Make a cup properly.

   Assist on the Order Counter, able to execute any order on Grocery Counter.

5. WEEK ENDS. Apprentices should wait on first hand or Manager whilst serving, etc., and listen how the Manager addresses and serves Customers, so that he can cultivate the proper manner of serving and speaking to a Customer when the time arrives for him to commence serving.

# First Year

### SECOND SIX MONTHS

**One Star**

1. Taught to serve on Grocery Counter, dress fittings, etc., and Counters. Unpacking and classifying all goods received, ready for checking.

2. At the end of a year the Apprentice should be able to serve right through on Grocery Counter, and have a general knowledge of all Grocery Lines stocked, and the correct prices of same.

# Second Year

## FIRST SIX MONTHS

APPRENTICES should be transferred to Provisions and taught his duties in the following order :—

1. Scrubbing down Counters, Lockers, etc.
2. Cleaning Windows and Scales, Tickets, Butter Stands, etc.
3. Turn out Butters, Lard and Marg., etc.
4. Keep all the Egg Baskets and shelves filled up, and serve on Butter Counter.
5. Taught the correct way to cut all Cheese and display, Scale and Price Joints, etc., correctly.
   How to open and turn out all Cooked Meats, etc., cut, and arrange displays without making any waste.

# Second Year

## SECOND SIX MONTHS

APPRENTICES should be able to carry out all the foregoing satisfactory and he should now be given charge of Cheese or Cooked Meats Dept., and assist in serving Bacon, etc.

TAUGHT HOW TO BONE THE FOLLOWING :—

Side of Bacon.

Bone and Roll Ham, or Gammon or Fore Hock.

Dissect a side of Bacon, giving number of Joints in detail Summer and Winter. Put all the Bacon through the machine and stack ready to go into window. Learn the names of the various cuts and prices.

Trussing Poultry, Skinning Rabbits, etc.

At the end of two years an Apprentice should be able to carry out any SHOP WORK with exception of Window Dressing.

Serve properly on either Counter, take orders, do any Counter and Shop Dressing and be able to weigh and correctly price PROVISIONS.

# Third Year

## FIRST SIX MONTHS

APPRENTICE should be taught the way to :—

Dress all windows correctly.

Learn all the clerical work of the Branch, including Book-keeping and Cash Desk Work, and ordering of Goods on proper Pads, etc.

Able to take 1st on Grocery or Provisions, take all weekly Stocks, etc., for Manager. Generally finished off properly, so that at the end of his Apprenticeship he should be able to fill any Senior position in any Branch.

# Third Year

## SECOND SIX MONTHS

### Two Stars

AT THE END OF APPRENTICESHIP, an Apprentice should be able to answer the following questions correctly, to gain further promotion. (To be confirmed by Inspector or H.O.)

Can you dress Grocery Window.

" " Grocery Counters and Fittings.

" take weekly Stocks and fill in all Order Pads correctly.

Have you an up-to-date knowledge of all Grocery Prices

Do you understand the working of the Cash Desk in all details.

How would you deal with weighed up Stock left over at week ends.

What articles in particular evaporate considerably after being preweighed and should be reweighed before selling.

What goods on Grocery Counter must be sold Nett Weight.

## EMPTIES

Describe how you would deal with these when returning to H.O. or MANUFACTURERS.

## *SAMPLE EXTRACTS FROM THE CITY'S RECORDS RELATING TO THE TRADE IN CHEESE AND BUTTER*

*(Such references are numerous)*

**Common Council 1 Dec. 1519**

Ordered that no freemen go outside the City and buy any cheese or butter barrelled or otherwise and bring it to the City for sale upon pain of forfeiture and imprisonment at the discretion of the Mayor and Aldermen but the citizens shall peacefully suffer the foreign owners, bringers or conveyers of such butter and cheese to this City by water to be sold, to sell the same upon the water of Thames in the vessells, and that the said foreigners shall bring examples of the same to the Mayor to set the price and they to sell the same out of the said vessels at the said price and in no other way upon pain of imprisonment.

**Court of Aldermen 13 Mar. 1533 (Rep. 8, fo. 277v.)**

The following prices of cheese were declared to Thomas Bekwyth, John Byrde, Thomas Malby, Henry Mopkyn, Thomas Barbour and William Herby, cheesemen, citizens of this City, and they entered into recognizances to the Chamberlain not to sell cheese to strangers:

Suffolk cheese ¾d a lb.
Essex cheese ½d a lb.
Butter 1¼d a lb.

**Court of Aldermen 14 Mar. 1543 (Rep. 10, fo. 319b.)**

The following persons acknowledged that they had certain quantities of butter and cheese in their hands and that they had bought but not yet received the other quantities specified:

<u>John Byrde, barbersurgeon</u>

66 wey of Suffolk cheese
30 " " Essex "
10 or 20 barrels of Butter
<u>coming</u>
20 wey of Suffolk cheese

<u>Thomas Malby, fishmonger</u>

57 wey of Suffolk cheese
8 " " Essex "
7 or 8 barrels of butter
<u>coming</u>
55 wey of Suffolk cheese
20 " " Essex "
6 or 7 barrels of butter

<u>Thomas Barbour, tallowchandler</u>

19 wey of Suffolk cheese
5 or 6 wey of Essex cheese
<u>coming</u>
40 wey of Suffolk cheese
20 " " Essex "
8 barrels of butter

<u>Geoffrey Fraunce</u>

20 wey of Suffolk cheese
1 " " Essex "
1 barrel of butter
<u>coming</u>
10 wey of Essex cheese
5 barrels of butter

**28 Mar. 1555 (Letter Book S, fo. 20b.)**

This day the Cheesemongers and all other citizens that have licences to provide and buy butter and cheese abroad in the country were charged to bring in here all the same licences the next court day after Easter and in the meantime to buy no manner of cheese out of the City to sell again within the City nor to make any manner of bargain for any such cheese or to send any cheese out of the City to any fair or market to be sold, on pain of disfranchisement.

# APPENDIX XIII – *THE POUND IN YOUR POCKET*

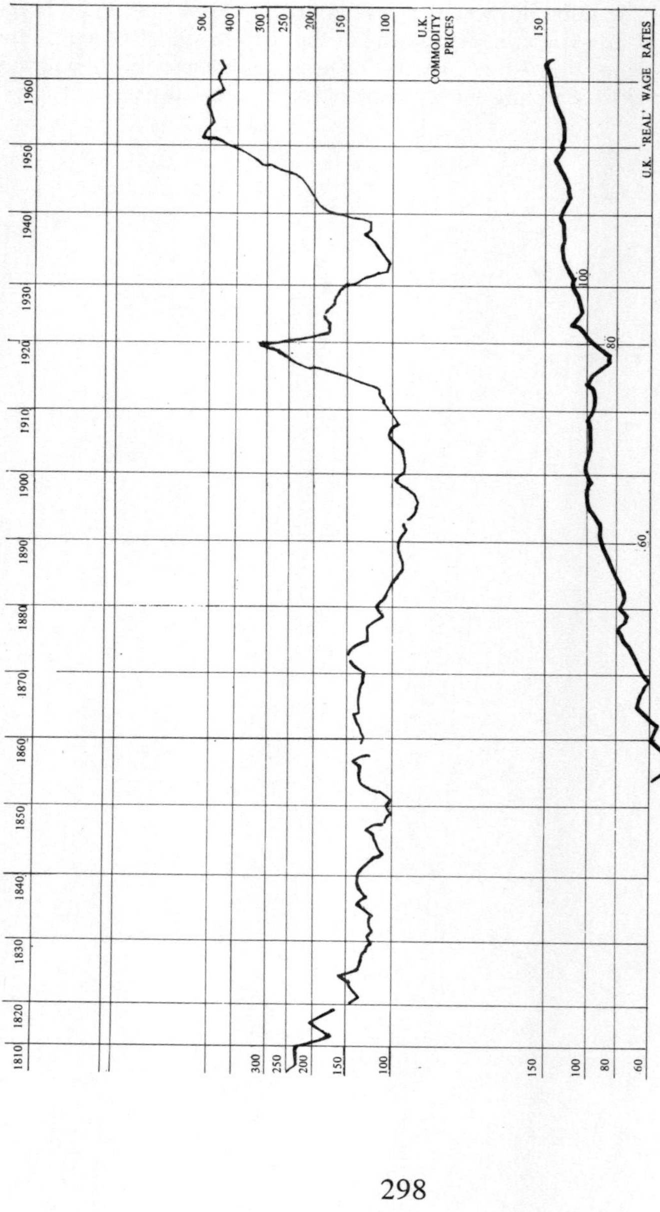


**Source of Figures:** *U.K. Commodity Prices*, Stanley Jevons to 1821. Thereafter Sauerbeck-Statist index of wholesale prices. *U.K. 'Real' Wages Rates*, G.H. Wood and A.D. Webb to 1891 on retail food prices and rent. Thereafter Wage Rates converted by Cost of Living Index or Retail Prices Index of Ministry of Labour (From 1919 onwards as published by London & Cambridge Economic Service). INDEX FIGURES are all on the basis of 1900 = 100

## APPENDIX XIV

### *FOOD PRICES*

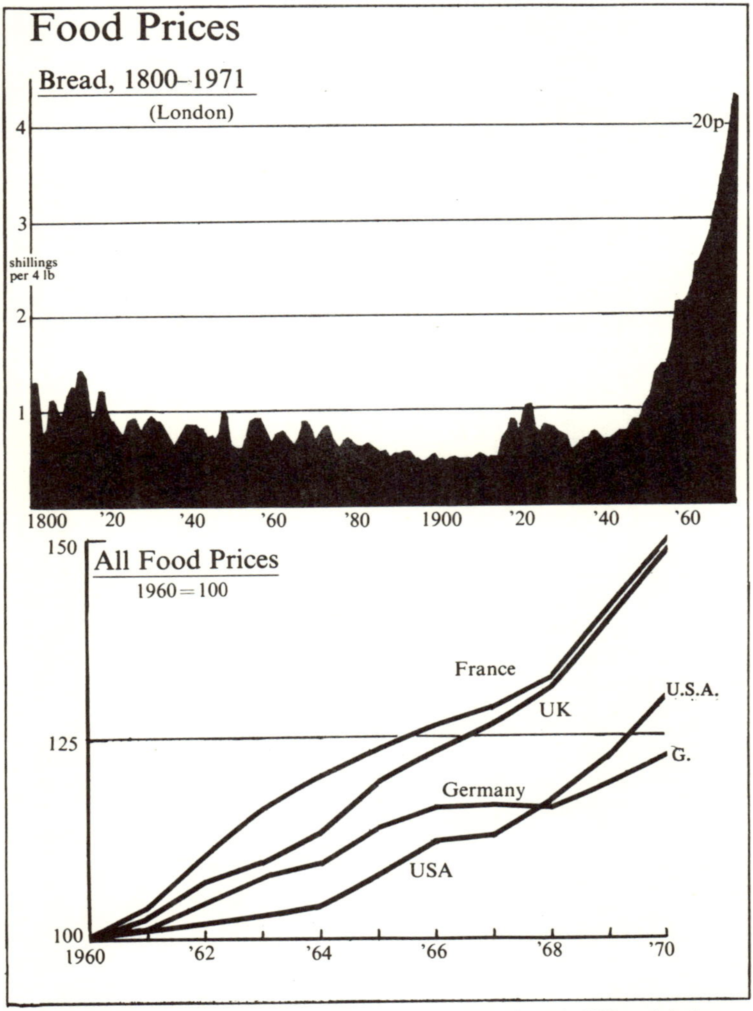


The price of bread showed little change, on balance, between the early 1800s and the late 1940s, since when it has about quadrupled. Over the 1960s the rise in general food prices in Britain was roughly the same as in France but greater than in Germany and the US.

*Sources: British Labour Statistics 1886-1968; OECD*

## *QUANTITIES OF MEAT SOLD ON SMITHFIELD AS AN OPEN MARKET (THE MARKET FAIR)*

| | |
|---|---|
| **MONDAY, 18th April, 1836** | |
| Beasts | 2,346 |
| Sheep and lambs | 15,010 |
| Calves | 94 |
| Pigs | 380 |
| **MONDAY, 25th April, 1836** | |
| Beasts | 2,304 |
| Sheep and lambs | 17,180 |
| Calves | 114 |
| Pigs | 450 |
| **MONDAY, 9th May, 1836** | |
| Beasts | 1,939 |
| Sheep and lambs | 12,650 |
| Calves | 120 |
| Pigs | 386 |
| **MONDAY, 16th May, 1836** | |
| Beasts | 1,939 |
| Sheep and lambs | 15,440 |
| Calves | 139 |
| Pigs | 395 |
| **MONDAY, 23rd May, 1836** | |
| Beasts | 1,839 |
| Sheep and lambs | 17,560 |
| Calves | 120 |
| Pigs | 423 |
| **MONDAY, 30th May, 1836** | |
| Beasts | 1,722 |
| Sheep and lambs | 20,560 |
| Calves | 153 |
| Pigs | 343 |
| **MONDAY, 6th June, 1836** | |
| Beasts | 2,226 |
| Sheep and lambs | 21,770 |
| Calves | 140 |
| Pigs | 355 |

As a comparison, the following supplies were received at Smithfield Market in the week ending 15th January, 1972.

| | |
|---|---|
| Beasts & Calves | 9,388 |
| Sheep and lambs | 46,400 |
| Pigs | 22,760 |

# APPENDIX XV

## *ORDINANCES OF THE CHEESEMONGERS*

**Common Council 27 May 1377. Letter Book H. Fol. lxii. (Latin and Norman French)**

To the honourable Lords, the Mayor, Recorder, and Aldermen of London, pray the Chesemongeres of London, that whereas our said Lord the Mayor has told them heretofore to devise and ordain how that the price of cheese and of butter may be amended, the said Chesemongeres therefore, by their common assent, have well considered how that the said price may be well amended; if our said Lord the Mayor, and his good Council, will put their hand to, confirm, and enrol, the points underwritten –

First – that foreigners who come to the City with cheese and butter for sale, in carts and upon horses, shall be charged to bring their wares into the market of the Ledenhalle, or the market between St. Nicholas Shambles and Neugate, and nowhere else, before Noon rung at such place where the purchase shall be made: and shall be charged that they shall not put away in houses or in rooms, privily or openly, either after Noon rung or before, any cheese or butter, on pain of forfeiting the same that shall be so put away.

Also – whereas those who carry or bring cheese or butter to the City by water, do sell it in secret to hokesters and to others, against the ancient usage, whereas they were wont heretofore to bring it to, and sell it in, the same markets; they do pray that from henceforth all such dealers shall be charged to bring such cheese or butter to the markets aforesaid, and there sell the same; on pain of forfeiting the thing so sold; and also, on pain of imprisonment, and of making fine at the will and ordinance of our said Lord the Mayor.

Also – divers bersters of cheese, from Hamme, Hakeney, and the suburbs of London, are wont to go to divers markets, and to buy up and forestal such wares, which ought to come to the hands of the working-men in London; and such bersters then bring the same into London, and go about through divers streets in the said city, and sell it, to the great damage of the commonalty; saying and affirming that it is the produce of their own cattle, and of their own making; they do pray therefore that from henceforth such forestallers, regrators, and bersters, and all other vendors of cheese or of butter, foreigners or freemen, shall be charged to sell the same at one of the said markets, on the pain aforesaid.

Also – whereas strangers do come and bring to the City cheese of Wales, called 'talgar', and house the same in Fletstrete and in Holbourne, and other places, as well within the City as without, and there sell it in secret, against the ancient custom, in manner aforesaid, and also, whereas two or three persons from Wales have their serving-men lying in wait in the City all the year through, and when any one from Wales brings talgar cheese to the City for sale, such men go and make false suggestions to the dealers in such cheese, and through such subtlety regrate the cheese in private, and then sell it by retail to the commoners, without it coming to such market, – that they may be charged to bring their wares to the said markets, in form and on the pain aforesaid.

Also, – whereas the hokesters and others who sell such wares by retail, do come and regrate such cheese and butter before Prime rung, and before that the commonalty has been served; may it be ordained that no such hokesters shall buy of any foreigner before the hour of Prime, on pain of imprisonment at the will of the Mayor, and of the wares being forfeited to the prisoners of Neugate, or in such other manner as shall seem proper to our said Lord the Mayor to be done.

Also, – that the good folks of the said trade shall be charged every year, at the Feast of St. Michael, to choose two of the most able men to oversee as to the points aforesaid, that they are well kept and observed in manner before stated. And that the persons so chosen shall have power to seize such manner of merchandize, so forfeitable, and to present the same before the Mayor, in amendment of the price aforesaid, to the great profit of the commonalty in time to come.

Also, – that each one of the said overseers shall make due execution of his office, without laxity, or doing wrong to any one; and that no one of them shall forestal any thing to his own private profit, against the common profit and the Ordinances aforesaid; on pain of paying 100s. to the use of Commonalty on the first default found against him; on the second default, 10l.; on the third default, 20 marks; and that, without any remission of the same, and that he who shall make prayer for such person found in default, shall pay to the use of the Commonalty 20s., without any remission thereof, as above stated.

Afterwards, on the 17th day of June in the 51st year of Edward III, William Sparke and Robert Whyte were here sworn well and trustily to oversee the Articles above-written, and here to present the defaults, if any such they should find.

<u>Royal Proclamation 20 Oct. 1550</u>

Setting price of butter and cheese
Sweet butter 1½d a lb.
Barrelled butter of Essex ½d and half farthing a lb.
" " " any other place ¾d a lb.
Cheese of Essex ½d and half a farthing a lb.
" " other places ¾d a lb.

# APPENDIX XVI

## *DETAILS FROM THE YEOMEN OF THE WATERSIDE IMPORTS INTO LONDON OF BUTTER AND CHEESE 1745*

One page of a book of fees collected by the Yeomen of the Waterside giving the names of persons importing Cheese and Butter, the name of the ship, the town from where the Cheese or Butter was exported and the quantity. Dec. 1745.

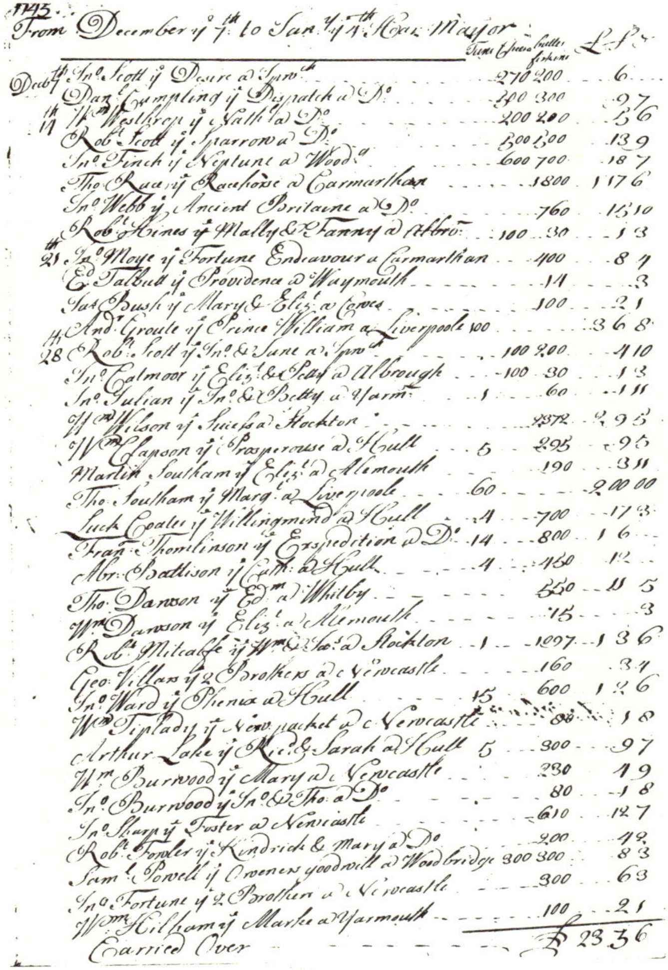

1745.
From December ye 7th to Jan. ye 4th Har. Mayor

| | | Tuns Cheese | Butter firkins | £ s d |
|---|---|---|---|---|
| Decr 7th | Jno. Scott ye Desire a Spwch | 270 | 200 | 6 |
| | Dan. Cumpling ye Dispatch a Do. | 300 | 300 | 9 7 |
| 14th | Wm. Westhrop ye Nath. a Do. | 200 | 200 | 5 6 |
| | Robt. Scott ye Sparrow a Do. | 300 | 300 | 13 9 |
| | Jno. Finch ye Neptune a Woodg. | 600 | 700 | 18 7 |
| | Tho. Ruay ye Racehorse a Carmarthen | | 1800 | 1 17 6 |
| | Jno. Webb ye Ancient Britaine a Do. | | 760 | 15 10 |
| | Robt. Hines ye Mally & Fanny a Albro. | 100 | 30 | 1 3 |
| 21th | Jno. Moye ye Fortune Endeavour a Carmarthen | | 400 | 8 4 |
| | Ed. Talbutt ye Providence a Waymouth | | 14 | 3 |
| | Jas. Bush ye Mary & Eliz. a Cowes | | 100 | 2 1 |
| | Andr. Groute ye Prince William a Liverpoole | 100 | | 3 6 8 |
| 28th | Robt. Scott ye Jno. & Jane a Spwch | 100 | 200 | 4 10 |
| | Jno. Calmoor ye Eliz. & Peggy a Albrough | 100 | 30 | 1 3 |
| | Jno. Julian ye Jno. & Betty a Yarm. | 1 | 60 | 1 11 |
| | Wm. Wilson ye Succefs a Stockton | | 4372 | 2 9 5 |
| | Wm. Clapson ye Prosperouse a Hull | 5 | 295 | 9 5 |
| | Martin Southam ye Eliz. a Alemouth | | 190 | 3 11 |
| | Tho. Southam ye Marg. a Liverpoole | 60 | | 2 00 00 |
| | Luck Coates ye Willingmind a Hull | 4 | 700 | 17 3 |
| | Fran. Thomlinson ye Expedition a Do. | 14 | 800 | 1 6 |
| | Abr. Battison ye Cath. a Hull | 4 | 450 | 12 |
| | Tho. Dawson ye Edm. a Whitby | | 550 | 11 5 |
| | Wm. Dawson ye Eliz. a Alemouth | | 15 | 3 |
| | Robt. Mitcalfe ye Wm. & Jas. a Stockton | 1 | 1097 | 1 3 6 |
| | Geo. Villars ye 2 Brothers a Newcastle | | 160 | 3 4 |
| | Jno. Ward ye Phenix a Hull | 15 | 600 | 1 2 6 |
| | Wm. Tiplady ye New packet a Newcastle | | 80 | 1 8 |
| | Arthur Lake ye Ric. & Sarah a Hull | 5 | 300 | 9 7 |
| | Wm. Burwood ye Mary a Newcastle | | 230 | 4 9 |
| | Jno. Burwood ye Jno. & Tho. a Do. | | 80 | 1 8 |
| | Jno. Sharp ye Foster a Newcastle | | 610 | 12 7 |
| | Robt. Fowler ye Kendrick & Mary a Do. | | 200 | 4 2 |
| | Saml. Powell ye Oweners goodwill a Woodbridge | 300 | 300 | 8 3 |
| | Jno. Fortune ye 2 Brothers a Newcastle | | 300 | 6 3 |
| | Wm. Hilham ye Marke a Yarmouth | | 100 | 2 1 |
| | Carried Over | | | £ 23 3 6 |

# APPENDIX XVII

## *FITCH LOVELL LIMITED*

### *Fitch Lovell Divisions*

**Bacon Curing /Manufacturing**
Bywater-Hollingsworth Ltd.
F.L. Miller & Sons Ltd.
Roberts & Birch Ltd.
Roberts & Birch (Evesham) Ltd.

**Bakery**
Hale Trent (Holdings) Ltd.
The Far Famed Cake Co. Ltd.
Hale Trent Cakes Ltd.

**Home & Export**
Fitch & Son Ltd.
Fitch & Son (Export) Ltd.
Edwin Bevington Ltd.
Carter (Produce) Ltd.
Thomas Forde & Co. Ltd.
Impey & Cyke Ltd.
J. & T.H. Staples Ltd.
C.C. Ryan (C & C) Ltd.
Robson & Son (Bmth) Ltd.
Southwark Bacon Drying Co.
Auguste Noel Ltd.
L. Noel & Sons Ltd.
Wholesale Catering Services
Pannett & Neden

**L.& C.**
Lovell & Christmas Ltd.
Lovell & Christmas (Northern) Ltd.
Lovell & Christmas (Bristol) Ltd.
Lovell & Christmas (Scotland) Ltd.
Rutzou Ltd.
Blue Cap Foods (Kent) Ltd.
Hamilton & Co. (Bootle) Ltd.
Lovell, Wall & Co. Ltd. (London)
Lovell, Wall & Co. Ltd. (Stockport)
John McCaskill Ltd.
Rogerson & Black Ltd.
McElderry & Moffett Ltd.

**I.B.S.**
I. Beer & Sons Ltd.
I.B.S. (Cash & Carry)
Alfred Mason & Co. Ltd.

**Poultry & Markets**
Golden Produce Chicken Ltd.
Golden Produce Hatcheries Ltd.
Golden Produce Sales Ltd.
Henry Gillham Ltd.
Keevil & Keevil Ltd.
Phillips & Co. (Smithfield) Ltd.
Webb & Fowler Ltd.

**Retail**
Barrow's Stores Ltd.
Brown & White (Produce) Ltd.
R. Gunner Ltd.
Key Markets Ltd.
West Layton Ltd.
The Worlds Stores Ltd.

**Timber etc.**
Machin & Kingsley Ltd.
Leyens Cardboard Box Co. Ltd.
Malex Ltd.
Austen & Griffin Ltd.

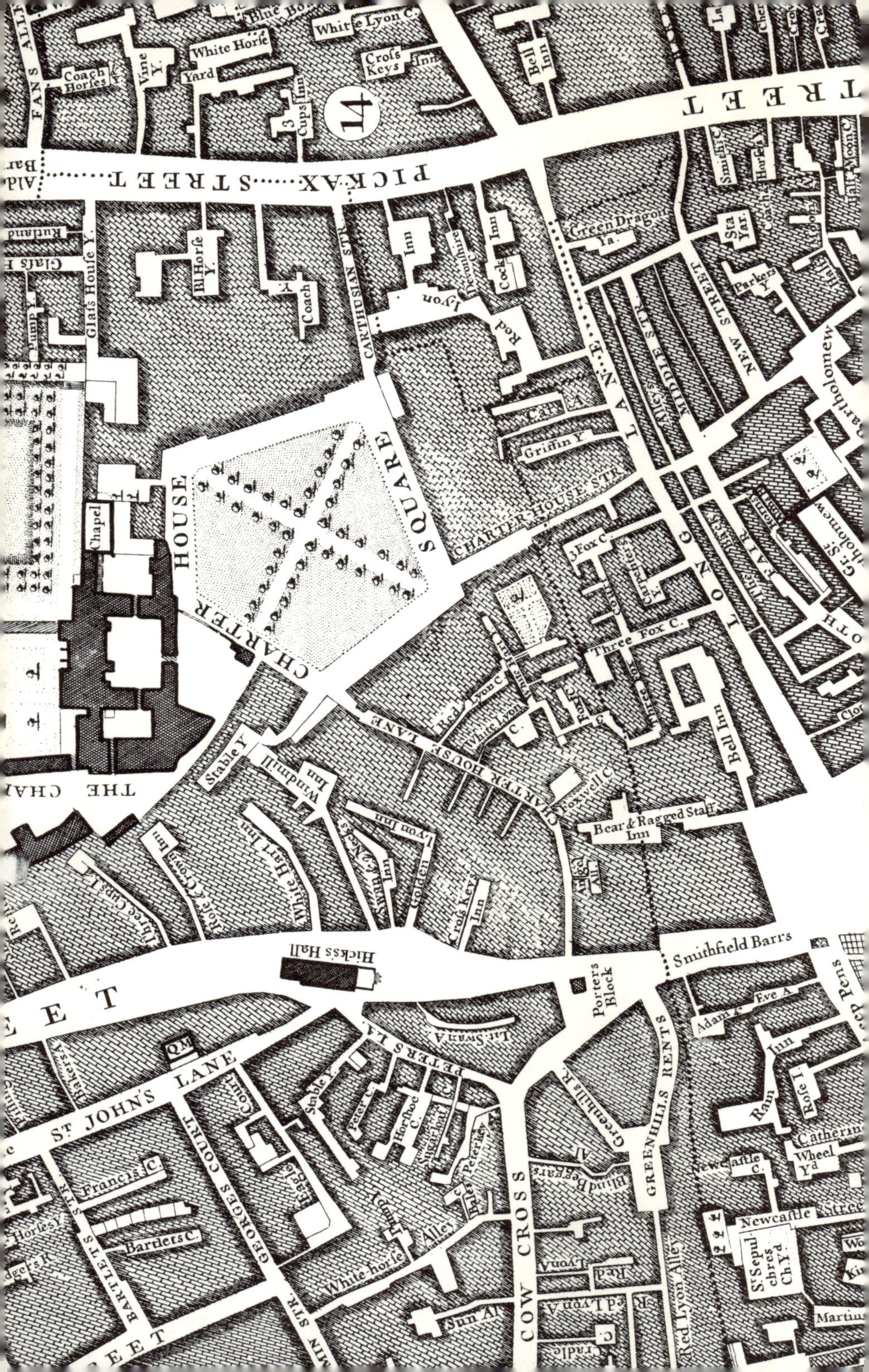

White Horse Yard
White Lyon C.
Cross Keys Inn
Coach Horses
Vine Y.
3 Cups Inn
Bell Inn
14
PICKAX STREET
STREET
Rutland
Glass House Y.
Bl Horse Y.
Coach Y.
CARTHUSIAN STR.
Inn
Devonshire
Cock Inn
Red Lyon
Green Dragon Ya.
Parkers Y.
NEW STREET
MIDDLE STR.
LONG LANE
Griffin Y.
CHARTER HOUSE STR.
CHARTER HOUSE SQUARE
Chapel
THE CHAR
3 Fox C.
Three Fox C.
Bell Inn
Stable Y.
Windmill Inn
CHARTER HOUSE LANE
Red Lyon C.
White Lyon
Foxwell C.
Bear & Ragged Staff Inn
White Hart Inn
Lyon Inn
Golden
Cross Key Inn
Angel All.
Smithfield Barrs
Hickss Hall
Porters Block
Lt. Swan A.
PETERS LA.
ST JOHNS LANE
GREENHILLS RENTS
Adam & Eve A.
Rain Inn
Rose I.
Wheel Yd
Newcastle C.
Newcastle
St. Sepulchres Ch. Yd.
Francis C.
Bartlets C.
GEORGES COURT
Horsshoe C.
Stable Y.
White horse Alley
COW CROSS
Blind Beggars A.
Red Lyon A.
Red Lyon Alley
Sun Al.
BARTLETS
STREET
Greenhills R.
Catherin
Martin